Explorations in Critical Studies of Advertising

This volume provides a thoughtful and wide-ranging exploration of approaches to the critical study of advertising. Current and impending practices of advertising have in many ways exceeded the grasp of traditional modes of critique, due at least in part to their being formulated in very different historical conditions. To begin to address this lag, this edited collection explores through critical discussion and application a variety of critical approaches to advertising. Authors address a variety of concrete examples in their chapters, drawing on existing research while presenting new findings where relevant. In order to maintain the relevance of this collection past this particular historical moment, however, chapters do not simply report on empirical work, but also develop a theoretical argument.

James F. Hamilton is the James Kennedy Professor of New Media, Head of the Department of Entertainment and Media Studies, and Director of the New Media Institute at the University of Georgia, USA. Among his published work is *Democratic Communications; Formations, Projects, Possibilities* (2009) and *Alternative Journalism* (2009), co-written with Chris Atton.

Robert Bodle is an Associate Professor of Communication and New Media Studies at Mount St. Joseph University and Adjunct Professor in the Department of Media, Journalism, and Film at Miami University, USA. He served as Co-Chair of the Internet Rights and Principles Dynamic Coalition at the UN Internet Governance Forum, and as a steering committee member of the IRP Coalition since 2010.

Ezequiel Korin is a PhD student in the Grady College of Journalism and Mass Communication at the University of Georgia, USA.

Routledge Research in Cultural and Media Studies

For a full list of titles in this series, please visit www.routledge.com

Explorations in Critical Studies of Advertising

Edited by James F. Hamilton, Robert Bodle, and Ezequiel Korin

LONDON AND NEW YORK

First published 2017 by Routledge

2 Park Square, Milton Park, Abingdon, Oxfordshire OX14 4RN
52 Vanderbilt Avenue, New York, NY 10017

Routledge is an imprint of the Taylor & Francis Group, an informa business

First issued in paperback 2019

Library of Congress Cataloging in Publication Data
CIP data has been applied for.

ISBN: 978-1-138-64952-1 (hbk)
ISBN: 978-0-367-87745-3 (pbk)

Typeset in Sabon
by codeMantra

For Cynthia (James)
For Jenn (Robert)
For Ana & Emiliana (Ezequiel)

Contents

Introduction
Critical Traditions

James F. Hamilton and Robert Bodle

This edited collection is prompted by the pressing need for a thoughtful and wide-ranging exploration of approaches to the critical study of advertising, which have been established through decades of scholarly work and commentary. Granting a number of valuable efforts ranging from single articles (Harms and Kellner 1991; Duffy 1994; McAllister and Smith 2012) to book-length and multivolume overviews and collections of "classic readings" (MacRury 2009; Turow and McAllister 2009; Moeran 2010; McAllister and West 2013; Wharton 2015), few areas of media research are as lacking in sustained critical reflection (McFall 2004), unlike similar topic areas such as critical approaches to marketing (Tadajewski and Cluley 2013).

Engaging in reflexive (re)evaluation is particularly necessary now, because of the extent to which current and impending practices of advertising seem to exceed the grasp of traditional modes of critique, due at least in part to their being formulated in very different historical conditions. The mass-culture thesis of social criticism, the culture-industry thesis of the Frankfurt School, theses of cultural imperialism, of semiotic criticism, and of simulacra (to name just a few) emerged at a time of and are premised upon advertising and media institutions, technologies, and practices up through the 1980s, which were comparatively nationalized as well as highly centralized, professionalized, and routinized.

However, the degree to which such characteristics describe advertising/media institutions, technologies, and practices today is increasingly in doubt. Indeed, even industry commentators claim with increasing frequency (granting some hyperbole) that, in the words of one, "advertising as we know it has come to an end" (Inamoto 2013). Some reasons for such a claim include:

- The expansion of advertising and promotion into ever-broader realms of society and experience
- The accelerating convergence and commercialization of here-to-fore discrete media industries, technologies, practices, and texts
- A growing digitally driven advertising ecosystem with an increasing dependence on marketing research for improving efficiency and value
- Consumer behavior tracking across ubiquitous computing environments in order to profile and thus personalize ad content

- Data-driven targeting, marketing, and consumer response, which raises to qualitatively different levels long-standing issues of privacy, autonomy, and the production of experience
- The steady incorporation of user activity in the forms of mobile media and social media, which renders less and less adequate binary conceptions of rank manipulation by an elite or of the implications of advertising as ones solely of false consciousness, misinformation, and the like

To acknowledge the growing need to grapple with these changes and thus confront critical approaches themselves as radically historical, this edited collection explores a variety of critical approaches to advertising in the context of current and anticipated future conditions. This book provides in-depth discussion and application of existing perspectives as well as insights into some key emerging perspectives. To maintain the relevance of this collection beyond this historical moment, chapters pay as much attention to the perspectives themselves and to their antecedents, varieties, and strengths as to their limitations. But, in doing so, many chapters address a variety of concrete examples, thus drawing on existing research while presenting new findings where relevant.

By combining theoretical argument and empirical example in this way, we hope that this book illuminates critical approaches to the study of advertising while also emphasizing more generally the constituent historicity of critique (Said 1982; Hardt 1992). Critical theories remain critical only to the extent they recognize themselves as historically constituted.

The balance of this introduction sketches a broad interpretation and analysis of various traditions of advertising criticism.

The earliest is what could be called a consensus critique, which was legitimized by the western European-derived critique of mass culture (Bennett 1982; Manning and White 1959). It reigns currently as the dominant touchstone for mainstream advertising criticism. As a consensus critique, it does not question the existence or place of advertising, but advocates instead simply for its ethical practice. Despite variations, this critique operates within liberal-pluralist political philosophies and Lockean rationalities that are formative in the conceptualization of communication (Peters 1989). Consisting largely of structural critiques of undue advertiser influence on journalism and psychological critiques of potent images foisted upon susceptible audiences, the consensus critique places at the forefront issues of individual freedom versus social control and truth versus deception while regarding as unproblematic the institution of advertising itself.

Popular consensus critiques are as old as advertising itself. Sampson cites in his 1874 book a variety of swindles and fakes by "advertising scoundrels" (312) that were successful due to their victims being either merely "credulous" or "selfishly and idiotically greedy for other folk's goods" (309). In either case, the onus is on the person swindled and certainly not on the publication in which the advertisement appeared, which, if expected to validate every claim of every advertiser, could hardly have resources left over to even publish (329). Variations of this view of powerful institutions and susceptible readers include press criticism that bemoans the influence of advertisers (as well as governments and politicians) on journalism (Sinclair 1919; Seldes 1929; Bagdikian 1983). A sub-genre of autobiographical reflection by former advertising executives (an example is Young 1946) lends this criticism an air of a public absolution of sins.

By the 1950s and the general dissemination of Freudian psychology into marketing research, popular consensus criticism of advertising was articulated through the terms of motivation psychology (Schwarzkopf and Gries 2010), which centered attention on the power of (fetishized) techniques and subliminal images to subvert free will (Packard 1957; Key 1973, 1980). The persistence of this consensus critique (sans Freudian motivation psychology, which remains as anathema to Anglo-American empiricists) is suggested by the 50-year trajectory of a staple textbook of advertising and society college courses in the United States, beginning as *The Role of Advertising* (Sandage and Fryburger 1960), then updated as *Advertising and Society* (Hovland and Wilcox 1989), and updated and revised again (Hovland, Wolburg and Haley 2007). A number of articles in the 1960 edition can be found in the 2007 version, suggesting the establishment of a core, timeless canon that requires little if any updating.

However, a second body of critical work on advertising can be labeled an oppositional critique. By oppositional, we mean it asks questions and focuses on issues that the consensus critique sets aside. Importantly, advertising is seen in the oppositional critique as a specific embodiment of commodity capitalism, outside of which advertising in its current form would not exist. Oppositional critiques thus take issue just as much with commodity capitalism as they do with advertising, with the critique of not only how advertising is conducted, but of the fundamental bases of commodity capitalism. Advertising in this view is not an accepted and natural if not also inevitable fact of modern life, but regarded historically as a particular manifestation, feature, and agent of capitalist societies in which the circulation of commodities occupies a central role while working against the ethical support and fulfillment of human lives and dignity.

Notwithstanding the fact that its theoretical bases were laid in the 19th century, by the 1960s and the New Left criticism of consumer culture and mediated marketing (Hayden 1962), the oppositional critique had come to be premised upon different theoretical and philosophical bases, consisting in the main part of combinations of Marxism, Critical Theory, structuralism(s), and critical-psychoanalytic approaches combined in many cases with an overtly historical perspective, although in some ways not a clear break in all cases from the consensus position.

Since its overt emergence, such work has taken many forms. An American example is historical work that draws upon the myth-and-symbol school of American Studies (Smith 1957; Marx 1972). Such work emphasizes a largely literary, idealist, textualist understanding of advertising as the perpetuation of archetypal stories about people and society, although often embedded within descriptions of material changes in the industry and in society (Marchand 1985; Lears 1994). Another influential stream of critical-historical work downplays the textualist focus in favor of a political and institutional focus informed in part by critical political economy (Strasser 1989; Ohmann 1996; Frank 1997; Laird 1998; Stole 2006; McGovern 2006; Schwarzkopf 2007; Spring 2011; Stole 2012).

Wedding a critique of advertising more deeply to theoretical and philosophical issues has been critical work informed more overtly by Marx, Freud, and their amalgam in the shape of the Frankfurt School (Adorno and Horkheimer 1989; Jay 1986). This literature pushes the consensus critique of mass culture to a deeper and more substantial level (Ewen 1976; Leiss, Kline and Jhally 1986; Jhally 1987; Ewen and Ewen 1992; Ewen 1999). Berger is an early application of the work of Walter Benjamin to the matters of advertising and publicity (Berger 1972, 129–55). An oft-quoted early essay by Williams (1980) eschews the Freudian connection in an interpretation of advertising aligned with notions of ideology as false consciousness.

In addition, oppositional critiques of advertising have been heavily indebted to structuralist approaches. While also focusing on the textual dimension of advertising and while acknowledging an interpretive approach launched by Goffman (1976, 1979), a structuralist approach views myth as a form of speech instead of a kind of content. Structuralist critiques of advertising were initiated by Barthes (1972) and elaborated since in individual essays and works by like-minded scholars (Williamson 1978) and popularized for classroom use (Berger 2000). The 1970s poststructuralist critique of structuralism has also made its mark in critical studies of advertising by demonstrating the value of destabilizing the boundaries that separate advertising from other cultural forms (Wicke 1988) and by destabilizing the issue of the meaning of advertising itself (Stern 1996).

Lastly, an important strain of oppositional criticism of advertising has come from critical-sociological studies of advertising cultures. Much work is based in large part on pioneering studies of popular culture done in the Center for Contemporary Cultural Studies under the direction of Stuart Hall (Hall et al. 1986). The feminist critique of work in the CCCS shapes studies such as Nixon (2003), which notes how the institution and creative process of advertising is gendered. McRobbie (2015) places the specific case of advertising within the general area of creative industries, while also drawing upon work of Foucault and issues of disciplinarity and governmentality as do a handful of others (prominent examples include Hackley 2002 and McFall 2004).

However, both the consensus critique and the oppositional critique as sketched above deserve critical attention, as the most recent works already acknowledge. Complicating the landscape of critical approaches to advertising has been the accelerating digitization of advertising practice, which has heightened abilities of surveillance and data-collection while reshaping how advertising itself is considered and practiced. As a result, the key critical task is to consider the full range of changes in advertising over the past recent decades and to critically reassess oppositional critiques in order to become more responsive to changes taking place, with Spurgeon (2008) and McStay (2009) early efforts in this regard.

The strategic logic of online advertising—amassing data about people to predict their future needs and to serve them with relevant ads—depends on ubiquitous surveillance; the monitoring of one's quotidian life online and off. Making ads relevant involves prediction; knowledge of past behavior can be used to indicate (and modify) future behavior. Tracking personally identifiable data, both behavioral and transactional, requires maintaining the identity of an individual over time (persistent identity), so that seemingly harmless disclosures can aggregate into a useful profile that can attain value over time ("data creep"; Reidenberg 2000). The adage, "If it's free, then you are the product," is frequently applied to no-cost digital media services like search engines and social network sites. Yet, less discussed are the implications of what it means to be a product and relatedly the implications of real time surveillance of one's life for commercial purposes ("dataveillance"; Clark 1988).

Online advertising practices and techniques increasingly center on surveillance, big data, and the instrumental role of algorithms to provide the analytical capabilities used to process and interpret that data. The move to surveillance and data-driven advertising has its roots in product placement and direct marketing, with the attendant features of customization and discrimination. Tailoring ads requires dividing customers, attracting some, repelling others. Today's advertising practices and institutional changes, like so many things digital, outpace user awareness, industry regulation, and theoretical models of critique.

Digital advertising practices and methods of data tracking, collecting, trading, and targeting spur an evolving ecosystem that consists of new and old: data tracking companies, data brokers, direct marketers, and media planners. The scale and scope of data collected also helps account for the complex structure of the third party ad ecosystem. This expanding constellation facilitates the vast and scalable exchange of customer data to enable, for example, real-time bids on user data to target ads for people as they navigate from site to site, device to device. These industrial practices are not only obscured by their structural complexity but also by the opaqueness or black boxing of technological processes that enable pop-up and banner ads, customer relationship media, ad personalization, collaborative filtering (Amazon.com), contextual advertising (Google, Facebook), behavioral targeting, and algorithmic "fortune telling and selling" (Zuboff 2016). What is clear is the centrality of surveillance in online advertising, with advertising as a driving force, and the instrumental use of people's data to achieve monetary ends.

If data is the new oil of the 21st century, to cite another prevailing adage of the digital economy, surveillance and big data serve the prerogatives of capital accumulation and profit. The surveillant qualities of digital media where every action leaves information about itself (or "digital enclosure," Andrejevic 2007) create transactional secondary information. And the exchange and exploitation of this information helps facilitate the growth of the information economy (Wall 2006). The relationship of big data to big capital also indicates a structural subset of Information Capitalism, "Surveillance Capitalism" (Zuboff 2016), marked by a "systemic logic of accumulation" in which profits derive from ubiquitous surveillance, the exchange of data, and the modification of human behavior. This model is by no means inevitable, and the surveillance-based marketing and advertising bubble may burst.

Part of this strategic logic involves getting people to accept dragnet surveillance by displacing consumer anxiety (Turow 2006), asserting predictability as a form of trust, or encouraging routinized compliance. The level of public trust in surveillance practices is at a crisis point. Predictive advertising, where ads follow people around, provides a "creep factor" (Schneier 2015), the popularity of adblocking and encryption products (apps and devices) are on the rise, and a recent survey of American attitudes toward commercial tracking and profiling finds 93% of adults surveyed are "not confident that records of their activity collected by online advertisers will remain private and secure" (Pew Research Center, 2015). The majority of respondents believe that it is important to be able to maintain privacy in their everyday lives, which includes their online activities. In effect, people care about online privacy as digital communication is a fundamental aspect of everyday, "ordinary" life (Kennedy 2016).

The significance of surveillance-based advertising and marketing practices requires further examination and theorization. Privacy and self-determination are two interrelated implications of surveillance-based ad practices. Decisional privacy, or the freedom from interference in one's choices and decisions, enables the right to make decisions and the ability to exercise free will (Tavani 2010). Informational privacy, which includes control of the flow of personal information—but also algorithmic control over the meaning of data (Beer 2009; Kitchin and Dodge 2014; MacKenzie 2008; Mayer-Schönberger & Cukier 2012; Neff & Nafus 2016)—requires further critique. Additional concerns include: online discrimination (Gandy 2003; Lyon 2003; Nakamura 2002; Sweeney 2013), the financial manipulation of the poor, uneducated, and the elderly (Angwin 2014), digital labor exploitation (Fuchs et al. 2012; Terranova 2000) and the loss of political freedom (Schneier 2015).

This edited collection seeks to ground further awareness of the diversity and rigor of critical approaches to the study of advertising. In doing so, it also seeks to renew critical thinking about these approaches. While each chapter makes a unique case for what is needed, the range of responses represented as a whole in this collection argues that new critical theoretical frameworks, methods, and approaches are needed to better understand surveillance-based advertising practices, to best account for their ethical, legal, and human rights dimensions, and to provide alternatives. This collection provides a foundation for further research, inquiry, and critique.

References

Adorno, Theodor, and Max Horkheimer. 1989. *Dialectic of Enlightenment,* translated by John Cumming. New York: Continuum.

Andrejevic, M. 2007. *iSpy: Surveillance and Power in the Interactive Era.* Lawrence: University Press of Kansas.

Angwin, J. 2014. *Dragnet Nation: A Quest for Privacy, Security, and Freedom in a World of Relentless Surveillance.* New York: Times Books.

Bagkidian, Ben. 1983. *The Media Monopoly.* Boston: Beacon Press.

Barthes, Roland. 1972. *Mythologies,* translated by Annette Lavers. New York: Hill and Wang.

Beer, D. 2009. Power through the Algorithm? Participatory Web Cultures and the Technological Unconscious. *New Media & Society* 11(6): 985–1002.

Berger, Arthur Asa. 2000. *Ads, Fads, and Consumer Culture: Advertising's Impact on American Character and Society.* Lanham: Rowman & Littlefield.

Berger, John. 1972. *Ways of Seeing.* Harmondsworth: Penguin.

Clark, R. 1988. Information Technology and Dataveillance. *Commun. ACM* 31, 5 (May): 498–512. Retrieved from http://dx.doi.org/10.1145/42411.42413.

Duffy, Margaret. 1994. "Body of Evidence; Studying Women and Advertising." In *Gender and Utopia in Advertising; A Critical Reader,* edited by Luigi Manca and Alessandra Manca, 5–30. Lisle: Procopian Press.

Ewen, Stuart. 1976. *Captains of Consciousness: Advertising and the Social Roots of the Consumer Culture.* New York: McGraw Hill.

———. 1999. *All Consuming Images: The Politics of Style in Contemporary Culture.* New York: Basic Books.

Ewen, Stuart, and Elizabeth Ewen. 1992. *Channels of Desire: Mass Images and the Shaping of American Consciousness.* Minneapolis: University of Minnesota Press.

Frank, Thomas. 1997. *Conquest of Cool; Business Culture, Counterculture, and the Rise of Hip Consumerism.* Chicago: University of Chicago Press.

Fuchs, C., K. Boersma, A. Albrechtslund, & M. Sandoval, eds. 2012. *Internet and Surveillance: The Challenges of Web 2.0 and Social Media.* New York: Routledge.

Gandy, Jr., O. 2003. Privatization and Identity: The Formation of a Racial Class. Retrieved from http://www.asc.upenn.edu/usr/ogandy/c53704read/privatization%20and%20identity%20i.pdf.

Goffman, Erving. 1976. "Gender Advertisements." *Studies in the Anthropology of Visual Communication* 3: 69–154.

———. 1979. *Gender Advertisements.* Cambridge: Harvard University Press.

Hackley, Christopher. 2002. "The Panoptic Role of Advertising Agencies in the Production of Consumer Culture." *Consumption, Markets & Culture* 5(3): 211–29.

Hall, Stuart, Dorothy Hobson, Andrew Lowe, and Paul Willis, eds. 1986. *Culture, Media, Language; Working Papers in Cultural Studies, 1972–79*. London: Hutchinson.

Hardt, Hanno. 1992. *Critical Communication Studies: Communication, History, and Theory in America*. London: Routledge.

Harms, John, and Douglas Kellner. 1991. "Toward a Critical Theory of Advertising." *Current Perspectives in Social Theory* 11: 41–67.

Hayden, Tom. 2005. *The Port Huron Statement: The Visionary Call of the 1960s Revolution*. New York: Thunder's Mouth Press.

Hovland, Roxanne, and Gary B. Wilcox. 1989. *Advertising and Society; Classic and Contemporary Readings on Advertising's Role in Society*. Chicago: NTC Business Books.

Hovland, Roxanne, Joyce Wolburg, and Eric Haley, eds. 2007. *Readings in Advertising, Society, and Consumer Culture*. New York: M.E. Sharpe, 2007.

Inamoto, Rei. 2013. "The End of Advertising as We Know It—And What to Do Now." *Co.Create* 27 June. Online at http://www.fastcocreate.com/1683292/the-end-of-advertising-as-we-know-it-and-what-to-do-now.

Jay, Martin. 1986. "The Frankfurt School's Critique of Marxist Humanism." In *Permanent Exiles; Essays on the Intellectual Migration from Germany to America*, 14–27. New York: Columbia University Press.

Jhally, Sut. 1987. *The Codes of Advertising: Fetishism and the Political Economy of Meaning in the Consumer Society*. New York: St. Martin's Press.

Kennedy, Helen. 2016. *Post, Mine, Repeat; Social Media Data Mining Becomes Ordinary*. London: Palgrave Macmillan.

Key, Wilson Bryan. 1973. *Subliminal Seduction; Ad Media's Manipulation of a Not So Innocent America*. Englewood Cliffs: Prentice-Hall.

———. 1980. *The Clam-Plate Orgy, and Other Subliminals the Media Use to Manipulate Your Behavior*. Englewood Cliffs: Prentice-Hall.

Kitchin, R., and M. Dodge. 2014. *Code/Space: Software and Everyday Life*. Cambridge: MIT Press.

Laird, Pamela Walker. 1998. *Advertising Progress: American Business and the Rise of Consumer Marketing*. Baltimore: Johns Hopkins University Press.

Lears, T.J. Jackson. 1994. *Fables of Abundance: A Cultural History of Advertising in America*. New York: Basic Books.

Leiss, William, Stephen Kline, and Sut Jhally. 1986. *Social Communication in Advertising: Persons, Products, & Images of Well-Being*. New York: Methuen.

Lyon, D. 2003. Surveillance and Social Sorting: Computer Codes and Mobile Bodies. In *Surveillance and Social Sorting: Privacy, Risk and Digital Discrimination*, edited by D. Lyon, 13–30.

Mackenzie, A. 2007. Protocols and the Irreducible Traces of Embodiment: The Viterbi Algorithm and the Mosaic of Machine Time. In *24/7: Time and Temporality in the Network Society*, edited by R. Hassan & R. E. Purser, 89–108. Stanford: Stanford University Press.

MacRury, Iain, ed. 2009. *Advertising*. New York: Routledge.

Marchand, Roland. 1985. *Advertising the American Dream: Making Way for Modernity, 1920–1940*. Berkeley: University of California Press.

Marx, Leo. 1972. *The Machine in the Garden: Technology and the Pastoral Ideal in America*. New York: Oxford University Press.

Mayer-Schönberger, V. and K. Cukier. 2013. *Big Data: A Revolution That Will Transform How We Live, Work, and Think*. Boston: Houghton Mifflin Harcourt.

McAllister, Matthew P. and Alexandra Nutter Smith. 2012. "Advertising and Promotion." *Oxford Bibliographies*. DOI: 10.1093.

McAllister, Matthew P. and Emily West, eds. 2013. *The Routledge Companion to Advertising and Promotional Culture*. New York: Routledge.

McFall, Liz. 2004. *Advertising: A Cultural Economy*. London: Sage.

McGovern, Charles F. 2006. *Sold American; Consumption and Citizenship, 1890–1945*. Chapel Hill: University of North Carolina Press.

McRobbie, Angela. 2015. *Be Creative: Making a Living in the New Cultural Industries*. Cambridge: Polity.

McStay, Andrew. 2009. *Digital Advertising*. London: Palgrave-Macmillan.

Moeran, Brian, ed. 2010. *Advertising: Critical Readings*. 4 vols. Oxford: Berg.

Nakamura, L. 2002. *Cybertypes: Race, Ethnicity, and Identity on the Internet*. New York, NY: Routledge.

Neff, G., and D. Nafus. 2016. *Self-Tracking*. Cambridge: MIT Press.

Nixon, Sean. 2003. *Advertising Cultures; Gender, Commerce, Creativity*. Thousand Oaks: Sage.

Ohmann, Richard. 1996. *Selling Culture: Magazines, Markets, and Class at the Turn of the Century*. New York: Verso.

Packard, Vance. 1957. *The Hidden Persuaders*. New York: D. McKay Co.

Peters, John D. 1989. "John Locke, the Individual, and the Origin of Communication." *Quarterly Journal of Speech* 75(4, November): 387–99.

Pew Research Center. 2015. *American Attitudes about Privacy, Security, and Surveillance*. Washington, D.C.. Retrieved from http://www.pewinternet.org/files/2015/05/Privacy-and-Security-Attitudes-5.19.15_FINAL.pdf.

Reidenberg, J. R. 2000. Resolving Conflicting International Data Privacy Rules in Cyberspace. *Stanford Law Review*, 52: 1315–1371.

Said, Edward W. 1982. "Travelling Theory." *Raritan* 1(3, Winter): 41–67.

Sampson, Henry. 1874. *A History of Advertising*. Edinburgh and London: Ballantyne.

Sandage, Charles H. and Vernon Fryburger, eds. 1960. *The Role of Advertising: A Book of Readings*. Homewood: R.D. Irwin.

Schneier, B. 2015. *Data and Goliath: The Hidden Battles to Collect Your Data and Control Your World*. New York: W. W. Norton.

Schwarzkopf, Stefan. 2007. "Transatlantic Invasions or Common Culture? Modes of Cultural and Economic Exchange between the American and the British Advertising Industries, 1950–2000." In *Anglo-American Media Interactions, 1850–2000*, edited by Joel H. Wiener and Mark Hampton, 254–74. New York: Palgrave Macmillan.

Schwarzkopf, Stefan, and Rainer Gries. 2010. *Ernest Dichter and Motivation Research: New Perspectives on the Making of Post-War Consumer Culture*. New York: Palgrave Macmillan.

Seldes, George. 1929. *You Can't Print That! The Truth behind the News 1918–1928*. New York: Payson & Clarke.

Sinclair, Upton. 1919. *The Brass Check: A Study of American Journalism*. Pasadena: Published by the author.

Smith, Henry Nash. 1957. *Virgin Land; The American West as Symbol and Myth*. New York: Vintage.

Spring, Dawn. 2011. *Advertising in the Age of Persuasion: Building Brand America 1941–1961*. New York: Palgrave Macmillan.

Spurgeon, Christina. 2008. *Advertising and New Media*. London: Routledge.

Stern, Barbara. 1996. "Deconstructive Strategy and Consumer Research: Concepts and Illustrative Exemplar." *Journal of Consumer Research* 23 (September): 136–47.

Stole, Inger. 2006. *Advertising on Trial: Consumer Activism and Corporate Public Relations in the 1930s*. Urbana: University of Illinois Press.

———. 2012. *Advertising at War; Business, Consumers, and Government in the 1940s*. Urbana: University of Illinois Press.

Strasser, Susan. 1989. *Satisfaction Guaranteed: The Making of the American Mass Market*. New York: Pantheon.

Sweeney, L. 2013 "Discrimination in Online Ads Delivery Study." Retrieved from http://dataprivacylab.org/projects/onlineads/1071-1.pdf.

Tadajewski, Mark, and Robert Cluley. 2013. *New Directions in Critical Marketing Studies*. 4 vols. London: Sage.

Tavani, H. T. 2010. *Ethics and Technology: Controversies, Questions, and Strategies for Ethical Computing* (3rd ed.). Hoboken, NJ: John Wiley & Sons, Inc.

Terranova, T. 2000. "Free Labor: Producing Culture for the Digital Economy." *Social Text*, 18(63): 33–58.

Turow, J. 2006. Cracking the Consumer Code: Advertisers, Anxiety, and Surveillance in the Digital Age. In *The New Politics of Surveillance and Visibility*, edited by K. D. Haggerty & R. V. Ericson, 279–307. Toronto: University of Toronto Press.

———. 2011. *The Daily You: How the New Advertising Industry Is Defining Your Identity and Your Worth*. New Haven: Yale University Press.

Turow, Joseph, and Matthew P. McAllister, eds. 2009. *The Advertising and Consumer Culture Reader*. New York: Routledge.

Wall, D. S. 2006. Surveillant Internet Technologies and the Growth in Information Capitalism: Spams and Public Trust in the Information Society. In *The New Politics of Surveillance and Visibility*, edited by K. D. Haggerty & R. V. Ericson, 340–62. Toronto, ON, Canada: University of Toronto Press.

Wharton, Chris. 2015. *Advertising: Critical Approaches*. London: Routledge.

Wicke, Jennifer. 1988. *Advertising Fictions: Literature, Advertisement & Social Reading*. New York: Columbia University Press.

Williams, Raymond. 1980. "Advertising: The Magic System." In *Problems in Materialism and Culture*, pp. 170–95. London: Verso.

Williamson, Judith. 1978. *Decoding Advertisements: Ideology and Meaning in Advertising*. London: Boyars.

Young, James Webb. 1946. *The Diary of an Ad Man: The War Years June 1, 1942-December 31, 1943*. Chicago: Advertising Publications.

Zuboff, S. 2015. "Big Other: Surveillance Capitalism and the Prospects of an Information Civilization." *Journal of Information and Technology*, 30: 75–89. Retrieved from http://www.palgrave-journals.com/jit/journal/v30/n1/pdf/jit20155a.pdf.

Part I
Critical Political Economy

1   Marketers' Influence on Media

Renewing the Radical Tradition for the Digital Age

Jonathan Hardy

The distinctive contribution of the critical political economy of media approaches has been to examine the implications of advertising as a system of financing media and the influence of marketers on media content, media provision, and access to communications. Classic contributions examined advertisers' influence on non-advertising content and media firms' behavior. The problems they identified are of central concern today, but critical political economy theory and analysis need to be updated to deal with transformations in the ways marketing communications are produced and circulated within the changing dynamics of media-advertising relationships. Key features include the expansion of marketers' self-promotion ("owned" media), the "disaggregation" of media and advertising, as marketers bypass media to target and reach consumers directly through online behavioral advertising, and the "integration" of media and advertising through product placement, sponsored stories, and native advertising (Turow 2011; Hardy 2013). This chapter explores the strengths and limitations of political economy perspectives and offers guidelines for the contemporary analysis and critique of marketer influences on communications.

Advertising and Political Economy Critiques

Political economy addresses how resources are organized in societies. Critical political economy (CPE) refers to approaches that examine and critique the unequal distribution of resources and the power relations that sustain and reproduce such inequalities. In media and communication studies, critical political economy forms a distinctive sub-field, articulated in writings from the 1970s onwards. Its central claim is that different ways of organizing and financing communications have implications for the range and nature of media content and the ways in which these are consumed and used (Murdock and Golding 2005; Hardy 2014). Critical political economists generally share broader critiques of advertising as the leading ideological agency for capitalism due to its role in promoting consumerism and possessive individualism and for its regressive, stereotypical representations of gendered, racial, and other identities. Advertising has been examined as part of a system of communications that "engineers consumption to match production and reproduces the ideological system that supports the prevailing status quo" (Faraone 2011, 189). My focus, though, will be on another path of CPE inquiry that considers the consequences of media dependence on advertising finance and marketers' influence on media content and on what range of content and services media provides. Such analysis of the *relationship between media and advertising* is where I argue CPE has made its most distinctive contribution (Hardy 2014, 2015).

Media and Advertising Relationships

The critical political economy literature has tended to advance instrumental or structural explanations of advertiser influence. Instrumentalist explanations focus on the intentional actions and behavior of actors who seek to control communications. These may range from marketers' efforts to shape specific content or actions to influence the editorial environment to efforts to influence the broader orientation of media firms' output and their allocation of resources for telling stories and reaching particular audiences. Numerous accounts such as Soley (2002) and Bagdikian (2004) examine instrumental power in the form of marketers intervening to censor or shape media content. Various studies have assessed advertisers' use of economic pressure and the threat or actual withdrawal of advertising as a means of influencing media coverage and the extent of acquiescence or resistance by staff (Nyilasy and Reid 2011).

Structuralist explanations suggest that advertising operates as an "impersonal force" (Curran 1986) created by the cumulative decisions of advertisers seeking the most cost-effective vehicles to reach target consumers, thus creating a source of finance that is unevenly distributed across media. Advertising subsidy functions as a *de facto* licensing system, determining which ad-dependent media have the resources to survive and thrive. One basis for structuralist explanations lies in economic analyses of ad finance, whilst another is rooted in historical scholarship that considers how the professionalization of marketing nevertheless resulted in a shift to less politicized and more "neutral" decision making about advertising effectiveness, as media planners relied more heavily on quantitative data over subjective judgments (Curran 1978, 1986). Advertising influence can be impersonal too in that the "licensing" effect arises from the innumerable decisions of individual advertisers:

> Advertiser influence is so built in to the market context that not only is it often difficult to prove, but advertiser influence frequently occurs without the advertiser's inducing it by any specific act, sometimes even without the advertiser's wanting it.
>
> (Baker 1994, 103)

The implications of the uneven distribution of commercial subsidy for media serving poorer, ethnic minority audiences in the US are explored by Gandy

(2000, 48; 1982, 2004) who finds: "[t]o the extent that advertisers place a lower value on gaining access to particular minority audiences, those who would produce content for that segment will be punished by the market...."

Accounts such as Herman and Chomsky's propaganda model combine structuralist and instrumentalist explanations, with advertising finance amongst the five "filters" that shape what news content is published by encouraging media to become advertising-friendly in order to compete for advertiser patronage (Herman and Chomsky 2008, 2, 15; Murdock 2011). Other studies have suggested that advertising influence is largely internalized by media management, influencing editorial strategies designed to maximize revenue (Curran 1978, 1986). For Baker (1994, 44), the influence of advertising on non-advertising content can include favorable editorial coverage of advertisers' products and corporate interests, creating an editorial environment conducive to marketers' promotions, favoring higher- income audiences and reducing partisan or controversial content that may divide or delimit target audiences (Baker 1994, 44).

The level of economic dependence on advertising revenue has always been a key factor shaping the structure and content of different media. Baker (1994: 45–49; see also Rinallo and Basuroy 2009) usefully summarizes factors that can affect the extent on advertising's influence within a given media outlet. These include the level and kind of economic dependence on advertising, whether widely distributed amongst many advertisers or concentrated on individual advertisers or organized groups. Another factor is the acceptability of advertising influence on content decisions (and the "cost" of public disapproval arising from knowledge of influence). When this "cost" is internalized by media managers and workers, the influence of "professionalism" may act to resist advertiser pressure, with "accepted industry practice" another factor influencing behavior. Consumer expectations and awareness of ad disclosure and ad separation from editorial are other, increasingly significant factors. Finally, Baker includes the implications of conglomeration, citing examples of advertisers applying pressure on one part of the conglomerate's business in order to influence another.

Political economists insist on examining interrelationships among corporate media, ad agencies, and big business. For example, the tobacco giant Phillip Morris held seats on News Corporation's board, while News Corp. head Rupert Murdoch remained on the Morris board for 12 years. The pharmaceutical giant Pfizer had directors on the boards of Time Warner, Viacom, and Dow Jones. Such corporate interlocks indicate the "continuing symbiotic relationship between news, advertisers, and advertising" (Bettig and Hall 2012, 165; Bagdikian 2004). The ways in which executive boards influence operations and editorial decisions require situated analysis, yet the corporate integration of advertising and media raises profound issues for democracy, media, and culture about the powers of commercial speech. Transnational communications conglomerates such as Aegis, Omnicom,

WPP, Havas, and Interpublic colonize media and political systems around the world (Sussman 2011).

Changing Conditions

The CPE literature is valuable both for its own efforts to address historical changes and as a resource for assessing changing conditions. It shows that the relations among marketers, media, and users are dynamic, suggesting in turn the need to consider different forms of power and influence by market-ers in specific situations. Nevertheless, some general trends are discernible. First, marketer influence has increased across commercial media and media systems where commercial media predominate. Second, the countervailing influence of professional norms and institutionalized practices to restrict advertiser influence has tended to weaken, or in some cases collapse. Third, a complex range of challenges for marketers can mitigate and limit advertiser power. These range from the inherent risk and instability of cultural tastes to highly volatile market conditions. There are also on-going challenges from technological aids and cultural practices of ad avoidance, from remote con-trol zapping (McAllister 1996) to contemporary ad blocking.

The results of surveys, interviews with practitioners, commentary, and analysis of corporate data indicate how pressures have increased on advertising-dependent media to comply with advertiser demands and offer a host of added benefits including exacting more and more "editorial support" beyond paid advertising (McAllister 1996, 2000). Studies of US news media show increasing advertiser pressures across local and national TV and con-vergent print/online news (PEW State of the News Media Reports at www.journalism.org; FAIR's Fear and Favour reports www.fair.org; McChesney 2013). The variant findings are important too, in that they highlight how different factors influence outcomes in specific settings. Price (2003) found that US national news correspondents felt insulated from advertisers, with only 7 percent reporting pressure to report a story because of advertisers, although that set a relatively high threshold for advertiser influence. Indeed, indirect advertiser influence may be captured in the 20 percent who reported owner pressure to cover or censor stories. De Smet and Vanormelingen (2011, 12) surveyed 100 news journalists in Belgium and found 35 percent experienced pressure from advertisers, with 13 percent often approached to favor marketers by one of the four agents identified (editor-in-chief, direct editor, marketing department, advertiser). Further, professional journalism norms such as the "firewall" between editorial and advertising established in US news journalism (Gans 1980) were never as firmly established in the entertainment business or in media sectors like consumer magazines, which were based on closer interdependencies between media and marketers. Far from being a uniform dynamic, the intensification of ad pressure has varied and met varying responses in changing work cultures and conditions, from resistance (Steinem 1990) to normalization.

New Contexts: Issues and Challenges for Critique

The intensification of marketing communications within media content has been accompanied by largely uncritical responses from academics, including within "critical" studies of convergence culture. The latter includes the convergence culture approach of Henry Jenkins (2006), Mark Deuze (2005), and others; the creative industries approach of John Hartley et al. (2013); and the "new" critical media industries approach of Amanda Lotz, Tim Havens, and others (Havens and Lotz 2012). My argument (Hardy 2014, 2016) is that, while this culturalist scholarship is valuable and needed, it offers a problematic evaluation of media and marketing derived from its largely positive and affirmative reading of shifts toward greater consumer empowerment under capitalism. For instance, Deuze (2005) regards journalists' defense of editorial integrity against marketers (the firewall) as part of a conservative ideology to resist change and welcomes greater accommodation and collaboration with marketers. Jenkins goes further by suggesting that marketers are involved in processes of innovative content creation and storytelling that serve consumers and empower users. The critical political economy tradition is needed here for its greater attention to power asymmetries under the structuring influence of capitalism and for its attention to regulation and governance, not least the weakening of protections designed to prevent advertisers who pay the piper from also playing the tunes and influencing the playlist.

Media and Advertising Integration and Disaggregation

Digital media is at the apex of two key trends: toward the *disaggregation* of advertising and media and toward their *integration*. The characteristic relationship between media and advertising in mid-20th century media was *integration with separation:* Advertisements appeared alongside editorial matter in publications or between broadcast programs. While advertisers controlled their ads, media businesses controlled editorial, packaging, and distribution of the ad-carrying media. It can be argued that this was in fact a short-lived period, between the advertiser-sponsored broadcasting of the early 20th century and the growth of integrated content, such as ad-financed television, from the 1990s. Yet *integration with separation* reflected norms that "advertising—as the major funding system of the mass media—should not unduly influence the non-advertising content" (McAllister 2000, 101). While there have always been pressures and opportunities to integrate, the principles of separation were generally upheld by journalists and creative professionals, supported by managers, underpinned by self-regulatory codes of conduct in both media and advertising, and subject to stronger statutory regulation in sectors such as UK broadcasting (Hardy 2010).

The emergent relationship is *integration without separation*. The integration of media and advertising takes various forms, many with long histories, such as product placement, coterminous with the birth of cinema.

However, the opportunities and challenges of convergence and digitalization, not least the struggles to finance an enormous expansion of media, has brought increased pressures from marketers and increased accommodation by media. Product placement, branded entertainment, advergames, and infomercials are the most familiar outcomes (Lehu 2009; Hardy 2010, 2013). The emergent form is *integration without separation*, but this coexists with trends toward *disaggregation* of media and advertising. Marketers are less dependent on the intermediary role of media and are able to profile, track, and target consumers directly, with the resulting demand to reduce their subsidy to media by paying only the costs of delivering an advertisement onto a selected platform (Turow 2011). The traditional subsidy supporting the news, information, or entertainment surrounding advertisements is diminishing, with profound consequences for communication resources, public media, and cultural pluralism (Couldry and Turow 2014). Both integration and disaggregation reflect a shift toward enhanced marketer power in an era of increased media dependence on advertising finance.

Convergence of Owned, Paid, Earned, and Shared

Marketing professionals identify four main types of media: paid, earned, owned, and shared. Traditional advertising means paying to insert advertisements into media vehicles or other advertising spaces. Earned media describes public relations activities to generate editorial coverage. The third area, owned media, refers to marketers' own content, and here exponential growth has occurred across digital publishing and the production of branded content for online and mobile platforms, which has the effect of also increasing pressures on media for greater accommodation in paid and earned media. Finally, shared media refers to the circulation of marketing communications across social media and online as messages are created, shared, and adapted between users of various kinds from professional to amateur, including "influencers" like vbloggers who can be encouraged to act on behalf of brands along a spectrum overlapping with paid media. *Shared* also highlights another axis here in terms of levels of control over communications.

Traditionally, earned media consisted of content derived from public relations activities and communications but still subject to editorial control exercised by the media outlet. How much control and how much dependency, especially on elite sources, is a major topic for critical media studies (Herman and Chomsky 2008; see Hardy 2014). Studies also show increasing journalistic dependence on PR materials. "Churnalism" is a term that emerged to describe the PR-inflected journalism increasingly appearing due to accelerating production pressures on news outlets—particularly under-resourced local and online-only news—to constantly churn out 24/7 content updates and the corresponding requirement to meet that need by any means possible (Jackson and Moloney 2015). The relationship between media and

PR sources varies across different cultures of journalism, with consumer and entertainment media tending to have much closer co-dependencies, while legacy professional news journalism exhibited much greater resistance to it. Ad spending has long been a factor in obtaining favorable editorial coverage, with some sectors such as US local news going further in offering editorial-ad packages as inducements for marketers. Today's growth in editorial content produced by or on behalf of brands marks the extension of owned and paid media into earned and shared media.

Branded Content and Native Advertising

Across digital media, new forms of integrated advertising are developing rapidly. Content marketing refers to the promotion of branded editorial content in marketers' own media and third-party media. According to the Content Marketing Association (2016) it is "the discipline of creating quality branded editorial content across all media channels and platforms to deliver engaging relationships, consumer value and measurable success for brands." Branded content ranges from *The Lego Movie* to Red Bull's high-altitude Stratos dive and other audiovisual, entertainment-based content, but another common form is native advertising, editorial-like material supported by an outside party or advertiser. Native advertising refers to promotional messages paid for by advertisers that match the form, behavior, and user experience of the digital media in which they are disseminated. Such ads appear in news feeds, publishers' websites, search results, posts in social media, e-mail, and other digital communications.

Native advertising is more integrated that its print-based antecedent, advertorials, reflecting the greater affordances and incentives for intermingling editorial and advertising online as well as the shifting conditions and normative values encouraging institutionalization of advertiser-editorial collaboration (Carlson 2015). However, while advertorials are labeled as advertising, much native advertising is intended to disguise its ad status, blend into surrounding editorial, and fool readers. As an AOL executive commented, it should "look and feel as similar as it possibly can to the surrounding content" (Ponsford 2014). A recent study tested native ads on 242 subjects and found that fewer than 8 percent were able to identify native advertising as a paid marketing message (Wojdynski and Evans 2015). Another study found that 33 percent of British readers tended to be disappointed or were very disappointed when they later discovered that an article had been sponsored by a company, a figure that reached 43 percent in the US where native advertising is more prevalent (Austin and Newman 2015).

Branded content has grown rapidly, becoming a major focus for marketers during the last five years. One report (Hoelzel 2014) estimates that native advertising will increase fourfold from $4.7b in 2013 to $21b in 2018, with spending in 2015 reaching $8b. In the UK, content and native advertising grew to £509m in 2014, accounting for 22 percent of all display ad spending (Internet Advertising Bureau 2015). Billed as the savior for newspapers losing traditional ad revenue, publishers from the *New York Times* to the *Daily Mail*, Mashable, and Refinery29 deploy editorial staff or special teams to create native ads. *The Guardian*'s Guardian Labs, for instance, worked on 400 branded content projects in 2015 (Hayday 2015). Where previously relations were formed among brands, marketing agencies and media sales, publishers are increasingly offering the agency functions themselves to brands integrated with in-house production. BuzzFeed, for instance, offers creative execution, cross-platform distribution, and data analytics to brands. Vice offers "sponsored content" packages through Virtue, its faux-distinct in-house marketing agency.

The key context for these changes lies in corporate responses to declining advertising revenues, the challenges of monetizing content in new market conditions, and the declining effectiveness of display, banner, and other visually distinct ad formats. Some of the digital native publishers like BuzzFeed have moved entirely from display advertising to branded content. On the technical side, media producers find it increasingly easy and inexpensive to format ads to match the surrounding content in contrast to traditional media. "The effect," says the US Federal Trade Commission (2015, 2), "is to mask the signals consumers customarily have relied upon to recognize an advertising or promotional message." Finally, such integrated advertising is expected to grow as a response to software assisted ad blocking.

Problems and Governance of Ad Integration

Advertising has long been the patron of commercial media, yet various regulatory and market mechanisms set limits on that patronage. Regulations and industry norms upheld principles of separation of advertising. Market arrangements tended to work against advertisers exercising direct, instrumental power over editorial content. Marketers controlled advertisements (paid media) but not the content around them. Public relations firms chased "earned" media that they could not fully control. While the shifts we are seeing certainly pre-date digitalization, marketers' control is extending increasingly from advertising forms to integrated editorial forms.

Importantly, again, the pressures and implications are complex, with differing practices giving rise to different problems, for instance according to whether the promotions are paid or unpaid, published by brands directly or integrated into third-party editorial content. Much branded content is owned media, such as *Meet Me at Starbucks*, a storytelling video released recently on YouTube. As another indication of this complexity, an estimated quarter of branded content is user-generated rather than created directly by marketers. The particular problems associated with integrated marketing communications range from concerns about disclosure, deception, economic surveillance, and privacy to concerns about advertiser and ad-finance influences on media content, creative control, aesthetic agendas, editorial agendas, and corporate decision making. Identification of advertising is an important issue, although by no means the only one, and here rules have been toughened in some media systems. In August 2015, the Advertising Standards Authority (UK) introduced new guidance for vbloggers' brand endorsements. The US Federal Trade Commission (2015, 2) brought in new guidelines for native advertising, reaffirming the principle that "advertising and promotional messages should be identifiable as advertising." However, industry pushback in the form of the Internet Advertising Bureau described the FTCs requirements for plain language in describing branded content as overly prescriptive. So, regulatory battles lie ahead over descriptions such as "partner content," "promoted post," and "promoted by." What is most notable, though, is that the FTC is not concerned about the implications of commercial sponsorship on media as such, but rather about the likelihood of consumer deception. If an article is sponsored but does not promote the sponsor's brand, the article is not deemed an ad and so consumers do not need to be informed (even though the FTC recognizes that sponsorship of the article is itself a form of advertising). More fundamentally, the FTC is not directly concerned with the impact of branded content on the quality and integrity of media channels. The concern is that, once we are past the hurdle of consumer recognition of native ads, little is left in the prevailing regulatory arsenal to support restrictions.

Media-Marketing Convergence

Media and marketing integration is arguably the next phase of convergence, following that of mass media, telecommunications, and computing. Donaton (2004) was an early celebrant of the merging of entertainment content and commerce that has gathered pace over the last decade, with marketers moving increasingly into content production. The integration of media and marketing is occurring across corporate ownership, joint ventures, operations, and practices, forms and formats, and relationships with users. This merging includes personnel, practices, and values oriented to profit-seeking activities on behalf of marketable goods and services, whether brands, celebrities, or media. Both commercial media and marketing firms recognize themselves as being in the same business, concerned with selecting and offering suitably engaging content to reach target consumers in the most cost-effective ways. For Carlson (2015: 861), media abundance has increased the strategic importance for news publishers of advertising content itself in generating audiences, accompanied by efforts to advance new normative justifications that redefine journalistic work around a "curational norm of providing a coherent mix of both editorial and advertising content." However, such convergence remains conflict-ridden and contested, especially where institutionalized values other than profitability counter the normalization of marketization. Key tasks for research are to examine the particular dynamics of changing practices and the conjunction of forces that drive and resist such shifts.

Media Integration and Media Studies

This next wave of convergence is something that media and communication studies are relatively ill equipped to address. Marketing communications and public relations have tended to be specialist sub-fields with limited overlap with the rest of the field. The overwhelming preponderance of academic output on marketing communications embraces "administrative" rather than "critical" research in Lazarsfeld's (1941) terms, thus seeking to assist marketers in improving advertising effectiveness. When not explicitly affirmative, such scholarship tends to be descriptive, with normative-evaluative debate subsumed under managerial and operational concerns (such as minimizing ad clutter or consumer resistance) or narrowed to ethical considerations. While media and advertising integration *is* addressed in mainstream economic and business literature, it offers limited articulation across the full range of dimensions that media studies grapples with, which include the economic, political, organizational, practice-based, ethical, symbolic, social, and cultural.

By contrast, such broader articulation of media and advertising integration *is* addressed by two key traditions, critical political economy, and culturalist scholarship. Culturalist approaches have emphasized people's immersion in branding and brand culture and turned away from what were regarded as crude, Marxian theories of domination. The culturalist critique makes valid points, but the attack is lopsided. Critical scholarship is not wedded to presumptions of strong ideological effects or manipulation associated with mass media domination paradigms. Instead, it is distinguished by the concern to identify and address problems arising from the manner in which resources, including communication resources, are organized in social life, problems that are downplayed in culturalist accounts celebrating market provision. The radical tradition can be renewed by addressing the ways in which marketer power can be realized and undermined, challenged and contested. This requires analysis of practices, policy (including regulation and governance), and problems (the formulation of critique).

Frameworks for Analysis

I have proposed a framework for analysis of marketers' influence (Hardy 2014, 2015) that seeks to map the factors that tend to strengthen advertiser influence on media communications as well as countervailing forces that can serve to mitigate or contest advertiser influence. Such an approach seeks to bring the insights of earlier accounts into a more appropriate framework for examining emergent practices in convergent media. It proposes a broader and more open analytical framework than those derived from mass media influence (radical functionalism) or reception (manipulation). To do so, it incorporates political economic dynamics, regulatory contexts, work cultures, and practices, as well as multiple sites of agency and user interaction.

This section summarizes but also develops that framework in the context of emergent trends in advertising and their implications for analysis.

Studies of how the various agents operate and reflect on rules of exchange, including automation, can better illuminate how contemporary media-advertising relationships are produced and negotiated. Intermediaries have always existed between marketers and media in such forms as multi-agency creative work, media planning, and buying. The digital era has added to the chains of intermediaries particularly through automation. As key examples of this, the growth of real-time bidding (RTB) and programmatic advertising show the rapid evolution and proliferation of ad management using computing technologies. Intermediaries between the advertiser and publisher now consist of agency trading desks, demand-side platforms, ad exchanges, and services from audience-targeting firms to verification and fraud prevention (World Federation of Advertisers 2014). As a result, analyses of advertiser influence on media need to take account of more complex attenuations of power, as agency work spreads across digital advertising networks and into automation, including ad content-recommendation engines used to place branded content onto publishers' websites. Granting that earlier accounts engage with instrumental and structural explanations of power, such approaches need to be extended to incorporate more complex networks of actors and processes of automation. For example, there is scope here to draw selectively on aspects of Actor-Network Theory (ANT) in examining the involvement of human and non-human actants in advertising networks, while sustaining critiques of ANT's relative neglect of the temporality, wider power dynamics, and social consequences of networks (see Couldry 2008). More synthesizing of critical scholarship might also draw on insights from "new institutionalism," "convergence culture," and media industry studies on the cultures, practices, and governance of institutions, individuals, networks, and groups. These themes are further developed in feminist, Marxist, and culturalist studies of digital labor, precarity, work practices, and performativity (Fuchs 2014). Greater attention to work cultures helps expand an account of governance, including how formal regulation and informal rules influence commercial integration.

While the radical tradition highlights key problems arising from media dependence on advertising finance, investigating and challenging these problems persuasively requires the examination of the configuration of influences in a more dynamic and open manner. Critical work needs a revised mapping of the main factors that tend to strengthen marketers' influence on media and communications services as well as a new mapping of countervailing forces in order to aid the creation of increasingly open interrogation of marketer influences operating in specific instances. Here, I draw on Curran (2002) in seeking to identify for media-advertising relationships what that essay considers for media in general. My focus is on the power of marketers to influence editorial, operational, or strategic decisions by communication providers in ways that favor marketers' messages and interests.

For each of the factors identified below, we need to consider a *structural* dimension (economic), *sectoral* dimensions (institutional cultures shaping relationships in how communication services are organized), and *behavioral* dimensions (interactions and relations among specific actors, such as particular brand marketers, agencies and media firms, and computer systems). We need to consider specificities of firms, forms, and formats, which have different norms and expectations influencing behaviors and which together form the institutional and cultural contexts.

The main factors that tend to enhance advertiser influence on (non-advertising) media content and services are: (1) the commercial orientation of the media entity and corporate level promotion of advertising revenue maximization; (2) the media entity's dependence on advertising finance; (3) the level of competition to attract marketing finance and the influence of competitor behavior; (4) corporate level relationships with marketers and marketing agencies; (5) institutional/operational level organization and promotion of advertising integration (technical, labor, content creation, media-marketer interactions and transactions); (6) professional/pro-am normalization of advertising integration; (7) user involvement, user support/acceptance of advertising integration; (8) regulation and governance arrangements that are permissive of advertising integration.

These should be addressed together with the main factors that constitute countervailing influences: (1) the non-commercial orientation of the media entity (public service, community, radical, etc.); (2) low dependence on advertising finance; (3) market conditions favoring media sellers rather than advertising buyers; (4) corporate/institutional level separations between media and marketers; (5) professional and pro-am practices, cultures, and norms resisting advertiser influence; (6) users' actual/predicted responses in regard to their capacities as consumers and influential publics; (7) governance and regulation restricting advertising integration; (8) civil society action and influence.

CPE attention to advertising as a support mechanism for media remains of central importance, but it needs updating as "possibilities for the direct influence of content keep changing" (Leiss et al. 2005, 120). The classic CPE frameworks conceive of marketers as external to media firms in ways that no longer fit emergent patterns of corporate and operational convergence of media and marketing. Where postmodernists have tended in the pre-digital past to argue that the separation of media and advertising is irretrievable (Wernick 1990), a revised radical approach can inform a more nuanced analysis of the conditions in which commercial communications and media content combine and influence one another.

The CPE tradition is guided by critical social theory to identify and address problems. The extension of advertiser power in the digital age, as well as its limits, cries out for further study and public discussion. Ambitions for critical scholarship must include gathering evidence for a persuasive case to influence public policy making, defending space to carry out that work in the academy, and drawing on the strengths of strong student interest in these topics to help counter the threats to provide courses that are entirely framed within affirmative, pro-industry perspectives. What is needed is critical scholarship, informed by the theoretical sophistication of culturalist media studies, that gives close attention to material practices but continues to ask and address larger, critical questions about the ways in which advertising shapes our communication environments. A new phase of convergence is underway and we should make it our business to address it.

References

Austin, Shaun, and Nic Newman. 2015. "Attitudes to Sponsored and Branded Content (Native Advertising)." Reuters Institute for the Study of Journalism, *Digital News Report 2015*. http://www.digitalnewsreport.org/essays/2015/attitudes-to-advertising/.

Bagdikian, Ben. 2004. *The New Media Monopoly*. Boston: Beacon Press.

Baker, C. Edwin. 1994. *Advertising and a Democratic Press*. Princeton: Princeton University Press.

Bettig, Ronald, and Jeanne. L. Hall. 2012. *Big Media, Big Money*, Lanham, Maryland: Rowman and Littlefield.

Carlson, Matt. 2015. "When News Sites Go Native: Redefining the Advertising–Editorial Divide in Response to Native Advertising." *Journalism* 16(7): 849–65.

Content Marketing Association. 2016. "Who are the CMA?" http://www.the-cma.com/about-us/.

Curran, James. 1978. "Advertising and the Press." In *The British Press: A Manifesto*, edited by James Curran, 229–67. London: MacMillan.

———. 1986. "The Impact of Advertising on the British Mass Media." In *Media, Culture and Society: A Critical Reader*, edited by Richard Collins, James Curran, Nicholas Garnham, Paddy Scannell and Colin Sparks, 309–33. London: Sage.

Couldry, Nick. 2008 "Actor Network Theory and Media: Do They Connect and on What Terms?" In *Connectivity, Networks and Flows: Conceptualizing Contemporary Communications*, edited by Andreas Hepp, Friedrich Krotz, Shaun Moores, and Carsten Winter, 93–110. Cresskill, NJ: Hampton Press, Inc.

Couldry, Nick, and Joseph Turow. 2014. "Advertising, Big Data, and the Clearance of the Public Realm: Marketers' New Approaches to the Content Subsidy." *International Journal of Communication* 8: 1710–26.

De Smet, Dries, and Stijn Vanormelingen. 2011. "Advertiser Pressure on Newspaper Journalists: A Survey." HUB Research Papers 2011/37.

Donaton, Scott. 2004. *Madison & Vine*. New York: McGraw-Hill.

Faraone, Roque. 2011. "Economy, Ideology and Advertising." In *The Handbook of Political Economy of Communications*, edited by Janet Wasco, Graham Murdock, and Helen Sousa. Oxford: Blackwell Publishing.

Federal Trade Commission. 2015. "Enforcement Policy Statement on Deceptively Formatted Advertisements." https://www.ftc.gov/system/files/documents/public_statements/896923/151222deceptiveenforcement.pdf.

Fuchs, Christian. 2014. *Digital Labour and Karl Marx*. Abingdon, Oxon: Routledge.

Gandy, Oscar. 1982. *Beyond Agenda Setting*. Norwood, NJ: Ablex.

———. 2000. "Race, Ethnicity and the Segmentation of Media Markets" in *Mass Media and Society*, edited by James Curran and Michael Gurevitch. London: Arnold.

———. 2004. "Audiences on Demand" in *Toward a Political Economy of Culture*, edited by Andrew Calabrese and Colin Sparks. Lanham, MD: Rowman and Littlefield.

Gans, Herbert. 1980. *Deciding What's News*. London: Constable.

Hardy, Jonathan. 2010. *Cross-Media Promotion*. New York: Peter Lang.

———. 2013. "The Changing Relationship between Media and Marketing." In *Promotional Culture in an Era Convergence: Consumers, Markets, Methods and Media*, edited by Helen Powell. Abingdon, Oxon: Routledge.

———. 2014. *Critical Political Economy of the Media: An Introduction*, Abingdon, Oxon: Routledge.

———. 2015. "Political Economy Approaches to Advertising." In *Advertising: Critical Approaches*, by Chris Wharton. Abingdon, Oxon: Routledge.

———. 2016. "Money, (Co)production and Power: The Contribution of Critical Political Economy to Digital Journalism Studies." *Digital Journalism*. DOI: 10.1080/21670811.2016.1152162.

Hartley, John, Jason Potts, Stuart Cunningham, Terry Flew, Michael Keane and John Banks. 2013. *Key Concepts in Creative Industries*. London: Sage.

Havens, Timothy, and Amanda Lotz. 2012. *Understanding Media Industries*, Oxford: Oxford University Press.

Hayday, Graham (2015) "Guardian Labs: Our New Year Resolutions for 2016." 21 December. http://guardianlabs.theguardian.com/blog/info/2015/dec/21/guardian-labs-our-new-year-resolutions-for-2016.

Herman, Edward, and Noam Chomsky. 2008 [1988]. *Manufacturing Consent: The Political Economy of the Mass Media*. London: Bodley Head.

Hoelzel, M. 2014. *The Native Advertising Report*. BI Intelligence.

Internet Advertising Bureau UK (2015) "IAB / PwC study: Digital Adspend up 14% to record £7.2 billion." http://www.iabuk.net/about/press/archive/iab-pwc-study-digital-adspend-up-14-to-record-72-billion.

Jackson, Daniel, and Kevin Moloney. 2015. "Inside Churnalism." *Journalism Studies* DOI: 10.1080/1461670X.2015.1017597.

Jenkins, Henry. 2006. *Convergence Culture*. New York: New York University Press.

Lazarsfeld, Paul. 1941. "Remarks on Administrative and Critical Communications Research." *Studies in Philosophy and Social Science* 9: 2–16.

Lehu, Jean-Marc. 2009. *Branded Entertainment*. London: Kogan Page.

Leiss, William, Sut Jhally, Stephen Kline, and Jackie Botterill. 2005. *Social Communication in Advertising*, 3rd ed. London: Routledge.

McAllister, M. 1996. *The Commercialization of American Culture*, Thousand Oaks, CA: Sage.

———. 2000. "From Flick to Flack: The Increased Emphasis on Marketing by Media Entertainment Corporations." *Critical Studies in Media Commercialism*, edited by Robin Andersen and Lance Strate. Oxford: Oxford University Press.

McAllister, M., and E. West. 2013. *The Routledge Companion to Advertising and Promotional Culture*, New York: Routledge.

McChesney, Robert. 2013. *Digital Disconnect*, New York: The New Press.

Murdock, Graham. 2011. "Political Economies as Moral Economies: Commodities, Gifts and Public Goods." In *The Handbook of Political Economy of*

Communications, edited by Janet Wasco, Graham Murdock, and Helen Sousa. Oxford: Blackwell Publishing.

Murdock, Graham, and Peter Golding. 2005. "Culture, Communications and Political Economy." In *Mass Media and Society*, edited by James Curran and Michael Gurevitch. London: Hodder Arnold.

Nyilasy, Gergely, and Leonard N. Reid. 2011. "Advertiser Pressure and the Personal Ethical Norms of Newspaper Editors and Ad Directors." *Journal of Advertising Research*, 51 (3): 538–51.

Ponsford, D. 2014. "Going Native: Why Journalists Need to Be Involved in Taming Advertising's New Wild West." 7 May. http://www.pressgazette.co.uk/content/going-native-why-journalists-need-be-involved-taming-advertisings-new-wild-west.

Price, Cindy J. 2003. "Interfering Owners or Meddling Advertisers: How Network Television News Correspondents Feel about Ownership and Advertiser Influence on News Stories." *The Journal of Media Economics* 16 (3): 175–88.

Rinallo, Diego, and Suman Basuroy. 2009. "Does Advertising Spending Influence Media Coverage of the Advertiser?" *Journal of Marketing* 73 (November 2009): 33–46.

Soley, Lawrence. 2002. *Censorship Inc.*, New York: Monthly Review Press.

Steinem, Gloria. 1990. "Sex, Lies and Advertising." *Ms.* July/August: 18–28.

Sussman, Gerald. 2011. "Introduction: The Propaganda Society." In *The Propaganda Society*, edited by Gerald Sussman. New York: Peter Lang.

Turow, Joseph. 2011. *The Daily You: How the New Advertising Industry Is Defining Your Identity and Your Worth*. New Haven, CT: Yale University Press.

Wernick, Andrew. 1990. *Promotional Culture*, London: Sage.

Wojdynski, Bartosz, W., and Nathaniel J. Evans. 2015. "Going Native: Effects of Disclosure Position and Language on the Recognition and Evaluation of Online Native Advertising." *Journal of Advertising* DOI: 10.1080/00913367.2015.1115380.

World Federation of Advertisers. 2014. *WFA Guide to Programmatic Media*. http://www.wfanet.org/media/programmatic.pdf.

2 Free-to-play Games and App Advertising
The Rise of the Player Commodity

David B. Nieborg

The global diffusion of mobile devices—smartphones and tablets—has fundamentally changed the way consumers interact with brands and vice-versa, how companies are using marketing strategies to position their products and services. On an average day, US consumers spend more time using mobile apps than they spend watching television. Tellingly, the two major digital advertising behemoths, Facebook and Google, derive the majority of their revenue from their mobile products, instead of their desktop services. As a subset of digital advertising, mobile marketing is a particular catalyst for growth. And within the wider mobile domain, app advertising is spearheading the transformation of advertising tools, technologies, and strategies.

More so than Fortune-500 companies, the game industry (i.e., game studios, game publishers, and associated marketing service providers) is keen to leverage the accessibility and ubiquity of mobile devices. Game developers are widely considered to be ahead of the curve in terms of exploring and exploiting mobile marketing related innovations. On the one hand, mobile games are played by hundreds of millions of players on a daily basis and can therefore offer advertising inventory (i.e., highly trafficked in-app real estate for advertising banners and videos). On the other hand, the market for game apps is extremely competitive. As thousands of new mobile games are released *every day*, effective app advertising has become a key competitive advantage for game developers and publishers. This chapter focuses on this second instance of mobile marketing: game developers using in-app advertising for their freemium or "free-to-play" (f2p) games to generate new installs or in industry terms, to "acquire users."

User acquisition as a form of mobile marketing raises important critical questions pertaining to the emergence of mobile platform-based advertising, the position of players, their data and, in the end, their play. To gain a deeper understanding of the political economy of app advertising my approach takes an institutional perspective on the advertising ecosystem and the commodification of audiences (Turow 2011; Meehan 2014; Napoli 2014). In the era of connective platforms (Van Dijck 2013), app advertising, one could say, closes the loop. As opposed to the inherent "waste" associated with mass-marketing campaigns, app advertising promises an ecosystem where every action, or "event," is fully attributable. For f2p games this means that every step of the "funnel"—from player acquisition, to player engagement (i.e., playing), retention, and, potentially, player monetization—can be tracked, analyzed, and optimized and comes with an array of highly granular metrics or "key performance indicators" (KPIs). This data-driven approach to advertising has historical roots and builds on technologies and practices rooted in desktop-based digital advertising. At the same time, app advertising for f2p games goes far beyond digital advertising of physical products as mobile games are *contingent cultural commodities*: they are constantly altered, sometimes in real-time, to improve KPIs based on player actions.

The reason to focus specifically on f2p games is not so much their popularity or the US$30 billion generated in global annual revenue (Newzoo 2015). Rather, my interest lies with the implications of the freemium business model and its inherent inequalities. Popular mobile games, such as *Clash of Clans* and *Candy Crush Saga*, predominantly generate revenue via optional virtual consumption; on average a percentage ranging between 1 and 10 percent of players are also payers. Because of this structural imbalance of payers-versus-players, f2p games favor economies of scale, requiring game studios to focus on mass-scale user aggregation. For f2p games to effectively generate revenue, every aspect of their production, marketing, and usage has to be measured and optimized (Voigt and Hinz 2015). In this sense, they are to be considered services rather than products as the instances of game development, distribution, and advertising constituting cultural commodities, which were previously relatively distinct, are fully intertwined (Nieborg 2015), up to a point where it is difficult, if not impossible, to tell where one phase starts and the other ends.

The chapter is organized as follows: First, I will position mobile marketing against relevant historical innovations in digital advertising. Attention is then paid to the economics underlying the f2p business model, with a particular focus on the relationship of app advertising to the configuration of the app stores operated by Apple and Google. Following this discussion, the third section unpacks the advertising practice specific to the f2p business model known as "user acquisition." In a nutshell, by using mobile marketing platforms, game developers are able to "buy players" (Luton 2013, 135) via complex performance-based advertisement campaigns aimed at transferring players from one app to another. This seemingly straightforward process masks a growing sub-segment of the app economy that relies on mass-scale data aggregation and the individual tracking and targeting of players, thus tying into my argument of f2p games as contingent commodities. The fourth and last part of this chapter connects user acquisition with critical political economic theory and builds on Smythe's (1977) conceptualization of the "audience commodity" to introduce the concept of the *player commodity*. The chapter ends with a review of the political economic implications of user acquisition for players and developers.

The analysis in this chapter is informed by three complementary sources of qualitative data. One is a close reading of industry material, including white papers, company brochures, blog posts, and seminar material. The second source consists of 25 semi-structured interviews conducted between 2013 and 2016 with industry professionals working at app advertising firms, including ad networks, app marketing platforms, app tracking providers, and app analytics firms. The final source was participation observation conducted at a game app developer and at key industry events in the US and Northern-Europe, the geographic breadth of which is a necessary move due to how global the app economy is, especially when compared to other segments of the game industry. This chapter begins a study of the globalization of the app economy by focusing on app stores operated by Google and Apple and on mobile marketing and app development in North America and Europe.

Online Advertising: From Click to Tap

The emergence of the free-to-play business model is fully intertwined with the evolution of online advertising strategies, the global diffusion of mobile devices, and the political economy of ad-supported social media platforms. Before offering deeper insight into the market structure of the mobile marketing ecosystem, let me briefly reflect on the recent history of online advertising as current app advertising efforts, and user acquisition in particular, find their roots in both digital and non-digital advertising. Digital advertising, and app advertising by extension, should be seen as a mix of both old and new companies, tools and technology, regulatory institutions, business models, and industry practices (Stole 2014).

The first instances of web-based advertising were fairly simple and consisted of banner ads that were sold on a "cost per mille" (CPM, with a "mille" indicating a thousand views) basis. Two subsequent innovations in the history of online advertising worth singling out are the implementation of browser-based cookie technology and the "click" as a mechanism to measure individual ad interaction (Turow 2011). Together, these developments helped advance advertising strategies involving behavioral targeting: "the monitoring of people's online behaviour to use the collected information to show people individually targeted advertisements" (Zuiderveen Borgesius 2014, 21). For targeting to work, intermediaries need to collect, store, analyze, and disclose data on an unprecedented scale. As will be discussed in more detail below, user acquisition strategies build on behavioral targeting tools, technology, and practices by successfully adapting them to the app-based mobile ecosystem.

By all accounts, the online advertising ecosystem is highly complex. While, from a neoclassical economic perspective, online advertising is still a market consisting of buyers and sellers of advertising, the arrival of new intermediaries, the changing role of incumbents, and the adoption of

Internet-enabled mobile devices resulted in an increasingly opaque multi-sided market structure. Its complex value network consists of thousands of individual actors roughly divided among three groups: advertisers, advertising "publishers" (i.e., ad-serving websites), and a myriad of intermediaries (i.e., media buying agencies, ad networks, ad exchanges, ad trackers, and data providers). To add chaos to complexity, marketing professionals routinely invent sometimes-obscure new terms for common business practices. One way to comprehend the sprawling power dependencies is through work in the field of management on "multisided" or "platform" markets (Rochet & Tirole 2003). In its embryonic 1990s form, online advertising constituted a straightforward two-sided market where intermediaries operated platforms that connected two "sides": ad publishers and ad buyers. However, during the last decades, the ability to track, store, analyze, sell, resell, and auction advertising "inventory" through cookie technology and various kinds of behavioral data has entangled company roles and data flows even more.

A number of key developments in the evolution of this complex marketplace should be noted. First, throughout the 1990s, search-engines introduced cost-per-click (CPC), which produced pricing models for ad inventory that were sold via online auctions (Evans 2009). Search engines evolved into platforms themselves, adding an extra side to the advertising market. For example, Google Search operates in a three-sided market, bringing together users, content providers (web pages), and advertisers (Rieder and Sire 2014). Second, in the realm of web-based display advertising, the introduction of real-time-bidding (RTB) and programmatic buying technology added new levels of sophistication and aggregation to both the ad publisher side and the intermediary side. RTB protocols operating with demand-side platforms (DSPs) constitute buyer-driven ad-exchanges that conduct real-time auctions on ad impressions. Supply-side platforms (SSPs) do essentially the same on the publishing side by offering access to ad inventory (Turow 2011). Fed by various forms of data (e.g., a current location), a DSP predicts, evaluates, and optimizes ad bids to engage in an automated (i.e., "programmatic") bidding process. As such, real-time-bidding markets advance behavioral targeting by facilitating billions of parallel auctions on individual ads. This most recent instance of digital advertising signals a shift from probabilistic models to deterministic ones, a changing emphasis from delivering impressions to prompting actions, and the resulting ascendance of a performance-based approach to individually targeted advertising.

Mobile and social media platforms expand forms of data collection, storage, analysis, and disclosure. However, mobile platforms handle data gathering and user tracking differently than the more open desktop environment. Instead of relying largely on cookies, mobile marketing relies on other forms of fingerprinting technologies such as device IDs and IP addresses. For example, every mobile device running Apple's iOS is outfitted with a unique advertising identifier, described as "an alphanumeric string unique to each device, used only for serving advertisements" (Apple 2014). As most mobile user activity takes places outside the mobile browser and in individual apps, these more persistent identifiers are vital components for mobile marketing campaigns and thus replace web-based tracking technologies. New identifiers such as these help solve the "attribution issue" (who served which ad to whom?), aid in tracking users across apps, and make behavioral targeting on mobile devices many times more effective.

These advantages were not fully recognized at the start. Mobile marketing has only recently seen widespread adoption. As late as 2009 it was considered a "sleeper advertising medium" that demonstrated enormous potential but was faced with a number of challenges such as lagging mobile Internet technology, a lack of user-friendly devices, and a dysfunctional relationship among key actors in the mobile ecosystem, chief among them mobile operators or "telcos" (Wilken and Sinclair 2009). Despite these challenges, mobile marketing soon expanded, due not only to innovations in tracking tools already noted, but also to the consolidation of technology. Indeed, one of the reasons advertisers embraced the iPhone is that Apple solved many of these structural issues by integrating Internet connectivity, introducing app stores, and offering user-friendly interfaces (Goggin 2009). The last two years have been a turning point for mobile advertising.

App Store Politics

Global app usage is soaring and mobile Internet penetration is reaching all-time heights. Yet, advertisers as well as app developers are faced with a trade-off as Google and Apple altered the game industry's competitive dynamics by creating a central role for the app store that has emerged as a key means of game distribution and user aggregation. During the last decade, the global market for games ballooned into a globally diverse market of players and platforms. More accessible tools for game production and the accessibility of app stores of widely diffused mobile devices constitute in one sense the on-going democratization of game production and distribution. At the same time, the requirement for upfront monetary investments has been lowered significantly and, with it, barriers to market entry. As a result, app developers face fierce competition in a highly competitive and hit-driven ecosystem, made even more dynamic by, in the case of free-to-play games, user choices driven by whim and game availability instead of price.

The advent of integrated application stores has been a crucial development in the evolution of the game industry. Coupled with the introduction of freemium business models (revenue models that offer basic functionality for free and complementary access or features at additional costs), these virtual stores lower transaction and search costs for consumers (Rietveld 2016). Their emergence has benefited game developers due to the stripping away of power in mobile game value networks from network operators.

Instead, platform holders increasingly exercise key power in a much more fragmented and rather impenetrable ecosystem (Feijoo et al. 2012). App stores make this possible by providing developers with a secure and integrated payment and billing system, as well as a broad range of first-party (i.e., platform-provided) and third-party development tools and services, such as game-related software, social network integration, analytics, and remote computing and content hosting (Cuadrado and Dueñas 2012). This integrated approach includes a wide range of tools, technologies, and services necessary for in-platform advertising and thus user acquisition. More importantly, mobile platforms grant both developers' and third-party marketing companies' access to crucial advertising related innovations, allowing for large-scale user tracking and targeting.

Despite organizing and streamlining app distribution, the current configuration of app stores is both a blessing and a curse for app developers. The integrated, unified storefronts lower a user's search costs by offering tools to navigate hundreds of thousands of apps via search capabilities, rankings, and other algorithmically or hand-curated sections. Yet, despite these mechanisms, many industry insiders consider app discovery fundamentally broken. Consider the layout of Apple's App Store, which feeds into risk-averse consumer behavior. For example, Apple biases consumer selection by anointing some games as an "editor's choice" in its Featured section. More generally speaking, app-store rankings and ratings skew consumer choices. A recent study on app selection by Dogruel, Joeckel and Bowman (2015) found that the vast majority of users tend to deploy "take-the-first" decision-making heuristics and take their cues mainly from app store ratings and rankings. Yet, aggregated user choices also drive others' choice, in ways such as how the heavily frequented Top Charts section, particularly the Top Grossing category, heavily favors incumbents.

The accessibility for consumers of mobile games is further boosted by the ability to download games free of charge. Compared to the more straightforward and fixed transaction-based model of pay-before-play, the "free-to-play" (f2p) model covers a combination of post-release monetization strategies that are still very much in flux. In many respects, the political economy of the free-to-play business model is organized by the Pareto principle (a rule of thumb that states that 80 percent of the output is generated by 20 percent of the input). Key elements such as app usage and revenue are disproportionally distributed. A handful of developers generate the majority of app-related revenue (Hyrynsalmi, Suominen, and Mäntymäki 2016). App usage is highly concentrated because of habit formation and network effects (Jung, Kim, and Chan-Olmsted 2014). In addition, only a small number of users interact with in-app advertisement or spend money on in-app-purchases (IAPs). Despite so few paying players, those who do pay tend to spend, on average, significant monthly sums. This dynamic of disproportionality requires developers to invest significantly in advertising campaigns that aim at not only acquiring high-spending users (known as "whales") but also enticing lapsed payers to return. This brings us back to the domain of user acquisition and reconnects app development with advertising.

User Acquisition

On the face of it, creating a company to develop, produce, and distribute a free-to-play game appears to be a losing proposition. However, it generates value by simultaneously gathering and analyzing data on players and using app advertising as a revenue source as well as a user acquisition strategy. A common formula used by industry professionals, LTV > CPA, captures this economic rationale for free-to-play games. Where LTV denotes the average revenue from a player over her/his lifetime, CPA is the price paid to get a player to install the game, which ranges between 50¢ to US$12 or more during holiday seasons or in competitive markets. Only when a player generates revenue (LTV) that exceeds the cost of getting a player to play (CPA) does it make sense for developers or game publishers to invest in paid-player advertising campaigns. But campaigns in this environment differ immensely from even the most targeted campaigns in conventional media. Access to the services of demand-side advertising platforms offer developers the tools to simultaneously set up thousands of highly granular campaigns, targeting hundreds of discrete audience clusters and user actions. When a user taps on an advertisement and subsequently downloads the advertised app in the app store, a series of transactions takes place among intermediaries. A demand-side advertising platform can automatically bid on players who not only installed an app but also opened it or finished the first level of a game. These interactions determine the cost of acquiring a player, with the more targeted and the more specific the player action or the more specific a player profile the higher the Cost Per Acquisition, requiring in turn revenue off that player that exceeds this cost in order to fit the imperative of LTV > CPA.

Whether such a business is sufficiently profitable depends heavily on a developer's ability to accurately measure the value generated by existing players and accurately forecast the spending patterns of future players. As a result, developers must try to track players over multiple play sessions and see how they play, when, and how often they come back. In addition, developers must create either predictive or real-time analytics with which to do this, which means in turn that getting consumers to download and play a free game is part of a much larger effort by game developers to use actionable data to optimize player engagement and to heighten a player's "willingness-to-pay" (Voigt and Hinz 2015).

To make their data as dependable as possible, developers use a number of tactics for gathering key metrics and thus actionable intelligence. One such tactic is to "soft launch" an app, which means distributing in a few selected countries a test version from which the developer formulates and pre-tests data strategies prior to a release worldwide. A soft launch is typically kicked off with a "burst campaign" (a brief in-app campaign) in order to quickly attract a sizable player base and gain actionable data. Soft launches can generate insights on key financial metrics, as well as a related set of "engagement metrics," such as the Opens or Events Per Install (OPI/EPI), and use that information to model player profiles. For example, there might be a correlation between app installs and men in their thirties owning an iPhone who "like" *The Daily Show* on Facebook. This would entice developers to invest heavily in an acquisition campaign specifically targeting that user profile (or have Facebook find "lookalike audiences").

More recently, industry attention has focused on retaining players and getting them to play habitually. Doing so is made more difficult due to the fact that players tend to lose interest in free-to-play games fairly rapidly. As a result, free-to-play apps have a very short life cycle, which requires developers to formulate new ways to battle user attrition. One solution to this dilemma is pushed by mobile marketing agencies who, due to it being cheaper to focus on player retention than on player acquisition, argue that app advertising is particularly useful in reaching lapsed players. In order to target them, developers run retention campaigns that rely even more heavily on behavioral targeting that uses the wealth of data already gathered on existing players.

An example of what a typical re-engagement campaign might look like can help clarify these complex institutional pressures and relationships. Voigt and Hinz (2015) found that app users represented higher future Lifetime Values (LTVs) if they made early in-app-purchases and spent significantly on those early purchases. Armed with this knowledge, while also leveraging existing player data such as e-mail addresses and device IDs, developers can use demand-side advertising platforms to set up campaigns that target such players with a specialized advertising message. Tailored ads can be served to each individual. For example, a game studio can serve a specific player who made an early in-app-purchase with an advertisement in, for example, the Facebook app, offering a 20-percent discount on a future in-app purchase. Using app deep-linking technology, once this ad is clicked or tapped, the device goes to the targeted app, and the player is taken to the in-game store then greeted by a customized prompt that encourages the player to buy discounted virtual items. In this way, the f2p model finishes what Turow (2011) calls "the long click." In addition to pinpointing a specific player and presenting a specific offer, app advertising tracks the holy grail of online advertising: the final purchase.

The Evolution of the Audience Commodity

For those journalists and industry insiders who championed the implementation of the "free" business model in all segments of the cultural industries (Anderson 2009), the dominance of the f2p business model seemed to reify their thesis. In the app economy, the lower barrier to market entry has indeed resulted in the proliferation of hundreds of thousands of free games. With this abundance, however, "comes a new scarcity: that of attention" (Lovell 2013, 22). A burgeoning mobile marketing ecosystem populated by hundreds of companies specialized in app analytics, re-engagement, ad-tracking, real-time bidding, programmatic ad buying, incentivized app discovery, customer relationship management, and ad yield (i.e., optimization) management stands at the ready to convince app developers about the spoils of data collection, user profiling and the power of predictive analytics. Or as the title of an industry brochure reads: "Mobile Games: Now You Can Predict the Future" (App Annie 2015).

Yet, the very existence of this massive marketing apparatus makes the notion of "free" in free-to-play disingenuous. Indeed, app advertising and user tracking at the heart of the f2p game is what produces users as commodities. Indeed, the highly individualized, performance-based nature of user acquisition as an emerging mobile marketing practice raises questions pertaining to the commodification of players. The institutional application of Smythe's (1977) work on the "audience commodity" to television by critical scholars Meehan (2014) and Napoli (2014), and recent work on the nature of the audience commodity for connective platforms such as Facebook (Cohen 2008) and Google (Rieder and Sire 2014), is particularly helpful for a critical materialist analysis of this process. In the same way that audiences were manufactured and being sold to advertisers in the golden age of broadcast television, the advertising strategy of user acquisition should be seen as a continuation, intensification, and individualization of the commodification of audiences.

Just like data generated by TV audiences, players of f2p apps are tradable commodities whose exchange value is determined by the complex interplay among third-party advertising intermediaries. In the case of broadcast TV, rating firms make the audience commodity visible by translating "viewers into a verifiable audience" (Meehan 2014, 81). Meehan's TV-based argument maps quite well on the app economy. Developers of f2p apps want players; app developers capture players; ad intermediaries and social media platforms measure (i.e., track and target) players, and demand-side platforms "deliver" installs or engagements for app developers. Seen in this way, players along with their data and their in-app actions constitute the *player commodity*. Similar to Facebook, f2p games do not dictate desires or player behavior as much as they shape and organize players' activity in order to meet the needs of business models (Cohen 2008, 17).

Despite these similarities, game apps, online ad networks, and social media platforms work at a granular level much finer than conventional audience commodity production. They produce intricate metrics about individual players based on behavioral data that make possible individual targeting through app-based advertising. Conventional aggregated exposure-based audience ratings are turned into individual profiles that measure a player's willingness to play, share, and pay, with players tracked, targeted, and sold on a per-person basis. Good illustrations of a player's exchange value are the monthly indexes for the Cost Per Install (CPI) and Cost Per Loyal User (CPLU) published by Fiksu. The CPI "measures the cost per app install directly attributed to advertising," whereas the CPLU stands for the average cost paid by brands for an in-app advertising targeted at a "loyal user," which is defined as a person who opens "an app three times or more" (Fiksu 2016).

As of early 2016, the Cost Per Loyal User hovered between US$3.50 and US$4, suggesting how precisely values can be assigned to audience commodities produced through this system. As the Fiksu example indicates, players generate exchange value, however small, through in-app interactions. But this value is increased by a persistent and likely pattern of interaction made possible by the ubiquitous and habitual use of smartphones, readily available identifiers such as IP addresses, device and advertising IDs, and location data. While game play is in once sense voluntary and highly engaging, by being integrated with the political economy of both mobile and social media platforms (Fisher 2015; Van Dijck 2013), f2p games commodify user sociality and connectivity through constant surveillance.

Discussion and Conclusion

At this early point in the development of f2p games, it is increasingly hard to imagine what the f2p business model would look like without recent developments in (big) data storage and analysis, online advertising, and mobile media. While not universally popular among either players or developers, the f2p model has become a seemingly natural choice for all but a handful of mobile studios. Regardless, the model holds significant short-term and long-term implications for players and developers. The most notable concerns for users relate to privacy and discrimination through (dynamic) pricing, with these challenges mirroring in many ways those in the online advertising ecosystem at large (Turow 2011). Free-to-play ad intermediaries and technology providers have been at the forefront of implementing dynamic pricing strategies that focus on affluent users, thus creating the potential for mass-scale (price) discrimination. The passive and ubiquitous nature of data collection raises concern about privacy. Compared to cookie-based tracking, which happens on the client side, app tracking and targeting occurs largely on the server side. While cookies can be deleted or disabled, few clear opt-out mechanisms exist for user tracking and commodification through mobile apps.

In the foreseeable future, changes are unlikely. As Peacock notes, "currently, incentives for transparent, limited and consensual personal data extractions are low, while profits for invisible web tracking and unlimited data storage are high, all the while costs for storage are decreasing" (Peacock 2015, 5). Even though Apple-device users can limit ad tracking via resetting the advertising ID, or make use of Apple's recent decision to allow ad-blocking technology, these options only affect a small part of mobile app-tracking practices. And ad-blocking plug-ins only affect browser-based mobile advertising, which works on the client side.

The potential for unlimited in-app-purchase revenue presents an unmistakable siren call to investors, policy makers, and new market entrants, helping spur a vibrant developer ecosystem in which hundreds of mobile games are published on a daily basis. Yet, because of competitive entry, the seemingly great accessibility of app stores is highly deceiving. Even though players are more diverse and plentiful than ever before, Rietveld's (2016) recent analysis shows that, when compared to premium games, freemium games may attract twice as many players who play less, translating to lower revenue compared to up-front payment models. In practice, app development is fraught with uncertainty, and the ecosystem is populated with mostly small teams that are able to exert a minimum of influence over the terms of distribution. After disintermediating the role of "telcos," the duopoly of Google and Apple has had little trouble setting technological standards and platform governance structures that benefit their own business models and interests.

The issue thus becomes to what degree user acquisition acts as a catalyst for inequality or as an opportunity for renewed competitiveness and diversity. I would argue that app advertising's high-capital requirements and knowledge-intensive nature suggest the former. Already we see a growing divide between two classes of f2p app developers. By far the largest group (let's call them "The 99%") consists of app developers that serve as ad publishers and rely on advertising as a source of income. Then there is the very select group of "Net Advertisers": well-capitalized start-ups, superstar game publishers, and studios that rely primarily on in-app-purchases as a source of income and have the know-how and monetary capital to engage in user acquisition campaigns of a mass, often global, scale. The f2p hit *Clash of Clans* is a suitable example of a game that is heavily advertised online and offline and that generates substantial revenue solely through the sale of virtual currency. As a member of a small inner circle of incumbents, the game shows remarkable staying power. It has been on top of the Top Grossing segment of the Top Charts section in Apple's App Store for years. Similarly, King Digital Entertainment, Machine Zone, and a handful of others have been quite skilled at long-term player retention.

In other words, Net Advertisers such as Supercell are becoming the "dust busters" of the app economy by vacuuming up as many players as possible while simultaneously looking for players that show a propensity to pay. Ironically, by serving as player aggregators, The 99% are sowing the seeds for their own demise. For the Net Advertisers, user acquisition serves as a means to an end, the goal being finding those players that are willing to spend lavishly on in-app-purchases. Yet, because both parties are active in the same ecosystem and their games are commonly outfitted with the same analytics and tracking tools, The 99% help pinpoint loyal p(l)ayers of whom there are so few. The premium price of loyal users makes app advertising increasingly competitive, creating a two-tiered system that reinforces power asymmetries in a growing segment of the game industry. Lastly, the arrival of "big brands" (such as retailers, travel companies, and movie studios) in the app ecosystem is likely to drive further demand for ad inventory. As mentioned previously in this chapter, the Cost Per Loyal User and Cost Per Install indexes have been rising steadily over the course of 2015. And while there are billions of mobile devices, the pool of loyal users, let alone "payers," is finite. The ability of The 99% of app developers to remain competitive in the marketplace for app engagement is already severely compromised.

To conclude, the great majority of players quite vocally loathe spending money on in-app purchases and, by doing so, they sustain the notion of f2p games as free. The integration of in-app advertising, and the emergence of user acquisition strategies in particular, turn the free-to-play descriptor into an inherently deceptive proposition. Just as advertising-supported broadcast television should not be considered free, f2p games should not be either. App advertising transforms, extends, and intensifies the process of audience commodification and the structure and nature of the cultural commodity form in multi-sided markets. The dynamic we see playing out in the realm of free-to-play app advertising—the contingent nature of cultural commodities and the inherent disproportionality associated with app stores and the freemium business model—is a harbinger of a future that is increasingly dominated by advertising-driven platforms and apps. Going forward, vital questions remain pertaining to the concentration of capital and power in the app economy as well as the long-term sustainability of new revenue models given the increasingly complex and capital-intensive nature of app advertising.

References

Anderson, Chris. 2009. *Free: The Future of a Radical Price*. New York: Hyperion.

App Annie. 2015. "Mobile Games: Now You Can Predict the Future." http://blog.appannie.com/app-adoption-cycle/.

Apple. 2014. "ASIdentifierManager." https://developer.apple.com/library/ios/documentation/AdSupport/Reference/ASIdentifierManager_Ref/index.html#//apple_ref/occ/cl/ASIdentifierManager.

Cohen, Nicole S. 2008. "The Valorization of Surveillance: Towards a Political Economy of Facebook." *Democratic Communiqué* 22 (1): 5–22.

Cuadrado, Félix, and Juan C. Dueñas. 2012. "Mobile Application Stores: Success Factors, Existing Approaches, and Future Developments." *IEEE Communications Magazine* 50 (11): 160–67.

Dogruel, Leyla, Sven Joeckel, and Nicholas D. Bowman. 2015. "Choosing the Right App: An Exploratory Perspective on Heuristic Decision Processes for Smartphone App Selection." *Mobile Media & Communication* 3 (1): 125–44.

Evans, David S. 2009. "The Online Advertising Industry: Economics, Evolution, and Privacy." *Journal of Economic Perspectives* 23 (3): 37–60.

Feijoo, Claudio, José-Luis Gómez-Barroso, Juan-Miguel Aguado, and Sergio Ramos. 2012. "Mobile Gaming: Industry Challenges and Policy Implications." *Telecommunications Policy* 36 (3): 212–21.

Fiksu. 2016. "Fiksu Recourses." March 21, 2016. https://www.fiksu.com/resources/fiksu-indexes.

Fisher, Eran. 2015. "Class Struggles in the Digital Frontier: Audience Labour Theory and Social Media Users." *Information, Communication & Society* 18 (9): 1108–22.

Goggin, Gerard. 2009. "Adapting the Mobile Phone: The iPhone and Its Consumption." *Continuum* 23 (2): 231–44.

———. 2014. "Facebook's Mobile Career." *New Media & Society* 16 (7): 1068–86.

Hyrynsalmi, Sami, Arho Suominen, and Matti Mäntymäki. 2016. "The Influence of Developer Multi-Homing on Competition between Software Ecosystems." *Journal of Systems and Software* 111 (January): 119–27.

Jung, Jaemin, Youngju Kim, and Sylvia Chan-Olmsted. 2014. "Measuring Usage Concentration of Smartphone Applications: Selective Repertoire in a Marketplace of Choices." *Mobile Media & Communication* 2 (3): 352–68.

Lovell, Nicholas. 2013. *The Curve: How Smart Companies Find High-Value Customers*. New York: Portfolio Hardcover.

Luton, Will. 2013. *Free-to-Play: Making Money From Games You Give Away*. San Francisco, CA: New Riders.

Meehan, Eileen R. 2014. "Ratings and the Institutional Approach; A Third Answer to the Commodity Question." In *The Audience Commodity in a Digital Age: Revisiting a Critical Theory of Commercial Media*, edited by Lee McGuigan and Vincent Manzerolle, 75–89. New York, NY: Peter Lang Publishing.

Napoli, Philip M. 2014. "The Institutionally Effective Audience in Flux: Social Media and the Reassesment of the Audience Commodity." In *The Audience Commodity in a Digital Age: Revisiting a Critical Theory of Commercial Media*, edited by Lee McGuigan and Vincent Manzerolle, 115–33. New York, NY: Peter Lang Publishing.

Newzoo. 2015. "The Mobile Gaming Landscape 2015. And the Power Users Who Shaped It." Trend Reports. http://www.newzoo.com/trend-reports/the-mobile-games-market-in-2015-report/.

Nieborg, David B. 2015. "Crushing Candy: The Free-to-Play Game in Its Connective Commodity Form." *Social Media + Society* 1 (2): 1–12. doi: 10.1177/2056305115621932.

Peacock, Sylvia E. 2014. "How Web Tracking Changes User Agency in the Age of Big Data: The Used User." *Big Data & Society* 1 (2): 91–107.

Rieder, Bernhard, and Guillaume Sire. 2014. "Conflicts of Interest and Incentives to Bias: A Microeconomic Critique of Google's Tangled Position on the Web." *New Media and Society* 16 (2): 195–211.

Rietveld, Joost. 2016. "Creating Value through the Freemium Business Model: A Consumer Perspective" (February 24, 2016). Available at SSRN: http://ssrn.com/abstract=2737388.

Rochet, Jean-Charles, and Jean Tirole. 2003. "Platform Competition in Two-Sided Markets." *Journal of the European Economic Association* 1 (4): 990–1029.

Smythe, Dallas. 1977. "Communications: Blindspot of Western Marxism." *Canadian Journal of Political and Social Theory* 1 (3): 1–27.

Stole, Inger L. 2014. "Persistent Pursuit of Personal Information: A Historical Perspective on Digital Advertising Strategies." *Critical Studies in Media Communication* 31 (2): 129–33.

Turow, Joseph. 2011. *The Daily You: How the New Advertising Industry Is Defining Your Identity and Your Worth*. New Haven: Yale University Press.

van Dijck, José. 2013. *The Culture of Connectivity: A Critical History of Social Media*. Oxford: Oxford University Press.

Voigt, Sebastian, and Oliver Hinz. 2015. "Making Digital Freemium Business Models a Success: Predicting Customers' Lifetime Value via Initial Purchase Information." *Business & Information Systems Engineering*: 1–12. doi: 10.1007/s12599-015-0395-z.

Wilken, Rowan, and John Sinclair. 2009. "'Waiting for the Kiss of Life' Mobile Media and Advertising." *Convergence: The International Journal of Research into New Media Technologies* 15 (4): 427–45.

Zuiderveen Borgesius, Frederik J. 2014. "Improving Privacy Protection in the Area of Behavioural Targeting." PhD thesis, Universiteit van Amsterdam.

3 Recovering Audience Labor from Audience Commodity Theory

Advertising as Capitalizing on the Work of Signification

Brice Nixon

A key critical theory that has been used to explain advertising's role in the processes by which communication is capitalized is the theory of the audience commodity, which claims that advertisers purchase audiences as commodities from media companies that thereby generate advertising revenue. In this chapter, I argue that while the theory of the audience commodity is an inaccurate representation of the process of capitalizing on communication through advertising revenue, the neglected concept of audience *labor* provides a critical means of understanding advertising. Versions of the audience commodity theory were first developed as an aspect of the critical political economy of communication in the 1970s and 1980s, beginning with Smythe (1977, 4), who explains advertising as a process by which mass media companies commodify audience labor power, i.e., audience capacity to "pay attention," in order to sell it to advertisers. Audience activities of consuming meaning by paying attention to, e.g., a commercial broadcast television program are treated by a broadcasting company and other media companies as a kind of audience labor. The advertising revenue of mass media companies is money advertisers pay to control audience labor, because it means they control what people pay attention to: Advertisers want people to pay attention to their advertisements.

Other scholars built upon Smythe's initial formulation, such as Jhally and Livant (1986), despite some differences. Meehan (1984) ignores the issue of audience labor, focusing instead on advertising revenue as money gained in exchange for audience commodities consisting of audience ratings, not the "actual audience" (Meehan 1993). More recently, Andrejevic (2002; 2011) and Fuchs (2010) note commodification or exploitation of digital-media labor, although neither considers the consumption activities Smythe termed audience labor.

However, none of these efforts moves us closer to comprehending the role of advertising in the capitalization of communication. While Smythe valuably recognized the materiality of signifying practices and the importance of noting the conditions of those practices, this chapter sets aside the audience commodity in order to focus on audience labor and its work of signification. Doing so means not hunting for a commodity but instead grasping how communication is capitalized. It develops the concept of audience labor within a political economy that describes the exploitation of that labor as the key process in turning communicative practices into the means for value appropriation and capital accumulation.

The chapter begins by describing a materialist and dialectical theory of signification that is a significant departure from the existing critical approaches to the production of meaning. It then uses that perspective to turn the undeveloped concept of audience labor into the basis for a theory of audience activities as the work of subjective signification. It concludes by outlining a political economy of signification that explains how audience labor is channeled and exploited in the advertising process. Accompanying is an illustration of the analytical power of this recovery of audience labor in a series of examples of industry efforts to capitalize on the audience labor of signification through advertising.

Toward a Materialist and Dialectical Theory of Signification

If neither the audience commodity nor digital labor provides an adequate explanation of advertising from the perspective of the political economy of communication (Nixon 2013), then what is needed is to radically materialize signification (Williams 1977, 92). As Peck (2006) demonstrates, this is precisely the move the critical approaches of the political economy of communication and cultural studies have yet to sufficiently make. Smythe's suggestion that audiences labor was a striking position to take, but audience activities are a kind of labor that cannot be commodified, as will be discussed. A deeper consideration of signifying practices makes possible in turn a deeper consideration of the nature of audience practices, which provides the means to further develop the concept of audience labor into a political economy of signification.

The fundamental premise of Marx's method is human activity: labor, in political economic terms (Marx 1978a, 143–45; 1978b, 149). Four years before Smythe's initial article on the audience commodity, Williams called for just this focus not on texts and meanings but on "the nature of a practice and then its conditions" (Williams 1980, 47, first published in *New Left Review* in 1973). As Schiller (1996) notes, communication theory has long been deformed by a definitional separation of meaning as mental/ideational concepts from material activities. By contrast, the "unified conceptual framework" of labor that Schiller proposes as an antidote informs the direction taken here. Williams says as much, urging us to "look at our actual productive activities without assuming in advance that only some of them are material (Williams 1977, 94). More specifically, Williams (1980b) urged recognition of the means of communication as means of production. Communicative practices are productive practices within the "whole social material process" (Williams 1977, 94) that is human life, with means of communication ranging "from the simplest forms of language to the most advanced forms of communications technology" (1980b, 50). Signification is "a practical material activity; it is indeed, literally, a means of production" (1977, 38).

Peck (2002, 2006) suggests that Sartre also proposes human signifying activity as a material process and as part of a dialectic of signification, with our signifying activity producing materialized and objectified significations but always in an encounter with others' significations. Sartre also notes the implications of materialized and objectified significations *on us*. In addition to our own meaning-making practices as material, these practices occur within a field of meanings produced by others and with the power to condition our own activity. This is what makes it a dialectical theory: We are "both signifying agents and the signified objects of the materialized results of our own activity" (Peck 2002, 152). All of our activity produces materialized significations, but all of our activity is also conditioned by materialized significations—a power that our activity gives to that "worked matter" (Sartre 2004, 122–25, 169, 183).

Particularly crucial for the critical study of advertising is Sartre's claim, as Peck (2006, 116) explains it, that our activity "inscribes matter with human significance," but that matter then "acquires the power to signify us and thereby determine a 'field of possibilities' that demand our action" as we encounter it through our actions. Advertisements are produced as materialized and objectified significations to condition our signifying activity. But they exist, and we act, in a field of materialized and objectified significations, so they can condition but not uniquely determine the result of our signifying activity. This power over meaning-making (and human activity in general), as uncertain as it is, is clearly enough power to convince advertisers to pay to gain it.

Audience Labor as the Work of Subjective Signification

The materialist theory of signification outlined in the previous section provides the basis for a slightly more concrete theory of the *labor* of signification. This is the basis for a political economy of signification. Here I am specifically concerned with what I seek to analytically distinguish as *subjective* signifying practices. Audience practices are signifying in a subjective sense, as the meaning produced is in the consciousness of the producer. Those audience practices constitute an audience labor of signification. An understanding of the audience labor process is a necessary basis for a political economy of signification that provides a critical understanding of advertising.

While Smythe (1978, 121) conceptualized audience labor as helping produce ideology and consciousness, he paid insufficient attention to the particularities of signification. Baudrillard's (1981; published in French in 1972) effort earlier in the 1970s to produce a "critique of the political economy of the sign" usefully highlights "the *labor* of signification" (93, emphasis added) and "ideological labor" (89) as something not accounted for in political economy, thus coinciding with a major part of the project of Western Marxism (Jacoby 1979). He was also correct in describing communication theory's inability to truly comprehend signification (Baudrillard 1981, 164–84), an observation that was also the basis of Smythe's (1977) theory and claim of a "blindspot" in Western Marxism. However, Baudrillard's theory retains the distinction between mental and material labor and rejects political economy (Baudrillard 1981, 112–14).

A materialist and dialectical theory of signification makes it possible to put Baudrillard's "labor of signification" back *within* political economy. Following Smythe, I focus on the audience aspect of this labor: the labor of *subjective* signification. While those practices involve the consumption of meaning as paying attention to materialized and objectified meaning, they also involve the production of meaning, as cultural-studies scholars have emphasized (e.g., Hall [1980] 2006; Fiske 1987). However, despite this recognition, this approach also has yet to fully recognize meaning making as material, just as much of the political economy of communication has neglected to see it as labor.

Revisiting the discussion of "labor" itself helps clarify how advertising capitalizes on the audience labor of signification (Nixon 2014). Marx's (1990, 283–92) theory of the labor process in Volume I of *Capital* has three elements: labor, objects of labor, and instruments of labor (284). Extending this into the audience labor process, these elements become signifying audience labor, signified objects of audience labor, and instruments of audience labor, which mediate audience labor and its signified objects. Like all labor processes, the audience labor process is productive through consumption (290). This is obvious in the audience labor process, as audiences are defined as the consumers of meaning. But, as a labor process, audience activity also produces something: meaning. This audience labor process differs from labor that is commodified in the production of commodities, because it entails individual, rather than productive, consumption. The product is "the consumer himself" (290), as the meaning produced is subjective. This is a primary reason the theory of the audience commodity is incomplete.

While audience labor cannot be commodified, I argue it can be exploited. The dialectic of signification makes clear how that is possible. Audience labor requires objects and instruments as its means of production (Marx 1990, 287)—communicative production or signification. The means of communication, as means of production, "are themselves always socially and materially produced" (Williams 1980b, 50). That fact allows producers of the objects and instruments of audience labor to direct the audience labor process. The signified objects of audience labor are materialized and objectified significations that, in the US, are copyrighted from the moment they materialize. Audience labor is not autonomous. It is conditioned by access to the signified objects it works on, and that access is restricted by intellectual property rights. The signifying activity of audience labor is also conditioned by the signifying activity of those signified objects it consumes and works on, which provides an additional determination on signification that is of particular interest to advertisers. A political economy of signification provides an understanding of how those processes occur in relation to advertising.

Advertising as the Exploitation of Audience Labor: Toward a Political Economy of Signification

What can now be seen is that the exploitation of audience labor is the core process by which communication is capitalized. The theory of that process can be seen as a political economy of signification, which accounts for how processes of surplus-value appropriation and capital accumulation occur through processes of signification. Subjective signification—the work of the audience—is the aspect of signification that is directly connected to the appropriation of surplus value and the accumulation of capital. Advertising is one way in which audience labor is exploited, with processes of communication (of consuming and producing meaning) also processes of capital accumulation. Despite drawbacks noted above, Baudrillard helped develop some key insights. For Baudrillard, the reified labor of signification was not comprehensible in the terms of political economy; it required a more general political economy of the sign. That is how he concluded that it is "absurd" to claim that "the mode of production of significations" is "the 'capitalist' mode of production" (Baudrillard 1981, 115). However, the terms of political economy provide a means of comprehending signifying activity as an aspect of material production, but only when political economy takes signification seriously and in its specificity as a kind of material activity.

Baudrillard (1981, 115) also asked the fundamental question of a political economy of signification: "In what social relation is [signification] produced?" The materialist answer to this question is the one explicitly rejected by Baudrillard, who separated "mastery of the process of signification" from "ownership of the means of production" (Baudrillard 1981, 116). Across a range of communicative practices, capitalist social relations are dominant, as this is specifically determined by ownership of the means of communicative production and signification. In the simple case of viewing a video, one also views commercials. As Baudrillard (83, 113–15, 147) insists, consumption is, indeed, a part of the labor of signification or sign production.

Audience activities of consuming objectified meaning and producing subjective meaning are conditioned in turn by a capital-labor relation of what can be called communicative capital and audience labor. A second capital-labor relation exists between communicative capital and what I term cultural labor, by which I mean the labor that produces the meanings audiences consume. However, the communicative-capital/*audience*-labor relation is where surplus value is appropriated and capital is accumulated because, like capitalizing on land, surplus value is appropriated by means of a "production-determining *distribution*" relation (Harvey 2006, 332, emphasis added) rather than through the exploitation of labor directly in the production process. The communicative production of objectified and materialized meanings as subjective signification is, like land in a different context, both "an indispensable *condition* of production" and "a *means* of production" (73, emphasis original). Control over objects of audience labor in turn conditions audience labor's productive process of signification. It is the materiality and dialectic of signification that determines audience labor.

Another piece deserving attention is the productive determination of the communication medium. While audience labor (the signifying activity) requires materialized and objectified meanings (signified objects) to consume and work on, the signifying work on those objects is mediated by an instrument of audience labor, which is a communication medium. The nature of this medium, then, also conditions audience labor. For example, a newspaper company in the US in the nineteenth century could require potential readers to pay for its news (a signified object) even though it was not protected by copyright, because that news was only available for consumption when it was materialized and objectified via printing (an instrument of audience labor). This is a direct process of exploiting audience labor, as it is the use of power over the conditions of audience labor to appropriate surplus value from that labor. It is surplus-value appropriation through a relation of distribution: the extraction of *rent*, which is surplus value appropriated in return for access to and use of but not ownership of means of production or other resources (Harvey 2006, 330).

Upon clarifying the communicative capital-audience labor relation of exploitation, advertising's role in the exploitation of audience labor and capitalization of communication can be better understood. Advertising is a more complex process of exploiting audience labor. A communicative capitalist such as a newspaper company can determine audience labor's signifying activities as well as how the consumption of signified objects occurs. Rather than create a condition of direct exploitation in which audience consumption and signification only occur in exchange for payment (the appropriation of surplus value as rent), a newspaper company creates a condition in which the consumption of news also involves an encounter with advertisements. This is what US newspapers in the nineteenth century increasingly chose to do. The signifying activity of audience labor is channeled into a field of materialized and objectified significations that includes news and advertisements. The appropriation of surplus value in this case occurs through an indirect process of exploiting audience labor and another relation of distribution: *interest*, with objects of audience labor now including advertisements. The surplus value extracted by the newspaper company in the process comes from advertisers, who pay to borrow space. In return for that loan, the newspaper company gains interest from the borrower as advertising revenue. The newspaper company treats its signified objects (measured in space) as valuable assets it lends (it controls the space and can lend it repeatedly over time) in return for that space plus additional value in the form of advertising revenue. This is an indirect process of audience-labor exploitation, because the surplus value extracted comes from advertisers, but it is power over the audience labor process that enables that extraction of surplus value.

Meanwhile, advertisers pay to channel audience labor toward specific signified objects that condition the subjective signification process. Advertisers transform the productive process of subjective signification in an effort to affect the product of that process. As Smythe (1977) argued, it is up to audience laborers themselves to produce demand for commodities through their audience labor. However, compared to the audience commodity theory that emphasizes capital's control over audience labor, the process as outlined here carries no guarantee that the meaning created will be in demand. However, audience members are never free from being conditioned by the meanings they encounter.

Advertising in the History of the Capitalist Mode of Communicative Production

The political economy of signification described above and based on a materialist and dialectical theory of signification helps generate new insights into the historical development of industries that seek to capitalize on communication. The history of capitalizing on communication involves a history of industries developing around the capacity to exploit audience labor, including through advertising. A number of examples from the US illustrate this perspective on communication history as, in part, a history of efforts to channel and capitalize on the work of subjective signification.

The theoretical insights of a materialist and dialectical political economy of signification make it possible to reconsider the commercialization of news in the US in the 19th century. Newspaper capital operates as a form of the communicative capital examined above, which seeks to exploit the news audience labor of signification through news consumption. While histories (Baldasty 1992; Mott 1962; Starr 2004) that describe how advertising replaced political patronage as the primary source of revenue for newspaper capitalists in the 19th century are accurate in one sense, the radical break they describe ignores the *similarity* between patronage and advertising. In the late 18th and early 19th centuries, newspaper capitalists of the "partisan press" (Baldasty 1992) essentially treated their news as fictitious capital (Harvey 2006, 347) by lending all of the space in their newspapers to a political patron. This was not a process of subsidizing the production of news (Baldasty 1992) as much as it was a process of channeling and exploiting news audience labor. In the 19th century, newspaper capitalists increasingly lent their fictitious capital to advertisers in order to appropriate surplus value as interest. Advertising revenue was also not a subsidy but rather the result of indirect news audience-labor exploitation.

Thus, newspaper capitalists moved from a group that wanted to channel the work of subjective signification to its partisan political meanings to a group that wanted to channel that work to its commercial meanings. In each case, newspaper capitalists used their power over news audience labor to indirectly exploit that labor. Political parties and advertisers set the conditions for audience practices of creating meaning through the consumption of news by placing audience labor in a field of partisan or commercially signified objects, whether news from their partisan perspective or news with advertisements. What is seen as a radical break in the business of news is better seen as a transformation in the fundamental process of exploiting audience labor in which one source of interest—political patrons—was replaced by a much more lucrative source—advertisers.

As a second example, the development of commercial radio broadcasting in the US involved a process of creating radio audience labor by turning most radio users into consumers and a process of indirectly exploiting radio audience labor by commercializing radio programming. The development of commercial radio broadcasting involved a class struggle in communication as a struggle over whether a process of communicative production and signification would be capitalized. The first struggle occurred over the development of the means of production and means of circulation that resulted in the mass of radio users being relegated to the position of consumer (listener). In the first decades of the 20th century, the portion of the electromagnetic spectrum used to communicate wirelessly was transformed from a common means of circulation to, in effect, a private means of circulation. The US government regulated use of the spectrum by allocating rights to what were still legally public airwaves (Starr 2004, 329). This helped end the two-way communication of amateur radio users by creating radio broadcasting, a one-way, one-to-many process. For those who did not have rights to the radio spectrum, radio as a means of communicative production was also transformed into an instrument of consumption, namely, the radio receiver. It was a means of production and instrument of labor only for the audience labor of signification through consumption. Their signification was only subjective; they could not broadcast themselves.

These developments enabled capital accumulation through the sale of radio receivers, but a second struggle turned radio communication itself into a process of capital accumulation: the fight over who would be granted broadcasting licenses and thus who would be able to exploit the radio-audience labor that had been created. While many groups fought in favor of non-commercial broadcasters who would not exploit radio-audience labor (McChesney 2008), the US government played a decisive role through a policy of favoring commercial broadcasters (Lloyd 2006), who gave some of their power over audience labor to advertisers by lending advertisers some of the time in which radio programming was broadcast. In sum, what comprises the development of commercial radio broadcasting was the ascendance of commercial broadcasters as radio capitalists who appropriated surplus value through the indirect exploitation of radio-audience labor, thus gaining advertising revenue as interest on their loan of time to advertisers. Radio listening then occurred in a field of commercially signified objects that conditioned the radio-audience labor of subjective signification.

The Exploitation of Digital Audience Labor: Capitalizing on Digital Communication through Advertising

The current newspaper crisis in the US can be better understood through a political economy of signification. The crisis is, more specifically, one of newspaper capital that arose from a decreased capacity to exploit news-audience labor. The response to the crisis by MediaNews Group, until recently the second-largest newspaper company in the US, can be seen to entail efforts to create the means to exploit *digital* news-audience labor (news audience labor that uses digital means of production). As noted above in the discussion of the commercialization of news in the 19th century, advertising revenue as a kind of interest gained through the indirect exploitation of audience labor has long been the primary source of newspaper capital accumulation. However, in the digital era, the crisis for newspaper capital has been precipitated by precisely the loss of power over news-audience labor. Newspaper capital has less control over the conditions of digital news-audience labor, because it has less capacity to control access to its digital news (the object of news-audience labor) and does not control digital media (the instrument of audience labor) the way it controlled paper. As a result, news-audience labor is comparatively empowered in its relation to newspaper capital. As a result, advertisers see less reason to pay to borrow some of newspaper capital's space (digital or print) because there is less power for them to gain over the signifying activity of news-audience labor.

Like other newspaper capitalists, MediaNews Group responded to the crisis of newspaper capital by creating a digital business model—particularly after its bankruptcy and subsumption by Digital First Media (Spector and Ovide 2010; Digital First Media 2011). These efforts revolved around the need to channel and exploit digital news-audience labor in order to capitalize on news. Many of MediaNews Group's strategies involved advertising such as on newspaper websites and through smartphone and tablet computer applications created for each of the company's newspapers. A "citizen journalism" strategy resembled many of the strategies employed by Google and social media companies: the use of freely provided signified objects of consumption as the basis for exploiting audience labor, including indirectly through advertising. However, the rate of interest MediaNews Group and other newspaper capitalists can charge advertisers to borrow some of their digital space is significantly less than what they could get for print space: The industry's overall advertising revenue has decreased from $47.4 billion in 2005 to $23.6 billion in 2013, while digital advertising accounted for $3.4 billion of the 2013 total (Newspaper Association of America 2014).

MediaNews Group also tried Google Consumer Surveys as another interest-based strategy. In this strategy, MediaNews Group loaned part of its digital space to Google, with the result that the conditions of news-audience labor included encountering surveys that provided information to Google, while MediaNews Group indirectly exploited news-audience labor to extract a payment from Google.

The recent proliferation of companies that capitalize on digital communication by providing generally free platforms for the production, circulation, and consumption of user-generated content while generating advertising revenue are yet another example of a new form of audience labor exploitation. Google is exemplary here, as its expansive efforts to capitalize on numerous digital communicative practices are mostly aimed at gaining power over digital audience labor in order to indirectly exploit that labor. These efforts extend the fundamental process of "old media" businesses like newspapers—the exploitation of audience labor—into the new media era (Nixon 2016). This key fact of the capitalization of digital communication is one for which the theory of digital labor has not accounted, particularly in relation to the advertising that accounts for the primary source of revenue for platform-based companies like Google and Facebook. Theories of digital labor have missed the fact that if advertising is key to capitalizing on digital communication, then digital communicative capitalists need people to *consume* advertisements. They need digital media users as consumers of meaning or as digital audience laborers.

Although Google directly exploits audience labor in some circumstances, such as all of the digital content in its Google Play store and its YouTube Red subscription service, it operates as a communicative capitalist primarily by indirectly exploiting digital audience labor to generate advertising revenue. This is what the notion of "platform" obfuscates. Google appropriates user-generated content to create the field of signified objects that attract, channel, and exploit audience labor. Google's search engine does this by copying and indexing the web content produced by others, appropriating those materialized and objectified significations so that it determines the conditions under which they are consumed, and providing free access to them as objects of audience labor while lending to advertisers part of the space in which search results appear. Google's YouTube long operated in the same way, describing itself as a place to "broadcast yourself," while Google appropriated the user-generated videos and treated them as the basis for indirect audience labor exploitation. This process of indirect digital audience labor exploitation, in which part of the space or time controlled by Google is borrowed by advertisers, occurs in many other aspects of Google's business, including e-mail, books, and news.

Considering the extent to which digital communicative activities are capitalized by means of advertising, an understanding of the political economy of signification and the specific process of indirect audience labor exploitation will be necessary to critical perspectives on advertising. This is something audience commodity theory cannot provide.

References

Andrejevic, Mark. 2002. "The Work of Being Watched: Interactive Media and the Exploitation of Self-Disclosure." *Critical Studies in Media Communication* 19 (2): 230–48.

———. 2011. "Surveillance and Alienation in the Online Economy." *Surveillance & Society* 8 (3): 278–87.

Baldasty, Gerald J. 1992. *The Commercialization of News in the Nineteenth Century*. Madison, WI: The University of Wisconsin Press.

Baudrillard, Jean. 1981. *For a Critique of the Political Economy of the Sign*. St. Louis, MO: Telos Press.

Digital First Media. 2011. "Journal Register Company Announces the Creation of Digital First Media Inc." Press Releases, September 7. http://www.digitalfirstmedia.com/journal-register-company-announces-the-creation-of-digital-first-media-inc/.

Fiske, John. 1987. "Active Audiences." In *Television Culture*, 62–83. London, UK: Metheun.

Fuchs, Christian. 2010. "Labor in Informational Capitalism and on the Internet." *The Information Society* 26 (3): 179–96.

Hall, Stuart. (1980) 2006. "Encoding/Decoding." In *Media and Cultural Studies: KeyWorks*, edited by Meenakshi, Gigi Durham, and Douglas M. Kellner, 163–73. Malden, MA: Blackwell Publishing Ltd.

Harvey, David. 2006. *The Limits to Capital*. London: Verso.

Jacoby, Russell. 1979. "The Inception of Western Marxism: Karl Korsch and the Politics of Philosophy." *Canadian Journal of Political and Social Theory* 3 (3): 5–33.

Jhally, Sut, and Bill Livant. 1986. "Watching as Working: The Valorization of Audience Consciousness." *Journal of Communication* 36 (3): 122–42.

Lloyd, Mark. 2006. *Prologue to a Farce: Communication and Democracy in America*. Urbana, IL: University of Illinois Press.

Marx, Karl. 1978a. "Theses on Feuerbach." In *The Marx-Engels Reader (2nd Ed)*, edited by Robert C. Tucker, 143–45. New York: W. W. Norton & Company, Inc.

———. 1978b. "The German Ideology: Part I." In *The Marx-Engels Reader (2nd Ed)*, edited by Robert C. Tucker, 146–200. New York: W. W. Norton & Company, Inc.

———. 1990. *Capital: A Critique of Political Economy: Volume I*. London: Penguin Books.

McChesney, Robert W. 2008. "The Battle for the U.S. Airwaves, 1928–1935." In *The Political Economy of Media: Enduring Issues, Emerging Dilemmas*, 157–80. New York, NY: Monthly Review Press.

Meehan, Eileen R. 1984. "Ratings and the Institutional Approach: A Third Answer to the Commodity Question." *Critical Studies in Mass Communication* 1 (2): 216–25.

———. 1993. "Commodity Audience, Actual Audience: The Blindspot Debate." In *Illuminating the Blindspots: Essays Honouring Dallas W. Smythe*, edited Janet Wasko, Vincent Mosco, and Manjunath Pendakur, 378–97. Norwood, NJ: Ablex.

Mott, Frank Luther. 1962. *American Journalism: A History: 1690–1960* (3rd ed.). New York, NY: The Macmillan Company.

Newspaper Association of America. 2014. "Business Model Evolving, Circulation Revenue Rising." *Trends and Numbers*, August 18. http://www.naa.org/Trends-and-Numbers/Newspaper-Revenue/Newspaper-Media-Industry-Revenue-Profile-2013.aspx.

Nixon, Brice. 2013. "Communication as Capital and Audience Labor Exploitation in the Digital Era." PhD diss., University of Colorado Boulder. ProQuest (UMI 3592351).

———. 2014. "Toward a Political Economy of 'Audience Labour' in the Digital Era." *tripleC: Communication, Capitalism & Critique* 12 (2): 713–34.

———. 2016. "The Old Media Business in the New: 'The Googlization of Everything' as the Capitalization of Digital Consumption." *Media, Culture & Society* 38 (2): 212–31.

Peck, Janice. 2002. "The Oprah Effect: Texts, Readers, and the Dialectic of Signification." *The Communication Review* 5: 143–78.

———. 2006. "Why We Shouldn't Be Bored with the Political Economy versus Cultural Studies Debate." *Cultural Critique* 64: 92–126.

Sartre, Jean-Paul. 2004. *Critique of Dialectical Reason: Volume I: Theory of Practical Ensembles*, Edited by Jonathan Rée. Translated by Alan Sheridan-Smith. London: Verso.

Schiller, Dan. 1996. *Theorizing Communication: A History*. New York: Oxford University Press.

Smythe, Dallas W. 1977. "Communications: Blindspot of Western Marxism." *Canadian Journal of Political and Social Theory* 1 (3): 1–27.

———. 1978. "Rejoinder to Graham Murdock." *Canadian Journal of Political and Social Theory* 2 (2): 120–27.

Spector, Mike, and Shira Ovide. 2010. "MediaNews Holding Company to Seek Bankruptcy Protection." *The Wall Street Journal*, January 15. http://online.wsj.com/article/SB10001424052748703657604575005813195786280.html.

Starr, Paul. 2004. *The Creation of the Media: Political Origins of Modern Communications*. New York, NY: Basic Books.

Williams, Raymond. 1977. *Marxism and Literature*. Oxford, UK: Oxford University Press.

———. 1980a. "Base and Superstructure in Marxist Cultural Theory." In *Problems in Materialism and Culture*, 31–49. London, UK: Verso.

———. 1980b. "Means of Communication as Means of Production." In *Problems in Materialism and Culture*, 50–63. London, UK: Verso.

4 Crisis and Contradiction

Promotional Authenticity in the Digital World

James H. Wittebols

A world of ubiquitous promotion has many consumers increasingly avoiding promotional messaging and imagery. The promotional culture industry's (PCI) response has been to reach further into consumers' consciousness to target them individually. Enabled by the interactivity of the digital world, it is clear that the old days of advertising and promotion, which at best sought groups of people with similar demographic characteristics, have given way to a new system that knows much more about individual consumers than many of those consumers are aware. This new promotional system also recognizes that people seek more from their consumption through a desire for greater authenticity in their lives and in their experiences (Zogby 2008).

This personalization of messaging and fetishism of authenticity results in a projected form of commercial or commodified authenticity. As these activities become blended or tied to together in an effort to personalize and/or naturalize promotional efforts, they create environments in which promotional efforts are kneaded or insinuated into other cultural events or arenas and thus are not perceived immediately as promotional clutter (Solis 2010). Coordinating the formerly separate activities of advertising, public relations (PR), marketing, etc. and the use of many platforms—both traditional and digital—results in what the PCI calls integrated marketing communications or strategic communications campaigns.

As this chapter argues, the human ideal of authenticity is adaptable and malleable. After a brief look at the history of authenticity, this chapter will detail the utility of promotional authenticity for the PCI and describe how authenticity is appropriated by the PCI for promotional purposes, largely by developing "authentic" methodologies of promotion and developing messaging and imagery that conveys an authentic aura around a person, product, idea, or experience.

The move toward promotional authenticity is a reaction to a crisis in promotional culture resulting from consumers' proliferating use of ad-avoidance technologies—digital video recorders, music players, and adblocking, for example. One of the responses to this crisis has been the development and growth of promotional culture conglomerates, which integrate the many former "standalone" activities of the PCI. Referring to these conglomerates as the promotional culture industry allows us to comprehend these many formerly separate activities as coordinated campaigns designed to reach consumers wherever they are and whatever they are doing. The PCI includes such areas as advertising, public relations, marketing, sports and celebrity representation, polling, political campaign management, and online digital promotion, but integrating and coordinating them to insure its reach is increasingly unavoidable.

An example includes PR giant Fleishmann-Hillard, which announced in April 2013 its transformation from PR to an integrated marketing communications agency offering advertising and social media as well as PR (Elliott 2013). Social media are quickly elevating the status of PR within the PCI, with the distinction between PR and advertising blurring as a result (McClellan 2011). Public relations firms seem to have become a recent favorite target for acquisition by holding companies, with WPP stating that 10 percent of its revenue now comes from PR firms in the group.

Discussion of authenticity in promotion strategies can be found on an almost daily basis in such industry-based websites as *Ad Age, CommPro, Daily Dog, PR Week,* and a range of online advertising, PR, and marketing-oriented publications under the *Media Post* (www.mediapost.com) banner. The in-house discussion within the PCI began to focus in the mid-2000s on authenticity as promotional strategy, with research on authenticity and branding emerging in business and marketing academic journals at about the same time (Napoli, Dickinson, Beverland, and Farrelly, 2014). The turn toward authenticity represents a drastically different approach to promoting and selling for the PCI. In addition to using a great deal of knowledge about individuals' lifestyles, preferences, and purchasing behavior, our online expressions are "mined" to develop individual "persuasion profiles" (Pariser 2012). Furthermore, the general goal of promotional activity is to seem less obviously promotional—embedding, disguising, and displaying promotional efforts.

Contemporary Disenchantment and the Thirst for Authenticity

Understanding the value of promotion in this way requires tracing the emergence of the relation between personal authenticity and the idea of the autonomous self, which is thought to be a product of the way Europe was evolving in the late 16th Century (Trilling 1972). According to Trilling, the idea of society, which was a form of social organization that came to usurp the naturalized hierarchical arrangements typified by the Church and monarchies, came into use in the late 16th and early 17th centuries. European cultural historians describe a "mutation" in humans taking place that was largely a product of the fall of feudalism and the rise of social mobility, the urbanization of Europe and Martin Luther's challenge to the authority of the Church. Individual autonomy was also encouraged through the emergence of a market economy (Guignon 2004; Potter 2010).

The rise of the market and the growth of consumer society would provide a secular form of enchantment that replaced the mysticism of religion. As the self emerged, how we present ourselves also became a concern for individuals in a market society. Golomb (1995) says all classical philosophical treatments of the authentic self start with the idea that authenticity in one's self is always a process—there is no authentic state of being, and that authenticity is not something that can be fully realized. Golomb furthermore identifies the following values as exemplary of authentic character: self-sufficiency, heroism, creative sublimation of instinct, intellectual tolerance, generosity, courage, self-control, faith in one's ability to accept contradiction, and a lack of bad conscience (1995, 76). Thus the "human ideal" version of authenticity can be seen largely as a process of critical reflection on oneself and one's cultural surroundings. Personal authenticity is the result of a dialectical process guided by self-critique (as opposed to self-consciousness) and one's sense of being in the world (Golomb 1995; Taylor 1991; Harter 2002).

Contemporary manifestations of the human desire for authenticity have increasingly become alienated from that ideal. Charles Taylor (1991) asserts that consumer society has transformed how we think about authentic being and living. He cites the rise of cost/benefit analysis as taking over the value system of society, leading to what he calls a narrowing and flattening of lives to material self-interest. Hyper-individualism carries with it consequences for how we relate to the social world. The implications of these developments include what Taylor calls the individualism of self-fulfillment, in which people engage in new modes of conformity while striving to be themselves (1991, 14–15). As we will see in the pages ahead, this fits nicely into the marketing of products, services, experiences, and people in which authenticity and being true to oneself play a central role.

However, authenticity in relation to the self has also transformed. The beginnings of what could be called a post-modern version of authenticity were produced by the advertising industry response to the social movements of the late 1960s and '70s (Banet-Weiser 2012). The civil rights, youth, women's, and environmental movements focused on individual freedom and autonomy and concern for the common good. The advertising industry began to adopt and appropriate these positions, to the point today that autonomy now means solely individual fulfillment. Guignon (2004) captures this transformation in the difference between the older ideal of authenticity as self-realization or actualization and the contemporary notion of self-fulfillment in the self-help culture so pervasive in the North America. He argues that conflict in today's world is a product of self-centeredness and extreme individualism fostered by self-fulfillment. Once the self is put at the center of experience, the emerging psychology of self-desire results in an endless cycle of temporary satisfaction followed by disenchantment, which in turn produces new desires. "Authentic" consumption thus becomes a temporary means of helping us feel alive in the midst of the standardized roles and mundane routines we move through in our everyday lives.

Scholarly Debates

A variety of scholars have explored this problem. For example, Guignon (2004) and Braman (2008) argue that the lack of social connections and solidarity require people to rush ever more toward the self-fulfillment authenticity ethic. Chaudhry (2007) agrees, arguing "the idea that every self is important has been redefined to suit the needs of a cultural marketplace that devalues community and self hood in favor of success." Outka (2009) argues that what is being sold when authenticity is the subject is not any single product but rather a new kind of identity and new ways to live that provide an outlet for the self-fulfillment ethic. She terms this "commodified authenticity," by which she means it is not a search for authenticity per se but a new way to express one's social mobility. In this view, striving to be authentic is a form of status projection. This commodified redefinition of the authentic self in the PCI world stands ironically in contrast to the self-actualization model posed by classic philosophy.

The thinness of the current authentic self was recognized some decades ago by Adorno (1973), who labeled the self-fulfillment ethic as a "jargon of authenticity"—a language that projects a closeness and homey-ness "committing itself to a philosophy of As If." (1973: 30). The nebulous nature of human authenticity makes it virtually impossible to verify. Those skeptical of authenticity as a core human value feel this impossibility makes the concept virtually worthless. As a way to analyze the motives and cognitions behind people's behavior, it may indeed offer little utility. But for the PCI, the notion that one can project authenticity without really being authentic is the basis of most if not all promotional culture campaigns.

Elaborating Adorno's characterization, the philosophical focus on authenticity is an attempt to address contemporary alienation resulting from issues of domination and control. Hardt (1993) cites the role media play in fostering mass society and identifies the search for personal truth "a lofty goal in the face of declining intellectual engagement and increasing cultural or political constraints" (p 51). Because we experience such domination and control in the world of work and through the institutions that govern society, the self is expressed in the contemporary world not through work but rather through leisure pursuits. Hardt argues this kind of authenticity is a retreat from the world. In such situations, people sacrifice freedom for belonging, with such a conformist strategy thwarting both democratic dialogue and authentic individuals. Mass advertising has inevitably played a role in fostering feelings of inauthenticity and alienation—self-expression through increasingly standardized tastes does not seem to even approximate an ideal of authenticity.

Potter (2010) describes this striving for authenticity as a self-defeating process that generates not self-fulfillment but narcissism that is anti-social, non-conformist, and competitive. Because this commodified form of authenticity involves self-absorbed individualism, it meshes well with most advertising messages that encourage consumption: "Because commercial transactions are motivated entirely by desire for private gain, human contact becomes thoroughly instrumentalized. We treat others as means to our own selfish ends, not as ends themselves" (Potter 2010: 89). Potter calls this kind of authenticity "conspicuous" authenticity.

Authenticity and the PCI

Understanding the post-modern self and the desire for authenticity helps us appreciate how people seek and/or project authenticity in the realm of consumption. Advertising largely addresses us as individuals and speaks to both our desires and fears. The PCI seeks to link the human desire for authenticity with the commercial means to realize it. The social standards for how to be authentic or "self- fulfilled" are thus provided in many ways by the PCI as ways to promote and sell. Authenticity's ambiguity, its applicability to both products and people, and its status as an enduring human value make it ripe for exploitation by promotional culture. Products based on tradition, nostalgia, originality, sincerity, design consistency, and those "artisanal" or "handcrafted" are some of the markers of a promotional strategy that mines authenticity (Napoli, Dickinson, Beverland and Farrelly 2014).

However, using authenticity as a promotional strategy carries with it the impossibility of its fulfillment. While advocating for using authenticity in the promotional world, Godin (2005) and Gilmore and Pine (2007) admit its use is fraught with difficulty. Godin says authentic promotion is about getting consumers to believe the lie they tell themselves—convincing themselves that a product or experience will be authentic. Gilmore and Pine theorize about how to commodify authenticity but admit: "commercializing any activity yields the inauthentic" (Gilmore and Pine 2007, 88).

The turn to authenticity by the PCI and the contradictions it poses reflect the larger dilemma the PCI faces. It must continually expand its reach and convince consumers they need to buy, because consumers are less enchanted by the world of promotional culture. This challenge is multifaceted; one key problem is that of clutter. The PCI continues to saturate cultural and physical spaces with promotional efforts while it colonizes each new digital technology. This saturation has resulted in a cluttered promotional environment where the volume of promotions tends to drown out the effectiveness of any one of them. Because of the clutter, more and more consumers actively avoid promotional messaging and environments. Zogby's (2008) survey work early on revealed how many Americans (and global citizens as well) are far less responsive to the techniques of the past. As a result, they are buying technologies that help them, such as digital music players that eliminate the banter of commercial radio and digital video recorders that help viewers reclaim nearly 20 minutes of their lives for every hour of TV aired. Finally, and perhaps due to sensing that clutter has led to disdain, clients of the PCI are demanding greater accountability and return on investment (ROI) for their promotional culture expenditures.

A variety of evidence that documents these three problems suggests the degree to which PCI practitioners are caught between audiences and clients. Clutter increasingly characterizes promotional communication, with a corresponding increase in coping mechanisms used by audiences. Advertising breaks on broadcast media take up more time than they did 40 years ago (Wittebols 2004). Nearly 20 minutes per hour of television time is absorbed in advertising and other promotional material. The increasingly shorter average times for commercials means more commercials are being aired during these breaks—some ads are as short as 7.5 seconds—thus making recall of ads even more difficult for consumers. As a result, advertising recall rates have dropped from 35 percent in the 1960s to 10 percent or less today (Saatchi 2006). Furthermore, one study of worldwide consumers found 63 percent reporting they are "highly annoyed" by the repetition and redundancy of ads on any media platform that engages in such tactics (Carufel 2015b). And as regards online, the Goo Online advertising survey found banner ads (73%), social media ads (62%), and search engine ads (59%) are largely ignored by consumers (Four of Five Americans 2015). Recent data from Track Maven found even "branded content," which is supposed to lure consumers into promotional environments, falls far short of the expectations: nearly half of all Facebook posts placed at product Facebook sites get fewer than 100 "interactions" (More is not better 2015).

A vicious circle has emerged as consumers use remote controls, digital video recorders, music players, and other technology to avoid promotional clutter, which has prompted PCI practitioners to pursue other channels and technologies of promotion. As people shift from traditional media such as radio, TV, and print to digital platforms, marketing gurus have focused on getting promotional material delivered on these platforms (Newman 2007). While the use of digital video recorders has exacerbated ad skipping, with the highest ad-skipping rates for TIVO owners are found among the more popular shows (Perlberg 2014), advertisers respond by increasing use of product placement and integration, text messaging, and pop-up ads on digital devices.

However, even efforts to promote on platforms such as Facebook and Twitter are being avoided, with some consumers wishing there was an "unlike" button on Facebook pages (Online marketing 2012). One exception to this is Pinterest, where consumers post photographs and other visual material, which is becoming more commercially oriented as members share consumption experiences and purchases (Megginson 2014). And while ad spending at websites and through mobile devices increases and traditional media ads are waning, people seem to be actively avoiding promotional pitches in the digital world as well (Kleinberg 2012; Young Consumers Switch 2012; Four of five Americans 2014). The solution seems to be to place promotions in ever-more obscure venues such as out-of-home marketing, which seeks to reach people at "gas stations, gyms, sports venues, hospital rooms and commuter trains" (Hayes 2008, 1).

As a result of this uneven success, the viability of social network sites as vehicles for promotional culture is being debated given people's efforts to avoid what they see as excessive efforts at promotion. Some analysts are asserting many social media like Facebook are too engaging and that the more people find the content engaging the more they ignore the ads (Gullov-Singh 2011). A J Walter Thompson survey from 2007 found 84 percent agreeing that too many things are hyped and 72 percent tired of "people trying to grab my attention and sell me stuff "while only 22 percent said they connect with advertisements (JWT Survey 2007).

Partially due to these trends of saturation and avoidance, the return on investment (ROI) for traditional PR and advertising is now being questioned (ROI remains 2016; ROI is dead 2015). Advertisers are now demanding ratings for advertisements, not just the ratings for the programs in which they appear (Mandese 2007). Data from these efforts show a decline in viewers during ad breaks (Steinberg 2007a & b). PCI clients are also concerned that the metrics often provided by the PCI firms they work with are dubious (Lots of sightings 2015). The proliferation of adblocking (which we will cover in our discussion of native advertising) and the amount of ad fraud is an increasing concern for PCI clients, who feel they may be overpaying for their services (Sharma 2014; Bilton 2014, What Will Win the Ad War? 2015).

Ad Blocking and Native Advertising

These three developments confronting the PCI have led it to identify projecting authenticity as a value and goal to remain relevant. The remainder of this chapter examines how the PCI attempts to exploit authenticity by looking at one of the latest authentic methods: the response to ad blocking through "native" advertising and by looking at a specific group—millennials—in terms of members' particular view of what constitutes the authentic.

Authentic promotional methods are tactics the PCI uses to disguise or embed advertising and promotional messaging. The goal is to have targets of these messages not realize that what they are seeing is an ad. The PCI has been trying to do this for a long time by employing some form of third-party delivery—having the promotional message delivered by someone thought to not benefit from the promotion (see for example, Third Party Content 2014).

In the online world, finding an authentic form for advertising captures the relationship between adblocking and native advertising. Adblockers are software/applications that block pop-up ads that disrupt a viewer's use of a website. Adblocking across an increasing number of gadgets/platforms has become a mass phenomenon around the globe. Page Fair, an anti-adblocking firm, estimates that 198 million people use adblockers (Morrison and Peterson 2015). In the US, 41 percent of 18–29 year olds use adblockers (One Answer to Ad Blocking 2015). And advocates for advertisements argue they lost $21.8 billion in revenue due to the increasing use of adblockers (IAB explores its options 2015).

The industry response to adblocking and other ad-avoidance techniques has been to move toward embedding advertising material directly into editorial copy. The term used for this is "native advertising" or "branded content" (Sass 2014). Most PCI practitioners admit native ads are designed to look like editorial copy—using the same fonts, layout presentation, and feel of editorial copy (Publishers, Agencies Say Native Ads 2013). Often the only thing distinguishing native ads from editorial copy is a simple phrase like "sponsored by." A recent analysis by *Advertising Age* (Media Brands Shy Away 2015) looked at 23 major news/publishing/social media sites and found numerous ways to refer to native advertising—using phrases that include "presented," "sponsored," or "brand publishing" but not advertising.

This development has prompted the Federal Trade Commission (FTC) to look into the practice of native advertising and how it is received and interpreted by consumers. A study by Contently (Lazauskas 2015) found that 63 percent of readers could not identify whether an "article" was actually an ad across six different versions of native advertising. Recently released FTC guidelines argue for a more specific identification of native advertising—including using the word "advertisement" when it is placed amongst editorial copy in order to eliminate any confusion for consumers (Ember 2015). Because this material is targeted at people based on the kind of lifestyle, preferences, and desires they express online through purchasing behavior, websites they visit, social media and e-mail, the PCI views this as an "authentic" way to get to consumers and a benefit to them. However, consumers see this kind of authenticity as having little to do with their desire for authentic living.

The Interactive Advertising Bureau (IAB) immediately objected that the FCC directives would need to be "technically feasible, creatively relevant and not stifle innovation" (The IAB is concerned 2015). It is clear from the resistance to the FTC that the PCI is not concerned about the authenticity of native advertising (whether it is labeled as an ad) and in fact rather openly admits the intended deception. They define it as authentic, however, because ads are "personalized" for the consumer.

Despite this, the PCI uses authenticity as a promotional tactic or strategy, because the concept is malleable enough to apply to any promotional situation. How the PCI approaches promotional efforts directed at millennials provides insight into the narrow line the PCI treads on when projecting authenticity. Many millennials (as well as most people) are wary of all the data gathered about them through the PCI's tracking efforts (Privacy: The Smartphone's Achilles 2015; Retail PR Conundrum 2015). But they seek a "personal" touch and like to have companies they patronize reflect their values (Johnson 2015; Carnoy 2015; Carufel 2015a & c). This is especially true when it comes to the environment and corporate social responsibility (CSR).

Millennials show a degree of loyalty toward brands at slightly higher levels than do other demographic segments (Reaching Millennials 2015; CSR Mandate 2015; Carufel 2015a). However, they are more demanding of real results from environmental efforts or "authentic" CSR. Convincing young people that buying a product is good for the environment or knowing that a company treats its workers fairly is important given millennials' emphasis on what goes into the product, how the people who made it are treated, and how much the environment is affected by the manufacture and use of the product. Furthermore, as this generation has emerged in the age of promotional authenticity, it reflects Boyle's (2003, 39) description of an "authenticity paradox"—it's like a drug: If you give people a taste of authenticity, they will clamor for more "until every hint of fake and implied lie is slung out."

A final point needs to be made about the fragility of authenticity as an advertising tactic. No matter how well the PCI projects authenticity, it can be undone when an inauthentic practice undermines the projections of corporate social and environmental responsibility so carefully cultivated through promotional messaging. So, while the PCI can project the appearance of authenticity, it frequently has problems delivering on it. Furthermore, doing it "wrong" creates a boomerang effect where it only further alienates consumers.

Conclusion

This chapter examined the role that authenticity plays in the promotional culture industries as a way of responding to increasing public desire to avoid promotional messaging. Recent moves and practices by the PCI illustrate how they are using authentic promotional strategies and endowing products, people, services, and experiences with authentic auras to foster consumption. However, as has been discussed, one might conclude that the PCI's use of authenticity is painting itself into a corner. The fact that the promotional culture industry and the market cannot be a source of authenticity by definition continues to impair its use by advertisers. Zogby's (2008) assertions about the American public's desire for more authentic lives show people are finding non-commodified means to realize a more authentic lifestyle once they realize the marketplace is not a genuine source of authenticity. At the same time, however, many people continue to treat something as authentic or define themselves as authentic through the use of a particular product that helps them express their "true self."

Will the PCI conclude that authenticity is a lie it has told itself? Will it conclude that it is better for consumers to seek out information about planned purchases when they want it, instead of bombarding their daily lives with promotional messaging that alienates them? Will the companies that "do" authenticity better than others win out? How the use of authenticity as a promotional strategy plays out may possibly change promotional culture into something more palatable to consumers, but only if the PCI recognizes that promotional authenticity is not very authentic at all.

References

Adorno, T. W. 1973. *The Jargon of Authenticity*. Evanston, IL: Northwestern University Press.

Banet-Weiser Sarah. 2012. *Authentic: The Politics of Ambivalence in a Brand Culture*. New York, NY: New York University Press.

Bilton, Nick. 2014, April 20. "Friends, and Influence, for Sale Online." *The New York Times*. Accessed April 22, 2014. http://bits/blogs.nytimes.com.

Boyle, David. 2003. *Authenticty: Brands, Fads, Spin and the Lust for Real Life*. New York: Harper Perennial.

Braman, B. 2008. *Meaning and authenticity*. Toronto: University of Toronto Press.

Carufel, Richard. 2015a, September 24. "The CSR Generation: Millennials Are the Most Ardent Supporters—Six Subsets of Gen Y Examined in Cone Study." Accessed September 24, 2015. http://bulldogreporter.com.

———. 2015b, June 29. Consumers to Brands: "The Louder You Scream, the Less We Care." *PR Newswire*. Accessed June 29, 2015. http://prnewswire.com.

———. 2015c, February, 10. "Millennial Messaging: Study Finds 62% of Millennials Feel Useful, Personalized Content Drives Brand Loyalty." *Bulldog Reporter*. Accessed February 19, 2015. http://bulldogreporter/dailydog.

Carnoy, Juliet. 2015, December 18. "Why Millennial Women Crave Authenticity." *Huffington Post*. Accessed December 21, 2015. http://www.huffingtonpost.com/julietcarnoy.

Chaudhry, L. 2008. "Mirror, Mirror on the Web." *The Nation*, Accessed January 29, 2008. http://www.thenation.com.

CSR Mandate. 2015, June 2. "CSR Mandate: Consumers Will Make Personal Sacrifices to Address Social, Environmental Issues, Cone Study Finds." *Bulldog Reporter*. Accessed June 2, 2015. http://bulldogreporter/dailydog.

Elliott, S. 2013, April 28. "The New Look of Public Relations." *The New York Times*. Accessed April 30, 2013. http://www.nytimes.com.

Ember, Sydney. 2015, December 22. "F.T.C. Guidelines on Native Ads Aim to Prevent Deception." *The New York Times*. Accessed December 23, 2015. http://nyti.ms/1S9c9OT.

Four of five Americans. 2014. "Four of Five American Consumers Ignore Online Ads Most Frequently." *Research Brief from the Center for Media Research*. Accessed February 25, 2014. http://mediapost.com/publications.

Gilmore, J., and B. Pine. 2007. *Authenticity: What Consumers Really Want*. Boston, MA: Harvard Business School Press.

Godin, S. 2005. *All Marketers Are Liars*. New York: Portfolio.

Golomb, J. 1995. In Search of Authenticity: From Kierkegaard to Camus. New York: Routledge.

Guignon, C. 2004. *On Being Authentic*. New York: Routledge.

Gullov-Singh, A. 2011, April 11. Is Social Media Too Engaging for Its Own Good? *Advertising Age*. Accessed April 11, 2011. http://adage.com.

Hardt, Hanno. 1993. "Authenticity, Communication and Critical Theory." *Critical Studies in Mass Communication* 10: 49–69.

Harter, S. 2002. "Authenticity." In *Handbook of Positive Psychology*. edited by C.R. Snyder & Shane J. Lopez, 382–94. New York: Oxford University Press.

Hayes, D. 2008. "NBC Sets Plans to Expand Ad Reach." *Variety*. Accessed: http://www.variety.com.

IAB Explores Its Options. 2015, September 4. "IAB Explores Its Options to Fight Ad Blockers, Including Lawsuits." *Advertising Age*. Accessed September 4, 2015. http://adage.com.

Johnson, Bryce. 2015, September 4. "How to Engage and Educate Millennials on Your Brand." *Engage: Millennials*. Accessed September 4, 2015. http;//mediapost.com/publications.

JWT Survey. 2007. "Madison Avenue, Main Street Don't Often Connect." *MarketingCharts.com* Accessed July 24, 2008. http://www.marketingcharts.com.

Kleinberg, A. 2012. "Don't Let Growth Fool You: Mobile Advertising is Still Failing." *Advertising Age*. Accessed December 19, 2012. http://adage.com.

Lazauskas, Joe. 2015, September 8. "Study: Article or Ad? When It Comes to Native, No One Knows." *Contently*. Accessed September 14, 2015. http://contently.com.

Lots of Sightings. 2015, August 28. "Lots of Sightings, Not a Lot of Ad Relevance." Center for Media Research. Accessed Aug 28, 2015. http://mediapost.com/researchbrief.

McClellan, S. 2011, 18 November. "Social Falls Short on Customer Loyalty; Traditional Methods Encouraged." *Marketing Daily*. Accessed November 18.2011. www.mediapost.com/publications.

Mandese, J. 2007, 20 June. "Media Auditors Subscribe to TiVo ratings, Increase Scrutiny of TV Ad Buys." *Marketing Daily*. Accessed June 20 2007. http://www.mediapost.com/publications.

Media Brands Shy Away. 2015, June 11. "Media Brands Shy Away from the A-word, When It Comes to Labeling Native Ads." *Advertising Age*. Accessed June 11, 2015. http://adage.com.

Megginson, Melissa. 2014, Jan 15. "How Pinterest Became the ROI King." *CommPRO*. Accessed January 17, 2014. http://www.compro.biz.

More Is Not Better. 2015, February 5. "More Is Not Better Without Effectiveness." *Research Brief from the Center for Media Research*. Accessed February 5, 2015. http://www.mediaost.com/publications.

Morrison, Maureen. and P. Peterson. 2015, Sept. 14. "Advertising. Now What?" *Advertising Age*. Accessed September 14, 2015. http://adage.com.

Napoli, J.,S. Dickinson, M. Beverland, and F. Farrelly. 2014. "Measuring Consumer-Based Brand Authenticity." *Journal of Business Research* (57): 2090–98.

Newman, E. 2007. "IBM Study: Marketers Must Adjust to Gadget Generation. *Brandweek*, Accessed December 31, 2007. http://brandweek.com.

One Answer to Ad Blocking. 2015. "One Answer to Ad Blocking is Fewer, (Yes Fewer), Better Ads." *Advertising Age*. Accessed August 20, 2015.http://adage.com.

Online Marketing. 2012, 29 October. "Online Marketing is Failing With Consumers." *Daily Dog*, Accessed October 29, 2012. www.bulldogreporter.com.

Outka, Elizabeth. 2009. *Consuming Traditions: Modernity, Modernisms and the Commodified Authentic*. New York: Oxford University Press.

Pariser, Eli. 2102. *The Filter Bubble: How the New Personalized Web Is Changing What We Read and How We Think*. New York: Penguin Books.

Perlberg, Steven. 2015. "Which TV Shows Have the Highest Rates of Ad Skipping?" *The Wall Street Journal.* Accessed December 28, 2015 at www.blogs.wsj.com.

Potter, Andrew. 2010. *The Authenticity Hoax: How We Get Lost Finding Ourselves.* Toronto: McClelland & Stewart.

Privacy: The Smartphone. 2015, March 3. "Privacy: The Smartphone's Achilles Heel—68% of US Users Concerned about Having Their Activity Tracked for Use in Targeted Ads." *Daily Dog.* Accessed March 3, 2015. http://bulldogreporter. com/dailydog.

Publishers, Agencies Say Native Ads. 2013, October 23. "Publishers, Agencies Say Native Ads Should Look More Like Editorial, Not Less." *Advertising Age.* Accessed October 25, 2013. http://adage.com.

Reaching Millennials. 2015, March 4. "Reaching Millennials: Young Adults Want Brands to Support Their Causes and Care about Social Issues that Matter to Them." *Daily Dog.* Accessed March 4, 2015. http:// bulldogreporter.com/ dailydog.

Report: For Every $3. 2015 "For Every $3 Spent on Digital Ads, Fraud Takes $1." *Advertising Age.* Accessed October 22, 2015, http://adage.com.

Retail PR Conundrum. 2015, March 12. "Retail PR Conundrum: U.S. Consumers Want More Personalized Retail Experience—But Don't Trust Targeting Tactics." *Daily Dog.* Accessed March 12, 2015. http://bulldogreporter.com/dailydog.

ROI Is Dead. 2013, March 4. "ROI is dead. A New Metric Is Needed for Customer Relationship." *Advertising Age.* Accessed March 4, 2013. http://adage.com.

ROI Remains. 2016, March 21. "ROI Remains a Tough Metric for CMOs" *Bulldog Reporter.* Accessed March 21, 2016. http://bulldogreporter.com.

Saatchi, M. 2006. "The Strange Death of Modern Advertising." *Financial Times.* Accessed June 21, 2006. http://ft.com.

Sass, Erik. 2014, March 1. "Native Ads: Thumbs up, Or Thumbs down." *MediaPost Weekend.* Accessed March 3, 2014. http://mediapost.com.

Sharma, Mahesh. 2014, February 13. "Facebook Accused of Defrauding Advertisers by Attracting Fake 'Likes'." *Sydney Morning Herald.* Accessed February 14, 2014 http://www.smh.com.

Solis, B. 2010. *The Hybrid Theory Manifesto: The Future of Marketing, Advertising and Communications (Part one).* Retrieved from: www.briansolis.com.

Steinberg, B. 2007a. "C3 Ratings Show 3% Decline between Ads and Program Audience." *Advertising Age.* Accessed October 16, 2007. http://adage.com.

Steinberg, B. 2007b. "Viacom to Start Measuring Audience Views Second by Second." *Advertising Age.* Accessed August 7, 2007. http://adage.com.

Study Reveals. 2011, 4 April. "Study Reveals Half of PR." *Daily Dog,* Accessed April 4, 2011. www.mediapost.com/publications.

Taylor, C. 1991. *The Ethics of Authenticity.* Cambridge, MA: Harvard University Press.

The IAB Is Concerned. 2015, December 29. "The IAB is 'Concerned" about the FTC's New Native Advertising Rules, but Publishers Play It Cool." *Advertising Age.* Accessed December 29, 2015. http://adage.com.

"Third Party Content Appears More Credible." *Research Brief from the Center For Media Research.* Accessed April 1, 2014 http://mediapost.com/publications.

Trilling, L. 1972. *Sincerity and Authenticity.* Cambridge, MA: Harvard University Press.

What Will Win the Ad War? 2015. "What Will Win the Ad War? Technology, or Creativity and Transparency? *Advertising Age.* Accessed October 10, 2015. www.adage.com.

Wittebols, J. 2004. The Soap Opera Paradigm. Lanham, MD: Rowman and Littlefield.

Young Consumers. 2012. Young Consumers Switch. *Advertising Age.* Accessed April 8, 2012. http://adage.com.

Zogby, J. 2008. *The Way We'll Be.* New York: Random House.

5 Toward an Ecological Critique of Advertising

David J. Park

Advertising is the most ubiquitous form of institutional propaganda in US society due to its being the primary means of stimulating sales of products in consumer-oriented economies (Jowett and O'Donnell 2006). Advertising campaigns educate people to buy and consume a set of goods that they may or may not have preferred prior to the advertising exposure (Heilbroner and Thurow 1998). Yet, the impact of advertising stretches far beyond individual consumers to the global and ecological. As a key contributing sector of human activity, the manufacture and transportation of vast quantities of advertised goods around the world expends unprecedented amounts of fossil fuels that increase greenhouse gas emissions, which constitute the underlying cause of global warming (American Association for the Advancement of Science 2014; Klein 2014). Advertising helps fuel a planetary environmental crisis, which according to Hansen (2009), is rapidly turning into one of the most pressing problems facing humankind.

Because advertising contributes to planetary decay by promoting over-consumption of natural resources, it must be reassessed, given the antagonism between the depletion of the Earth's resources via extractive consumer societies and the sustainability of the planet. In fact, understanding advertising in this light may be necessary for humanity's survival, and given the limited amount of time to alter consumption and production habits to ensure planetary survival (Anderson 2012), this challenge becomes increasingly urgent.

This chapter seeks to reflect upon and contribute to what could be called an ecological critique of advertising. After describing the historical contexts of ecology and advertising, it explains how scholars began to focus on emerging concepts and relationships among advertising, production, consumption, and economic growth against the backdrop of expanding capitalist production capabilities and evolving phases of industrialization. Upon tracing how these relationships created significant environmental externalities, the chapter moves on to the digital/post-industrial era of capitalist expansion, with the net effect of empowering advertisers and marketers at the expense of consumers, widening wealth disparities and creating new environmental challenges. This chapter concludes by proposing an "ecologically-just" model for advertising as a means of addressing the climate crisis.

Historical Contexts of Ecology and Advertising

Advertising and ecology developed independently, with the ecological critique of capitalist relations predating any significant discussion of advertising. Given their deep structural relation today, this may be surprising. However, tracing their development suggests how these independent fields of understanding and practice converged.

Ecology as a scientific discipline developed to explain how social-productive systems interact with the ecological systems in which they are embedded. In 1866, Haeckel coined the term "ecology" as an equivalent to Darwin's "economy of nature" concept, which focused on understanding complex plant communities (Foster 2015). Also during this period, Marx drew on the work of German chemist Justus von Liebig and physician Roland Daniels to introduce the concept of "social metabolism," which connected human labor processes (society) to the environment (nature). Marx also attended lectures by British physicist John Tyndall, who discovered that carbon dioxide emissions contributed to the greenhouse effect. Marx eventually identified an irreparable rift in the interdependent process of social metabolism, one constituted by capitalist production treating nature as boundaries to be subsumed, thus undermining the ecological foundations of human existence (Foster 2015).

In succeeding decades, concepts of social metabolism, metabolic rift, and finite planetary space were elaborated into foundations of a critical ecological perspective. Foster (2015) notes that in the 1880s, British zoologist E. Ray Lankester and botanist Arthur George Tansley followed Marx's work by creating a powerful ecological critique of capitalism; Tansley went on to develop the ecosystem concept in 1935. In 1926, V.I. Vernadsky explored the spatial limitations of production processes, noting that life exists on a limited and self-contained planetary sphere. By the 1940s onward, scholars became better armed with improved science, demonstrating how human action contributes to climate change and global warming. Today, ecology "focuses on the human disruption of ecosystems from the local to the global" (Foster 2015, 3).

In comparison, while not yet a significant mechanism in capitalist relations during Marx's time, the development of advertising paralleled the various stages of industrialism and capitalist production capabilities. Since the beginning of the industrial revolution, commodity production has led consumption, at a comparatively small scale (Hamilton 2009). Early on, advertising operated on the periphery of the economy and mainly consisted of simple proclamations and announcements (Dyer 1982). In the 19th-century economy characterized largely by localized and competitive markets, advertising accounted for well below one percent of the US GDP. However, the first wave of industrialization increased productive capacity, which resulted in a need for more consumers. As a result, as early as the 1840s, advertising was recognized as a means of expanding markets, thus already moving from periphery to center of capitalist economies (Northrup 2003, 319).

Electrically powered production ushered in a second phase of industrialization during the late 1800s to the early 1900s, which further divided labor and flooded markets with a more diverse array of products, thanks in part to advertising. During this period, advertising increased tenfold (Northrop 2003, 320). By the early 1900s, scientific methods to gauge consumer opinion were developed, while business schools began to teach strategies and tactics of advertising. Following WWI, advertising continued to grow significantly, with businesses doubling their advertising budgets. The national reach of the new commercial broadcast media system starting in the 1930s led to a massive expansion of advertising, which paralleled the rise of corporate capitalism (McChesney 2004). Advertising drove commercial media expansion, while cultivating desire for consumer products, now at the national level, which would further expand productive capacities for manufacturers.

In the third stage of the industrial revolution post-WWII, new technology and further automation increased productive output while creating a major manufacturing base. Despite increasingly vocal criticism of advertising, which painted unflattering pictures of admen as greedy con-men or hucksters, advertising grew apace, thanks to national markets created through commercial television networks. The pattern for developments in the recent decades, despite their great differences from the era of mass markets, had therefore been laid.

As the centrality of advertising has increased, scholarship and social criticism of the relationships among advertising, capitalist production, and ecology have as well, with the majority of this work appearing in the third stage of industrial/capitalist expansion. By this time, scholars generally accepted the proposition that capitalist/growth/profit-oriented production requires consumption, which in turn requires advertising to spur consumption. Packard (1960) noted how overabundance of commodities required heightened consumption, with manufacturers creating advertising that convinced consumers to purchase products they wanted but did not necessarily need. Galbraith (1969) identified how increasing production required an increase in consumer desire, which he referred to as the Dependence Effect. More recently, scholars such as Jhally (1997), Faraone (2011) and Sukhdev (2012) emphasize both the unparalleled extent of commodity production and the central role of advertising as part of an even more developed system of encouraging consumption to match production.

Scholars also developed a structural critique of advertising as an integral part of the logic by which commerce is moved forward. Dyer (1982) argues how advertising serves a key structural role in modern industrial capitalism by organizing and ensuring markets for its goods. The equation of consumerism and patriotism can be seen in US presidential exhortations from Eisenhower to George W. Bush, which position consumption as not only part of economic growth, but also as fulfilling national purpose. Indeed, the "contemporary political economy is, in fact, built on the grounds of a consumption-dependent framework" (Comor 2008, x), with consumption the driving force of capitalist economies and economic growth (Goodman and Cohen 2004) while also providing norms of behavior appropriate to current economic conditions and existing political and economic control (Faraone 2011). Finally, the structural centrality of advertising corresponds to the increasing centrality of decision-making power about what products are to be produced, and how they are produced, to a small and powerful group of businesses, and away from consumers, a trend noted some decades ago by Mills (1956).

Advertising and the Environment

The important point about advertising on which the above scholars and critics focus is how production and consumption required advertising to sustain growth in economic performance. However, new insights also emerged about the environmental dimension. For example, while Packard (1960) viewed advertising's promotion of affluence as threatening to bring a decline in the quality of American life, he also began to envision advertising's influence on the decline of the planet's ability to sustain human life.

Since Packard and others, the relationship between capitalism and the environment has been clarified. Daly's (1993) Impossibility Theorem posits that infinite growth on a planet with a finite environment is a contradiction, impossible to achieve, and an approach that will eventually lead to environmental disaster. What's more, the ideal of consumerism emerged in the West, which constitutes only 10 percent of the world's population, with North America and Western Europe alone consuming about 60 percent of everything that is produced (Comor 2008). The United States alone with 5 percent of the world's population constitutes 32 percent of total consumption while using 25 percent of the Earth's bio-capacity (Comor 2008; Wackernagel and Rees 1996). Environmental impact is stratified by class, with those of highest income or net worth likely to consume the most. The Congressional Budget Office (2007) estimated that the carbon footprint for the top quintile of the US economy was more than three times that of the bottom quintile. Ultimately, the planet cannot sustain the same level of consumption the Western nations currently enjoy. If only India and China develop the same ecological footprint as the United States, the entire planet will be stripped of its resources within a few decades, with the equivalent of two planet Earths needed just to sustain their two economies (Wackernagel and Rees 1996). Ironically, with a shift of global manufacturing, the wealthy countries of the world have outsourced much of their manufacturing, and thus carbon emissions, to poor and emerging economies (Sato 2012).

Structural factors encourage environmentally destructive consumerism. Profit-driven manufacturing is often cheaper than Earth-friendly and sustainable production. Labor costs of manufacturing goods from materials that harm the planet are often cheaper (Foster 2013). Making products that wear out after a few years is more profitable, but they also extract unnecessary natural resources and create surplus environmental waste while, as Packard (1960) recognized earlier, transforming Americans into wasteful and compulsive consumers. Although he only indirectly connects the advertising and resource depletion in his earlier works, Galbraith also believed that environmental despoliation rises along with production (Berry 2013, 129). Of course these kinds of production processes are not limited to growth-oriented capitalist economic systems and exist in other systems as well.

With the infinite accumulation of capital as a main motivating force and goal, capitalism ultimately creates environmental havoc locally, regionally, and globally (Magdoff 2011). They promote consumption beyond human needs, which simultaneously ignores the limits of non-renewable energy resources and challenges the Earth's waste capacity. Besides environmental decay, unlimited growth also creates competition between countries for global natural resources, adding to environmental threat heightened political instability. Packard (1960) projected how increased consumption would exhaust natural resources and increase a reliance on other countries' resources, which would encourage their eventual colonization to continue the extraction of additional raw resources. Forty years after Packard, Jhally (1997) argues that advertising is partly responsible for creating a global struggle for scarce natural resources, which will likely exacerbate conflict between countries.

Unlimited growth is not the only option, as other scholars have noted. For example, Daly (1993) argues that the concept of "development," instead of growth, is more conducive to sustainability because it emphasizes qualitative improvement for humanity rather than an economic gain for business. Daly (1993) goes on to note that even "green growth" is unsustainable because it implies economic growth, and that the present scale of growth-oriented economies is unsustainable, eventually leading from unsustainability to collapse. While Packard (1960) also advocated a "tuning down" of the economy, he correspondingly argued for a more modest and less wasteful lifestyle in such ways as buying functional items and generic drugs, avoiding fashion, learning how to repair consumer goods, recycling materials, changing tax laws, and rejecting planned obsolescence in order to limit diminishing natural resources.

Digital/Postindustrial Advertising

Environmental externalities resulting from post-WWII era relationships have accelerated in the recent digital/postindustrial era of capitalist expansion. Since the privatization of the internet through the US Telecommunications Act of 1996, the digital era has been marked by the empowering of corporate and advertising sectors in the online world at the expense of consumer welfare. Publishing companies, marketers, and advertisers are individualizing online content based on the surveillance of user identities, which in turn more effectively targets and engages consumers. The digital era developed to a point that the extraction and sale of personal data for advertising purposes is a defining characteristic.

The post-1996 digital era has seen at least two significant changes for society. First, it enhanced advertising, retail sales, and consumption while creating an explosively profitable new industry in data mining whose purpose is to better influence individual online purchasing decisions. These enhanced sales and consumption patterns lead economic growth while opening new pathways such as price customization for advertisers and companies to extract an even greater surplus. Price customization (also known as dynamic pricing) creates unique online prices for different people who view the same product. Second, the digital era boosts the redistribution of wealth to corporate sectors, increases economic inequity, and disempowers consumers.

As the data show, advertising in the digital/post-industrial era is front and center of economic growth and the sales effort. US digital advertising reached $51 billion (out of $700 billion globally) in 2014 (World Federation of Advertisers 2015), which was more than was going to all print media. By 2018, it is expected to increase to $82 billion annually (eMarketer 2014b). Revenues to global advertising media owners are expected to reach $536 billion in 2015, while the US is expected to pull in $165 billion (IPG Mediabrands 2014). Advertising spending, particularly in the US, has been very successful in terms of generating significant sales. According to eMarketer (2014a), US retail sales in 2013 topped $4.53 trillion. These sales are leading economic growth, which in 2013 represented 27 percent of nominal US GDP.

While these are significant sums, advertisers, marketers, and new technology companies have realized there is still more money to be made by expanding the abilities of advertisers and the online sales effort. Perhaps the most efficient way of doing this is through data collection and price customization, which are major growth areas for corporate profits. In fact, the surveillance of online consumers is one of the fastest-growing businesses on the internet (Angwin 2010). Data mining can increase operating margins by 60 percent (Manyika, Chui, Brown, Bughin, Dobbs, Roxburgh, and Hung 2011), while the overall financial benefits of exploiting data, especially personal data within existing databases, is estimated to be around $600 billion (Mosco 2014). With the advent of new information technologies, advertising and customization are regarded as growth areas (Office of Fair Trading 2010). Price customization maximizes corporate profits (Elmaghraby and Keskinocak 2003; Ghose and Huang 2009; Obermiller, Arnesen and Cohen 2012), often up to 8 and 25 percent (Sahay 2007), and is considered superior to other forms of consumer capital extraction (Armstrong & Vickers 1999). One estimate by Jupiter Communications placed the value of price customized e-commerce transactions at $7 billion dollars for 2004 (Reinartz 2002).

While these changes benefit industry, they have fewer benefits for the public and the planet. With few exceptions, this new advertising and marketing-driven system of online price customization means higher over-all prices for consumers compared to models where prices are competi-tive, openly displaced, and advertised (Ellison and Fisher-Ellison 2009; Newman 2015; Hannak et al. 2014). In order to work well, price discrimi-nation must be fairly secretive and difficult for online consumers to detect (Hannak et al. 2014). The overall effect of price customization decreases total consumer surplus (Ghose and Huang 2009) and harms consumer welfare (Klock 2002).

Furthermore, data mining, big data, and individual behavior profiling allow companies to know more about consumers than those consumers know about their marketplace options. This rising information asymmetry also contributes to overall social and economic inequity by having lower socio-economic status households pay more than wealthy households (Newman 2014; Stigliz 2002). Consumer exploitation is not only enabled by price customization, it is also aided by the monopoly status of social media firms like Facebook and search engines like Google. Part of the exploitation process means consumers in monopoly non-competitive markets such as those dominated by Google share their data at too low a price (Newman 2014). One industry-oriented estimate placed the value of personal data to advertisers as up to $5,000 per person per year (Fottrell 2012).

Digitally enabled advertising and marketing boost ubiquity, effective-ness, and, as a result, the ecological impact by many times its reach. The cost of the production, use, and disposal of commodities within consumer culture leading up to the beginning of the digital era has led to the degradation of over 60 percent of the world's eco-systems (Jackson 2010). The evolving digital era enhances this decline through at least four recent trends, one being how the surveillance of online users, data-mining, and individually tailored messages, as well as a number of additional strate-gies and tactics, more effectively sells products and services enhancing consumption.

A second trend is how the additional revenue generated during the digital era enriches a small segment of the population that consumes items requir-ing larger carbon footprints. Global billionaires are recently increasing their spending on luxury items, especially super-yachts, which are boats at least 80 feet long. Sales of these boats rose by 40 percent in 2015 (Kollewe 2016). Wealthy Americans also appear to be splurging with high-end con-sumption habits. Luxury automakers like Bentley and Porsche report rising sales and luxury hotels are seeing increased sales, while wealthy Americans are expected to continue increasing spending on luxury hotels and resorts (by 17 percent), home entertainment and electronics (by 17 percent), watches (by 10 percent), and automobiles (by 18 percent) (Tuttle 2013). Spending on items and experiences that require elevated amounts of carbon emissions (such as air travel) will continue to increase in the future as the number of ultra-high net-worth individuals is expected to rise 41 percent to 263,500 by 2025, while the population of millionaires is expected to increase from 13 million in 2016 to 18 million by 2025 (Knight Frank Research 2016).

Third, the production and disposal of digital devices by which advertisers target consumers in the digital era (meaning computers, cell phones, tablets, and other items) are expected to do significant environmental damage by 2020 (Maxwell and Miller 2012). Not surprisingly, it is often more profitable to design an item with cheaper components to break down after a few years instead of building a product to last for several decades (Packard 1960). Apple does something similar by keeping its "older" phones from being able to run newer software, apps, or other features. Even if someone's phone works, he or she will have to buy a new one in order to access up-to-date features. Apple spent almost $1 billion advertising its goods in 2012, but it was really essentially advertising newer and improved versions of goods most people already had (Taylor 2014).

One calculation puts the annual turnover rate of electronic products at 17 percent (Grossman 2010). Indeed, hundreds of millions of still-working items that constitute billions of pounds of hazardous waste are thrown away every year (Leonard 2011). By 2007, between 20 and 50 million tons of e-waste were generated annually, with the majority coming from televisions, computers, and cell phones (Maxwell and Miller 2012). Most electronics are thrown into incinerators and dumps and even when converted to waste are highly toxic. The business strategy of forcing consumers to continually upgrade electronic gadgets by making many of their functions obsolete unnecessarily drains an immense amount of natural resources.

Fourth, the data centers that acquire consumer information to better target and advertise online, combined with the electronic devices needed for this surveillance, require a massive amount of energy to function. Mosco (2014) points out that the rates of electrical consumption for data centers and electronic devices are ultimately unsustainable. By 2013, data centers used 2 percent of all of the electricity consumed in the world, and their carbon emissions are set to quadruple by 2020 (*Data Center Journal* 2013). A single data center can use more power than a medium-sized town (Glanz 2012). The elevated levels of energy required also contribute to greenhouse gas emissions. For example, Facebook built a data center in central Oregon that was serviced by a utility that primarily used coal-fired power stations, which are the largest sources of greenhouse gas emissions in the United States (Greenpeace International 2010). The power demands of data centers grew by 56 percent between 2005 and 2010, and they continue to expand and require more energy (Maxwell and Miller 2012b). Apart from data centers, the phones, tablets, computers and other electronic items, which add up to over 10 billion devices, use 15 percent of all global residential energy. They will require 30 percent of the world electrical grid by 2022 and 45 percent by 2030 (Maxwell and Miller 2012b).

An Ecologically-Just Model for Advertising

The digital/postindustrial era is on a path to increasingly exceed sustainable energy usage. Yet, it is only the latest component in a longer history of capital expansion and industrialization, with advertising closely intertwined with each of these eras. Given this and the evidence supporting global warming that is now thoroughly established and largely undisputed among scientists, it is time for new thinking, solutions, and action. Because advertising grew in a symbiotic and mutually dependent relationship with capitalist production, altering one would likely change the other. If jettisoning perpetual growth-oriented economies proves too difficult on its own, eliminating or reimagining advertising could also help forestall global warming by helping jumpstart the necessary changes.

One way of doing so is to recall that advertising does not have to create negative consequences for the Earth. Indeed, it may be able to decrease consumption, as in time of war, or promote environmentally sustainable products. New advertising systems may be able to promote products that are made with sustainable resources and penalize those that are not. Advertising may be able to affect consumption in ways that are harmonious with the planet. In fact, advertising can be part of a much larger link in a chain that can slow down and stop the impending planetary environmental crisis. As such, developing an "ecologically just" model for material commodity/product advertising is one strategy that could help address global warming. Possible contributions of advertising agencies should not be underestimated or dismissed out of hand.

An "ecologically just" advertising system could promote products that maintain a healthy and sustainable planetary ecosystem. Six criteria of such a system could constitute its foundation and of course be regularly revised as needed. First, such a system would measure the self-sufficiency of the production process. Second, it would measure the percentage of recycled and recyclable materials that constitute the commodity to be advertised. Third, it would measure the product's ability to be recycled. Fourth, it would measure the percentage of workers/employers/employees who use public transportation, collective transportation, or walk or bicycle to get to work. Fifth, it would create fees for businesses wanting to advertise that have not divested in holdings from fossil fuel companies. Six, it would measure the degree to which the production process of the commodity to be advertised is intentionally created to break down or expire over a short period of time, and thus require replacement.

Next, grounded in these six criteria, the system would create fees for advertising based on the amount of environmental damage created by the production processes of the commodity to be advertised. As labor costs of producing products from materials that harm the planet are often less (Foster 2013), levying significant fees on advertising would create an incentive for manufacturers to use non-polluting production processes and sustainable material. Because most US industries (including the advertising industry) exist within oligopolies, the resources required to regulate and measure the six components of the model would be reasonable.

This regulatory process is quite similar to other commonly found practices that exist within a variety of sectors throughout societies around the world. For example, driving a car requires a license. Practicing medicine requires significant education and testing. An unlicensed driver is more likely to kill someone on the road, while an untrained person practicing medicine could kill his or her patient. This same concept should apply to the advertising world. Without some sort of formal assessment/testing, it is likely the production process of the product to be advertised is harming the environment, which by default will harm the human race. Therefore, the "ecologically just" advertising model would use the advertising system as the gatekeeper through a system of fees to incentivize manufacturers to produce environmentally sustainable products that do not harm the Earth's eco-systems.

While the growth-oriented economic system and profit-centered production processes can be viewed as the amplifier of environmental destruction, advertising should be regarded as their megaphone, with the ability to convey powerful pro-consumption messages 24 hours a day, seven days a week in nearly every nook and cranny around the world. In order to address this system, communications scholars now need to generate new normative models, policy recommendations, and regulatory frameworks that connect advertising to ecology. As outrageous as this may sound to many, advertising may be able to play a part in saving the planet instead of expediting its demise.

References

American Association for the Advancement of Science Climate Science Panel. 2014. "What We Know: The Reality, Risks, and Response to Climate Change." American Association for the Advancement of Science.

Anderson, Kevin. 2012. "Climate Change Going Beyond Dangerous – Brutal Numbers and Tenuous Hope." *Development Dialogue* 61: 16–40.

Angwin, Julia. 2010. "The Web's New Gold Mine: Your Secrets: A Journal Investigation Finds that One of the Fastest-Growing Businesses on the internet Is the Business of Spying on Consumers." *Wall Street Journal*, July 30, 2010. Accessed March 30, 2015. http://www.wsj.com/articles/SB10001424052748703940904575395073512989404.

Armstrong, M. and J. Vickers. 2001. "Competitive Price Discrimination." *RAND Journal of Economics* 32(4): 1–27.

Baran, Paul, and Paul Sweezy. 2013. "Theses on Advertising." *Monthly Review* 65(3): 34–42.

Berry, Mike. 2013. *The Affluent Society Revisited*. Oxford, UK: Oxford University Press.

Carey, James. 1960. "Advertising: An Institutional Approach." In *The Role of Advertising: A Book of Readings*, edited by Charles Sandage and Vernon Fryburger. Homewood, Illinois: Richard D. Irwin Inc.

Comor, Edward. 2008. *Consumption and the Globalization Project: International Hegemony and the Annihilation of Time*. New York: Palgrave MacMillan.

Congressional Budget Office. 2007. "Trade-offs in Allocating Allowances for CO_2 Emissions." Economic and Budget Issue Brief: 1–8. Accessed March 18, 2015. http://cbo.gov.

Daly, Herman, and Kenneth Townsend. 1993. "Sustainable Growth: An Impossibility Theorem in Valuing the Earth." In *Valuing the Earth, Economics, Ecology, Ethics*, edited by Herman Daly and Kenneth Townsend. Cambridge: MIT Press.

Data Center Journal. 2013. "Industry Perspective: Energy Efficiency and Renewable Sources for the Data Center." *Data Center Journal*. Accessed March 1, 2016. http://www.datacenterjournal.com/industry-perspective-energy-efficiency-and-renewable-sources-for-the-data-center/.

Driver, John, and Gordon Foxall. 1984. *Advertising Policy and Practice*. New York: St. Martin's Press.

Dyer, Gillian. 1982. *Advertising as Communication*. New York: Methuen & Co.

Dyer-Witheford, N. 1999.*Cyber-Marx: Cycles and Circuits of Struggle in High-Technology Capitalism*. Chicago, IL: University of Illinois Press.

Ellison, G., and S. Fisher-Ellison. 2009. "Search, Obfuscation, and Price Elasticities on the Internet." *Econometrica* 77 (2): 427–52.

Elmaghraby, Wedad, and Pinar Keskinocak. 2003. "Dynamic Pricing in the Presence of Inventory Considerations: Research Overview, Current Practices, and Future Directions." *Management Science* 49(10): 1287–1309.

eMarketer. 2014a. "Total US Retail Sales Top $4.5 Trillion in 2013, Outpace GDP Growth." *eMarketer*, April 10. Accessed November 10, 2015. http://www.emarketer.com/Article/Total-US-Retail-Sales-Top-3645-Trillion-2013-Outpace-GDP-Growth/1010756.

eMarketer. 2014b. "Total US Ad Spending to See Largest Increase Since 2004: Mobile Advertising Leads Growth; Will Surpass Radio, Magazines and Newspapers This Year." eMarketer, July 2. Accessed November 10, 2015. http://www.emarketer.com/Article/Total-US-Ad-Spending-See-Largest-Increase-Since-2004/1010982.

Faraone, Roque. 2011. "Economy, Ideology, and Advertising." In *The Handbook of Political Economy of Communications*, edited by Janet Wasco, Graham Murdock, & Helena Sousa. Oxford: Blackwell Publishing.

Foster, John. 2013. "The Epochal Crisis." *Monthly Review* 65(5): 1–12.

———. 2015. "Marxism and Ecology: Common Fronts of a Great Transition." *Monthly Review* 67(7): 1–13.

Fottrell, Q. 2012. "Who Would Pay $5,000 to Use Google? (You)." *Smartmoney* Jan 25. Accessed November 10, 2015. http://blogs.smartmoney.com/advice/2012/01/25/who-would-pay-5000-to-use-google-you/.

Galbraith, John. 1958. *The Affluent Society*. Rev. ed. Reprint, Boston: Houghton Mifflin Company, 1969.

Ghose, A. and K.W. Huang. 2009. "Personalized Pricing and Quality Customization." *Journal of Economics & Management Strategy* 18(4): 1095–1135.

Glanz, James. 2012. "Power, Pollution, and the Internet." *New York Times*, September 22. Accessed November 10, 2015. http://www.nytimes.com/2012/09/23/technology/data-centers-waste-vast-amounts-of-energy-belying-industry-image.html.

Goodman, Douglas, and Mirelle Cohen. 2004. *Consumer Culture*. Santa Barbara: ABC-CLIO, Inc.

Greenpeace International. 2010. "Making IT Green: Cloud Computing and Its Contributions to Climate Change." *Greenpeace International*. Accessed November 9, 2015. http://www.greenpeace.org/international/Global/international/planet-2/report/2010/3/make-it-green-cloud-computing.pdf.

Grossman, Elizabeth. 2010. "Tackling High-Tech Trash: The e-Waste Explosion and What We can do about it." *Demos*, November 22. Accessed November 12, 2015. http://www.demos.org/publication/tackling-high-tech-trash-e-waste-explosion-what-we-can-do.

Hamilton, Clive. 2009. "Consumerism, Self-Creation and Prospects for a New Ecological Consciousness." *Journal of Cleaner Production* 18(6): 571–75.

Hannak, Aniko, Gary Soeller, David Lazer, Alan Mislove, and Christo Wilson. 2014. "Measuring Price Discrimination and Steering on e-Commerce Web Sites." In *Proceedings of the 2014 Conference on Internet Measurement Conference*, 305–18. ACM.

Hansen, James. 2009. *Storms of My Grandchildren*. New York: Bloomsbury.

Heilbroner, Robert, and Lester Thurow. 1998. *Economics Explained: Everything You Need to Know about How the Economy Works and Where It's Going*. New York: Touchstone, 1998.

Horowitz, Daniel. 1994. *Vance Packard & American Social Criticism*. Chapel Hill: University of North Carolina Press.

IPG Mediabrands. 2014. "MAGNA GLOBAL Forecasts Global Advertising Revenues to Grow by +4.8% to $536 billion in 2015." *IPG Mediabrands*, December 8. Accessed November 2, 2015. http://news.ipgmediabrands.com/article_display.cfm?article_id=1666.

Jackson, T. 2010. *Prosperity without Growth? The Transition to a Sustainable Economy*. London: Sustainable Development Commission.

Jhally, Sut. 1997. *Advertising and the End of the World: The Movie*. PDF Transcript. Media Education Foundation. Accessed March 17, 2015. https://www.mediaed.org/assets/products/101/transcript_101.pdf.

Jowett, Garth, and Victoria O'Donnell. 2006. *Propaganda and Persuasion*. Thousand Oaks, CA: Sage.

Klein, Naomi. 2014. *This Changes Everything: Capitalism versus the Climate*. New York: Simon & Schuster.

Klock, Mark. 2002. "Unconscionability and Price Discrimination." *Tenn. L. Rev.*, 69: 317.

Knight Frank Research. 2016. "The Wealth Report." *Knight Frank*. Accessed March 7, 2016. http://content.knightfrank.com/research/83/documents/en/wealth-report-2016-3579.pdf.

Kollewe, Julia. 2016. "World's Super Rich Keep Buying up Luxury Goods in Face of Wealth Decline." *Guardian*, March 1. Accessed March 1, 2016. http://www.theguardian.com/business/2016/mar/02/global-super-rich-luxury-goods-yachts-wealth-report-knight-frank.

Leonard, Annie. 2011. *The Story of Stuff: How Our Obsession with Stuff Is Trashing the Planet, Our Communities, and Our Health-and a Vision for Change*. New York: Free Press.

Magdoff, Fred. 2011. "Ecological Civilization." *Monthly Review* (62)8: 1–25.

———. 2014. "An Ecologically Sound Socially Just Economy." *Monthly Review* 66(4): 23–34.

Manyika, James, Michael Chui, Brad Brown, Jacques Bughin, Richard Dobbs, Charles Roxburgh, and Angela Hung. 2011. "Big Data: The Next Frontier for Innovation,

Competition, and Productivity." *McKinsey & Company*, May. Accessed on March 8, 2016. http://www.mckinsey.com/insights/business_technology/big_data_the_next_frontier_for_innovation.

Maxwell, Richard, and Toby Miller. *Greening the Media*. 2012a. New York: Oxford University Press.

———. 2012b. "Greening Starts with Us." *New York Times*, September 24. Accessed March 7, 2016. http://www.nytimes.com/roomfordebate/2012/09/23/informations-environmental-cost/greening-starts-with-ourselves.

McChesney, Robert. 2004. *The Problem of the Media*. New York: Monthly Review Press.

Mills, C. Wright. 1956. *The Power Elite*. New York: Oxford University Press.

Mosco, Vincent. 2014. *To the Cloud: Big Data in a Turbulent World*. Boulder, Colorado: Paradigm Publishers.

Newman, Nathan. 2014. "The Costs of Lost Privacy: Consumer Harm and Rising Economic Inequality in the Age of Google." *William Mitchell Law Review* 40(2): 850–88.

———. 2015. "Data Justice: Taking on Big Data as an Economic Justice Issue." *Data Justice*. March. Accessed November 1, 2015. http://www.datajustice.org/sites/default/files/Data%20Justice-%20Taking%20on%20Big%20Data%20as%20an%20Economic%20Justice%20Issue.pdf.

Northrup, Cynthia Clark. 2003. *The American Economy*. Santa Barbara: ABC-CLIO, Inc.

Obermiller, C., D. Arnesen, & M. Cohen. 2012. "Customized Pricing: Win-win or End Run?" *Drake Management Review* 1, 2: 12–28.

Office of Fair Trading. 2010. "Online Targeting of Advertising and Prices: A Market Study." *Office of Fair Trading*. Accessed on March 3, 2016. http://webarchive.nationalarchives.gov.uk/20140402142426/http:/www.oft.gov.uk/shared_oft/business_leaflets/659703/OFT1231.pdf.

Packard, Vance. 1960. *The Waste Makers*. New York: David McKay Company.

Reinartz, W. 2002. "Customizing Prices in Online Markets." *Symphonya Emerging Issues in Management* 1: 55–65.

Rotzoll, Kim, James Haefner, and Charles Sandage. 1976. *Advertising in Contemporary Society: Perspectives toward Understanding*. Columbus: Grid.

Sahay, A. 2007. "How to Reap Higher Prices with Dynamic Pricing." *MIT Sloan Management Review*. Accessed November 7, 2015. http://sloanreview.mit.edu/article/how-to-reap-higher-profits-with-dynamic-pricing/.

Sato, Misato. 2012. "Embodied Carbon in Trade: A Survey of the Empirical Literature." *Grantham Research Institute on Climate Change and the Environment: Working Paper* 77: 1–39. Accessed March 12, 2015. http://cccep.ac.uk.

Sayers, Dorothy. 1947. *Creed or Chaos?* London: Methuan.

Shapiro, Steven. 2014. "Poor People, Poor Planet: The Psychology of How We Harm and Heal Humanity and Earth." In *Toward a Socially Responsible Psychology for a Global Era*, edited by Elena Mustakova-Possardt, Mikhail Lyubansky, Michael Basseches, and Julie Oxenberg. New York: Springer.

Stiglitz, Joseph. 2002. "Information and the Change in the Paradigm in Economics." *The American Economic Review* 92, 3: 460–501.

Sukhdev, Pavan. 2012. "Sustainability: The Corporate Climate Overhaul." *Nature* 486, 7401: 27–28.

Taylor, Astra. 2014. *The People's Platform: Taking Back Power and Culture in the Digital Age*. London: Fourth Estate.

Tuttle, Brad. 2013. "The Splurge Surge: Luxury Spending on the Rise." *Time Magazine*. May 1. Accessed March 1, 2016. http://business.time.com/2013/05/01/the-splurge-surge-luxury-spending-on-the-rise/.

Valentino-Devries, Jennifer, Jeremy Singer-Vine, and Ashkan Soltani. 2012. "Websites Vary Prices, Deals Based on Uusers." *Wall Street Journal*, December 24. Accessed November 7, 2015. http://on.wsj.com/Tj1W2V.

Wackernagel, Mathis, and William Rees. 1996. *Our Ecological Footprint: Reducing Human Impact on Human Health*. Gabriola Island, B.C., Canada: New Society Publishers.

World Federation of Advertisers. 2015. "What Is the WFA?" *World Federation of Advertisers*. Accessed November 10, 2015. http://www.wfanet.org/en/about-wfa.

Part II
Ideology Critique

6 On the Futility of Advertising Critique
Searching for Alternatives

Olga Fedorenko

This chapter questions the effects and limitations of advertising critique today. In the first half, I argue that advertising critique does little to disrupt advertising as a capitalist institution. Instead, it mediates the critics'—academic and otherwise—practical acquiescence to the very effects targeted by advertising critique, albeit from a critical distance. The theoretical foundation of this argument comes from Slavoj Žižek's theorizations on how ideology works by disidentification and how, counterintuitively, literal identification with ideological claims is subversive. In the second half of the chapter, I suggest what a truly corrosive engagement with advertising might look like. To that end, I flesh out two instances, one from the United States and a second from South Korea, in which the smooth operation of advertising was disrupted.

Accomplishments of Advertising Critique?

"People no longer believe that there's any truth in advertising—even though deceitful ads are both illegal and simply bad business," lamented a contributor to one marketing blog, under the title, "How to Please Cynical Consumers" (Owens 2013). That consumers do not believe advertising has been a long-standing complaint of advertising agencies, their clients, and marketing experts. New technologies and media infrastructures have tremendously increased advertisers' knowledge about potential consumers and multiplied venues where to reach them, but these new opportunities have not necessarily improved advertising effectivity or made it more appreciated. A 2012 Gallup poll revealed that advertising was among the 10 industries US consumers hated most (Sauter and Frohlich 2012), whereas other studies confirmed again and again that the majority of consumers ignore advertising, consider it irrelevant, and are suspicious of advertisers' motives (e.g., Ligerakis 2004; GooStudy 2014). As one marketing-advice book notes, "Shooting down the advertising has become a kind of sport, designed to show that the participants are not stupid enough to be manipulated, particularly by those without enough respect for their intelligence to at least make the sport challenging" (Bond and Kirshenbaum 1997, 3).

So commonplace is the cynicism about advertising that it found its way to one of the biggest celebrations of the advertising industry. Comedian Jerry Seinfeld, a 2014 recipient of an honorary CLIO Award and a celebrity endorser for Apple, Microsoft, and Acura, began his address with a confession, "I love advertising because I love lying" (O'Hare 2014). He continued to "roast" advertising for the disconnect between its promises and actual consumption experiences by paradoxically over-identifying with advertising's ultimate promise of fulfillment through consumption. According to the media reports, some of the advertising dignitaries did seem uncomfortable, but Seinfeld was neither thrown out of the room nor robbed of his award, and the advertising audience did applaud his speech.

It is tempting to interpret such widespread skepticism about advertising as a victory of advertising critique—but should we? Just as advertising practitioners did not quit in droves after hearing Seinfeld's denouncements, so we consumers of advertised commodities are not so far from knowing that advertising often lies, exaggerates, and manipulates. We continue to buy advertised products and participate in consumerist rituals, such as Christmas shopping or Black Friday. Stampedes at the launches of Apple products are evidence that today's consumers, despite their penchant for "shooting down" ads, are no wiser to "commodity aesthetics," enhancements of commodities' desirability through aesthetic and marketing tactics to maximize sellers' profits (Haug 1986). There have been movements for "fair trade" and local shopping, which problematize individual consumption choices; nevertheless, they do not disturb the centrality of consumption to contemporary life and often fold into an assertion of class status or assuagement of liberal guilt (Littler 2011; Miller 2001). After decades of denouncing conspicuous consumption and commodity-mediated distinction, contemporary societies are no less consumerist. Some would argue that we late-capitalist subjects are more than ever invested in our "small salaries and various little techno-gadget toys" (Johnston 2004, 266). Held as fetish-objects, commodities seduce us to disregard the actual conditions of material reality, such as the alienating, disciplinary regimes of many workplaces (Johnston 2004, 266–68).

Moreover, popular familiarity with advertising deficiencies does not prevent advertising from being a five-hundred-billion-dollar industry globally—and growing (Statista 2014; Sebastian 2015; Johnson 2014). With the wide spread of the Internet and refinement of tracking technologies, users' information and attention have been commodified and sold to advertisers with ever greater efficiency and precision (Fuchs 2014). Already by the 1980s, the global advertising industry had grown increasingly concentrated and influential as advertising agencies merged, acquired each other, and became publicly traded (Mattelart 1991). Connecting manufacturers, mass media, financial markets and politicians, advertising became a "network of networks" (Ibid., ix), whose influence went beyond shaping commodity choices. Those tendencies continued in the 21st century as political advertising became even more extensive, while governments and politicians became increasingly reliant on professional public relations firms to promote their causes.

In a word, if the purpose of advertising critique has been to reform advertising, to make it less problematic from the standpoint of commodity consumers or democratic citizens, its achievements are unimpressive. True, there were considerable victories with regulating advertising of dangerous substances, medications, and unhealthy foodstuffs as well as with limiting advertising to vulnerable groups, such as children. Yet many advocates and critics would argue that regulation could go much further (e.g., Livingstone 2012; Rubie-Davies et al. 2013). Far from being subject to stringent regulation, advertising industries all over the world are increasingly governed by voluntary codes of ethics, whose enforcement is up to the industry itself and is often slow and lenient (Cronin 2004; Shaver and An 2014). There were also some successes in policing advertising depictions, such as orchestrating intolerance for sexism or demeaning representations of minorities (e.g., Boddewyn and Loubradou 2011; Shankar 2015), but that has been an overall trend in the media and social sensibilities, not a development particular to advertising. Moreover, with advertising's politics of representation, those very victories were ambivalent because they contributed to depoliticizing the subcultures advertising thus acknowledged, transforming their agendas into lifestyle choices achieved by choosing the right brand while displacing collective popular politics into individual politics of shopping (e.g., Cronin 2004; Klein 2000). The more ambitious goals of advertising critique—diverting pursuits of self-realization from consumption or preventing advertisers' interests from setting agendas for advertising-dependent media—in most locales were all but abandoned. For example, historian Inger Stole (2006) argues that in the US the debates about the desired parameters of advertising as a social institution have been excluded from public debate since the 1930s, when consumer movement to regulate "business propaganda" was defeated by heavy lobbying from business circles and nasty ad hominem attacks on consumer activists.

How can we understand this gap between the ubiquity of advertising critique and its limited accomplishments? The following section offers an answer by relating discourses and practices of advertising critique to the pervasiveness of a cynical sensibility, an oft-noted feature of late capitalism (e.g., Sloterdijk 1987; Žižek 1989). Drawing on Žižek's work of ideology and insights from workplace resistance studies, I contend that advertising critique, rather than being disruptive of advertising as a capitalist institution, mediates the critics' complicity with consumerism and other practices that the critique targets.

Ideology, Advertising and "Decaf Resistance"

Marxist philosopher Slavoj Žižek's theorizations of ideology (Žižek 1999a, 1999b; Dean 2006) offer a potent tool for interrogating the limits of advertising critique. Žižek leaves behind the critique of ideology as "false consciousness" and focuses on ideology as externalized in material practices, rituals and institutions. The crucial move in such an analysis is to privilege what Žižek terms the "objective" materiality of belief in a particular ideology—people's actions as well as assumptions they betray—over consciously held "subjective" convictions, which often reject the logic of the "objective" actions.

For example, that is how Žižek frames commodity fetishism, a phenomenon when social relations between people appear as relations between commodities. As he stresses, "in Marx's notion of fetishism the place of the fetishist inversion is not in what people think they are doing, but in their social activity itself" (Žižek: 1997, 105). Namely,

> a typical bourgeois subject is, in terms of his conscious attitude, a utilitarian nominalist—it is in his social activity, in exchange on the market, that he acts as if commodities were not simple objects but objects endowed with special powers, full of "theological whimsies. (Ibid.)

In other words, as a normative doctrine, commodity fetishism hardly has any avowed followers. Few consciously believe that commodities have special powers. Yet we "practically" believe it by participating in the rituals and institutions of consumer society.

Drawing on Lacanian psychoanalysis, Žižek also emphasizes that for an ideology to take hold of a subject, compliance with ideological injunctions must be *enjoyable*. Žižek treats ideological formations—socialist, capitalist, fascist—as economies of enjoyment, which reproduce relations of domination by channeling subjects' desire. Each offers an explanation of the ontological lack (posited as the constitutive of a subject in the psychoanalytic framework) and suggests a path to bridge it; though it is an impossible promise, the pursuit is enjoyable enough to bind subjects to a certain set of relations and hierarchies. In Žižek's example, Nazism got a grip on subjects not because its doctrines were logically convincing but because they were supported by an ideological fantasy of a natural community where social contradictions could be overcome, and Jews were cast as the obstacle toward the achievement of this enjoyment of a harmonious, contradiction-free communal life (Dean 2006, 61–62); whereas on the mundane level, this ideological formation produced "little nuggets of enjoyment" for subjects, who complied with its externalized practices, in following orders and fulfilling their ideologically defined duties (Dean 2006, 68). Advertising, too, can be analyzed as an ideological fantasy that supports a capitalist economy of enjoyment: it incites mundanely enjoyable consumption while promising sublime fulfillment (Stavrakakis 2006; Fedorenko 2012, 16–24).

From the inevitable gap between what ideologies promise and what they deliver, it follows that a certain disidentification with an ideology's literal message, far from being detrimental, is essential for the ideological fantasy to be operational (Žižek 1999a, 61–62). A certain detachment allows subjects to engage in the practices that the ideology prescribes without confronting the logical leaps that the ideological formation contains and without feeling compelled to change those practices. To put it differently, ideological belief is sustained by a cynical distance, which Žižek, building on philosopher Peter Sloterdijk (1987), proclaims the very formula of ideology today, "They know very well what they are doing, yet they are doing it" (Žižek 1999a, 62).

The insight about the crucial role of disidentification in binding subjects to an ideological fantasy has been provocatively applied to studying workplace resistance, to point out that employees' minor non-compliance with rules, irony, and sarcasm about corporate values seldom prevent those employees from trying to succeed in the organizations they mock, so that in the end cynical employees end up reproducing the system they criticize (Fleming and Spicer 2003; Contu 2007). In the context of liberal-capitalist workplaces Alessia Contu defines this dynamic as "decaf resistance," after decaffeinated coffee, which lacks the essential coffee ingredient, caffeine: "Decaf, because it threatens and hurts nobody" (Contu 2007, 370); it is "a resistance without the acid that can destroy the machine of power" (374). Instead of shaking the existing order, decaf resistance reproduces it by allowing a space for disidentification, so that resisting subjects can maintain a fantasy of themselves as "liberal, free, and self-relating human beings to whom multiple choices are open and all can be accommodated" (370)—which ultimately allows them to participate in the very practices they condemn. In sum, far from causing a disturbance, an ironic distance between individual convictions and what is perceived as official ideology enables the subject to participate in the practices in which the ideology is externalized.

These arguments have direct relevance for understanding our everyday engagements with advertising. Though most of us know full well that advertising often exaggerates, misleads, and manipulates, we compliantly subject ourselves to advertising, consider it in our consumption decisions, buy advertised commodities, and seek enjoyment in them. In other words, whatever our convictions, as long as we participate in advertising-mediated consumption we "objectively," materially believe advertising and end up reproducing the system of which advertising is a part. Moreover, our ironizing about advertising, to mirror Contu's argument, falls under decaf resistance, which frees the ironic to shop for holiday gifts, communicate status through purchases, and perform other consumption-related rituals. That irony about advertising has little disruptive power is evidenced by how the advertising industry has embraced mocking advertising as a creative tactic— for example, an ad that parodies the advertising cliché of "beer and babes" by featuring a belching and farting "babe" ("Best beer commercial ever?" 2007) or a commercial that advertises a restaurant by ridiculing its menu (Nudd 2012).

The charge of decaf resistance holds for much of advertising critique as well. In so far as those pronouncing those critiques continue to participate in the marketplace as if they believed in the consumerist dream, it is still decaf resistance. In particular, the critique feeds the fantasy of the critic as somehow being more immune from advertising than those who, presumably naïvely, follow the injunction to buy. Such references to naïve others work as a displacement of belief: having critiqued the naïve others for their uncritical vulnerability to advertising, advertising critics are free to engage in precisely the practices those naïve others are allegedly tricked into (cf., Žižek 1997, 105.)

Does this mean that all advertising critique is futile? No. There is no denying that there is value in contesting problematic advertising representations, which normalize gender or ethnic stereotypes, for example. Yet such interventions are not fundamentally about advertising. They might be of some help in addressing the social problems of inequality and discrimination. Yet they do nothing to disturb commodity fetishism or to challenge the discretion of corporations over what advertising gets to exploit for sales purposes. Nor do they raise questions about the role of advertising in society. To the contrary, in so far as corporations voluntarily offer to respect politics of representation, such interventions shield companies from binding regulations (Cronin 2004). In other words, advertising critique is consequential in so far as the goal is to police representations. Yet if its goal is to problematize the social formation for which advertising stands—capitalism—it ends up a case of decaf resistance, when the critic feels superior to those who presumably are unaware of advertising habitual transgressions and is free to engage in consumerist rituals from a critical distance. This is the kind of resistance that costs nothing but possibly advances academic and journalistic careers. What kind of intervention then has the corrosive power to challenge advertising as a social institution?

Searching for Alternatives: Subversive Identifications

While disidentification is the very tool through which ideological formations are maintained, what proves subversive is too literal an identification, Žižek argues. His example is the protagonist of *The Good Soldier Schweik* by Czech writer Jaroslav Hasek. When WWI breaks out, Schweik, a resident of Prague, at the time a part of Austro-Hungarian empire, wishes to enlist, and he is so eager to serve the emperor and support the war effort that the authorities cannot tell whether he is a naïve fool or a crafty saboteur. Schweik's enthusiasm about participating in the war and his eagerness to follow orders literally exposes the absurdity of the war machine, and hence he is constantly in trouble and under suspicion. For Žižek, Schweik is "an exemplary case of the subversion-through-identification" (Žižek 1999b, 99). To give another example and return to workplace resistance, a subversive literal identification would be "work-to-rule" industrial action, when employees follow safety and other regulations literally while doing exactly the minimum specified in the rules of their contracts, which tends to disrupt regular operations or at lease cause a slowdown.

To apply this to advertising, the most destabilizing act would be complete identification with advertising narratives and with the self-glorifying discourses of the advertising industry. In other words, a subversive position toward advertising would not be in asserting that advertising distorts reality, or in mocking advertising messages, or in critiquing advertising's stifling influence on mass media, but in expecting and demanding that consumption of advertised commodities brings exactly the satisfactions that advertising shows and in expecting and demanding that advertising as an institution serve the consumer just as its official ideologies claim it does.

> In Žižekian terms, this would be an "impossible demand,"
>
> To demand consistency at strategically selected points where the system cannot afford to be consistent is to put pressure on the entire system. The art of politics lies in making particular demands which, while thoroughly realistic, strike at the core of hegemonic ideology and imply much more radical change. Such demands, while feasible and legitimate, are de facto impossible.
>
> (Žižek 2013, 11)

To demand that advertising consistently live up to its official justifications—to provide useful information about commodities, to prioritize human needs, to serve public interest and democracy—is such a demand. It seems fulfillable and reasonable, but ultimately it implies a radical challenge: a disruption of commodity circulation and of the alliance between capital and mass media. In the remainder of the chapter, I turn to two instances in which the smooth operation of advertising was indeed destabilized by literal identification.

"Red Bull gives you wings:" Really?

Red Bull is an energy drink, which, its trademark claims, "vitalizes body and mind." The promise of enhanced performance has been expressed through the slogan, "Red Bull gives you wings." A series of humorous cartoon commercials illustrated protagonists facing a vexing situation, growing wings after consuming the drink, and then resolving the issue. A man gets pooped on by a pigeon but then drinks a Red Bull, grows wings, flies over the bird and takes his revenge ("Redbull—Pigeon 1" 2012). A frog drinks a Red Bull offered by a hopeful but unsightly princess and turns into a prince—but only to grow wings and fly away to check out other princesses ("Redbull—Frog Prince" 2007). A widow, after learning of her late husband's will to leave his possessions to another woman, drinks a Red Bull, grows wings and flies to heaven to presumably have the will changed ("Redbull—Last Will"

2010). To enjoy these ads, one needs to interpret them metaphorically and not expect miraculous results.

One Red Bull consumer, however, refused to assume such a complicit distance. A self-declared regular Red Bull drinker since 2002, Benjamin Careathers sued the company in a class-action suit, taking issue with its advertising's promise. The lawsuit claimed that the advertising that stated that "Red Bull gives you wings" was "deceitful and fraudulent" (*Benjamin Careathers v. Red Bull North America, Inc.* 2014, 6). Specifically, the complaint stated,

> The Red Bull Defendants prey upon consumers by promising that, among other things, "Red Bull gives you wings" by providing a mixture of ingredients that, when ingested, significantly improve a consumer's physiological and mental performance beyond what a simple cup of coffee or caffeine pill would do for a consumer's physiological and mental performance. (Ibid., 2)

Careathers's wording is ambiguous enough as to whether he literally expected to grow wings. The core of the suit was to point out that the caffeine was the only active ingredient in the drink, and its concentration was less than in a cup of Starbucks coffee, though its price was considerably higher. Because the higher price was justified by claims about the uniqueness of energy-giving ingredients, it was false advertising, the suit argued:

> Defendants spend millions of dollars misleading customers about the superiority of their "functional beverage" and its ability to "give you wings" and provide energy and vitality. (Ibid., 5)

Rather than disprove the accusations, the advertiser chose to settle. The settlement offered a compensation, either in cash or in products, to whoever claimed to have been a consumer since 2002, until the $13 million settlement fund ran out. Red Bull also had to stop using its "Red Bull gives you wings" tagline in the US. Media quoted a Red Bull representative saying, "Red Bull settled the lawsuit to avoid the cost and distraction of litigation. However, Red Bull maintains that its marketing and labeling have always been truthful and accurate, and denies any and all wrongdoing or liability" (Quirk 2014).

The lawsuit and Careathers himself attracted lots of media attention and ridicule. Some commentators insinuated that it was an attempt to take advantage of the company. Others called the plaintiff "an extremely idiotic consumer" (Falletti 2014) and showing naiveté "greater than typically exhibited by young children" (Corbett 2014).

The point I wish to stress is not whether or not consumers cognitively believed that they would sprout wings, but that advertising actually said it—counting on consumers not to believe it. Or rather to believe it enough to consume Red Bull and enjoy it but not enough to expect wings. The question of whether Careathers expected literal wings is unimportant if, with Žižek, we focus on the materiality of belief. Careathers—just as other Red Bull drinkers—"believed" not because he was "subjectively" convinced that Red Bull would give him wings but because he "objectively" bought and drank Red Bull. It was about the material act of consuming, not about conscious expectations. For the purpose of advertising critique, what is important is that Careathers's lawsuit forced observers to confront the fact that advertising did not tell the truth about products and, more disturbingly, consumers—us—have been complicit with those untruths.

In *Age of Propaganda*, psychologists Anthony Pratkanis and Elliot Aronson expose sly propaganda strategies, including those of advertising, and seek an alternative to both, "native acceptance of the fruits of propaganda" and "total cynicism combined with a lust for entertainment," to defend democracy, which, they insist, needs citizens who rely on logical persuasion, as opposed to manipulative propaganda, to make rational consensual decisions (2001, xiv). Among other strategies, the authors suggest asking advertisers to provide proofs of their claims in writing (118, 347), and Careathers's intervention could be interpreted as an extreme case of this anti-propaganda, pro-democracy strategy. Just as Schweik's literal identification with the militarist ideology spread mayhem, so did Careathers's naïveté about advertising promise. His lack of complicit distance from advertising messages exposed the absurdity of what advertising habitually says—and what consumers usually acquiesce to by assuming an abetting distance.

"Advertising Terrorism" in South Korea

In South Korea, a Schweikian disruption of advertising was enacted by civil society group, Korea Press Consumerism Organization (official English name), or KPCO. The literal translation of the organization's name would be "Mass Media Consumer Sovereignty Organization" (*Ŏllon sobija chukwon tanch'e*), and it was "consumer sovereignty" they were fighting for, literally identifying with the business truism that the consumer is king. As I detail the story elsewhere (Fedorenko 2012, ch 1), KPCO challenged how companies allocate their advertising budgets among newspapers of different ideological orientation. They wished to redirect some of the advertising contracts of the three rich right-wing "conservative" dailies to the two struggling oppositional "progressive" dailies.

To provide some context, the three "conservative" newspapers, the *Chosun Ilbo*, the *Dong-A Ilbo* and the *JoongAng Ilbo*, were national leaders in circulation and readership numbers; however, according to the trio's many critics, what those numbers reflected was not the readers' preference for the right-wing editorial bias. Rather, the critics argued, the "conservative" dailies attracted many readers because they printed more pages, provided entertainment news, published extensive lifestyle sections, and offered munificent gifts to incentivize subscriptions—all of this possible because they received generous advertising contracts from big business. Advertising thus was a bloodline of the alliance of large conglomerates, right-wing politicians who advanced their interests, and the three dailies, which promoted the right-wing, pro-conglomerate agenda. The two oppositional newspapers, the *Hankyoreh* and the *Kyunghyang Shinmun,* on the other hand—pro-union, critical of big business, and ready to expose corporate abuses—received few advertising contracts and scrambled financially.

KPCO attempted to challenge the right-wing hegemony from the position of concerned consumers whose sovereign rights were being trampled. KPCO activists argued that, as consumers of media, they were entitled to news sources that represented a diversity of opinions, and the conservative "bias" of the right-wing press violated that. More provocatively, they insisted that, as consumers of advertisers' commodities, they were entitled to have a say where companies spend their advertising budgets. According to KPCO, whether to support the oppositional media was not an ethical, voluntary choice of advertisers but their obligation. In the KPCO discourses, consumer sovereignty was evoked to exert hierarchy over corporations in a way akin to popular sovereignty. These demands, however, were formulated with, not against, the dominant neoliberal ideologies, which anointed the consumer and her choices as the ultimate arbiter in the marketplace and privatized society. With Schweikian subversive naïveté they insisted that corporations acknowledge that the "consumer is always right" and realize the will of the consumers—even if that means supporting the newspapers that criticize those very corporations.

KPCO conducted two rounds of advertiser boycotts, in the summers of 2008 and 2009. In the first round, activists made a list of advertisers that advertised only in the conservative press, posted the list online and encouraged supporters—membership surpassed 40 thousand within days of KPCO's emergence as an online forum—to call the offices of those advertisers and tell them to stop advertising in the conservative dailies, under a threat of consumer boycott. Tens of thousands of angry calls were made per day, according to KPCO, and advertisers' offices were paralyzed. Some of the calls, according to a later investigation, got out of hand and included foul language and even death threats. Many advertisers yielded, and the conservative dailies had to reduce their number of pages. The campaign petered out after the police began an investigation into KPCO activities. Two dozen activists were charged and eventually found guilty of "obstruction of business," a criminal offense. The court, however, ruled that consumers were lawfully entitled to boycott newspapers' advertisers to sway editorial policies. The angry calls and threats were illegal.

For the second round in summer 2009, KPCO activists boycotted "conservative" advertisers one at a time. They would hold a press conference to announce the boycott target and then post online updates about not buying the company's products. Some members picketed in public places with boycott posters, but no phone calls were made. The first boycott target, a medium-size snack manufacturer, committed to advertising in the progressive dailies within hours after the boycott announcement. KPCO's next target was Samsung, South Korea's biggest conglomerate, which more or less shrugged the boycott off. Though about ten thousand Koreans publicly pledged to avoid Samsung products, the boycott was unlikely to dent Samsung's profits, because of the conglomerate's global scale and the sheer unavoidability of Samsung products in South Korea. Despite the limited scope and effects of the second round of boycotts, KPCO leaders were again prosecuted by police.

Predictably, the boycotts provoked vehement criticism from the right wing. One newspaper went as far as to call KPCO "advertising terrorists," and another suggested that the movement leader get a mental health check. Such reactions are telltale signs of KPCO activism becoming Schewikian politics of subversive imbecility, which disrupts the ideological fantasy through literal identification. KPCO activism aired some "obscene dirty secrets" (Žižek 1997, 55), whose disavowal is essential for consumer capitalism: On the one hand, KPCO openly based its intervention on the power of advertising to set political agenda and define media bias—a power that is publicly disavowed to keep the ideal of democratic public sphere compatible with the media's dependence on advertising. On the other, KPCO revealed that in neoliberal South Korea the consumer wasn't king after all, and advertisers were not eager to listen to consumers. To put it differently, KPCO activists' mental health was questioned, and terrorist intentions were alleged because they posed a Žižekian impossible demand. To demand that consumers be kings, corporations be their subjects, and advertising distribution prioritize political preferences of consumers, not corporations, is a subversive demand that a consumer capitalist society cannot accommodate.

Conclusion

With the development of mobile technologies, the spread of social media, and refinement of user tracking techniques, advertising as a genre might seem to be crumbling (Hamilton et al. 2014). However, it is not because advertising is disappearing, but rather because advertising is subsuming other media forms, as producers of media content compete to commodify their audiences and sell their consumer profiles and attention to advertisers. Advertising critique is ever more needed at such a moment. Yet, as I showed in this chapter, the expository critique that reveals the manipulative, exploitative practices is not enough, as it is easily coopted into a decaf resistance, which, far from disrupting systems of domination, offers a safety valve for integrating critically minded subjects. If advertising critics are serious about challenging advertising as a social institution, the way forward is through refusing to take a cynical distance from advertising promises and official ideologies—Schewikian imbecility, whose disruptive potential for advertising I illustrated with the stories about Red Bull held accountable to its promise to give wings and about Korea Press Consumerism Organization standing up for democratic media.

Acknowledgements

This essay began in 2008 as a term paper for a reading course with Ken Kawashima. I wish to thank him for introducing me to critical theory and for encouraging me to explore theoretical issues beyond the usual confines of East Asian Studies.

References

Benjamin Careathers v. Red Bull North America, Inc., 2014. Case No. 1:13-CV-00369 (KPF). United States District Court Southern District of New York4.

Best Beer Commercial Ever? 2007. Posted by RM2Static on May 9, 2007. https://www.youtube.com/watch?v=2S2VUCdbhg0.

Boddewyn, Jean J., and Esther Loubradou. 2011. "The Control of 'Sex in Advertising' in France." *Journal of Public Policy & Marketing* 30(2): 220–25.

Bond, Jonathan, and Richard Kirshenbaum. 1998. *Under the Radar: Talking to Today's Cynical Consumer*. Adweek Magazine Series. New York: Wiley.

Cantu, Alessia. 2007. "Decaf Resistance: On Misbehavior, Cynicism, and Desire in Liberal Workplaces." *Management Communication Quarterly* 21(3): 364–79. doi: 10.1177/0893318907310941.

Corbett, Jonathan. 2014. "Objection by Class Member Jonathan Corbett." *Professional Troublemaker*. October. https://tsaoutofourpants.files.wordpress.com/2014/10/careathers-v-red-bull-objection.pdf.

Cronin, Anne M. 2004. *Advertising Myths: The Strange Half-Lives of Images and Commodities*. London and New York: Routledge.

Dean, Jodi. 2006. *Žižek's Politics*. New York: Routledge.

Falletti, Tim. 2014. "Redbull Sued Because It Doesn't Give You Wings." *The Acrimonious Clown*. October 14. http://www.chicagonow.com/acrimonious-clown/2014/10/redbull-sued-because-it-doesnt-give-you-wings.

Fedorenko, Olga. 2012. "Tending to the 'Flower of Capitalism:' Consuming, Producing and Censoring Advertising in South Korea of the '00s." PhD Dissertation. University of Toronto, East Asian Studies. http://hdl.handle.net/1807/33994.

Fleming, Peter, and Andre Spicer. 2003. "Working at a Cynical Distance: Implications for Power, Subjectivity and Resistance." *Organization* 10(1): 157–79. doi: 10.1177/1350508403010001376.

Fuchs, Christian. 2012. "Dallas Smythe Today - The Audience Commodity, the Digital Labour Debate, Marxist Political Economy and Critical Theory. Prolegomena to a Digital Labour Theory of Value." *tripleC: Communication, Capitalism & Critique* 10(2): 692–740.

"Goo Study: Most of Us Ignore Online Ads." 2014. *Goo Create*. February 11. http://goocreate.com/goo-study-most-of-us-ignore-online-ads.

Hamilton, James F., Robert Bodie, Helen Kennedy, and Andrew McStay. 2014. "Critical Approaches to the Study of Advertising." *Culture in Conversation: A Critical and Cultural Studies Round Table.* March. https://cultureinconversation.word-press.com/2014/03/01/critical-approaches-to-the-study-of-advertising.

Haug, Wolfgang Fritz. 1986. *Critique of Commodity Aesthetics: Appearance, Sexuality, and Advertising in Capitalist Society.* Social and Political Theory from Polity Press. Cambridge: Polity Press.

Johnson, Bradley. 2014. "What You Need to Know about the Global Ad Market." *Advertising Age,* December 8. http://adage.com/article/global-news/global-ad-market/296104.

Johnston, Adrian. 2004. "The Cynic's Fetish: Slavoj Žižek and the Dynamics of Belief." *Psychoanalysis, Culture & Society* 9: 259–83. doi: 10.1057/palgrave. pcs.2100014.

Klein, Naomi. 2000. *No Logo: No Space, No Choice, No Jobs: Taking Aim at the Brand Bullies.* Toronto: A.A. Knopf Canada.

Ligerakis, Maria. 2004. "Consumer Resistance at All Time High: US Study." *B&T Weekly,* May. EBSCOhost (13157956).

Littler, Jo. 2011. "What's Wrong with Ethical Consumption?" In *Ethical Consumption: A Critical Introduction,* edited by Tania Lewis and Emily Potter, 27–39. New York: Routledge.

Livingstone, Sonia. 2012. "Advertising Regulation and Childhood Obesity." In *Media Regulation: Governance and the Interests of Citizens and Consumers,* edited by Peter Lunt and Sonia Livingstone, 143–62. London, UK: SAGE Publications.

Mattelart, Armand. 1991. *Advertising International: The Privatization of Public Space.* Vol. Rev. English language. London; New York: Routledge.

Miller, Daniel. 2001. *The Dialectics of Shopping.* The Lewis Henry Morgan Lectures; Chicago: University of Chicago Press.

Nudd, Tim. 2012. "Could Ads Convince Hipsters to Go to Applebee's Ironically?" *AdWeek,* July 24. http://www.adweek.com/adfreak/could-ads-convince-hipsters-go-applebees-ironically-142142.

O'Hare, Kate. 2014. "Jerry Seinfeld Slams Ad World While Receiving Advertising Award." *Breitbart.* October 3. http://www.breitbart.com/big-hollywood/2014/10/03/jerry-seinfeld-slams-ad-world-while-receiving-advertising-award.

Owens, Matthew. 2013. "How to Please Cynical Consumers." *iMedia Connection.* July 24. http://www.imediaconnection.com/content/34551.asp.

Pratkanis, Anthony, and Elliot Aronson. 2001. *Age of Propaganda: The Everyday Use and Abuse of Persuasion.* Vol. Revised. New York: W. H. Freeman and Company.

Quirk, Mary Beth. 2014. "Red Bull Will Pay $13 Million to Settle False Advertising Lawsuit." *Consumerist.* October 6. http://consumerist.com/2014/10/06/red-bull-will-pay-13-million-to-settle-false-advertising-lawsuit/.

Redbull—Frog Prince. 2010. YouTube Video. Posted Jan 17 by MeLikeRedBull. https://www.youtube.com/watch?v=SHdL4BgSz_U&index=10&list=PL3C3D65 A5C2686781.

Redbull—Last Will. 2010. YouTube Video. Posted Jan 17 by MeLikeRedBull https://youtu.be/XlG4VAFIGFw?list=PL3C3D65A5C2686781.

Redbull—Pigeon 1. 2012. YouTube Video. Posted by Internet Epicness on Sep 30. https://www.youtube.com/watch?v=ZDHaGB_pXO4.

Rubie-Davies, Christine M., Sabrina Liu, and Kai-Chi Katie Lee. 2013. "Watching Each Other: Portrayals of Gender and Ethnicity in Television Advertisements." *The Journal of Social Psychology* 153 (2): 175–95. doi: 10.1080/00224545.201 2.717974.

Sauter, Michael B., and Thomas C. Frohlich. 2012. "America's Most Hated Industries." *Yahoo Finance.* August 24. http://finance.yahoo.com/news/america%e2%80%99s-most-hated-industries.html.

Sebastian, Michael. 2015. "Marketers to Boost Global Ad Spending This Year to $540 Billion." *Advertising Age,* March 24. http://adage.com/article/media/marketers-boost-global-ad-spending-540-billion/297737/.

Shankar, Shalini. 2015. *Advertising Diversity: Ad Agencies and the Creation of Asian American Consumers.* Duke University Press.

Shaver, Mary Alice, and Soontae An, eds. 2014. *The Global Advertising Regulation Handbook.* Armonk, NY: M.E. Sharpe.

Sloterdijk, Peter. 1987. *Critique of Cynical Reason.* Minneapolis: University of Minnesota Press.

Statista. "Global Advertising Revenue from 2007 to 2016 (in Billion U.S. Dollars)." *Statista.* Accessed November 25, 2015. http://www.statista.com/statistics/237797/total-global-advertising-revenue.

Stavrakakis, Yannis. 2006. "Objects of Consumption, Causes of Desire: Consumerism and Advertising in Societies of Commanded Enjoyment." *Gamma* 14: 83–106.

Stole, Inger L. 2006. *Advertising on Trial: Consumer Activism and Corporate Public Relations in the 1930s.* History of Communication. Urbana: University of Illinois Press.

Žižek, Slavoj. 1989. *The Sublime Object of Ideology.* London: Verso.

———. 1997. *The Plague of Fantasies.* Wo Es War. London; New York: Verso.

———. 1999a. "The Spectre of Ideology." In *The Žižek Reader,* edited by Slavoj Žižek, Elizabeth Wright, and Edmond Leo Wright, 53–86. Oxford, UK; Malden, MA: Blackwell Publishers.

———. 1999b. "Fantasy as a Political Category: A Lacanian Approach." In *The Žižek Reader,* edited by Slavoj Žižek, Elizabeth Wright, and Edmond Leo Wright, 87–102. Oxford, UK ; Malden, MA: Blackwell Publishers.

———. 2013. "Trouble in Paradise." *London Review of Books,* July 18. http://www.lrb.co.uk/v35/n14/slavoj-Žižek/trouble-in-paradise.

7 Art for Fun and Profit

The Political Aesthetics of Advertising

Nicholas Holm

Advertising exists at the crossroads of naked capitalism and artistic aspiration: a fraught position, neatly captured in Raymond Williams's description of it as "the official art of modern capitalist society" (2005, 207). Even as advertising's gradual migration into online spaces fuels the persistent demand that its aesthetic aspects have now been superseded by the algorithmic, advertising continues to exist and exert its influence as a vast constellation of images, narratives, spectacles, music, rhetoric, and sensual experiences. Advertising thus looks set to remain a significantly aesthetic form for the near future, albeit one absolutely entangled in the economic priorities of capitalism. This unstable combination of the economic and the aesthetic is not unique to advertising—the resulting conflict is one of the central themes of art, if not all culture, under capitalism—but it is particularly prominent in that context due to advertising's inescapable indebtedness to the marketing and sales process. As a consequence, advertising has never been the most highly esteemed object of study in the critical humanities and has instead frequently figured as an utterly corrupted form of culture (if indeed it qualifies as culture at all).

In the critical Marxist tradition, which has been the historically dominant mode for approaching advertising as a cultural form, commentators have unsurprisingly tended to emphasize advertising's implication in the operation of consumer capitalism and the well-documented wealth of tragedies and abuses generated by that way of life. From Max Horkheimer and Theodor Adorno to Juliet Schor and Sut Jhally, advertising appears as little more than the cultural expression of capitalism: a direct delivery system for ideology that distorts and perverts anything it touches. While such critical analyses are as valuable as they are influential, in their incisive focus upon certain political economic aspects of advertising they tend to overlook the textual and formal nature of the advertisements themselves, let alone the relations and means by which advertising is produced. This failure to attend to actually existing forms of advertising leads to a premature, pre-critical collapse of the distinction between advertising and capital, one that ignores rather than accounts for the other side of the binary: the advertising industry's ambitions toward provocation, inspiration, and even outright "art-ishness."

In order to address this oversight, this chapter will reassess the political aesthetic possibilities of advertising with particular respect to the concept of subsumption as a means to conceptualize the extent of advertising's integration into the structural logics of capitalism. Revisiting the bleak prognosis of Horkheimer and Adorno's account of advertising as part of the Culture Industry, I will suggest that the cultural status of advertising under capitalism is potentially more idiosyncratic than has traditionally been acknowledged. As a consequence of advertising's counterintuitive position with respect to wider capitalist processes, I will then argue that it can potentially be productively addressed in the terms of aesthetic intervention that cultural Marxism has historically reserved for more sanctified or immediately autonomous art. The purpose of such an approach is in no way to "redeem" advertising or exonerate its consumerist impulses, but rather to consider how attending to the complexities of advertising aesthetics is a necessary step to understanding the form's cultural, social, and political effects in a non-reductive manner and, moreover, to more generally illuminate the political possibilities and problems of aesthetic forms in the context of capitalism.

Advertising does not have a glowing reputation in the critical tradition. Horkheimer and Adorno's declaration that advertising is nothing more than "a pure representation of social power" (1973, 163) is both a foundational statement of the critical approach to adverting and an exemplary demonstration of that approach's reductive tendencies. In this particular critical tradition, the meaning and purpose of any given advertisement is always known in advance and known in its entirety: the advertisement exists to promote capitalism through the presentation of commodities and commoditized life in place of more materialist, democratic, or rational ways of living. For example, Henri Lefebvre asserts that advertisements exist in order to promote false needs (2008, 161–62); for Williams, "advertising is the consequence of a social failure to find means of public information and decision over a wide range of economic everyday life" (2005, 216); Michael Schudson suggests that "advertising is capitalism's way of saying 'I love you' to itself" (1986, 232), and Sut Jhally identifies advertising as "the theft and re-appropriation of meaning" (2006, 89). Notably, these critics speak of specific concrete advertisements only in broad strokes, if at all, when constructing their arguments. They write in terms of types and themes, rather than specific details, and none of them offers in-depth analysis of any particular advertisements. Instead, this critical tradition takes its lead from "Adorno [who had] no interest in explicating works because in commercial culture there are not works to critique or meanings to be found" (Brown 2014, 455). Even as other commercial mass cultural forms become the subjects of sustained inquiry, it remains accepted practice to speak of advertising *tout court* in ways that are largely unacceptable in the study of popular film, TV, music, and other media. Furthermore, on the rare occasions when scholars working in this tradition do engage with advertisements in a sustained fashion—probably the best example of such analysis is Judith

Williamson's ground-breaking *Decoding Advertisements* (1995)—they tend
to find exactly what one might expect when following Adorno's lead: equal
parts vacuity and domination.

The purpose of this quick summary of the Marxist critical tradition in
advertising studies is not to dismiss such an approach, but instead to draw
attention to the extent to which the ultimate political economic horizon
of capitalism has tended to over-determine the critical analysis of advertising. Regardless of the time, location, or producer, all that advertisements
can and ever do communicate is capitalist (and sometimes also patriarchal,
imperialist, or racist) ideology. Again, in drawing attention to this tendency,
I do not seek to challenge the importance or accuracy of this conclusion:
advertising is certainly (almost always) primarily about capitalism. However, while such a conclusion is not incorrect, it is potentially incomplete
due to the premature rejection of the other half of the equation: advertising's yearning toward the cultural status and function of art. Even if we
are deeply skeptical of the motivation and potential for realization of such
artistic desires, they play such a fundamental role in the self-conception of
historical and contemporary advertising (Berger 1983; McStay 2013; Nixon
2003; Pray 2009) that to dismiss them out of hand is to, at best, overlook a
central aspect of advertising discourse and, at worst, perpetuate groundless
prejudice and elitism. In addition, the persistent belief in the artistic nature
of advertising has real material and structural consequences for the way
in which advertising is produced: in almost all agencies, "Creatives" are
not only segmented into their own department, but also afforded particular
privileges and prestige in the production process (Malefyt and Morais 2012,
21; McFall 2004, 22; Hackley and Hackley 2015, 116). Operating at the
levels of both discourse and institution, advertising's artistic aspiration constitutes a significant aspect of advertising practice: one that has been widely
neglected in historically dominant Marxist accounts.

To further investigate how advertising might be understood as an aesthetic phenomenon, I now turn to Marx's concepts of formal and real subsumption as a way to characterize advertising's relation to its wider capitalist
context. Marx's explication of the two forms of subsumption can be found
in "Results of the Immediate Process of Production": a section excluded
from earlier translations of *Capital* that was only available in English
from the late 1960s (Mandel 1976, 943) and which has recently enjoyed
a resurgence in critical Marxist theory (quite likely as a consequence of
that concept's central role in Michael Hardt and Antonio Negri's *Empire*
where "real subsumption" names the process whereby global society, in its
entirety, becomes rebuilt according to the logic of capitalism in the moment
of "Empire" [2001]). Marx's subsumption refers to the process whereby
the labor process becomes encompassed by, and thereby subject to, the
governing logics of capitalism. The twinned terms—formal and real—refer
to different moments in this process of incorporation distinguished by the
extent and therefore the nature of their incorporation. Formal subsumption

refers to "the takeover by capital of a mode of labour developed before the emergence of capitalist relations" (Marx 1982, 1021): the process by which an industry is drawn into wage-labor and the exchange relations of capitalism through the sale of surplus product but in which the actual processes of production remain consistent. Marx's example is a peasant farmer who becomes an agricultural day laborer: swapping quasi-bondage for wage-labor but with the actual work methods unchanged (Marx 1982, 1020). In contrast, real subsumption is the transformation of the production process in accordance with the demands of capitalism through such means as the division of labor, increases in scale, the introduction of machinery and the rationalization of time and space in order to improve efficiency and thereby increase profit (Marx 1982, 1024). Formal subsumption thus refers to the initial entry into the market relations of capital where production continues through traditional methods, but the products are sold on the market; while in the case of real subsumption, traditional means and modes of production are abandoned as labor practices are rationalized in the pursuit of greater profits.

The relevance of such a model for advertising will become more apparent when we consider the subsumption of cultural production in the context of capitalism. Nicholas Brown argues that although Marx believed that "the arts are, by their very nature, unsuitable candidates for real subsumption," that is exactly the situation that Horkheimer and Adorno describe in their formative account of the Culture Industry, wherein cultural production is completely orientated toward exchange and profit (2014, 458–59). With the adoption of the division of labor, the proliferation of formulas and repetition, and the targeting of audiences as demographics, culture becomes a commodity: the production of which is carried out entirely according to the edicts of capitalist profit and thereby *really* subsumed. For Horkheimer and Adorno, however, some cultural production, such as modernist art, can remain somewhat outside of this capitalist process: while it may certainly be bought and sold in a marketplace, and thus is a commodity, it nonetheless is not produced *for* the market. In is this distinction, Brown suggests, that informs Horkheimer and Adorno's contrast between the latter novels of Walter Scott—written for the market in order to settle up debts—and Beethoven's latter quartets, which Adorno describes as an "extreme renunciation of the market" that were nonetheless sold, in Brown's words, in an act of "*ex post facto* patronage" (Horkheimer and Adorno 1973, 157; Brown 2009, 97). Beethoven's quartets may be exchanged for money, but they were not written in order to be exchanged: they are therefore indicative of a form of cultural production that is *formally* subsumed, but not really subsumed. The introduction of a distinction between formal and real subsumption thus allows us to more carefully distinguish between the different extents to which capitalism determines the production and form of culture: such a distinction thereby introduces the possibility of aesthetically experimental and politically meaningful culture even in the context of market exchange.

What is not entirely clear, however, is whether the distinction between the formal and real subsumption of cultural production is still relevant under the conditions of postmodern cultural capitalism. For Horkheimer and Adorno, the maintenance of non-really subsumed culture into the twentieth century was the result of a "cultural" lag in pre-Fascist Europe due to the uneven global development of capitalism, which "left intellect and creativity some degree of independence and allowed its last representatives to exist" (1973, 132). The underdevelopment of such cultural backwaters allowed for the persistence of non-market oriented culture production through an obstinate resistance to complete capitalist subsumption. However, as Brown notes following Fredric Jameson, under the conditions of postmodern capitalism "aesthetic production today has become integrated into commodity production generally": a state of affairs that means previously exempt cultural spaces are now also subject to real subsumption (Brown 2014, 456–57). Following the erasure of non-market oriented cultural production, we are thus faced again with the most despairing conclusion of the Culture Industry thesis: that, under capitalism:

> Culture would no longer be culture … it would be completely assimilated to the regime of accumulation. It would be design, or pornography, or advertising: a mood-altering commodity and nothing more, and there would be no particular reason to study it.
>
> (Brown 2009, 97)

Tellingly, it is at the moment when culture looks most threatened that we witness the re-insertion of advertising back into the argument as emblematic of the aesthetic impoverishment of completely and really subsumed culture. Indeed, it is against advertising (and design and pornography) that Brown stages the possible redemption of artistic culture through a commitment to the assertion of autonomy from the market (2009, 98–99; 2014, 461–64). Thus, while "the work of art is a commodity like any other" insofar as it is formally subsumed, it can escape real subsumption through the rejection of the cultural market in favor of a commitment to the limitations and possibilities of its formal properties. The work of art can avoid being reduced to the like of design, pornography, or advertising provided it turns its back on the market (2014 Brown, 449, 464). Such a summary dismissal of advertising should not be particularly surprising or unusual: it is simply another evocation of advertising as the nadir of culture in the critical tradition in the style of Adorno, Williams, and Jhally where advertising appears as a caricature—the cultural bête noire of the critical tradition—rather than as a fully realized subject of study.

What is absent here though is any consideration of how the concept of subsumption might complicate, rather than reinforce, the reductive truisms of critical advertising studies. While advertising is certainly formally subsumed within capitalism, the fact of its real subsumption is less clear cut. At the level of formal subsumption, advertising is not only produced within the context of wage relations and profit, but it is also fundamental to the wider promotional practices of contemporary consumer capitalism. Advertising is thus doubly formally subsumed in that it not only is produced in terms of capitalist relations of production but is also more widely bound up in the relations of production and promotion as they apply to other goods and services. However, as has been discussed above, formal subsumption does not guarantee real subsumption. It does not necessarily follow that because a production process is part of capitalism that its operations and products will be automatically entirely over-determined by capitalist logic. This gap between the two levels of subsumption opens up a conceptual space in which we can rethink the aesthetic and political possibilities of advertising with respect to capitalism.

It is well recognized in the critical tradition that, by virtue of its formal subsumption, advertising is inextricably tied up with our commoditized world. It promotes commodities and is a key part of the process of commoditization while working as well to transform its audiences' attention into a commodity (Smythe 1981). However, while advertising is clearly a central aspect of commodity culture, it does not necessarily follow that advertising itself is a commodity. Unlike films, video games, DVDs, toys and other merchandise, comics, books, online content streaming services, and popular music (in the form of MP3s, vinyl, or CDs), advertisements are not bought (or rented) and sold in a market. Nor are advertisements actively designed to cultivate as large or as specific an audience as possible, as is the case with broad and narrowcast media: instead, it is designed to address those audiences only once they've been gathered by those other means, or other equivalents such as data tracking. The possible exception to this rule is the rise of digital viral advertising, which is intended to be engaged with and enjoyed as content in its own right and then distributed through social media and other networks. Such a desire speaks to advertising that is meant to attract an audience through its own aesthetic merits. While the rise of this form is celebrated by some as the replacement of interruption and reposition with permission and engagement (McStay 2009, 1–3), in its direct appeal to the cultural market, viral advertising threatens to open the door for the conditions of real subsumption. Despite this possible exception, while advertisements are certainly produced in order to appeal to audiences, they are not produced (with the exception of the most aspirationally viral examples) in order to compete against other texts in a market in the same way as commoditized culture. Instead, they are distinct from other types of cultural commodities because they are not purchased and consumed in the context of a competitive cultural market. Thus, although advertisements are certainly deeply implicated in the construction and promulgation of exchange value of commodities, they themselves are not exchanged. Indeed, contrary to Marx's definition of a commodity, in the case of advertisements it is the use-value—the ability to persuade consumers to purchase specific goods and services—the predominates, rather than the exchange-value: that is the advertisement's ability to be exchanged for other goods and services in a market (Marx 1982, 179). Advertisements, because they are not produced to be exchanged, are not commodities: and insofar as they are not produced as commodities, advertisements are not a really subsumed form of cultural production. Instead, advertising as an industry fits within the larger economic context of the current moment where "the revival of contract work, home working and the like in our times indicates that some reversion to formal kinds of subjection and subsumption is entirely possible" (Harvey 2010, 174).

In order to consider the ramifications of this point—and how advertising's counterintuitive cultural exceptionalism operates—it is productive to consider in more depth the political economic and organizational structures involved in its production. In terms of the subsumption, the primary political economic fact of advertising is that, as a non-commodity, advertisements are not expected to turn a profit through exchange on a market. Certainly, it is exceedingly rare that an audience pays to encounter an advertisement. Producers of advertising are not seeking to recoup the costs of production, let alone turn a profit, by directly exchanging access to advertisements for currency. Instead, the costs of production and distribution are borne by corporate clients who commission advertising agencies to produce advertisements in order to promote their goods and services. Granted, this promotion is intended to then produce profit indirectly through the increased sale of the advertised goods, but any inferred connection between advertising and direct sales is tenuous at best. There is a long-standing and widely documented difficulty of identifying, let alone guaranteeing, whether any given advertising campaign actually works to increase sales (Cronin 2004, 59–64). In the absence of such information, decisions to commission advertising therefore are not and cannot be made on the basis of any rational calculation of profit.

Further indicative of the detachment of advertising from the market conditions of really subsumed cultural production is the relative unimportance placed upon knowing or pleasing the consumer. While much has been made in the critical tradition of the ability of marketers and consumer researchers to successfully manipulate consumers through the use of empirical research and psychological methods, in practice such research is often regarded with skepticism within the industry. Some agencies do not even include dedicated research departments (Frank 1997, 227; Hackley and Hackley 2015, 113–14; Mayer 2011, 81; Sullivan 2012, 248–53). Symptomatic of this dismissive attitude toward research is the extensively reproduced (although nearly undoubtedly apocryphal) aphorism of "ad legend" Bill Bernbach: "We are so busy measuring public opinion, we forget we can mold it. We are so busy listening to statistics that we forget we can create them" (Sullivan 2012, 244, 249). The underlying message of Bernbach's words—that, rather than seek to appeal to its audience's proclivities, advertising should seek to shape them—represents an almost radical rejection of the demands of the mass market and the consumer subject in favor of a project of autonomous artistic production.

Instead, if there is any party advertising seeks as a source of production funding, it is not a rationalized vision of the mass market consumer, but rather the more idiosyncratic and specific figure of the corporate client. As such, the successful securing of funding to produce advertising is widely understood to be as much, if not more, about appealing to the tastes and predilections of the client as it is about demonstrating an ability to appeal to the possible audience (Cronin 2004, 61, 64; Malefyt and Morais 2012, 19). However, in contrast to the pre-capitalist figure of the artistic patron, the figure of the client is frequently the subject of open ridicule in the industry and how-to guides are replete with advice on how to bamboozle or ignore clients (Hegarty 2014; Ogilvy 2004; Sullivan 2012, 239–47). Thus, neither the market, nor the client is regarded as the ultimate audience for an advertisement. Even if such skepticism regarding audiences and clients is not completely born out in practice, the persistent circulation of such sentiment reflects a desire toward autonomy at odds with the slavish culture of production ascribed to advertising in the critical tradition.

By taking into account the particular political economic coordinates of advertising's production, we can thus see how the non-commodity form of advertising arises from an orientation away from the market: an inclination that bears more in common with Brown and Adorno's model of the work of art than their concept of commodity culture. Advertising may be deeply formally subsumed under capitalism, but in real terms it remains surprisingly autonomous. A major consequence of this non-real subsumption is that, as a form of cultural production, advertising has the potential to retain a high degree of aesthetic autonomy—especially relative to those other media forms that are more directly implicated in the commodity-form. In light of this crucial distinction, there is therefore a need to rethink the way in which advertising is traditionally denied any possibility of critical aesthetic function. Such critiques mistake the formal subsumption of advertising—its use to sell products within the market—for its real subsumption. When we understand advertising in this non-reductive manner, it therefore opens up a conceptual space in which to make sense of not just the aesthetics of advertising but also the critical perspective and possibilities that the aesthetic freedom of advertising might allow.

In this new political-aesthetic conception of advertising I am proposing, the advertising industry functions less as a means of mass ideological indoctrination and more in a manner akin to Jeremy Gilbert's account of laboratories and artistic bohemias as "protected zones of experimentation which capital must keep close to itself if it is to find new resources for accumulation" (2008, 115). While Gilbert does not use the language of subsumption, his suggestion that capital cultivates such spaces "outside the circuits of capitalist accumulation" in order to feed off their potential for non-profit-driven invention and experimentation can be understood in terms of formal, but non-real subsumption (2008, 109). In addition, Gilbert's account also furnishes an explanation of how non-real subsumption is not simply an instance of spontaneous resistance, but rather can be interpreted as part of the larger logic of capitalist accumulation. Sites of invention and creation, such as advertising, are so desirable in their non-subsumed form that they are consequently sheltered from the capitalist system's transformative, rationalizing power that might hinder their productivity. Nonetheless, even though such explanation forestalls an account of such protected zones as somehow inherently or automatically resistant to capitalism, this does not mean that they are therefore politically neutered. Rather, such enclaves' forestalling of real subsumption means that capital "cannot always direct and capture what comes out of them, although it will try. When it cannot, when they become connected to other forces, progressive social change can ensue" (Gilbert 2008, 109).

In closing, then, and in stark contrast to the received critical tradition, I want to suggest one way that we might conceptualize advertising's potential role as a site of progressive social change. Key to this interpretation of advertising as a site of possible critique is its previously discussed inescapable orientation toward the market. Due to its deep formal subsumption, advertising is a cultural form that cannot ignore capitalism. Unlike other forms of cultural production, advertising always has to acknowledge its place in the market. However, in conjunction with its potential for aesthetic autonomy and formal experimentation, advertising's inevitable suturing to its economic context should not be read as problem to be escaped. Instead, this combination marks advertising as a potentially productive aesthetic space, because it is one in which the formal game of autonomy can lead to new ways of presenting and thinking through the world, while never being able to turn away from lived economic reality. This brings us back to Horkheimer and Adorno's account of how "Beethoven hurled away a novel by Sir Walter Scott with the cry: 'Why the fellow writes for money'" (1973, 157). For Horkheimer and Adorno, Beethoven's aesthetic superiority to Scott is not simply because of his non-real subsumption, but because he also acknowledges the contradictions of cultural production under capitalism by integrating an awareness of the market into his art. In contrast, "those who succumb to the ideology are precisely those who [like Scott] cover up the contradiction instead of taking it into their consciousness of their own production as Beethoven did" (1973, 157). Following the logic of this position, advertising appears as the aesthetic successor to Beethoven—one of Adorno's gold standards for critical autonomous aesthetics—because it cannot help but take up the contradiction between its real autonomy and formal subsumption into its consciousness. Unlike other forms of cultural production, there is absolutely no chance that advertising can cover up this contradiction, because by its very nature it is always about capitalism. Adverting is the cultural form that both acknowledges and (potentially) rebuffs its capitalist context.

However, simply because advertising is compelled to speak about capitalism, this does not mean that it will necessarily be critical. Indeed, such a claim would be obviously false and easily disproven through reference to majority of existing advertisements. Yet while aesthetic freedom does not equate to critique, it does create the conditions wherein critique can be realized without over-determination by the commodity form of the work. A concrete example of this possibility is "one of the most analysed, discussed, and admired campaigns in the industry's history, studied in introductory marketing classes and including in advertising retrospectives of all kinds [but almost entirely absent in the critical tradition]": Doyle Dane Bernbach's 1959 "Think Small" campaign for Volkswagen (Frank 1997, 60). In almost all aesthetic aspects, the original "Think Small" advertisement reflects a deep investment in the formal game of style that Brown argues is a key marker of autonomous art (2014, 458–60): its commitment to minimalism through a sans-serif font, use of excessive white space, and a tiny, off-set photo is a stark rejection of prevailing industry standards of the period that demonstrate how an advertisement can take its formal cues in competitive relations to the antecedents and history of its specific genre. Moreover, the Think Small advertisement is not simply a formal experiment but executes its aesthetic innovation as a crucial part of its larger cultural critique. Drawing comparisons between the ad's copy and the writing of critical theorists Herbert Marcuse, Frank argues that the "Think Small" advertisement display an "awareness of and deep sympathy with the mass society critique" as part of a wider denouncement of the waste and excess of consumer society (1997, 62–64). Hence, while the wider "Think Small" campaign certainly needs to be understood as part of a campaign to sell cars, that fact does not countermand its legitimate potential to "demystify the techniques of admaking" and undermine the demands of consumer society: that is to say the formal subsumption does not undercut the potential for a critical intervention (Frank 1997, 65).

Frank's reading of the "Think Small" campaign can thus be interpreted as an example of the potential of non-real subsumption in action. More than just formal difference or social comment, "Think Small" combines both aspects in a manner that illustrates the power of the aesthetic to intervene in political questions. This intervention can thus be considered an example of Rancière's assertion that aesthetic forms can disturb and reapportion the manner in which we understand and engage with the world or, in his own (translated) words, "the way in which the practices and forms of the visibility of art ... distribute spaces and times, subjects and objects, the common and the singular" (2009, 25). Even more provocatively in light of the critical tradition, this example of advertising can even by read as indicative of Adorno's argument that social and political problems can manifest formally as "the unsolved antagonisms of reality return in artworks as immanent problems of form" (2004, 7).

In advertising, we therefore find the potential for a critical manifestation of aesthetics that aligns with the categories that Cultural Marxism and aligned critical traditions have historically reserved for the more sanctified form of high culture. Nor is this simply an instance of advertising mimicking the forms and conventions of fine art in order to stake a claim to authority and dignity (Berger 1983, 135–38): rather this is advertising now understood as capable of doing the sorts of political aesthetic work that has historically been considered only the purview of the most critical and incisive expressions of creative practice. To approach advertising in this way is to follow Jameson's injunction to abandon Modernism's search for an ultimate pure aesthetic dimension and instead approach the politics of aesthetics as those of a historical, social, and thus always compromised phenomenon (1979, 133–34). Hence, when we refuse to reduce the political aesthetics to simply the reproduction of capitalism, we thus become alert to how it can function as a complex, contingent, and critical site of possibility under the contemporary cultural conditions of capitalism.

Yet, in closing, it is vital to note that it is certainly possible to overstate this critical potential. Contrary to the line of argument developed here, a significant portion of advertising practice could probably be characterized as really subsumed, with production taking place along distributed conveyer belt lines, especially historically. In addition, although it was critical for its time, the "Think Small" campaign no longer has much of a revelatory or radical kick now that it has been absorbed into marketing history and education as an example of "authenticity." Therefore, if we are to identify any contemporary potential in the non-real subsumption of advertising, there is a need for new examples of concrete critique. These will almost surely be more difficult to locate than in the past due to the dispersion and expansion of the industry into tinier niches and darkest reaches of online media. Moreover, algorithmic targeting means that many consumers may not ever encounter them, limiting their political aesthetic influence.

Nonetheless, while I don't want to naively put aside these problems and others, including questions of immaterial labor, and the neoliberal celebration of creativity, these concerns shouldn't automatically invalidate the critical potential of advertising. While the above concerns need to be taken into account, as I have argued the prospects for non-real subsumption means that the formal, aesthetic aspects of advertising can potentially transcend the well-documented limitations of the form. Most advertising does not change the world: but then neither does all, or indeed, most art, however much it might wish to. What the model of subsumption draws our attention to is how advertising provides a space to rethink the relations between modes of production and aesthetic conventions and possibilities: between the economic and the symbolic and the cognitive. In doing so, we can gain a sense of how advertising not only saturates our lives but might also change them: how through an engagement with the political aesthetic conditions of its production, advertising can be approached, now without the implicit scare quotes, as the art of capitalism.

References

Adorno, Theodor. 2004. *Aesthetic Theory*, translated and edited by Robert Hullot-Kentor. London: Continuum.

Berger, John. 1983. *Ways of Seeing*. London: BBC and Penguin.

Brown, Nicholas. 2009. "One, Two, Many Ends of Literature." *Mediations*24 (2): 91–100. http://www.mediationsjournal.org/one-two-many-ends-of-literature.

———. 2014. "The Work of Art in the Age of its Real Subsumption under Capital." In *Contemporary Marxist Theory*, edited by Andrew Pendakis, Jeff Diamanti, Nicholas Brown, Josh Robinson, Imre Szeman, 449–68. London: Bloomsbury.

Cronin, Anne M. 2004. *Advertising Myths*. London: Routledge.

Frank, Thomas. 1997. *The Conquest of Cool*: Chicago: University of Chicago Press.

Gilbert, Jeremy. 2008. *Anticapitalism and Culture*. Oxford: Berg.

Hackley, Chris, and Amy Rungpaka Hackley. 2015. *Advertising and Promotion*. London: Sage.

Harvey, David. 2010. *A Companion to Marx's Capital, Volume 1*. London: Verso.

Hegarty, John. 2014. *Hegarty on Creativity: There Are No Rules*. London: Thames & Hudson.

Horkheimer, Max, and Theodor Adorno. 1973. "The Culture Industry: Enlightenment as Mass Deception." In *The Dialectic of Enlightenment*, translated by John Cumming, 120–67. New York: Allen Lane.

Jameson, Fredric. 1979. "Reification and Utopia in Mass Culture." *Social Text* 1: 130–48.

Jhally, Sut. 2006. *The Spectacle of Accumulation*. New York: Peter Lang.

Lefebvre, Henri. 2008. *Critique of Everyday Life*, translated by John Moore. London: Verso.

Malefyt, Timothy de Waal, and Robert J. Morais. 2012. *Advertising and Anthropology*. London: Berg.

Mandel, Ernest. 1976. "Introduction to 'Results of the Immediate Process of Production'." In *Capital, Volume One*, 943–47. Middlesex: Penguin.

Marx, Karl. 1982. *Capital, Volume One*, translated by Ben Fowkes. Middlesex: Penguin.

Mayer, Roger. 2011. "The Advertising Agency." In *The Practice of Advertising*, edited by Adrian R. Mackay, 69–91. London: Routledge.

McFall, Liz. 2004. *Advertising: A Cultural Economy*. London: Sage.

McStay, Andrew. 2009. *Digital Advertising*. London: Palgrave MacMillan.

———. 2013. *Creativity and Advertising*. London: Routledge.

Nixon, Sean. 2003. *Advertising Cultures*. London: Sage.

Ogilvy, David. 2004. *Confessions of an Advertising Man*. Frensham: Southbank.

Pray, Doug. 2009. *Art & Copy*. DVD. Original Concept by Gregory Beauchamp and Kirk Soulder. New York: The One Club.

Rancière, Jacques. 2008. *Aesthetics and Its Discontents*, translated by Gabriel Rockhill. New York: Continuum.

Schor, Juliet B. 2000. "The New Politics of Consumption." In *The Consumer Society Reader*, edited by Juliet B. Schor and Douglas B. Holt, 446–62. New York: The New Press.

Schudson, Michael. 1986. *Advertising, the Uneasy Persuasion*. New York: Basic Books.

Smythe, Dallas. 1981. "On the Audience Commodity and Its Work." In *Dependency Road: Communication, Capitalism, Consciousness and Canada*, 22–51. Norwood: Ablex.

Sullivan, Luke. 2012. *Hey Whipple Squeeze This!: The Classic Guide to Creating Great Ads*. Hoboken: Wiley.

Williams, Raymond. 2005. "Advertising: The Magic System." In *Culture and Materialism*, 170–95. London: Verso.

Williamson, Judith. 1995. *Decoding Advertisements:* London: Marion Boyers.

8   Control and the Rhetoric of Interactivity in Contemporary Advertising Theory and Practice

Chris Miles

Interactivity and the apparent empowerment that it affords consumers has become a powerful watchword in contemporary discussions around advertising as well as in marketing theory and practice. Since the advent of marketing's engagement with the Internet, researchers, commentators, and practitioners have fixated upon the way in which the interactive environment that is at the heart of the World Wide Web signals a shift in the balance of power between brands and consumers. As Hoffman & Novak (1996) put it, "it affords the foundation for consumer control that is impossible in traditional, passive media" (64), along with the need for significantly different communication approaches. What is perhaps surprising is that some of the most forthright of these claims about rising consumer empowerment come not from consumer groups but from within the academic marketing discipline itself, which increasingly promotes the importance of the "co-creation of value," whereby brands acknowledge that it is customers' interactions with their products and services that produce value rather than value being something that the brand exclusively creates (Vargo and Lusch 2004). This perspective also stresses the importance of adopting marketing communication models based upon mutually beneficial, power-symmetrical dialogue rather than the old-fashioned, hypodermic-inspired monologue patterns beloved of traditional advertising (Ballantyne 2004; Duncan and Moriarty 1998; Grönroos 2000, 2004).

However, the way these developments have been framed, promoted, and discussed obscures the struggle for control in modern marketing communication theory and practice. Formulations of consumer empowerment, understandings of what interactivity is and what it represents, what "has" it and what doesn't, definitions of control—all of these are discursively constructed by academics and practitioners even though they are often treated as what Skålén et al. (2008) call "external, independent marketing reality" (119). To explore what this process of discursive construction suggests about interactivity in advertising and marketing, this chapter views both as rhetorical constructions, both in the sense of the discourse around them being an arena of rhetorical strategy and also in the broader sense of them as objects of knowledge and tools of practice that are produced through rhetoric (Hackley 2001; Miles 2010, Nilsson 2015; Skålén et al. 2008).

Despite a few attempts to give rhetoric a prominent position in formulations of marketing communication (Tonks 2002; Miles 2013) and investigations into the rhetorical and stylistic components of advertising executions (McQuarrie and Mick 1996; Phillips and McQuarrie 2002; Tom and Eves 1999) as well as of academic marketing writing itself (Brown 1999, 2004; Miles 2014), mainstream academic marketing research largely avoids what Simons (1990) has dubbed the "rhetorical turn," remaining largely under the spell of the belief that marketing, if not being so now, might "one day establish itself as a 'science'" (Tadajewski 2006, 183). Indeed, clear rhetorical advantages to one party or another exist in treating dynamic, discursively generated ideas as fixed, external realities. Accordingly, I hope to show that the theory and practice of contemporary advertising is suffused with attempts to control the understanding of "fetish" terms such as interactivity, empowerment, control, and dialogue and that the control of such understandings can be seen to afford distinct discursive advantages.

Accordingly, this chapter first examines the historical relationship of the discipline of marketing communication with the idea of control, one that also suffuses theory and practice of advertising. Then I will trace the link among control, interactivity, and consumer empowerment. Here, I will particularly examine the way in which early, foundational theoreticians of advertising on the Internet like Hoffman and Novak (1996) and Rodgers and Thorson (2000) position traditional advertising in opposition to the potentially egalitarian communication channels of the Internet. Next, I will discuss the burgeoning perspectives in current marketing theory regarding relationship and service, both of which containing clear exhortations against manipulative "traditional" advertising practices and call for interactive, dialogue-based communication approaches. This foundation helps clarify the rhetorical underpinnings of thinking about contemporary interactive advertising practices such as viral marketing and social media marketing.

While some of the discourse covered here is ostensibly concerned with "marketing" (such as Hoffman & Novak's 1996 paper on marketing over hypermedia environments or Vargo & Lusch's 2004 piece on the Service-Dominant Logic), it very much focuses on advertising when discussing aspects of marketing communication. In particular, such authors define interactive, networked marketing communication in *opposition* to traditional, persuasive advertising. As shown below, this opposition is part of a rhetorical strategy to package interactive advertising as something potentially revolutionary, even to the extent of avoiding the term "advertising" itself (as old-fashioned, manipulative, and something to reject) in the description of such new approaches that are being rhetorically re-positioned under the broader rubric of marketing practice. Additionally, many advertising practitioners take care not to distinguish too strongly between advertising and other forms of marketing communication. Advertising agencies specializing in digital, for example, do not only deal with simple online display advertising but will also be integrating their campaigns across blog marketing, social media dialogue and content efforts, and even gamification strategies. I will note further the significance of this point in the conclusion.

Marketing Communication and Control

Marketing is a discipline founded upon the urge to control the wild, mysterious, uncertain forces of the market. Most commonly, over the discipline's more than 90 years, that control has tended to manifest itself in the adoption of a "scientific" approach to the analysis of the functions and variables that beset the enterprise of bringing successful products to market, thus reflecting the peccadilloes of the larger discipline of management. Indeed, Taylor (1911) was a culmination of a number of streams of research that had been moving from the start toward a more "rational" approach to the management of industry. As Burris (1989) shows, it was part of scientific management's attempt to establish organizational control structures, "which work together to insure managerial control of the labour process, subordination of the workforce, and legitimation of this subordination" (1), with "science" a modish, discursively constructed framework informing the search.

Modern marketing communication conceptions possess an additional historical influence that locates control even more strongly at its disciplinary heart. Ewen (1996) cogently describes the way in which propaganda techniques of WWI, as rooted in the "publicity" practices of Ivy Lee, Theodore Vail and Walter Lippmann, became transfused into the American advertising and emerging public relations industries. Consequently, marketing communication from the 1920s onwards becomes far more focused upon the "manufacturing of consent" (to use Lippmann's phrase) as it employs new tactics of "psychological manipulation [and] seductive appeals to the subconscious recesses of mental life" (132).

The control orientation of marketing communication practitioners and scholars has also been buttressed by the way in which the burgeoning social sciences modeled human communication, considering as Varey (1993) does how "the work of Shannon and Weaver and of Schramm remains ... the main basis of the prevailing orthodoxy in the consideration of the communication aspects of marketing and management" (330). Despite Schramm's (1954) more nuanced elaboration upon Claude Shannon's (1948) model of communication, both approaches remain fundamentally linear by focusing upon the correct transmission and reception of meaning contained within a message and carried over a medium. Both models contain versions of a feedback path between sender and receiver and so display inklings of the interactivity that is such a central part of contemporary communication technologies. However, crucially, feedback is always a tool to determine whether a message has been *correctly received* and therefore an essential means of controlling for correct understanding.

Consequently, the communication models that have had such an influence on the development of marketing communication tend to treat the faithful and monological transmission of a message as the ideal. While some scholars have challenged such control assumptions in marketing communication, the mainstream marketing academic and practitioner understandings of communication continue to revolve around the control of intentions and meanings. This is, ironically, particularly evident in the realm of interactive marketing, to which I will now turn.

Interactive Marketing and Control

Hoffman and Novak (1996) is suffused with optimism at the prospect of the "revolution" that is "dramatically altering" the "passive one-to-many communication model" (50) of traditional marketing. The interactivity that is at the heart of the Web, and that allows consumers to communicate widely their own content about products and brands, renders "impossible the blind application of marketing and advertising approaches that assume a passive, captive consumer" (65).

However, even this classic argument for the revolutionary nature of marketing on the Internet strongly retains a control orientation. While empowering consumers to produce content and meaning with brands, the state of "flow" generated through hypermedia computer-mediated environments more effectively screens out "irrelevant thoughts and perceptions" so that "the consumer focuses entirely on the interaction" (58). Indeed, the bulk of Hoffman and Novak (1996) describes ways in which marketers can ensure that consumers are brought into the state of flow through careful attention to the design of the online experience. Interactive affordances that gently challenge the consumer's skill help manipulate the consumer into the most receptive state possible for marketing messages. Ironically, web users' perception of how much control they have over the hypermedia environment correlates strongly with entering the flow state, with a marketing emphasis on generating flow states leading to a greater perceived sense of control, the impact of which on "intentions and actions is more important than real control" (64). Seen this way, the approach is fundamentally manipulative despite being framed in a celebration of the equalizing, democratizing nature of the web. All that the new interactivity has brought to marketing communication, it seems, is a new site for control, with new variables and new processes to manage. Despite a handful of attempts to interrogate, evolve, or provide alternatives to the model of interactive marketing communication, it has become a foundational document for subsequent scholarship on digital marketing communication.

Rodgers and Thorson's (2000) article outlining their Interactive Advertising Model has also gained foundational status in the study of interactive marketing communication. Like Hoffman and Novak (1996), it also places control at the center of the online advertising experience. By "distinguish[ing] between aspects of the Internet that are consumer-controlled and those that are advertiser-controlled," they argue not only that "the initiation of Internet use ... completely under the consumer's control" but that "users are in the driver's seat throughout the entire online experience" (28). To demonstrate this, they delineate key factors in the online advertising experience that are consumer-controlled and advertiser-controlled. Given the highly optimistic manner in which they start the paper, it should come as no real surprise that their model leaves very little control in the hands of advertisers. Only "structures" are controlled by advertisers, by which Rodgers and Thorson mean advertisement types (product/service, corporate, PSA, etc.), formats (pop-up, interstitial, etc.), and features (objective/subjective). Consumers, on the other hand, control functions (such as motives and mode), information processes (i.e., the cognitive tools of attention, memory, and attitude), and outcomes (the wide variety of "consumer responses" that might be stimulated by advertisements, such as clicking on an ad link, emailing the advertiser, forming an opinion toward the product, etc.).

However, even such a cursory listing of these elements suggests the presence of a very curious, if not naive, approach. What does it mean to say, for example, that attention is under the control of the consumer, if it is also seen as the prime battleground for all forms of advertising (Nyilasy and Reid 2009)? What does it mean to say that the outcomes of exposure to advertising are under the control of the consumer if the advertising industry itself is also premised upon influencing these outcomes? Indeed, in their detailed explication, Rogers and Thorson do not really consistently maintain the distinction between what is consumer and advertiser-controlled. The labeling of "outcomes" as consumer-controlled, for example, has little significance to their description of the various "responses" that the stimuli of advertising are attempting to elicit. In this sense, "controlled" simply means "originating with," as in a response originating in the consumer but stimulated by the advertiser. Yet, Rodgers and Thorson continue to view empowerment as a self-evident result of the fundamentally interactive nature of the Internet, arguing that it "allows the user to participate in the persuasion process by changing the structural elements themselves" (39–40).

While one might wonder if this is not akin to allowing a goat to choose between a bolt to the head or a knife to the throat, the more important point is that the vaunted uniqueness is largely chimerical. One example that makes this point clearly includes the claim that "online, a customer can choose to click on a banner or not" (40). Of course, as an advertisement in itself, it may entice a user to click it for more information but, whether or not it is clicked, it is already fulfilling its job as advertising. A second, parallel example is the claim that a consumer can "choose" to attend to, and act upon, any traditional piece of interruption marketing. Indeed, a print advertisement vies for the attention of the reader, but the reader might ignore it, only pay it a small amount of attention, attend to it closely but balk at its claims, or as a consequence of any of some of these reactions decide to seek out further information about the product or the brand. No substantive difference exists between interaction with a print or a banner ad, with the possible exception of the speed with which this takes place. Yet another aspect of the ostensibly unique empowerment afforded by advertising on the Internet is how a consumer can actively "seek out advertising websites" (ibid.), ignoring the fact that many readers of special interest magazines purchase them to see the latest product information, advertising, and PR from the relevant brands (as any reader of a guitar magazine will be able to assure you).

Perhaps the only aspect of Rodgers and Thorson's view of how the Internet "allows the user to participate in the persuasion process" that might be considered to be "unique" is personalization, which enables a consumer to "customize ads to their own liking" (40). Yet, from the perspective of control, to whom this choice belongs is very arguable. The provision of customization affordances is something that the advertiser does, after all. The advertiser encourages the user to personalize his/her view in order to attract attention and keep her/his interest—in other words, customization is a variable that one can alter in order to meet a particular intention, rather than something solely at the hands of the consumer. While browsers allow us to alter the appearance of websites and writing CSS stylesheets to format any page or page element, the vast majority of consumers can no sooner write their own CSS style sheets as tell you what the acronym URL stands for. By far the most common form of customization of advertising that modern users perform on the Internet is the use of an adblocker (Kantrowitz 2015), which speaks volumes regarding the extent to which online advertising has successfully engaged with the concept of an empowered, interactive consumer but perhaps in ways quite unintended by industry advocates.

Rodgers and Thorson (2000) and Hoffman and Novak (1996) are only two of the better known studies that emphasize the empowered nature of the online consumer. Unlike Hoffman and Novak (1996), who almost in the same breath go on to outline an approach for marketers to more effectively control this wild component, Rodgers and Thorson attempt to build up a model of interactive advertising that aggrandizes consumer-controlled elements and diminishes advertiser-controlled ones. In sum, both of these classics of academic marketing's engagement with the online environment exhibit similar rhetorical gambits by going to great lengths to give the impression that the Web necessitates a sea-change in marketing's approach to control. They describe (to their readership of academic marketers) how technologies of interactivity empower consumers and make the "old" assumptions of marketing control untenable; yet they then end up describing new ways (or just the same old ways) to bring the consumer to heel.

Interactivity and the Relationship Marketing Vocabulary

One area in which academic marketing research has seemed to keep faith with the celebrated emancipating spirit of network technologies is in the field of relationship marketing and, latterly, the broader "service perspective."

Predating the Internet, since its emergence in the late 1980s and early1990s relationship marketing has consistently championed a fundamentally inter-active and non-controlling approach to communicating with stakeholders. For Gummesson (1987), interactivity differentiates a new relationship ori-entation from what he calls the "Old Marketing Concept." Because services, as he notes, are co-produced within the interaction of the customer and the firm, it makes little sense to maintain a dictatorial, control-oriented approach to a stakeholder with whom you are in a co-production rela-tionship. Similarly, as Grönroos (1994) argues, a relationship marketing perspective inevitably "leads to an interest in emphasizing *dialogues* and creating, for example, advertising campaigns that facilitate various types of dialogue with identified customers" (10, emphasis in the original). He later explains that, for the processes of relationship marketing to work, "the par-ties in a relationship will have to be able to share information and listen to each other, and not rely on persuasion and manipulation" (Grönroos 2000, 6). Such a dialogue-oriented approach requires the participation of both par-ties, "and hence there are no senders or receivers, there are only participants in the dialogue process" (7).

Present here is an implicit claim that marketing communication at the service of relationship building cannot afford to be dedicated to the control of the consumer. This valorizing of non-manipulative communi-cation is seen in the work of many other researchers allied to the rela-tionship and service marketing agendas. For example, in their exposition of a communication-based model of marketing relationship management, Duncan and Moriarty (1998) argue for a clear differentiation between "persuasion" and "communication" in the realm of marketing. The tradi-tional, short-term, "transaction marketing" understanding of persuasion, they note, "is manipulative" and "one way" (2). However, in marketing, preferable relationships are built not upon *persuasion* but *communication*, "where *listening* is given as much importance as *saying*" (ibid., emphasis in the original).

Many of these positions exist together in Vargo and Lusch (2004), which outlines a Service-Dominant Logic, which re-formulates and re-packages the precepts of relationships and service marketing into a set of easier-to-digest foundational premises based around the core concept of the co-creation of value between the firm and its stakeholders. Instead of one-way, mass mar-ket messaging, Vargo and Lusch argue that "promotion will need to become a communication process characterized by dialogue, asking and answering questions" (2004, 13). The traditional balance of power between firm and customer is also consequently upset, as a service-centered view "means col-laborating with and learning from customers and being adaptive to their individual and dynamic needs" (p. 6).

With little seeming room for manipulation and control in such an under-standing of marketing communication, the RM and service literature iron-ically provides a far more developed, and consistent, approach to the place of interactivity in modern marketing communication than does the foundational literature devoted to the specifics of advertising on the Internet. Yet, a clear opposition is also being constructed in this area of marketing thinking, as traditional advertising approaches are painted with the rhetoric of control and manipulation whilst the shining new relationship and service perspectives are constructed as supporting equitable, dialogue-based conversations with no persuasive intent. Paradoxically, perhaps, this rhetorical strategy persuasively emphasizes the revolutionary nature of the new marketing paradigm in a manner similar to that of foundational researchers in interactive marketing. Additionally, we might wonder just how this type of orientation towards non-controlling communication survives when it interfaces more directly with the practices of the network technologies that seem to afford its most promising efflorescence.

In the first half of this chapter, we have seen how advertising has been used to characterize a form of marketing communication obsessed with control and manipulation. This has often led to advertising being used as an oppositional "straw man" by researchers and theoreticians, in that it allows them to define an approach to marketing communication that is non-manipulative by pointing to traditional advertising practice as the exemplar of what should not be done. However, as has been discussed, even when interactive network technologies such as the Internet are held up as potential routes to non-manipulative, equitable marketing communication practice, rhetorics of control still seem to infect such formulations and understandings. The second half of this chapter investigates ways in which such rhetorics influence the forms of strategic advice offered by more recent academic voices concerned with marketing communication practices on the social web. I will be examining a number of voices that are representative of the way in which social media and other online platforms, while ostensibly being held up as opportunities for consumer empowerment and egalitarian dialogue, are then re-framed as sophisticated arenas of control.

Social Media and the Persuasive Gambit of Conversation

Social media provide an apparently perfect venue for the creation of equitable, symmetrical, and non-manipulative relationships between firms and customers. After all, these media are built upon platforms of connection and interaction instead of passive reception. As Rybalko and Seltzer (2010) argue, "social networking sites such as Twitter would seem to be capable of providing an organization with a wide range of opportunities to engage their publics in dialogic communication" (337). Yet, research has consistently shown that the opportunities that embedded interactivity affords advertisers have largely not been enthusiastically adopted. Instead, advertising on social networks continues to be much as the Facebook-using respondents in the study by Sashittal et al. (2012) describe it—"annoying, intrusive, insensitive to their needs, and peripheral to their interests" (499).

Academic advice to marketing communicators regarding effective strategies for using social media often undercuts the egalitarian language emanating from the relationship and service theoreticians. For example, Hanna et al. (2011) speak of how interactive digital platforms have "empowered consumers to connect, share, and collaborate" and made them "expect to be active participants in the media process" (267). Yet, the advice the authors proffer their readers is rooted firmly in the old transmission assumptions of mass media manipulation. The "critical questions" that online marketers have to ask are: "Who is/are the target(s)?" On what platforms do these targets live? "What marketing content (story) does the company want to tell?" and then "How can marketers propagate or feed this content throughout the ecosystem?" (269). Where has the interaction gone? Where has the active participation gone? Instead, the consumer is a target (once again) that has to be *fed the right message* by the marketer.

Sometimes the language of control and influence saturates the academic voice from the start. Kumar and Mirchandani's (2012) discussion of how to increase the ROI of social media marketing presents a seven-step approach that asks marketers to "first identify the net influence wielded by a user in a social network and then to predict that user's ability to generate the viral spread of information [so that] businesses can identify the 'right' individuals to engage in social media conversations to promote WOM" (56). The language employed here suggests a heavily manipulative attitude toward the consumer. Most importantly, only certain consumers are to be considered worth engaging with in dialogue. The "right" consumer—one who deserves the dialogic attention of the firm—is one who has influence over others. The motivation for engaging such consumers is entirely self-interested; they are to be used by the firm to relay their message in the most effective way across the network. Kumar and Mirchandani make this clear when they describe how these "right" consumers will have to be "incentivized" by the firm to spread their message. Such incentives "can be tangible (such as discounts and freebies), intangible (such as recognition in a social network) or both" (57). In these scenarios, traditional marketing attempts of control are simply shifted onto selected consumers who become proxy (traditional) marketers. There is no revolution of empowerment here, and there is certainly no attempt to give up the persuasive, manipulative mode of one-way communication. What persists is an attempt to finesse the network and bend it to the control-oriented thinking of traditional marketing.

A tension exists in academic marketing writing on social media. While initial celebrations of the dialogue-enhancing abilities of the platforms are common, they less commonly and completely promote the use of non-manipulative, mutually beneficial relationship strategies. Indeed, this tension perhaps simply mirrors the general practitioner response to social media. As Schultz and Peltier (2013) have noted, engagement on social media, "the way it is seemingly being defined and practiced today by marketers, and supported by academic studies, often seems to be nothing more than a re-invention of one of the oldest tools in the marketing arsenal, sales promotion" (90). The heavy use of "follow us," "post a picture of yourself with our product," "use our hashtag," as well as incentivizing discount codes, along with the form of influencer targeting that Kumar and Mirchandani (2012) encourage, constitute the dominant modes of contemporary social media marketing. While such practices are, in one sense or another, taking advantage of the interactivity that online platforms provide, they are largely riffs upon the old themes of manipulative, persuasion-based, mass marketing communication practices. Getting consumers to take your packshots for you in return for a 10% discount off their next purchase is simply a cheap form of outsourcing, instead of the sort of marketing communications revolution that the luminaries of the service perspective have been calling for (though it does, perhaps, take Gummesson's notion of the "part-time marketer" to its logical conclusion).

Infection and Control

The manner in which influencer targeting has spread through advertising theory and practice regarding interactive systems is a bold indication of the aggressive customer-as-resource thinking that has tended to underlie marketing communication's reaction to the supposedly "empowered" consumer. As I have argued elsewhere (Miles 2014), viral marketing promotes a "turning away from interaction with the customer" (4). While many theoreticians and gurus speak of the need to engage stakeholders in open-ended, exploratory dialogue in order to build up long-term relationships of trust and mutual benefit, the sort of contagion-inspired manipulation of targeted influencers that the viral version of word-of-mouth has generated is entirely antithetical to this approach. Viral marketers and influence marketers understand dialogue as a prime vector of infection instead of as a realm in which the firm and the consumer meet on equal terms. Indeed, all forms of influencer marketing shift the conversational dyad away from the consumer-firm and toward the customer-influencer. In these scenarios, the firm is not a transparent conversational agent but rather an *éminence grise* skulking behind the influencer.

The figurative violence of the viral metaphor measures in key ways the exasperation felt by marketing communicators (both academics and practitioners) when confronted by consumers who will not listen, cannot be found, or refuse to be interested in the persuasive messages prepared for them. Whichever is the case, viral marketing is substantively different in its implied conception of communication from the dialogue approach of the service and relationship marketing voices discussed above. For example, Kaplan and Haenlein (2011) typify this when they advise that the desired "growth pattern" of a viral campaign should be "similar to major epidemics such as the Black Death in the 14th century, Spanish Flu in the 20th century, and Swine Flu in the 21st century" (255). The language is controlling, violent, and confrontational—relegating the consumer to the role of helpless victim. The marketing virus effectively "punishes" them for their networked lifestyle.

Viral and influencer approaches might get people talking *about* the brand, but that is not the same as talking *with* the brand. Here, too, the control paradigm central to traditional marketing communication is replicated in the dominant forms of contemporary online advertising and academic research in these areas. The general strategy in this work typically seems initially to celebrate the empowering nature of modern two-way digital communication but then to suggest ways of undercutting it as effectively as possible.

Conclusion

There is currently a marked division in academic marketing research between scholars who champion an approach to marketing communication, which is non-manipulative, dialogic, and exploratory, and those who seek to explicate and promote control-oriented, persuasion/influenced-based marketing messaging. Ironically, those in the latter group are most represented in marketing communications research on interactivity. Many researchers have been responding to emerging practices in the marketplace, attempting to define and delineate new practices and techniques. In doing so, it is no surprise that they are led by the nature of these practices. Certainly, the ways in which advertising practitioners have responded to the promises of interactivity have inevitably been influenced by their own traditions and path dependencies. Additionally, despite the prominence of the dialogical turn in the service perspective, it is predominantly a theoretical one. So far, few attempts have been made to buttress the call for non-manipulative marketing dialogue with concrete frameworks or toolsets. Yet, the fact remains that, in the realm that should surely most engender discussion of non-control-oriented, non-manipulative, relationship-focused marketing communication, we find instead discourse saturated with uncritical assumptions of control and hierarchical influence.

In this way, the concept of interactivity serves as a rhetorical strategy in both marketing communication theory and practice. It is constructed as a "game-changer" in order to both excite managers and scholars alike but also to threaten them with the new, the unknown, and the uncontrolled. It is used to present the prospect of non-manipulative dialogue between firm and consumer while at the same time being framed within the promotion of strategies and tactics that focus on manipulation, interruption, persuasion, and control-by-proxy. In other words, it works as a warning flag. By praising the prospect of two-way, equitable communication, it raises the prospect of such loss of control in the minds of its audience. It celebrates this wonderful thing while at the same time showing us how to avoid its inevitable "excesses." In this way, powerful keywords such as "empowerment," "interactivity," and "dialogue" act as discursive grounds for a fearful re-dedication to the goal of control.

Advertising has become a key focus of such rhetorical efforts. The word "advertising" now functions as a strategic signifier of practices from which, for various reasons, it is now convenient for the discipline of marketing and the profession of advertising to distance themselves. Persuasive communication directed at mass audiences is seen in the service and relationship marketing literature, as well as in much of the thinking behind the promotional use of the Web 1.0 and 2.0, to be inappropriate if not counter-productive. "Advertising" thus risks becoming supplanted by terms and descriptors that position their supporters as non-controlling and enlightened. Yet, the adoption of such a "cleansed" vocabulary in no way ensures that the resulting communication strategies are truly egalitarian or non-manipulative. The "social media marketing" techniques that now surround us in the digital realm are sufficient evidence that (when presented with the possibilities of interactive communication technologies) marketing is quite capable of forcing them to the persuasive, control-seeking ends that many voices from within and outside it have come to associate with traditional advertising. The final lesson here, perhaps, is that there is nothing *inherently* liberating about the hypermedia computer-mediated environment and nothing that *necessarily* empowers anyone (other than, perhaps, the owners of the network).

References

Ballantyne, D. 2004. "Dialogue and Its Role in the Development of Relationship Specific Knowledge." *Journal of Business & Industrial Marketing* 19(2): 114–23.

Brown, S. 1999. "Marketing and Literature: The Anxiety of Academic Influence." *Journal of Marketing* 63(January): 1–15.

———. 2004. "Writing Marketing: The Clause That Refreshes." *Journal of Marketing Management* 20(3–4): 321–42.

Burris, B. H. 1989. "Technocratic Organization and Control." *Organization Studies* 10(1): 1–22.

Duncan, T., & Moriarty, S. E. 1998. "A Communication-Based Marketing Model for Managing Relationships." *Journal of Marketing* 62(2): 1–13.

Ewen, S. 1996. *PR! A Social History of Spin.* New York: Basic Books.

Grönroos, C. 1994. "From Marketing Mix to Relationship Marketing." *Management Decision* 32(2): 4–20.

———. 2000. "Creating a Relationship Dialogue: Communication, Interaction and Value." *The Marketing Review* 1(1): 5–14.

———. 2004. "The Relationship Marketing Process: Communication, Interaction, Dialogue, Value." *Journal of Business & Industrial Marketing* 19(2): 99–113.

Gummesson, E. 1987. "The New Marketing—Developing Long-term Interactive Relationships." *Long Range Planning* 20(4): 10–20.

Hackley, C. 2001. *Marketing and Social Construction: Exploring the Rhetorics of Managed Consumption.* London: Routledge.

Hanna, R., A. Rohm, & V. L. Crittenden. 2011. "We're All Connected: The Power of the Social Media Ecosystem." *Business Horizons* 54(3): 265–73.

Hoffman, D. L., & T. P. Novak. 1996. "Marketing in Hypermedia Computer-Mediated Environments: Conceptual Foundations." *Journal of Marketing* 60(3): 50–68.

Kantrowitz, A. 2015. "Publishers Watch Closely as Adoption of Ad Blocking Tech Grows." *Advertising Age* February 13 2015. URL: http://adage.com/article/digital/adoption-ad-blocking-tech-grows/297101/ [Accessed 30th March 2016].

Kaplan, A. M., & M. Haenlein. 2011. "Two Hearts in Three-Quarter Time: How to Waltz the Social Media/Viral Marketing Dance." *Business Horizons* 54(3): 253–63.

Kumar, V., & R. Mirchandani. 2012. "Increasing the ROI of Social Media Marketing." *MIT Sloan Management Review* 54(1): 55–61.

McQuarrie, E. F., & D. G. Mick. 1996. "Figures of Rhetoric in Advertising Language." *Journal of Consumer Research* 22(4): 424–38.

Miles, C. 2010. *Interactive Marketing: Revolution or Rhetoric?* London: Routledge.

———. 2013. "Persuasion, Marketing Communication, and the Metaphor of Magic." *European Journal of Marketing* 47(11/12): 2002–19.

———. 2014. "The Rhetoric of Managed Contagion: Metaphor and Agency in the Discourse of Viral Marketing." *Marketing Theory* 14(1): 3–18.

Nilsson, T. 2015. *Rhetorical Business: A Study of Marketing Work in the Spirit of Contradiction.* Lund: Lund University.

Nyilasy, G., & L. N. Reid. 2009. "Agency Practitioner Theories of How Advertising Works." *Journal of Advertising* 38(3): 81–96.

Phillips, B. J., & E. F. McQuarrie. 2002. "The Development, Change, and Transformation of Rhetorical Style in Magazine Advertisements 1954–1999." *Journal of Advertising* 31(4): 1–13.

Rodgers, S., & E. Thorson. 2000. "The Interactive Advertising Model: How Users Perceive and Process Online Ads." *Journal of Interactive Advertising* 1(1): 26–50.

Rybalko, S., & T. Seltzer. 2010. "Dialogic Communication in 140 Characters or Less: How Fortune 500 Companies Engage Stakeholders using Twitter." *Public Relations Review* 36(4): 336–41.

Sashittal, H. C., R. Sriramachandramurthy, & M. Hodis. 2012. "Targeting College Students on Facebook? How to Stop Wasting Your Money." *Business Horizons* 55(5): 495–507.

Schramm, W. 1954. The Process and Effects of Mass Communication. Urbana, IL: University of Illinois Press.

Schultz, D. E., & J. (Jimmy) Peltier. 2013. "Social Media's Slippery Slope: Challenges, Opportunities and Future Research Directions." *Journal of Research in Interactive Marketing* 7(2): 86–99.

Shannon, C. 1948. "A Mathematical Theory of Communication." *The Bell System Technical Journal* 29 (July & October): 379–423 & 623–56.

Simons, H. W. 1990. "The Rhetoric of Inquiry as an Intellectual Movement." In *The Rhetorical Turn: Invention and Persuasion in the Conduct of Inquiry,* edited by H. Simon. London: University of Chigaco Press.

Skålén, P., M. Fougère, and M. Felleson. 2008. *Marketing Discourse: A Critical Perspective.* London: Routledge.

Tadajewski, M. 2006. "The Ordering of Marketing Theory: The Influence of McCarthyism and the Cold War." *Marketing Theory* 6(2): 163–99.

Taylor, F. W. 1911. *The Principles of Scientific Management.* New York: Harper & Brothers.

Tom, G., & A. Eves. 1999. "The Use of Rhetorical Devices in Advertising." *Journal of Advertising Research* 39(4) 39–43.

Tonks, D. 2002. "Marketing as Cooking: The Return of the Sophists." *Journal of Marketing Management* 18(7–8): 803–22.

Varey, R. 1993. "A Critical Review of Conceptions of Communication Evident in Contemporary Business and Management Literature." *Journal of Communication Management* 4(4): 328–40.

Vargo, S. L., & R. F. Lusch. 2004. "Evolving to a New Dominant Logic for Marketing." *Journal of Marketing* 68(1): 1–17.

9 Captains of Habit Formation
Marketers' Emerging Models of the Consumer Mind

Anthony Nadler and Lee McGuigan

Internet users have grown increasingly conscious of the fact that they are subject to ubiquitous monitoring and data gathering by marketers and other commercial entities. A recent study by the Annenberg School for Communication at the University of Pennsylvania found that 84 percent of Internet users surveyed "strongly or somewhat agreed that they want to have more control over what marketers could learn about them," while 65 percent "agreed that they had come to accept that they had little control over it" (Turow, Hennessy, and Draper 2015, 14). As users express suspicion and resignation in regards to mass consumer monitoring, media researchers have been probing the implications and significance of this monitoring through perspectives that focus on it as both a form of social control (e.g., Gandy 1993; Andrejevic 2007) and a method of exploiting valuable information generated largely by unpaid labor (Cohen 2008). Web protocols and the structures of major media and social media sites are designed to fulfill marketers' and advertisers' prerogatives as they seek to capture more information about our online activities (Turow 2012). Simultaneously, more and more devices and procedures are allowing marketers to monitor our activity in ostensibly "offline" spaces through GPS tracking, a new wave of sensor technologies, shoppers' cards, and many other forms of inputs (Turow, McGuigan, and Maris 2015).

As critical media scholars, it behooves us to closely examine the stories marketers and advertisers are telling themselves and their clients about mass monitoring and how this information can help them exercise greater control over consumers. In this chapter, we focus on what our ongoing research is revealing about the stories marketers and advertisers are telling amongst themselves and to their clients about prospects of enhanced capacities for control of consumers. Specifically, we explore a discourse revolving around promises to apply insights from behavioral economics and related behavioral sciences to emerging marketing strategies. Some see behavioral economics as providing marketers with a new—or newly refurbished—model of the consumer mind that illuminates levers of human decision-making previously ignored or poorly understood by marketers (Rubinson 2010; Willcox 2015a).

Voices that advocate bringing behavioral economics into advertising and marketing offer a strategic vision that diverges significantly from the fundamental premises of what might be considered the "traditional" approach to advertising and branding. This traditional approach focuses on creating meanings and emotional/affective associations with products or brands. Such an approach has, for understandable reasons, been subject to the most criticism from scholars and cultural commentators. Scholars influenced by cultural studies and critical theory traditions, as well as many social and cultural historians studying advertising, have primarily seen advertising as an art of semiotic manipulation and meaning-making (Williamson 1994; Williams 1960; Lears 1995; Jhally 1990). For many critics, the essence of modern advertising and marketing is a particular kind of myth-making, one that devotes enormous resources to telling stories and creating images linking commercial products and brands with emotionally charged meanings—visions of the good life, fulfillment of deep human desires, personal identities and status, and escape from anxieties.

Much of today's advertising and branding efforts continue to focus on such semiotic incantations, and this is likely not something that will disappear or greatly diminish any time soon. Nonetheless, those incorporating insights from behavioral economics are mapping out a quite different approach to consumer persuasion—an option that is becoming more tempting with the aid of endless troves of consumer data. Instead of treating consumers as fundamentally driven by stories and emotions, the behavioral economic approach suggests consumers are creatures whose decisions are driven by habit and cognitive heuristics. This does not mean that such advertising substitutes traditional advertising's magic promises for utilitarian information about products that are now calibrated toward people's actual material needs through careful targeting. Nor, however, does it fit with a vision of the "irrational" consumer driven by unconscious desires and easily swayed by symbols invoked by Freudian-influenced marketing and PR gurus like Edward Bernays or Ernest Dichter. One way of characterizing the conception of consumers offered by behavioral economics, famously coined by the economist Dan Ariely (2008), is that humans are "predictably irrational." For Ariely and like-minded economists, this means that humans generally strive toward economic decisions that maximize their self-interest, but empirical studies reveal deep and abiding systematic flaws in how we misapprehend our self-interest while making decisions. Advertisers and marketers see opportunity in trying to anticipate and intervene upon the cognitive processes that drive such decisions through a type of *behavioral programming*.

So far, we have offered only a quick sketch of this viewpoint; important qualifications are required, as key disagreements on the nature of human rationality exist among behavioral economists themselves. Further, marketers promoting and applying behavioral economic approaches to their own trade are not merely applying a fixed set of ideas based on academic knowledge. Rather, they are creatively interpreting and appropriating these ideas. In the following sections of this chapter we analyze marketers' discourse on the promises of incorporating insights from a new wave of behavioral sciences into their trade, place the rise of behavioral economics' model of the consumer within a historical context of advertisers' evolving strategies for exerting influence and control, and make a case for why critical scholars and citizens should investigate and raise concerns about this emerging vision for a future of advertising and marketing.

Advertising and Psychological Research and Theory

By the late 19th and early 20th centuries, advertising agencies in the US and UK were reconfiguring their operations to directly serve manufacturers while developing systematic promotional techniques to court consumers through invoking desire, fantasy, anxiety, and playfulness rather than emphasizing utilitarian information about products and prices (Williams 1960; Ewen 1976; Leach 1993). Before standardized, branded products became integral in the material culture of everyday life (see Strasser 1989), business conditions, as Daniel Pope suggests, "did not demand complex theories of persuasion" (1983, 232). The recognition that advertising strategy requires an understanding of how mass communication relates to market fluctuations contributed to the establishment around the last decade of the 19th century of full-service advertising agencies, complete with dedicated research departments (Pope 1983; Beniger 1986). Soon these agencies became convinced that national brand advertising implied a shift from simply promoting products to strategically persuading consumers, with the crafting of messages becoming a major preoccupation (Leiss et al. 2005). Whereas advertising protocol previously had been to address readers plainly with straight-forward information, the exigencies of mass production and consumption created a business climate in which "advertising that did not evoke a desire to buy was simply not doing its job" (Pope 1983, 237). To initiate desires that would generate purchases sufficient to match the output of national manufacturers, advertisers required intimate knowledge of consumer behaviors and the triggers that might reliably and predictably influence them.

Around the same time, department store merchants tapped into customers' fantasies, using display techniques to usher in what William Leach (1993) calls the "democratization of desire." A new American dream was forged in the first part of the 20th century in which the goods acquired, and the stories advertisers and marketers told about those goods, said a lot about a person's identity and place in society (Marchand 1985). With advances in industry (e.g., innovations in power generation, communication, and logistics) an ideology favoring consumption was needed to match productive capacity (Ewen 1976; Beniger 1986). Advertising and commercial media were seen as vital tools for teaching citizens to live as consumers (Smythe 1981). Efforts to understand consumers' behavior and motivations were of singular importance in this task.

When most advertising alerted readers to the particular inventory and prices of a local merchant, consumers were generally imagined to be rational, knowledgeable, and already in the market for certain goods or services. Trade proceeded, at least formally, with an assumption that buyer and seller were on equal footing. With national advertising of branded products, these assumptions and strategies were recalibrated to a new environment that required new theories of consumer behavior and persuasive communication. Moving away from an emphasis on rationalism, advertising practice started to absorb several, sometimes clashing, perspectives on the consumer psyche. Already by the 1890s, George Rowell, founder of *Printers' Ink*, had anticipated a psychological turn in advertising (Leiss et al. 2005, 139), and before the century's close, psychologists at the University of Minnesota designed experiments to test responses to advertising messages (Vargas and Yoon 2004, 54).

Hardly a decade later, Walter Dill Scott, professor at Northwestern University, made a more lasting contribution in a number of books and articles by pairing applied psychology with advertising. Scott argued, most forcefully in *The Psychology of Advertising in Theory and Practice* (1908), that suggestibility exists alongside rationality, leaving humans subject to strategic influence by persuasive messaging. "Man (sic) has been called the reasoning animal," Scott wrote, "but he could with greater truthfulness be called the creature of suggestion" (quoted in Pope 1983, 241). Recognizing that informing consumers about products fell short of stimulating demand, Scott insisted that advertisements be crafted to tap both rationality and suggestibility, "designed to persuade and to motivate" (Leiss et al. 2005, 139). In 1912, the J. Walter Thompson agency commissioned a study by a research team that included John B. Watson, considered by many "the father of behaviorism." A year later, psychologists at Columbia University reported to the New York Advertising Men's League that ad messages could be considered part of a stimulus-response chain, further embracing the vocabulary of behavioral science (Pope 1983, 241). A mail-order merchant from Detroit put it bluntly: "It is a favorite superstition that because reason is peculiar to the human being it is his prevailing guide to action. Nothing could be much farther from the truth. Man ... actually ... is a creature of habits" (ibid, 240).

Famed copywriter Claude Hopkins similarly regarded consumers as acting non-rationally. In his 1927 autobiography, he compared shoppers to "sheep," yet he regarded "common people" with some admiration (Pope 1983, 249–50). Pope describes Hopkins's views as indicative of deeper tensions: "Advertising men saw the public as impulsive and irrational, but preached that consumer choices (suitably influenced by national advertising) should dictate economic activity" (250). In essence, as far as advertisers and their agents were concerned, consumers were competent enough to navigate markets without protective intervention (such as prohibitions on persuasive speech), but suggestible enough to warrant most any effort or expense thought to influence their buying behaviors.

Such ambivalence regarding the sovereign status of consumers and the role of advertising has persisted for decades. Not long after progressive economists critiqued mainstream assumptions about consumer "sovereignty" and the pure communicative function of advertising– (Galbraith, 1958; Scitovsky 1962), advertising practice underwent a "creative revolution" in which irreverent copy confronted consumers judged to be wily and cynical about advertising—evidenced most famously by DDB's Volkswagen ads. The expectation that consumers were hip and savvy—but still prone to being persuaded to align their identities with brand significations—infiltrated agencies and reversed some power dynamics between creatives and researchers (Frank 1997).

Disagreements between advertising (as meaning-making) and marketing (as a science) remain salient. Consider, for example, the perspective Sergio Zyman articulates in his book, *The End of Advertising as We Know It*. According to this former Chief Marketing Officer at Coca-Cola, "Advertising is not an art form. It's about selling more stuff more often to more people for more money. Success is the result of a scientific, disciplined process, and absolutely *every single* expenditure must generate a return" (Zyman 2003, 1; original emphasis). On the other hand, an artistic ethos emphasizes creative and experiential dimensions of advertising and marketing (Lopez 2009; Schmitt 2009; Spurgeon 2008).

While competing perspectives remain discernable today, the development of interactive and digital advertising has given credence to Zyman's views. The information harvesting capacities of digital technologies enable unprecedented feedback of market-related behaviors. In a paper for the National Bureau of Economic Research, two Stanford economists write, "Practically everything on the internet is recorded. ... When you shop on Amazon or eBay, not only every purchase, but every click is captured and logged. When you read a newspaper online, watch videos, or track your personal finances, your behavior is recorded" (Einav and Levin 2013, 2). Furthermore, techniques for tracking our movements, transactions, and patterns in physical spaces all contribute to "the data footprint that we now leave behind us" (ibid). This mindset is ushering sweeping changes in marketing thought and in media industries.

The Behavioral "Revolution" in Economics

While advertising and marketing have had a long, if fickle, engagement with psychological research, mainstream economics kept a steadier distance from psychology from the early 20th century until the last few decades. Neoclassical economists, who have dominated the discipline during this period, have largely imagined market behavior to be governed by a self-interested and rational drive to maximally satisfy one's own preferences. Economists like Milton Friedman (1953) have argued that economic activity can be understood—to the degree necessary for accurate prediction and development of economic theory—through deductive reasoning (Sent 2004; Hands 2009). Yet an increasingly influential discourse on behavioral economics (BE) represents a challenge to this approach; it complicates neoclassical economists' notion of what drives individual choices. BE ties economics to experimental psychology and other behavioral sciences. Some economists believe behavioral economics has the potential to radically disrupt dominant disciplinary assumptions (Berg and Gigerenzer 2010). However, the group of behavioral economists who have been gaining great influence within the discipline—through appointments to prestigious university faculties, Nobel prizes, and government positions—largely see room for compatibility between BE and the neoclassical economic outlook (Sontheimer 2015).

This influential group of behavioral economists has drawn on research from fields ranging from neuroscience to evolutionary psychology and, to a lesser degree, sociology and anthropology. Nonetheless, the focal point of their attention has been on experimental cognitive psychology, especially research by or inspired by the psychologists Amos Tversky and Daniel Kahneman. Reflecting on decades of research with the late Tversky, Kahneman (2003, 1449), winner of the Noble Prize in economics in 2002, says the pair set out to discover "the systematic biases that separate the beliefs that people have and the choices they make from the optimal beliefs and choices assumed in rational-agent models." Such a starting point framed the behavioral patterns they found as deviations from rational choice models. Cognitive psychologists and behavioral economists use psychological experiments to reveal patterns that illuminate how human decision-making processes systematically differ from neoclassical assumptions of rational, self-interested economic agents. For example, in one experiment, most subjects are unwilling to take a bet with a 50-percent chance of losing $10 and a 50-percent chance of winning $11, though standard economic models would generally predict that rational agents would choose to take the bet (Rabin 1998). Drawing on experimental evidence such as this, behavioral economists move from empirical observations to abstract models of heuristics and decision-making processes. Relating to the example above, repeated experiments have suggested a pattern that researchers call *loss aversion*—a tendency to place greater value on avoiding losses rather than seeking gains within certain ranges of monetary value (Kahneman 2011).

Detailed information about current and potential customers is an indispensable strategic resource for enterprises proceeding from an understanding of consumer behavior as predictably irrational. Toward realizing this logic, marketing theorists and strategists urge practitioners to reconstruct the marketing environment by engineering media interfaces that take full advantage of digital systems' capacities to harvest, analyze, and exploit behavioral data. Marketers are reorienting their priorities and organizational structures around the personalized and pervasive management of customers.

Applying the Behavioral Sciences to Marketing

The trajectory of advertising research and the corresponding conceptions of consumers from rational decision makers to emotional buyers subject to suggestion has more recently come to embrace behavioral economics. The industrial logic directing much of the churn in digital media industries defines audiences as *individual consumers* and assembles the tools and strategies necessary to monitor them and evaluate their observed (and predicted) consumption behaviors. Analysts at Forrester Research have declared ours the "Age of the Customer," one in which marketers must become "customer obsessed" (Cooperstein 2013). Forrester research suggests further that brand advertising should take a back seat to investments in "real-time actionable data" and "contextualized customer experiences" (Cooperstein 2013, 1). In other words, rather than building identities around brands, companies should focus on building marketing platforms that extract "identities" from customers' behaviors and then use this feedback to reorganize the platforms based on algorithmic predictions of customers' situational responses to specific stimuli—whether a discount, a mode of presenting product information, or preferred payment and delivery options. Researchers writing in the *Journal of Consumer Behavior* capture the spirit of digital marketing with reference to three primary beachheads for such designs:

> As we collect more sophisticated data on individuals' consumption patterns, say via credit cards, online marketplaces, or supermarket membership discount programs, we can more effectively tailor and convey advertisements directly to specific individuals.
> (Perrachione and Perrachione 2008, 310)

Manufacturing a comprehensive profile of an individual consumer thus requires extensive monitoring of people. As analysts at Forrester suggest approvingly, "Every interaction, every communication, every touchpoint creates a digital breadcrumb—a piece of data that can be analyzed and manipulated" (Khatibloo and Hopkins 2014, 2). Using customer analytics techniques, marketers not only respond to "wants and needs," but also "uncover end goals and desires" (Heffner 2014, 3). Since "[a]ny data that can be related to a known customer might be leveraged to engage with the customer" (p. 3), marketers must collect information whenever and wherever possible. Some of that data collection, of course, will be used for straightforward targeting, trying to match advertisements with likely buyers based on predictions relative to demographic and psychographic groupings or individual profiles. However, marketers' interests in BE and related sciences suggest an expanded array of strategic possibilities.

Discussions of BE among marketing researchers and advertising and marketing firms and professional organizations suggest BE offers at least three types of resources for marketers and advertisers. First, it helps promote and direct attention toward an experimental approach for understanding consumer decision processes. Marketers have long used focus groups, surveys, and other research techniques. Yet whereas much of this other research probes how consumers make meanings and associations, the BE model specifically pulls focus around research detailing how decisions are made. Like earlier behavioral research, pervasive monitoring attempts to bypass subjects' ostensibly unreliable accounts of their motivations. Second, BE research describes particular heuristics that people rely upon for making economics decisions, such as loss aversion. Marketers might end up using such theories in unpredictable ways and conducting further consumer research based on BE principles.

Lastly, behavioral economists also offer a general model of human cognition. Kahneman (2003; 2011) outlines core structures of the human mind underlying the BE framework. Mental operations are fundamentally bifurcated into two cognitive systems, which Kahneman describes as "System 1" and "System 2." System 2 is responsible for much of what is commonly thought to represent the "higher orders" of thought, including self-conscious reflection, difficult calculation, and analysis of complex problems. System 2 has the potential for recognizing uncertainty and being self-critical. Since System 2 is effortful and deliberately controlled, while System 1 is automatic and feels effortless, it is System 1 that serves as humans' default system. Kahnneman frames this preference as a matter of energy conservation with System 1 corresponding roughly with what we think of as intuition. Nonetheless, its judgments are not simply innate; they can be shaped by experience and deeply ingrained practices and cultural assumptions (Kahneman 2011, 38). Yet, System 1's speediness comes at a cost. Much of Kahneman's research, which has set a trajectory many behavioral economists have followed, shows System 1 regularly distorts perceptions. This system frequently leads people to make decisions that fail to optimize their self-interest in accord with assumptions made by traditional rational choice theorists.

In addition to this line of cognitive research, another avenue for intervening in consumer behavior that has stimulated much hype and some consternation develops from a strain of neuroscience research that feeds into what has become known as "neuromarketing" (Ariely and Berns 2011). Proceeding from the proposition that "The brain is responsible for all our consumer behaviors" (Morin 2011, 134), neuromarketing is "the application of neuroimaging techniques to sell products" (Lee et al. 2007, 200). These techniques involve tools for detecting brain activity in response to certain stimuli. The most common of these are electroencephalography (EEG), magnetoencephalography (MEG), and functional magnetic resonance imaging (fMRI)—all of which vary in the precision with which they capture either the spatial or temporal details of brain activity. Echoing behaviorists' distrust of measures such as self-reporting—essentially the dismissal of all evidence apart from observation of behavior—Christophe Morin (2011) celebrates neuromarketing for offering "cutting edge methods for directly probing minds without requiring demanding cognitive or conscious participation" (131).

In a widely cited article, Kenning and Plassmann (2005) suggest that this line of inquiry has followed behavioral economics' insurrection against certain tenets of neoclassical economics—specifically, the belief in perfectly rational actors who maximize utility based on a perfect understanding of complete information. Neuroscience, they propose, "implies a totally different idea of man [sic]" from mainstream economic theory; against *homo oeconomicus*, they put forward "*homo neurobiologicus*, whose behavior and social and economic nature are the result of neurobiology" (344). The goal of neuroeconomic research, they claim, is to "provide a descriptive decision-making theory, which is not restricted to economic theory and more realistic than that of the homo oeconomicus" (353).

The cognitive psychology and neuroscience traditions drawn upon by BE-influenced marketers suggest humans often do not understand the motivating factors behind their choices. The belief that preferences and motivations are hidden has been an assumption of some behaviorists since the early 20th century. Yet BE and neuromarketing, in contrast to behaviorism, take human cognition and brain activity seriously, not reducing human action to mechanistic reactions to stimuli. Nonetheless, these approaches remain skeptical of data that is not an objective outcome of behavior or its neurological substrate. A writer in *Advertising Age* summarizes the starting point for neuromarketing: "Amid the many vagaries of marketing research, one this is clear: Consumers lie. About what they want. About what they need. Sometimes they do it purposely. Most often they simply don't seem to realize what they're doing at all" (Frazier 2007).

Selling BE to Marketing Clients: The Institute of Decision Making

In 2010, one of the largest global advertising agencies, Daftfcb (later renamed Foote Cone and Belding), launched the Institute of Decision Making (IDM) in order to provide clients with "behaviorally based insights on how to influence consumer choice" ("Institute of Decision Making" 2015). Under the directorship of Matthew Willcox, the institute has partnered with psychologists and behavioral scientists not only to work with specific clients but to further basic research into the application of behavioral sciences to marketing (Elliott 2010). They have also pressed hard to make the case to potential clients that the rapidly changing media landscape calls for a new approach to marketing, one driven by a scientific knowledge of how humans make choices. The IDM's website ties together many themes found in marketing literature on behavioral economics and tells a powerful story about why today's advertisers need an agency that pays heed to the latest developments within the behavioral sciences.

Willcox (2015a) warns that too many marketers have mistaken their trade for the brand building. In Willcox's view building brands should be a means—and not the only means available—rather than an end for marketers. Citing evidence indicating that brands have become "significantly less trusted, liked, and respected and salient" in the preceding years, Willcox (2015a, 6) draws on a behavioral economic framework that might suggest today's consumers may be valuing branding less "as a no-questions-asked shortcut in their decision making" than in the past. The IDM promises to pursue the best insights from behavioral economics, evolutionary psychology, and neuromarketing to understand how contemporary consumers really make their decisions.

While IDM's claims about the benefits of behavioral science for marketing need to be interpreted as part of a sales pitch, this pitch reveals the ways in which a marketing discourse is appropriating the discursive and intellectual resources of a set of behavioral sciences—particularly a stream of thought within behavioral economics, evolutionary psychology, and neuroeconomics. Willcox maps how each of these sciences contributes complementary knowledge: "If Behavioral Economics reveals *what* drives our choices, and Neuroeconomics reveals *how* our brain processes choice, then Evolutionary Psychology is providing the framework to help us understand *why* we make the choices we do" (2015b). The language the IDM uses to promote a vision of marketing driven by behavioral science conflates conceptual distinctions that might be important in scientific discourses. Most prominently, IDM staff frequently refers to cognitive patterns identified by behavioral economists as "instincts." The use of this term—rarely employed in the disciplinary literature in behavioral economics—not only suggests, too easily, that evolutionary mechanisms can explain empirical observations; it also plays to a resonant mythology among marketers that figures consumers as instinct-driven in an animalistic sense. Yet, Willcox's notion of instinct differs significantly from previous conceptions in marketing discourses; in his view, human instincts cannot be grasped intuitively or reduced to fundamental drives for sex or other appetites. The thinking patterns that, as Willcox (2015a, 8) says, "make choices intuitive, or instinctive, in effect making them 'no-brainers'" have to be discovered by careful cognitive science.

Marketing as Behavioral Programming

While marketers see ways to apply scientific insights across all sorts of media campaigns, the behavioral economic framework holds particular promise for environments rich with consumer monitoring data. Andrew Pole, a consumer analyst working for the Target Corporation, provided what has become the most memorable example of emerging data-driven marketing strategies, thanks to the revelatory work of *New York Times* journalist and author Charles Duhigg. Pole devised an algorithm for Target to identify customers who were pregnant, which became infamous after a father complained to Target about the baby-related advertisements targeting his teenage daughter, only to learn she was already pregnant. To make such predictions, Pole's analysis drew on Target's extremely large database of consumer purchase records. Pole examined the purchasing patterns of customers who had used Target's baby registry and then identified "about 25 products that, when analyzed together, allowed him to assign each shopper a 'pregnancy prediction' score" (Duhigg 2012). This algorithm, according to Duhigg, could estimate a consumer's due date with surprising accuracy, so that Target could send carefully timed coupons and promotions.

The story of Target's pregnancy prediction struck a nerve. The story traveled widely through mentions in blogs and other publications, and it has become a frequent reference for advocates decrying commercial surveillance. It is not only the intimate nature of the data analysis that makes this case revelatory of the disturbing potential of data-intensive marketing; it is also the strategy behind it. Target's interest in predicting who was pregnant was based on a marketing plan to *program the habits and heuristics* of these consumers. Inspiring Target's strategy, according to Duhigg, was an empirical study conducted by researchers at UCLA. Its results suggested that consumer habits for mundane purchases tend to be difficult to change, but they are most vulnerable to marketing interventions at moments of major life changes, such as moving to a new home, a marriage or divorce, or, most of all, having a baby. That's why Pole's work was so valuable; it pointed to an opportunity to reprogram consumer habits at an especially susceptible moment. Target was not simply trying to identify a niche set of consumer needs around pregnancy. Rather, it used a niche promotion as bait for longer-term habit formation. Target wanted to bring new parents into the store to use baby-related coupons, expecting they would start buying all sorts of items on such a visit during a harried time, and hoping this would imprint a habit that could last for decades to come.

Conclusion

New conditions have spurred new approaches to advertising research, which in turn require new approaches to their critique. The attention given here to the historical emergence of these new conditions and approaches has examined discussions and debates within the industry itself. Tuning into insider discourses provides a detailed means of recognizing how much has changed. Digital retail environments equipped with consumer data mining capabilities allow marketers to have greater and more finely tuned control than ever before over the contexts in which consumers make decisions, through personalized promotions, discounts, and price adjustments. As data monitoring and electronic communication are increasingly deployed in physical retail spaces (Turow 2016), here too digital technologies afford marketers and retailers greater opportunities to construct the contexts in which consumers form habits and make decisions.

Cultural critics and scholars have pointed to several reasons for public concern regarding consumer monitoring and data-driven promotional strategies, including: the likelihood of targeted advertising to reinforce a prejudicially narrow range of options based on consumer profiles (Turow 2012), the potential of targeted promotion to further fracture social solidarity and democratic common experience along lines drawn for marketing purposes (Couldry and Turow 2014), the potential of consumer data to fall into the hands of criminals or over-reaching government agencies, as well as concerns about the exploitation of unpaid user labor that produces the extremely valuable data. Other than marginalizing all of these concerns, the digital advertising industry's most effective strategy for keeping critics at bay has been to promote targeted advertising as a convenience, promising "more relevant" advertisements for targets. However, looking at marketers' uptake of behavioral economics reveals another strategy for putting consumer data to use. Instead of matching consumers with advertisements presumed to fit their interests, advertising and promotion is geared toward manipulating the contexts in which consumers express preferences. These behavioral nudges do not entail any utility or preference maximization for consumers, only a chance for marketers to vie for control over the means by which consumers exercise their choices.

References

Andrejevic, Mark. 2007. *iSpy: Surveillance and Power in the Interactive Era.* Lawrence, KS: University Press of Kansas.

Ariely, Dan. 2008. *Predictably Irrational: The Hidden Forces That Shape Our Decisions.* New York: Harper Collins.

Ariely, Dan, and Gregory S. Berns. 2010. "Neuromarketing: The Hope and Hype of Neuroimaging in Business." *Nature Reviews Neuroscience* 11(4): 284–92.

Beniger, James R. 1986. *The Control Revolution.* Cambridge, MA: Harvard University Press.

Berg, Nathan, and Gerd Gigerenzer. 2010. "As-If Behavioral Economics: Neoclassical Economics in Disguise?" *History of Economic Ideas* 18(1): 133–66.

Cohen, Nicole S. 2008. "The Valorization of Surveillance: Towards a Political Economy of Facebook." *Democratic Communiqué* 22(1): 5–22.

Cooperstein, David M. 2013. *Competitive Strategy in the Age of the Customer.* Cambridge, MA: Forrester Research.

Couldry, Nick, and Joseph Turow. 2014. "Advertising, Big Data and the Clearance of the Public Realm: Marketers' New Approaches to the Content Subsidy." *International Journal of Communication* 8: 1710–26.

Duhigg, Charles. 2012. "How Companies Learn Your Secrets." *The New York Times,* February 16. http://www.nytimes.com/2012/02/19/magazine/shopping-habits.html.

Einav, Liran, and Jonathan D Levin. 2013. *The Data Revolution and Economic Analysis.* National Bureau of Economic Research Working Paper No. 19035. Cambridge, MA. http://www.nber.org/papers/w19035.

Elliott, Stuart. 2010. "A Quest to Learn What Drives Consumer Decisions." *The New York Times,* June 29. http://www.nytimes.com/2010/06/30/business/media/30adco.html.

Ewen, Stuart. 1976. *Captains of Consciousness: Advertising and the Social Roots of the Consumer Culture.* New York: Basic Books.

Frank, Thomas. 1997. *The Conquest of Cool.* Chicago: University of Chicago Press.

Frazier, Mya. 2007. "Hidden Persuasion of Junk Science?" *Advertising Age,* September 10. http://adage.com/article/news/hidden-persuasion-junk-science/120335/.

Friedman, Milton. 1953. *Essays in Positive Economics*. Chicago: University of Chicago Press.

Galbraith, John K. 1958. *The Affluent Society*. Boston, MA: Houghton Mifflin.

Gandy, Oscar H. 1993. *The Panoptic Sort: A Political Economy of Personal Information. Critical Studies in Communication and in the Cultural Industries*. Boulder, CO: Westview Press. http://eric.ed.gov/?id=ED377817.

Hands, D. Wade. 2009. "Economics, Psychology and the History of Consumer Choice Theory." *Cambridge Journal of Economics* 39(5). doi: 10.1093/cje/bep045.

Heffner, Randy. 2014. *A Radical Rethink of Data Architecture For Customer Engagement*. Cambridge, MA: Forrester. July 17.

"Institute of Decision Making." 2015. Accessed September 16. (http://www.instituteofdecisionmaking.com/about-us/.

Jhally, Sut. 1990. *The Codes of Advertising: Fetishism and the Political Economy of Meaning in the Consumer Society*. New York: Routledge.

Kahneman, Daniel. 2003. "Maps of Bounded Rationality: Psychology for Behavioral Economics." *The American Economic Review* 93(5): 1449–75.

———. 2011. *Thinking, Fast and Slow*. New York: Macmillan.

Kenning, Peter, and Hilke Plassmann. 2005. NeuroEconomics: An Overview from an Economic Perspective. *Brain Research Bulletin* 67: 343–54.

Khatibloo, Fatemeh, and Brian Hopkins. 2014. *Big Data's Big Meaning For Marketing*. Cambridge, MA: Forrester. May 28.

Leach, William. 1993. *Land of Desire: Merchants, Power, and the Rise of a New American Dream*. New York: Vintage.

Lears, Jackson. 1995. *Fables of Abundance: A Cultural History of Advertising in America*. New York: Basic Books.

Lee, Nick, Amanda J Broderick, and Laura Chamberlain. 2007. "What Is 'Neuromarketing'? A Discussion and Agenda for Future Research." *International Journal of Psychophysiology* 63: 199–204.

Leiss, William, Stephen Kline, Sut Jhally, and Jacqueline Botterill. 2005. *Social Communication in Advertising: Consumption in the Mediated Marketplace*, 3rd edition. New York: NY: Routledge.

Lopez, Herman. 2009. "Why Interactive Advertising Needs a Creative Revolution." *Advertising Age*, Jun. 15. Retrieved Mar. 10, 2011 from: http://adage.com/article/digital/interactive-advertising-a-creative-revolution/137246/.

Marchand, Roland. 1985. *Advertising the American Dream*. Berkley: University of California Press.

Morin, Christophe. 2011. Neuromarketing: The New Science of Consumer Behavior." *Society* 48 (2): 131–35.

Perrachione, Tyler K, and John R Perrachione. 2008. "Brains and Brands: Developing Mutually Informative Research in Neuroscience and Marketing." *Journal of Consumer Behavior* 7: 303–18.

Pope, Daniel. 1983. *The Making of Modern Advertising*. New York: NY: Basic Books.

Rabin, Matthew. 1998. "Psychology and Economics." *Journal of Economic Literature* 36(1): 11–46.

Rubinson, Joel. 2010. "What Behavioral Economics Can Teach Marketing Research." *Journal of Advertising Research* 50 (2):114–17.

Scott, Walter Dill. 1908. *The Psychology of Advertising in Theory and Practice*. Boston, MA: Small, Maynard & Company.

Schmitt, Garrick. 2009. "The Last Campaign: How Experiences Are Becoming the
. New Advertising." *Advertising Age*, Nov. 10. Retrieved Apr. 18, 2011 from: http://
adage.com/article/digitalnext/experiences-advertising/140388/.

Scitovsky, Tibor. 1962. "On the Principle of Consumers' Sovereignty." *The American
Economic Review* 52(2): 262–68.

Sent, Esther-Mirjam. 2004. "Behavioral Economics: How Psychology Made Its
(Limited) Way Back into Economics." *History of Political Economy* 36(4):
735–60.

Smythe, Dallas W. 1981. *Dependency Road*. Norwood, NJ: Ablex.

Sontheimer, Kevin. 2015. "Behavioral Versus Neoclassical Economics." In *Handbook of Contemporary Behavioral Economics: Foundations and Developments*,
237–56. New York: Routledge.

Spurgeon, Christina. 2008. *Advertising and New Media*. New York: Routledge.

Strasser, Susan. 1989. *Satisfaction Guaranteed: The Making of the American Mass
Market*. New York: Pantheon.

Turow, Joseph. 2012. *The Daily You: How the New Advertising Industry Is Defining
Your Identity and Your Worth*. New Haven, CT: Yale University Press.

———. 2016. *The Aisles Have Eyes: How Retailers Track Your Shopping, Strip Your
Privacy, and Define Your Power*. New Haven, CT: Yale University Press.

Turow, Joseph, Michael Hennessy, and Nora Draper. 2015. *The Tradeoff Fallacy:
How Marketers Are Misrepresenting American Consumers and Opening Them
Up to Exploitation*. A Report from the Annenberg School for Communication,
University of Pennsylvania. Philadelphia, PA.

Turow, Joseph, Lee McGuigan, and Elena R. Maris. 2015. "Making Data Mining
a Natural Part of Life: Physical Retailing, Customer Surveillance and the
21st Century Social Imaginary." *European Journal of Cultural Studies* 18 (4–5):
464–78. doi: 10.1177/1367549415577390.

Vargas, Patrick T, and Sukki Yoon. 2004. Advertising Psychology. In *Encyclopedia
of Applied Psychology: A-E, Volume 1*, edited by CD Spielberger. Boston: Elsevier
Academic Press. pp. 53–64.

Willcox, Matthew. 2015a. *The Business of Choice: Marketing to Consumers'
Instincts*. Indianapolis, IN: Pearson FT Press.

———. 2015b. "Welcome to The Institute of Decision Making." *FCB Exchange*.
September 1. http://fcbexchange.com/institute-of-decision-making/about_us/.

Williamson, Judith. 1994. *Decoding Advertisements*. Reissue edition. London:
Marion Boyars Publishers Ltd.

Williams, Raymond. 1960. "The Magic System." *New Left Review* 4(July–Aug):
27–32.

Zyman, Sergio. 2003. *The End of Advertising as We Know It*. Hoboken, NJ: Wiley.

10 A Critical Theory of Advertising as Surveillance
Algorithms, Big Data, and Power

Robert Bodle

Introduction

Online advertising practices have outpaced critical advertising studies due to the changes brought by an online environment characterized by ubiquitous surveillance (tracking, monitoring), big data (mining, collecting, profiling, sorting), participatory cultures (user-generated content production and social sharing), and behavioral advertising (serving, personalizing, targeting). Behavioral advertising is a subset of online personalization services that caters to the prior actions of the user in an algorithmically generated feedback loop. Examples of personalization services include targeted ads (Turow 2011), Google's personal search (Luca, Wu, Yelp Data Science Team 2015), featured recommendations on Amazon.com, taste preferences on Netflix, Twitter Trends, and Facebook's News Feed. Personalized marketing and advertising can be useful, relevant, and entertaining, when served with content that we ourselves help to generate. However, personalization requires identification, tracking, and predictive analytics and should be considered a new and important modality of surveillance (La Rue 2013). Negative consequences of commercial surveillance can include online discrimination, financial manipulation, labor exploitation, coercion, political polarization, the erosion of personal autonomy, and the loss of political freedom.

This chapter theorizes the implications of surveillance-based advertising including the loss of privacy, autonomy, and various forms of social control (both panoptic and bureaucratic). Recent interdisciplinary work in software and information studies helps explain the sociotechnical dynamics of predictive analytics used to personalize ads (Beer 2009; Kitchen and Dodge 2011; MacKenzie 2008; Mayer-Schönberger & Cukier 2012). Empirical studies in social science and communication fields suggest how seemingly neutral and opaque machine processes can reveal corporate agendas (Bucher 2012; Gillespie 2011). Political economy critiques of social media provide insight into the ways personal information helps facilitate the growth of the information economy (Wall, 2006), where surplus value and profit derive from surveillance, exchange of personal data, and instrumental uses of data for behavioral modification. This analysis applies a critical political economy perspective to identify the operational logics and underlying social relations among users, online services, and advertisers. Critical theories of surveillance (Andrejevic 2002, 2007, 2012; Gandy 1993, 2012; Turow 2005, 2006;) and privacy studies (Solove 2002, 2006; Tavani 2011; Westin 1967) provide further insight into recognizing the exploitative potential in power asymmetries. Empirical observation of online advertising practices, including tracking, use of predictive algorithms, and big data analytics, provides a basis for critique and resistance.

Surveillance-Based Advertising

Serving relevant ads involves making predictions, with knowledge of past behavior can indicate (and modify) future behavior. The tracking of personally identifiable data, both behavioral and transactional, depends on the ability to fix one's identify over time so that seemingly innocuous disclosures can culminate in a useful and valuable profile. Online advertising practices have evolved from the rudimentary and ineffective pop-up and banner ads, to involuntary and invasive adware installations, to more recent data-driven techniques such as collaborative filtering, contextual and personalized advertising, and behavioral targeting. These latter techniques are increasingly dependent on commercial surveillance, big data accumulation, and analytics to process, interpret, and serve ads. The move to surveillance-based, data-driven advertising has grown out of direct marketing and product-placement retail campaigns that utilize information for customization of ads and the discrimination of customers. Some critics suggest online advertising is "the original sin of the Web" (Zuckerman 2014), because it established an ad-based business model for otherwise free online services and platforms. The "sin" of digital advertising, which includes data tracking, collecting, and trading, is the ongoing surveillance of people while they seek and impart information online.

Online social networks provide ideal empirical case studies to identify and assess commercial surveillance and personalization services, which includes the automatic collection of user-generated content (e.g., big data), the application of data analytics (algorithms), and the economic imperative of advertising as a driving factor. Facebook is the dominant social network site (SNS) and can be a useful indicator of trends in similar Web 2.0 services. Advertising practices on the social network site culled from industry press and empirical observation are used to theorize the implications of surveillance and personalization, to examine power asymmetries, and to help formulate user empowerment.

Black Boxing and the Limits of Analysis

Industrial practices are obscured not only by their structural complexity but also by the opaqueness or black-boxing of technological processes. Research on online ad practices is often limited by the opacity of the underlying technological processes of surveillance and personalization

(Beer 2009; Feuz, Fuller, & Stadler 2011; Bucher 2012). This limitation is an early indication of asymmetrical power relations between the social network site, advertisers, and users. This power asymmetry suggests a pattern where selective insights about users are shared with advertisers, but not with people who are generating this information in the first place. Secrecy is common in ad-dependent industries where "Marketing is a war of knowledge, insight, and asymmetric advantage" (Nichols 2012, 8). Scientific data about how surveillance and personalization actually work lie outside the scope of this study, with a focus on general processes and their implications.

A Critical Political Economy of Communication

A critical political economy of communications approach makes an effort to theoretically and empirically identify industrial practices in the context of "domination, asymmetrical power relations, resource control, social struggles, and exploitation" (Allmer 2015, 87). This approach can be used to examine the potential conflicts of interest between market logic and user needs; for example, when companies "sometimes need to surreptitiously betray public trust to meet other resource goals" (Turow 2008, 282). Analysis of asymmetrical relationships among online services, advertisers, and users also points to the commodification of social labor (playbor), where personal information is turned into product, and the consumer becomes the (unpaid) producer (Terranova 2000; Mosco 2009; Wasco & Erickson 2009). "With its focus on institutional structures and practices," offers Bettig, "the political economy of communications is poised to help explain the forces driving these processes and to offer up predictions about their implications" (1996, 1).

Tracking users is an imperative for advertising-based business models and is evident in terms of service and privacy statements; "we may use all of the information we receive about you to serve ads that are more relevant to you" (Facebook 2013). "Privacy statements," Fernback and Papacharissi conclude in a discourse analysis of four web 2.0 sites, "pose virtually no restriction on businesses to profit excessively from the collection and use of consumer information" (2007, 730). The underlying market logic of surveillance is to provide user information to serve well-tailored and well-placed ads, to guide online interactions toward monetary goals. A critical political economy perspective will guide an empirical analysis of data-driven advertising practices on Facebook.

Surveillance, Big Data, and Algorithms

The personalization services on the web rely on amassing extensive customer data and predictive algorithms to tailor content generated, in part, by the prior actions of the user. Personalized services serve content relevant to one's prior interests and activities, and filter out content that is not. In an ad-funded online ecosystem, companies track and collect user data to serve personalize search results and ads for products and services. This collection of valuable data has given rise to an online advertising industry that consists of digital advertising networks and marketing firms, data-brokers, data-mining, tracking, and optimization companies (e.g., RapLeaf). These companies help comprise and sort through "digital dossiers" (Solove 2002) identify people's browsing, viewing, and purchasing habits, in order to personalize content. Cloud applications, web cookies, and Open APIs (application programming interfaces) including social plug-ins (e.g., the "Like" button) enable companies to track people's activities from site to site and across devices (Bodle 2011). The social sharing encouraged by social networks (Bucher, 2012; Bosker, 2013) produces an on-going trail of data harvested in real time, as secondary information products shared, traded, and sold for personalization services. Algorithms then help interpret the data in order to make inferences, correlations, and predictions about future behavior.

In 2009, Google introduced personal search results based on a user's semantic history (search terms run and results selected), location, time of year, language, and linked social networks (Notess 2012, 43). This search history helps drive Google's ad business that sells "personalized audiences" (Feuz, Fuller, and Stadler 2011, 7) to advertisers (AdSense for search, AdWords for syndicated texts, and DoubleClick for graphics). Research suggests that personal search results benefit advertisers more than the public, by pushing people toward "criteria predefined by Google" (Feuz, Fuller, and Stadler 2011, 7). Like Google, Facebook's advertising business is built on surveillance, tracking content used to predict and shape "what people want or don't want even before they realize it" (Simonite 2012, 7).

Facebook collects information about its users from its social network (clicks, likes, hides, shares, posts, comments, check-ins, RSVPs, apps used, friend activity) across multiple devices, to personalize ads that can result in cost-effective ad placements (ROI—Return on Investment). Personalized ads are more likely to be paid attention to if they are relevant and correspond to peoples' existing tastes, preferences, and habits. Perhaps highly targeted Sponsored Ads and Suggested Posts on Facebook can "reach people in a way that feels good, that's not intrusive," suggests Facebook COO, Sheryl Sandberg (Frier and Stone 2015).

Facebook generated $17.08 billion US dollars in ad revenue model in 2015, 95% of its global revenue (http://www.statista.com/statistics/271258/facebooks-advertising-revenue-worldwide/). Facebook only accounts for 3% of the total advertising market (http://www.cnbc.com/2015/11/05/why-facebooks-ad-revenue-can-keep-growing-analyst.html) and stands to grow its ad revenue while managing the creep factor of its tracking, which includes a recently introduced tracking tool that measures the time people linger on a particular post. One way of managing anxiety over surveillance is to make ads increasingly relevant with the help of predictive analytics (algorithms). A well-targeted ad is more likely to make a favorable impression. Surveillance, data analytics, and personalization tools can help grow ad revenue by providing relevancy without causing too much anxiety for Facebook users.

Facebook also shares selected targeting parameters with third-party advertisers that include location targeting (country, city, IP address, and zip code—within the US), age and birthday, interests (likes, interests, and topics), education (college, university, major, graduation year), and connections and/ or friends of connections (Facebook 2012a). A brand can use these criteria to broaden or narrow the level of personalization and reach. Facebook also provides third-party access to members' anonymized aggregate data. Yet, Turow aptly observes, "when companies simply strip the name and address off of data that is sorted and labeled and combined with a telephone number—its claim that you are anonymous is meaningless" (2011, 190).

With over 1.49 billion members, Facebook harvests billions of interactions daily on the site, which feed an adaptive set of algorithms that learn how to encourage more interaction, which has "increased people's likes, clicks, and comments by 50%" (Bosker 2013). Facebook provides real-time tracking (via the Insights API) of "News Feed Post Performance" (clicks, likes, comments, and shares), "Virality" (organic propagation) and "Negative Feedback" (unlikes and hides; Constine 2012). Facebook improved its social advertising services by integrating ads among user-generated content, providing greater targeting options for advertisers, and via personalization algorithms. Advertising began on Facebook in 2009 with "Marketplace ads"—essentially banner ads featured on the right-hand margin of a Facebook page. The direct-response ads averaged click-through rates (CRTs) of 0.051%, "half as much as the industry standard of .1%," which was already extremely poor (ibid). Facebook partnered with Nielsen Co. to create a new rating system that measures sales, awareness, and reach (ibid). "Marketplace ads" were gradually replaced by "Sponsored Stories," "Page Post ads," and "Premium ads" that also occupied the right-hand margin of the page. However, the newer ads resembled native posts in both visual design and functionality, allowing the ability to comment, share, and like. "Suggested Posts," completed the native integration of ads within the social network environment by appearing within the center column of the News Feed alongside friend's photos and posts. The result of "Suggested Posts" was immediately evident—ads appearing in the News Feed averaged higher CTRs (1.0%–7.0% CTR) than those occurring in the right-hand column (0.04%–0.05%; McDermott 2012); with mobile ads generally earning higher CTRs than desktop (ibid).

Enhanced tracking techniques increase the value of the online user as a social audience commodity (Smythe 2006) and directly fuel the data trading industry (Anwin 2014, 31). However, predictive algorithms help make those data useful for personalized advertising. Algorithms are a digital mode of statistical analysis programmed with an adaptable set of procedural inputs, instructions, and rules used to draw meaning from large data sets

(McStay 2011). Algorithms should not be considered merely "cameras" but "engines" that "performatively enact" (MacKenzie 2008) the "intentions of the programmers" (Introna 2013). Facebook's algorithms filter posts generated by friends and group pages and filter who/what is seen and who/what is made invisible in order to curate relevancy and ultimately generate future interaction (McGee 2013). The algorithms' "exact workings and logics ... include more factors than is publicly known" (Bucher 2012, 1172).

Facebook's predictive algorithms process "the most extensive data set ever assembled on human social behavior" (Simonite 2012, 3), which includes user-generated information on Facebook, online activity external to the SNS through social plug-ins (e.g., the "Like" button) and cookies (e. g., Facebook Exchange), and personal information gathered offline provided by data brokers (e.g., Acxiom), as well as demographic and psychographic data (Turow 2008, 299). According to the Electronic Frontier Foundation, Facebook's algorithms analyze personal and public information such as "names, addresses, phone numbers, and details of shopping habits" (2013). Facebook's predictive algorithms "are ultimately geared towards commercial and monetary purposes" (Bucher 2012, 1169). The underlying goals of predictive algorithms may go well beyond predicting the "cause and effect relationships between advertising and purchasing" (Nichols 2012, 1) to manipulating them. The company's algorithmic control over how information is disseminated on the social network has implications for user privacy, autonomy, and freedom.

The Political Economy of Algorithmic Power

A better understanding of the political economy of algorithmic power can help inform user participation and agency. Although Web 2.0 rhetoric celebrates an era of disintermediation, predictive algorithms have been interposed as society's new gatekeepers, information filters, social shapers, and causal agents (Mayer-Schönberger & Cukier, 2013). Algorithms are not neutral or "a-political" prediction engines, suggests McStay (2011, 138). Seemingly neutral and inscrutable machine processes have political effects that reveal corporate agendas (Bucher 2012; Gillespie 2011). They are "codified politics" (McStay 2011, 138), "ideological formulations about social relations embodied in code, insulated from political debate, about which most people are unaware" (Bucher 2012, 1171). Algorithms infer, filter, and correlate big data for a wide range of purposes: discriminate people for targeted ads (Turow 2011), regulate incivility on news sites (Morozov 2013), shape social behavior by rewarding sharing online (Bucher, 2012), guide public opinion (Sunstein 2009), and act as an ideological filter (Pariser 2011). Surveillance and algorithmic control over user data reveals power asymmetries, "The seemingly abundant existence of data does in no way mean that it is available" (Ulbricht and von Grafenstein 2016). Although people generate surplus value for social media sites from their online participation, they have very little access, control, ownership, understanding, or awareness of the instrumental use of their data that may account for social inequality, discrimination, censorship, and other potential abuses.

Insights into the operational logics of Facebook's algorithm reinforce an understanding of the company's underlying business model that is predicated on tracking users and amassing data tied to fixed identities. Close examination of Facebook's data-driven personalization practices reveals the fundamental inequality among members, advertisers, and the Internet company. Recognizing Facebook's asymmetrical algorithmic power can provide insights into the implications of personalization for informational privacy, personal autonomy, critical thinking, and civic engagement.

Implications of Surveillance-Based Advertising (Panoptic and Non-Panoptic)

Typologies and definitions introduced by critical Internet privacy and surveillance studies can help recognize user exploitation and control; otherwise "naming and taming" the economic force of surveillance-based advertising (Zuboff 2015). In 2014, Janet Vertesi, a professor of sociology at Princeton University, attempted to hide the fact that she was pregnant from advertisers on the Internet: "The average person's marketing data is worth 10 cents; a pregnant woman's is $1.50" (Petronzio 2014). Vertesi's struggle to avoid being tracked, and to control her own data, illustrates two social theories of privacy adapted by Allmer as a typology of Internet privacy studies. The objective theory of privacy involves a rights-based conception of restricting or limiting society's ability to access people or information ("restricted access definition of privacy"; Allmer 2015, 70). The subjective theory focuses on individual control over information about one's self ("limited control definition of privacy"; ibid). Vertesi's experience was a research experiment and a means by which to raise awareness about how difficult it is to elude surveillance-based advertising online. The two social theories of privacy encompass and overlap ethical (Tavani 2011) and legal (Prosser 1960) conceptions of privacy: 1) a right to be free from interference in one's choices and decisions (decisional privacy, privacy of autonomy-appropriation), 2) right to be left alone, free from intrusion (accessibility privacy, privacy of space-intrusion), a 3) the ability control information about one's self (informational privacy, privacy of information-public disclosure). For Allmer, all three ethical-legal distinctions can fit into objective and subjective conceptions given the interpretative emphasis, in order to highlight the limitations of each and to ultimately arrive at an integrative approach (Allmer 2015).

The benefit of the objective approach is the very practical focus on unwarranted intrusion from social structures outside of an individual, which should be protected by law, conceived of as a normative right to privacy or data protection. Objective approaches can be narrowly defined, defensive, and static. The benefit of the subjective approach is the focus on self-determination as an ideal, with a focus on individuals' control over knowledge about themselves not just a defensive right but a positive condition of life for interpersonal relationships, autonomy, identity, and personal development. The limitation of the subjective approach is that the focus on privacy as an individual issue based on choice overlooks structural invasions of privacy, frames privacy within notions of possessive individualism, and lacks the normative critique that privacy should be protected from unwarranted intrusion by the state or commercial forces. Critical surveillance studies identify both panoptic (Foucault and Orwell) and non-panoptic theories used to define surveillance within the context of modern society. The context for surveillance studies, whether panoptic or non-panoptic, must account for the following:

- surveillance capacities have grown exponentially
- surveillance is automated, systematic, and disembodied though tied to individual identities
- the increased ability for companies to collect, share, and analyze data (sort, sift, profile, categorize, classify) big data
- commercial and political surveillance overlap

The panoptic definition always conceives of Internet surveillance in narrow terms, as always negative and instrumental for "coercion, repression, discipline, power, and domination" (Allmer 2015, 85). Non-panoptic definitions of surveillance identify a broader notion of surveillance as a neutral and technical process. Panoptic definitions that focus on domination recognize the power that institutions, such as corporations and governments, have over resources that put individuals at a massive disadvantage. Non-panoptic definitions tend to recognize surveillance as dispersed, conducted by many bureaucratic agencies (police, security, commercial, and administrative), with the possibility that surveillance is benign or even positive and beneficial (i.e., watching over a child). The two distinct theories can shed light on the implications of surveillance-based advertising that is inhuman, technical, and database driven, while recognizing the potential abuse of modern surveillance for domination, coercion, and control, without the means for informed consent, recourse, or due process (i.e., a Kafkaesque nightmare). The final section of this chapter will theorize the implications of privacy and surveillance-based advertising to identify: "domination, asymmetrical power relations, resource control, social struggles, and exploitation" (Allmer 2015, 58).

Implications of Surveillance-Based Advertising

Informational Privacy, Privacy of Information-Public Disclosure

Facebook provides real-time insights of user engagement with ads, to advertisers to improve performance, however the company does not provide users access to their own information, revealing an important power asymmetry. Access to one's own data is an integral component of autonomy and self-determination (Froomkin 2000, Tavani 2010). Withholding what information is known about a person and how it is used prevents people from anticipating consequences and making informed decisions. Predictive analytics undermines human volition by making decisions for people, affecting their freedom to self-actualize (Pariser 2011, 112). The ability to control information about one's self has been recognized as a precondition for the development of identity and intimacy and an essential component in interpersonal relationships.

Facebook's business logic relies on tracking users and amassing data to fixed identities, and thus enforces a "real-name only" policy that prevents the use of pseudonyms. Pseudonyms have been found to provide safety and security for the most vulnerable in society—victims of sexual abuse, children, the elderly, people oppressed for their sexual orientation or religious beliefs, protestors, whistleblowers, and dissidents. Yet the social network claims, "We take the safety of our community very seriously. That's why we remove fake accounts from the site as we find them" (Facebook 2012b). The SNS's adherence to real-name only principles and norms undermines user privacy and relative anonymity that can provide protection from reprisal for expressing one's self, including one's political beliefs (UDHR 1948). If social networks and advertisers can identify its users, so can repressive state security forces.

Decisional Privacy, Privacy of Autonomy-Appropriation

Surveillance-based advertising can provide relevancy and convenience, but it can also limit one's exposure to information outside of one's range of experience, habits of behavior, and fields of expertise. In *The Filter Bubble* (2011), Eli Pariser is surprised to find that the political views of his conservative Facebook friends are filtered out of his News Feed and are made invisible to him. Algorithmic filtering prevents exposure to competing views, which can reinforce and maintain "confirmation bias—the tendency to believe things that reinforce our existing views, to see what we want to see" (Pariser 2011, 86). More recently, many people found posts of the ice bucket challenge to raise money for ALS while missing news of protests over the death of Michael Brown in Ferguson, Missouri, although they were both happening at the same time. Access to a wide range of news and views can encourage an active and informed citizenry and provide the preconditions for a vibrant public dialog and debate that is robust, wide open, and uninhibited. Public deliberation is most likely to occur, suggests deliberative democracy theory, when we are exposed to diverse and antagonistic sources of information, not only to perspectives and to information that confirm our pre-existing knowledge base and opinions (Bollinger 2010).

Advertising-driven analytics can act as a gatekeeper, filtering out political points of view in addition to filtering incivility ("violence, racism, flagrant profanity, and hate speech"; Morozov 2013, 164). Facebook is impoverished as a networked public sphere if competing points of view, including incivility, are filtered out—which can contribute to group polarization. Vaidhyathan suggests that when "using Facebook or Google, we're more likely to come across like-minded posts from like-minded people. A republic works better when we make the extra effort to engage with a variety of points of view" (2012). The impact of algorithmic gatekeeping can be far reaching in shaping how people think and come together to solve problems. We are more free when we are presented with the options of what is possible, suggests Benkler (2001). As our options become limited, so does our ability to shape our world and ourselves.

A recent survey, "Social Networks and Politics," suggests that people are likely to block, un-friend, and hide someone who posts political opinions and views they disagree with or otherwise find offensive (Pew Research Center 2012a). Selective exposure can occur in traditional media use as well as online environments that fine-tune political, commercial, and cultural flows of information. The survey found that people are discouraged from expressing political views when their real names are attached (2012), which can encourage people to remain silent from fear of social isolation for fear of holding a minority view (Noelle-Neumann 1974). When minority views are silenced they are also erased, which can give rise to a false majority view and prevent a true majority view from emerging. Social network sites could encourage democratic participation if algorithms enhanced one's exposure to diverse opinions, rather than filter them.

Facebook's predictive analytics filter diverse opinions, which can also reinforce homophily, or the tendency to seek sameness in one's associates. The network filters waning friend activity in the name of relevancy, which can reinforce the tendency to shut out difference. Homophilous online environments that discourage people from seeking diverse opinions and social standpoints can reinforce sociological trends offline (Bishop 2008) where "physical communities are [also] becoming more homogenous" (Pariser 2011, 66). Personalized ads that discriminate users can deepen social divisions among people based on race, age, class, education, region, and political beliefs. Increased social divisions are likely to result in a less tolerant society, where prejudice and hatred of the other can flourish. People may also feel pressure to filter out their own differences in order to assimilate within homogenous online communities. Nakamura suggests that the cyber-topian promise of "liberation from marginalized and devalued bodies" often leads to a "postbody ideology" that reinforces racial and gendered stereotypes, leaving white male as the default (2002). As Facebook becomes a more global platform, the reinforcement of social divisions and the filtering of diversity (by users and the SNSs) can have far reaching implications for intercultural awareness, interaction, and respect.

Algorithmic guesses about people can also reinforce traditional patterns of discrimination in the market place, where some groups are not valued as highly as others. Predictive analytics can arrive at the same correlations about demographics that reinforce cultural stereotypes (Nakamura 2002). For example, studies have found "statistically significant discrimination in ad delivery based on racially associated names," including search results that associate names with criminal arrest records (Sweeney 2013). Such predicted results can hurt one's ability to get a job, apply for a loan, and make new friends.

Racially targeting advertising can be used to guide media consumption that draws on feelings of in-group accountability and "reinforce a consumer's identification with a commodity" (Gandy 2003, 5). Market segmentation can reinforce boundaries between social groups, including macroscopic traditional identity categories (gender, race, class, nationality, and sexuality; McStay 2013; Terranova 2004), and reinforce disparities as a result. Consistent with a political economy critique, categorization is in the best interest of advertisers to narrowly define "consumers" who gain power from consumption rather than citizens of networked publics and members of social movements, who gain power from concrete political gains.

The market logic of surveillance, and the operational logic of predictive analytics, is to predict future actions from past interactions to provide surplus value. Algorithms can infer inaccurate notions about who people are; online profiles can be flawed, incomplete, and dead wrong, with harmful results. Predictive analytics might also overlook the relevancy of one's aspirational self; the full breadth of one's values, goals, ideals, and notions about the good life.

Facebook has the algorithmic power to make decisions about people's online environments, to reinforce patterns of inclusion, and to set social agendas. The social network has enough data on members' desires and interests to tailor online experiences in ways that can manage their interactions and coerce outcomes. Rather than merely conforming to the prior interests of people, personalization services may be exploiting one's need to fit in, preventing access to the information needed to make meaningful decisions, self-actualization, and personal freedom.

Conclusion

This chapter evaluated the implications of surveillance-based advertising on Facebook, including the role big data and predictive algorithms play in establishing asymmetrical relations of power among people, companies, and advertisers. Commercial values and market logic embedded in predictive analytics can mitigate against user autonomy, privacy, and freedom of expression. Moreover, this analysis suggests that surveillance and algorithmic filtering can discriminate against categories of historically vulnerable populations, prevent one's exposure to difference, undermine respect for diversity, and discourage democratic participation.

Studies suggest that the more people understand how personalization works, the more they oppose it (Pew Research Center 2012b; 2015). In order to help provide people with greater understanding of the implications of surveillance-based advertising, Facebook's on-going process of tracking and filtering should be made more transparent. People should have greater control over their data, a better understanding of how their information is used, and the choice to opt out of tracking and personalization altogether, by default.

Research that helps account for the power asymmetries among companies, advertisers, and private citizens can restore and protect human agency. International principles on the application of human rights online and consumer protection laws can guide the regulation of social media, advertising, and big data industries. By restoring informational and decisional privacy, people might be empowered to reject the original sin of ad-driven surveillance online—both panoptic and bureaucratic—in an effort to achieve a more free and participatory society.

References

Allmer, T. 2015. *Critical Theory and Social Media between Emancipation and Commodification.* New York, NY: Routledge.

Andrejevic, M. 2007. *iSpy: Surveillance and Power in the Interactive Era.* Lawrence, KA: University Press of Kansas.

Angwin, J. 2014. *Dragnet Nation: A Quest for Privacy, Security, and Freedom in a World of Relentless Surveillance.* New York, NY: Times Books.

Beer, D. 2009. "Power through the Algorithm? Participatory Web Cultures and the Technological Unconscious." *New Media & Society* 11(6): 985–1002.

Benkler, Y. 2001. "Siren Songs and Amish Children: Autonomy, Information, and Law." *New York University Law Review*, 76(23): 23–113.

Bettig, R. 1996. *Copyrighting Culture: The Political Economy of Intellectual Property.* Boulder, CO: WestviewPress.

Bishop, B. 2008. *The Big Sort: Why the Clustering of Like-Minded America Is Tearing Us Apart.* New York, NY: Houghton Mifflin Company.

Bodle, R. 2010. "Assessing Social Network Sites as International Platforms: Guiding Principles." *Journal of International Communication*, 16(2): 9–24.

———. (2011). "Regimes of Sharing: Open APIs, Interoperability, and Facebook." *Information, Communication & Society*, 14(3): 320–37.

Bollinger, L. C. 2010. *Uninhibited, Robust, and Wide-Open: A Free Press for a New Century.* New York, NY: Oxford University Press.

Bosker, B. 2013, May. "Zuckerberg: Folks on Facebook Are Happy with All the Ads We're Showing Them." *The Huffington Post.* Retrieved from http://www.huffingtonpost.com/2013/05/01/zuckerberg-facebook-ads_n_3196195.html.

Bucher, T. 2012. "Want to Be on the Top? Algorithmic Power and the Threat of Invisibility on Facebook." *New Media and Society*, 14(7): 1164–80.

Calo, M. R. 2011. "The boundaries of Privacy Harm." *Indiana Law Journal*, 86(3). Retrieved from http://papers.ssrn.com/sol3/papers.cfm?abstract_id=1641487.

Clark, R. 1988. "Information Technology and Dataveillance." *Commun. ACM* 31(5, May 1988): 498–512. Retrieved from http://dx.doi.org/10.1145/42411.42413.

Cochran, T. 2013, May. "Personal Information Is the Currency of the 21st Century." *All Things D.* Retrieved from http://allthingsd.com/20130507/personal-information-is-the-currency-of-the-21st-century/.

Cohen, J. 2012. "Facebook's Two New Promos: Reach Generator, Logouts." Retrieved from http://allfacebook.com/facebook-reach-logout_b79918.

Constine, J. 2012, April. "EdgeRank Checker Hustles, Builds Tool Just Five Days after Facebook Real-Time Insights API Goes Live." *TechCrunch*. Retrieved from http://techcrunch.com/2012/04/25/facebook-real-time-insights-api/.

Delo, C. 2013, May. "Facebook: 30% of Our Revenue Now Comes from Mobile Ads." *AdAge Digital*. Retrieved from http://adage.com/article/digital/facebook-30-revenue-mobile-ads/241240/.

Electronic Frontier Foundation. 2013. "The Disconcerting Details: How Facebook Teams Up with Data Brokers to Show You Targeted Ads." Retrieved from https://www.eff.org/deeplinks/2013/04/disconcerting-details-how-facebook-teams-data-brokers-show-you-targeted-ads.

Ess, C. 2009. *Digital Media Ethics*. Cambridge, UK: Polity Press.

Facebook 2012a. Targeting Options. *Facebook Help Center*. Retrieved from www.facebook.com/business/help/433385333434831.

———. 2012b. "Disabled – Fake Names." *Facebook Help Center*. Retrieved from https://www.facebook.com/help.249092175207621.

Facebook. 2013. *Facebook Data Use Policy*. Retrieved from https://www.facebook.com/full_data_use_policy.

Fernback, J., & Z. Papacharissi. 2007. Online Privacy as Legal Safeguard: The Relationship among Consumer, Online Portal, and Privacy Policies. *New Media & Society* 9(5): 715–34.

Feuz, M., M. Fuller, & F. Stadler. 2011, February. Personal web searching in the age of semantic capitalism: Diagnosing the mechanisms of personalization. *First Monday* 16(2). Retrieved from http://firstmonday.org/article/view/3344/2766.

Frier, S. & B. Stone. 2015, September. Facebook Ads Are All-Knowing, Unblockable, and in Everyone's Phone. *Bloomberg Technology*. Retrieved from http://www.bloomberg.com/news/articles/2015-09-28/facebook-ads-are-all-knowing-unblockable-and-in-everyone-s-phone.

Froomkin, M. 2000. The Death of Privacy? *Stanford Law Review* 52(5): 1461–1543.

Fuchs, C. Boersma, K, Albrechtslund, A & Sandoval, M, eds. 2012. *Internet and Surveillance: The Challenges of Web 2.0 and Social Media*. New York, NY: Routledge.

Gandy, Jr., O. 2003. "Privatization and Identity: The Formation of a Racial Class." Retrieved from http://www.asc.upenn.edu/usr/ogandy/c53704read/privatization%20and%20identity%20i.pdf.

Gillespie, T. 2013. "Can an Algorithm be Wrong?" *Limn* 2. Retrieved from http://limn.it/can-an-algorithm-be-wrong/.

Greenstein, R. & A. Esterhuysen. 2006. "The Right to Development in the Information Society." In *Human Rights in the Global Information Society*, edited by R. K. Jørgensen, 281–302. Cambridge, MA: The MIT Press.

Introna, L., & Nissenbaum H. 2000. Shaping the Web: Why the Politics of Search Engines Matters. *Information Society* 16(3): 169–85.

Kitchin, R., & M. Dodge. 2014. *Code/Space: Software and Everyday Life*. Cambridge, MA: The MIT Press.

La Rue, F. 2013, April. "Report of the Special Rapporteur on the Promotion and Protection of the Right to Freedom of Opinion and Expression." Human Rights Council, United Nations. Retrieved from http://bit.ly/1OIqJna.

Lyon, D. 2003. "Surveillance and Social Sorting: Computer Codes and Mobile Bodies. In *Surveillance and Social Sorting: Privacy, Risk and Digital Discrimination*, edited by D. Lyon, 13–30. New York: Routledge.

Mackenzie, A. 2007. "Protocols and the Irreducible Traces of Embodiment: The Viterbi Algorithm and the Mosaic of Machine Time." In *24/7: Time and Temporality in the Network Society*, edited by R. Hassan & R. E. Purser, 89–108. Stanford, CA: Stanford University Press.

Manjoo, F. 2012, April. "The Morning after: What's Next for Facebook? Trying to Make Enough Money to Justify that $100 Billion Valuation." *Fast Company*: 222–23.

Mayer-Schönberger, V. & K. Cukier. 2013. *Big Data: A Revolution That Will Transform How We Live, Work, and Think*. Boston, MA: Houghton Mifflin Harcourt.

McChesney, R. 2007. *Communication Revolution: Critical Junctures and the Future of Media*. New York, NY: The New Press.

McStay, A. 2011. *The Mood of Information: A Critique of Online Behavioural Advertising*. New York, NY: Continuum.

McStay, A. (2013). *Creativity and advertising: Affect, events and process*. New York: Routledge.

Morozov, E. 2013. *To Save Everything, Click Here: The Folly of Technological Solutionism*. New York, NY: PublicAffairs.

Mosco, V. 2009. *The Political Economy of Communication* (2nd ed.). Thousand Oaks, CA: Sage Publications Ltd.

Nakamura, L. 2002. *Cybertypes: Race, Ethnicity, and Identity on the Internet*. New York, NY: Routledge.

Neff, G., & D. Nafus. 2016. *Self-Tracking*. Cambridge, MA: The MIT Press.

Nichols, W. 2013, March. "Advertising Analytics 2.0." *Harvard Business Review*. Retrieved from http://hbr.org/2013/03/advertising-analytics-20/.

Noelle-Neumann, E. 1974. "The Spiral of Silence: A Theory of Public Opinion." *Journal of Communication*, 24, 43–51.

Notess, G. R. 2012. "Searching in Disguise." *Online*, 26(1): 43–46.

Pariser, E. 2011. *The Filter Bubble: What the Internet is Hiding from You*. New York, NY: Penguin Press.

Peterson, T. 2012, October. "Another Agency Claims Facebook Changes." *Adweek*. Retrieved from: http://www.adweek.com/news/technology/another-agency-claims-facebook-algorithm-changes-144405.

Petronzio, M. 2014 April. How One Woman Hid Her Pregnancy from Big Data. *Mashable*. Retrieved from http://mashable.com/2014/04/26/big-data-pregnancy/#9YhK2nqpkaqP.

Pew Research Center. 2012a. *Social Network Sites and Politics*. Washington, D.C., Author. Retrieved from http://bit.ly/zrzR0q.

———. 2012b. *Search Engine Use 2012*. Retrieved from http://bit.ly/yj7QMP.

———. 2015. *American Attitudes About Privacy, Security, and Surveillance*. Washington, D.C. Retrieved from http://www.pewinternet.org/files/2015/05/Privacy-and-Security-Attitudes-5.19.15_FINAL.pdf.

Prosser, W. 1960. Privacy. *California Law Review* 48(3): 383–423.

Reidenberg, J. R. 2000. "Resolving Conflicting International Data Privacy Rules in Cyberspace. *Stanford Law Review* 52: 1315–71.

Rheingold, H. 2012. *Net Smart: How to Thrive Online*. Cambridge, MA: The MIT Press.

Schneier, B. 2015. *Data and Goliath: The Hidden Battles to Collect Your Data and Control Your World*. New York, NY: W. W. Norton & Company, Inc.

Simonite, T. 2012, June. "What Facebook Knows." *MIT Technology Review*. Retrieved from http://www.technologyreview.com/featuredstory/428150/what-facebook-knows/.

Solove, D. 2002, July. "Digital Dossiers and the Dissolution of Fourth Amendment Privacy." *Southern California Law Review* (75). Retrieved from http://www-bcf. usc.edu/~usclrev/pdf/075502.pdf.

Steiner, C. 2012. *Automate This: How Algorithms Came to Rule Our World*. New York, NY: The Penguin Group.

Sunstein, C. 2009. *Republic.com 2.0*. Princeton, NJ: Princeton University Press.

Sweeney, L. 2013. "Discrimination in Online Ads Delivery Study." Retrieved from http://dataprivacylab.org/projects/onlineads/1071-1.pdf.

Tavani, H. T. 2010. *Ethics and Technology: Controversies, Questions, and Strategies for Ethical Computing* (3rd ed.). Hoboken, NJ: John Wiley & Sons, Inc.

Terranova, T. 2000. "Free Labor: Producing Culture for the Digital Economy." *Social Text*, 18(63), 33–58.

———. 2004. *Network Culture: Politics for the Information Age*. London: Pluto Press.

Turow, J. 2006. "Cracking the Consumer Code: Advertisers, Anxiety, and Surveillance in the Digital Age." In *The New Politics of Surveillance and Visibility*, edited by K. D. Haggerty & R. V. Ericson, 279–307. Toronto, ON, Canada: University of Toronto Press.

———. 2011. *The Daily You: How the New Advertising Industry Is Defining Your Identity and Your Worth*. New Haven, CT: Yale University Press.

Universal Declaration of Human Rights, The. (1948). Retrieved from: http://www. un.org/en/documents/udhr.

Vaidhyathanan, S. 2012, April 17. Voting against the Algorithm. *Slate*. Retrieved from http://slate.me/IQpeF0.

van Dijck, J. 2009. "Users Like You: Theorizing Agency in User Generated Content." *Media, Culture, & Society*, 31(1): 41–58.

Wall, D. S. 2006. "Surveillant Internet Technologies and the Growth in Information Capitalism: Spams and Public Trust in the Information Society." In *The New Politics of Surveillance and Visibility*, edited by K. D. Haggerty & R. V. Ericson, 340–62. Toronto, ON, Canada: University of Toronto Press.

Wasco, J. & M. Erickson. 2009. The Political Economy of YouTube. In *The YouTube Reader*, edited by P. Snickars & P. Vonderau, 372–86. Stockholm, SW: National Library of Sweden.

Wasserman, T. 2011, January 31. "Facebook Ads Perform about Half as Well as Regular Banner Ads." *Mashable*. Retrieved from http://mashable.com/2011/01/31/facebook-half-click-throughs/.

Zuboff, S. 2015. "Big Other: Surveillance Capitalism and the Prospects of an Information Civilization." *Journal of Information and Technology* 30: 75–89. Retrieved from http://www.palgrave-journals.com/jit/journal/v30/n1/pdf/jit20155a.pdf.

Zuckerman, E. 2014, August. The Internet's Original Sin: It's Not Too Late to Ditch the Ad-Based Business Model and Build a Better Web. *The Atlantic*. Retrieved from http://www.theatlantic.com/technology/archive/2014/08/advertising-is-the-internets-original-sin/376041/.

Part III
Critical Textual Analysis

11 Signification Advertising and Its Evolution

Felip Vidal Auladell

This chapter addresses the concept of "signification advertising" (Caro 1993) in order to elaborate key developments in textual approaches to the critical study of advertising. In doing so, it also explores the implications of new advertising techniques and strategies that have changed brand-creation mechanisms by creating a consumption experience that is increasingly produced by consumers themselves. These new techniques and tools of advertising provide a brand with imaginary signification and a material representation of it in order to give it consistency and to make semiotic production invisible.

During the past two decades, brand advertising that creates consumption experiences has gradually developed through two stages. First, brands' goal was to offer simple and previously prepared consumption experiences ready to be consumed. More recently, however, Web 2.0 and big-data technologies have resulted in increased consumer involvement and content customization. As a result, consumers co-create their own consumption experience as brand partners who add value to brands and corporations.

Advertising and Semiotics

A key premise of a semiotic approach to advertising is that it is not simply an instrumental tool for enterprises and corporations but also an artifact in which economic, social, and cultural factors are interrelated (Williams 1980; Ewen 1991; Fowles 1996; Goldman 1992; Goldman and Papson 1996; 2011; Jhally 1987; Leiss, Kline and Jhally 1990; Twitchell 2005; Williamson 1978; Zukin 2005; Eguizábal 2007; 2009; Caro 2009; 2010). Thus, advertising is both an element of symbolic representation and a symptom of structural changes taking place in the means of social and cultural production. Advertising is thus an ideal text through which to study contemporary society. It helps construct and legitimize the ideology of consumption on which late capitalism (Jameson 1991) is largely based. It also expresses a key societal shift from the production of goods to the consumption of signs (Lash and Urry 1994).

To remain effective in the midst of this shift, advertising assists in the consumption of signs by creating an emotional bond between the brand and

the consumer. As many scholars have argued, when products are functionally identical, advertising must instead mine consumers' emotional experience as a source of imaginary content for promotion (Schmitt 1999; Pine
and Gilmore 1999; Rifkin 2001; Norman 2004; Gobé 2005; Roberts 2004;
Press and Cooper 2003; Lenderman 2006). When advertising is seen as the
semiotic production of brand imagery, its semiotic analysis reveals how
brands and their imaginary signification are built. Likewise, it also reveals
how, today, consumers are brand partners in co-creating advertising that is
participative and experience-oriented.

The value of semiotics for the critical analysis of advertising became clear
with the work of Barthes (1957, 1982). His approach combined linguistic
science with cultural criticism. As Rodríguez and Mora (2002, 23) put it,
advertising "became a scientific subject on which various analysis methods
are applied but also subject of a trenchant and devastating critique." The
French semiotic tradition following Barthes includes contributions by
Péninou, Baudrillard and Floch. Péninou (1972) sought to conceptualise
the functions of the advertising message (distinctive, predicate, and implicated function). According to this classification, a product becomes a unique
brand through advertising, differentiates itself from its rivals in the market,
and represents the brand positively. Baudrillard (1977) emphasized the signification process that takes place when the product-object is replaced by
the product-sign in the context of the current economic scenario in which
goods are produced as signs. Floch (1991) furthered this approach by showing the constructive nature of the signification processes that take place
when building brand imagery. Every discourse uses connotation to produce
a referential illusion, which correlates a brand as a particular type of sign
with reality. An advertisement does not represent reality so much as produce
a reality effect, thus emphasizing that semiosis is always a construction of
meaning, not a transparent reflection of reality. Goldman and Papson (1996,
2011) note similarly that advertisements are not information-delivery but
sign-creation processes. Equally significant contributions have emerged
from Latin America scholars such as de Morentin (1984), who pointed out
that the main task of advertising is to generate an enthusiasm for relating to
reality as well as to create a world in which products have a prominent role.

Signification Advertising

The function and focus of advertising has changed over the past few
decades, which means new mechanisms for the semiotic production of a
brand. In order to understand these mechanisms, it is necessary to consider these changes. According to Caro (1993, 92–96; 1994, 119–23),
a key distinction exists between referential advertising, which ascended in
the 19th century and industrial capitalism, and signification advertising,
which corresponds to commodity capitalism. This classification drew upon
a categorization by Ibáñez between structural advertising and referential

advertising (1994, 233–34). While referential advertising is essentially informative advertising that tries to convince and persuade the target audience of the superiority of the advertised product over the competition, signification advertising builds a brand and attributes to it the most appropriate meaning, which is why the semiotic production of a brand plays a key role.

This difference in turn means that advertising no longer is best seen as a problem of commerce or manufacture, but a problem of meaning. Eguizábal (2007, 129) notes as much by arguing that "the advertising process becomes a semiotic process in which objects are no longer attributed a meaning but given an outward appearance." In other words, the product is perceived as "the object representing the brand-sign" (Caro 1998, 685), which entails that "the nature of the brand as a sign depends less and less on the *reality* preceding the product" (Caro 1994, 142). Semiotic production consists of a "genuine" production that results in a self-referential semiotic entity. While the brand of the product is materialized, the product is set aside and vanishes. As Benjamin (2005, 681) points out, "any trace of production of the object of consumption must be removed, as if it had never been produced whatsoever." Consequently, the product becomes a tangible representation of the symbolic content attributed to the brand. Signification advertising conceives the product as a road or journey to emotions and experiences. Emotions have taken the role that was once occupied by utility. The consumption of a specific product provides consumers with experiences tht in turn help construct their identity. Signification advertising conveys and contains elements that allow some degree of self-construction of consumers' identities through experiences contained in brand imagery. More generally speaking, we are witnessing the development of a whole range of techniques, strategies, and tools that are symptomatic of a major transformation, creating a new way of understanding traditional advertising. Over the last 15 years, a new set of techniques, strategies, and tools help advertising remain effective even in the face of consumer criticism. These include branded content, buzz marketing, street marketing, viral marketing, guerrilla marketing, and increasingly interactive and dynamic POS displays, all of which have significant experiential dimensions.

These changes have in turn been brought about by a number of new conditions. The growing importance of branding due to the decline in functional differences between products requires advertising that creates a strong bond between consumers and the brand that will make them have unforgettable experiences (Gobe 2005; Roberts 2004; Schmitt 1999; Lenderman 2006). Neuromarketing has expanded (Lindström 2012) in order to address the increased interest in the attention economy (Davenport and Beck 2001). Increasing clutter requires advertisers to look for new forms of advertising that are more subtle (Bermejo 2013). The rise of Web 2.0 and social media has made advertising increasingly interactive and multidirectional, which means significant changes in the role of consumers, a development foreseen some decades ago (Toffler 1980). Finally, the emergence of big-data technologies helps effectively optimize decision making in organizations, especially when it comes to branding, marketing, and advertising strategies (Mayer-Schönberger and Cukier 2013; Schmarzo 2014).

Granting new tools and techniques, analysis of signification advertising requires attention to the semiotic production of brand imagery in new ways (Vidal 2016). The new social and technological conditions described above have resulted in new ways of engaging in the semiotic production of brand imagery that virtualizes and dematerializes brands. These new ways include a) the use of distinct media and/or interfaces that may or may not be used for advertising, b) the use of narrative, and c) the embodiment of the brand through consumer activity.

On the one hand, these new ways of building brand equity, that make possible signification advertising, go hand in hand with the *significatization* process of the economy (Caro 2009). This means that in the transition process from *referential* to *signification advertising*, at present advertising is mainly a tool to build increasingly virtual brands. On the other hand, as was noted above, during the last few years there has been an increase in the use of emotional and experiential elements in advertising. It is worth mentioning that this should not only be understood as a trend but also as a strategy in response to the dematerialization of products. These two developments come into relation in signification advertising, in which a brand seeks to become well defined, to materialize, to underscore its imaginary qualities, to be present, and to become a material entity through objects, different supports and spaces, narrative, and their consumers' activity.

These new ways of carrying out semiotic production occur first of all as a result of the need for giving brands consistency or some real qualities. If these were lacking, brands would run the risk of being seen as a pipe dream by the consumers, as something vague with only a fictitious nature. Second, these new ways of semiotic production hide the brand's constructed and fictional nature from consumers, thus making it invisible or self-evident. Doing so allows the building of a brand discourse that proves the authenticity of the consumption experience of brands, despite the aim of commercializing that experience.

In order to better understand these new ways of semiotic production, it is useful to look at the brands of Lego and Foscarini, which both exemplify the use of these new techniques. Key characteristics make them work well as examples. First of all, both brands attach great importance to the design of a product, i.e., to its formal layout and to how it is advertised at the point of sale. Second, storytelling is crucial for both brands. As a result, they give their stories narrative form through interviews with the designers, who explain the origin and creation of their product lines, and which are then distributed as videos on YouTube or on specific sections of their websites. Third, both brands encourage consumers to generate communicative content or to customize the product they are going to buy. To do so, for instance, consumers can use Lego's website to create what they call *custom toys* or Foscarini's *Do you light?* application.

Toward a New Consumption Experience

Advertising now faces a situation in which there are new means of communication that encourage and make easier consumers' active involvement in building both the consumption experience and the brand imagery, with this co-creation forming a key basis for value creation. Therefore, the brand collaborates with consumers to create value by extracting the economic value resulting from this collaboration (Prahalad and Ramaswamy 2004, 4). It is thus worth considering how consumers have become a key player in co-creating value in the new developments of signification advertising. Hence, as Ollé and Riu have pointed out, at present branding cannot only consist of "making an investment in time to create an intangible differentiation in the medium term" (2000, 163). On the contrary, it must allow consumers to contribute to the brand's meaning to allow the market to become a conversation between brands and consumers (Levine et al. 2000).

Thus, currently it is more and more common to find advertising campaigns in which multiple channels are simultaneously used and which pursue a high degree of interaction with their target audience using the multiple possibilities of brand equity co-creation (Sanders and Simons 2009). This strategy is what has given rise to the new ways of building brand equity described above, particularly the third one. Today, brands encourage consumers' participation through events, microsites, and social networks to create content and customize and even design products.

Examples of this trend include the latest mobile applications and the competitions for designing products organized by BMW co-creation Lab, and the experiences co-created by P&G Connect + Develop. These and similar examples show that both consumers' involvement in constructing the brand imagery and the intensification of the use of emotional and experiential elements in modern advertising are not superfluous but essential to the product, brand, and consumer. Consumers' involvement is in many ways ontological in consisting of a (sometimes) fictional co-creation of experiential authenticity as brand equity (Vidal 2013).

Guerrilla, event, and social marketing are also examples of this trend as they are part of a transmedia narrative universe that can be used to create a more coherent and expansive brand (Scolari 2013). Brand imagery is built through multiple channels that enrich each other. In addition, the hybridization of genres in such forms as branded content often makes it difficult for consumers to distinguish among advertising, entertainment, and information.

In this sense, brands adopt participatory culture practices (Jenkins 2008), which are used to obtain content from "groups of consumers with a common interest" (Van Dijk 2011, 45–46). One can distinguish between creators who are active and provide brands with valuable content and the rest of the users, who are more passive. Nevertheless, in both cases the aim is to create in consumers an emotional investment in the brand, which implies a profound change in the way consumption is perceived (Potts et al. 2008).

Consumers and Emotional Investment

Bearing in mind all these considerations, it could be stated that value creation has shifted from the product to the brand and from the brand to the customization of the consumption experience. Consequently, user-generated content (UGC) can be seen as one instance of self-made media, which is necessary for enabling consumers' creation of value through co-creation.

As has been noted, in referential advertising, brands used to reflect and support their products, and a product was represented by its brand. However, that is not the case today, as signification advertising means that brands project not only their image but also our own. This means that brands must show, make visible, and ultimately represent consumers—or, more specifically, being represented by consumers—as many examples from current advertising show. For instance, Twitchell (2005) notes in a recent Levi's campaign that the brand does not represent a product and its effects on consumers, but consumers are represented in the brand through a product that distinguishes them. The aim is therefore to use emotional arguments and attributes so that consumers identify themselves with the brand and experientially invest themselves in the brand through its imagery.

The emotional investment achieved through advertising differs from the idea that mass consumption is ruled exclusively by the classic process of distinguishing and differentiating products by referring to their unique features. Although it is true that the products consumed are social signifiers and a sign of social aspiration, consumption has become more and more related to the individual autonomy and even to the construction of identity. Hence, it seems that the contributions of Veblen (1971) and Bourdieu (1991) via their models based on stratification and distinction do not exhaust all the possibilities of this field of analysis. On the contrary, they open the door to new models that develop concepts such as emotional experience (Maffesolí 1990).

In any case, technological advances have made it possible for consumers to not only become the target audience of advertising campaigns, but to get involved in them and to co-create with them through user-generated content and interactive microsites. These and other techniques are used to make consumers become actively involved in building brand discourse and sometimes also in creating the product they will buy afterwards. However, the use of Web 2.0 does not guarantee that the participation of consumers creates brand value and equity. Brands thus need to make sure they have the right tools to transform consumers' involvement into brand equity.

However, consumer involvement is far from certain. As noted earlier, when a brand launches a campaign that includes Web 2.0 tools, most consumers do not take part in the communities created for that campaign nor do they generate content, which shows in turn that not all activity on Web 2.0 results in the real involvement of consumers (Deuze 2008). This situation poses two questions: What is the actual scope of Web 2.0 tools? And, can one guarantee that the use of Web 2.0 tools in campaigns results in an effective and significant contribution toward building brand imagery?

Despite few users in a target market actually participating and creating content, the originality and effectiveness of the tools and strategies these websites use does not rest on the massive involvement of users in advertising campaigns but in the co-creation of a discourse on experiential authenticity as part of brand equity. Therefore, success is not determined by how many people participate so much as it is to promote the participation of few consumers who resemble the brand's target audience, some of whom are sometimes chosen by the brand itself.

In doing so, the aim is to achieve both the embodiment of the brand and customers' identification with the brand. But this takes place both directly, with some consumer co-creation, and indirectly with the rest of the target market experiencing others' co-creation. A kind of fictional co-creation of the experiential authenticity comes to stand for brand equity. Its effectiveness does not depend on direct participation as much as on the creation of a discourse about the above-mentioned authenticity. In this sense, it is possible to argue that the advertising tools provided by Web 2.0 and big data form a second stage in the process of brand experience creation and that, as a result, they contribute to an increased use of emotional and/or experiential elements in advertising.

From the Emotion-Brand to Big Data

The emergence of big data has brought about an evolution in the historical development of the representative function of the brand, with brands not representing the advertised product as much as the consumer who purchases it. This is now more possible than ever due to big data's allowing brands to make more accurate predictions, improve their own decision-making processes, and form new brand experiences by taking into account the data consumers have provided based on their own consumption experiences.

The first step in the evolution in the brand experience has been the formation of an emotional relationship or a memorable experience that would make the product be perceived as functionally useful (Schmitt, Rogers and Vrotsos 2004; Michelli 2007). During the past decade, extensive literature on branding and experiential marketing has stressed that consumption—and not solely agency-driven strategic planning—should create this relationship.

The second step in this evolution has been via Web 2.0 the closer relation of the consumer experience with the consumer identity. Interaction and participation made possible by social media tools developed from Web 2.0 have been amplified further with the emergence of big data, which in turn expands the forms of traditional marketing. The collection and analysis of Google searches, Facebook posts, Twitter messages, shopping reviews and opinions, navigation routes, participation rates in sites, and the customization of products and services allow increasingly personalized promotions. To make them even more powerful, these technologies have been gradually integrated into many types of media, supports, and forms of advertising. Screens have been integrated outdoors (Schaeffler 2008; Keslen 2010) and have become mobile devices.

The digitalization of advertising through digitization and big data has thus resulted in its redefinition. The information provided by big data allows: a) an intensification of the use of emotional elements in building brand imagery that had already been observed in the first stage of experience creation, b) an expansion in the constructed nature of the consumer identity based on consumption experience, and c) an elaboration of the possibilities for even greater interaction and consumer involvement.

This situation represents a challenge for advertising. Increased client demands for greater cost effectiveness and ROI requires that agencies delve more deeply into the tools and possibilities available through Web 2.0. Consumer interaction through social networks, augmented reality, information coming from big data, and increasingly interactive POS displays represent the most appropriate tools to counterbalance comparatively higher costs of traditional media. At the same time, big data from such sites as mobile phones, GPS, social networks, and the participation in websites provide a great amount of information generated by consumption experiences.

Not only does the use of big data address the economics of advertising. It also provides information that can be used to consider new techniques and strategies for offering new consumer experiences and, through them, constructing consumers' identities. This capability is a milestone in the evolution of the production/consumption conditions, because it poses many questions about its possibilities at the same time as it highlights the need for a new strategic approach by agencies. How consumer experiences are valued in branding is changing, due to big data and new tools, which offer greater interactivity and consumer information.

The usefulness of Web 2.0 tools and big data contributes to yet another key development, which is the increased ability of consumers to contribute to building advertising discourse and brand imagery. At the same time, consumers are more able to examine the production of their own consumption experiences by defining consumption as self-discovery and emphasizing the constructive nature of consumers' identities. For these reasons, consumers can be regarded as brand "partners" working in concert with advertisers instead of autonomous "prosumers" (Denison 2011) who create entirely separately and independently from advertisers. Indeed, understanding them as partners allows a more incisive analysis of the current practices of building brand imagery and creating consumption experience. The notion of consumer as a brand partner is more useful than that of prosumer as suggested by Toffler (1980) in describing the current situation. A partner differs from a prosumer given the fact that it allows an analysis of techniques and instruments on which advertising is based in a relational, existential, and non-essentialist point of view. What's more, consumer involvement as brand partner has now expanded to many fields and activities that not only inform consumers but also promote their participation in events, microsites, or social networks in order to create content, representing something more than a process of "self-discovery" (Campbell 2004, 35) or acknowledgment. It is best understood as identity construction, without which consumers would not effectively adhere to brand imagery.

Ultimately, it is very important to understand this update of advertising as part of the context of a new stage of development of capitalism and as a result of the logic of the economic system in the process toward an experience economy (Pine and Gilmore 1999), one of whose best-known manifestations can be obversed in experiential marketing (Schmitt 1999; 2004). Developments such as these cause our very existence to be commercialized.

Conclusions

As has been discussed here, consumers are not simply the recipients of advertising campaigns anymore. They have become the co-creators of their own consumption experience, through which they create added value for brands and corporations. On this basis, one could argue that the constructive nature characteristic of discovering one's self through consumption has been made possible by new and powerful tools that allow consumers to become brand partners. In doing so, the techniques and tools discussed above and that make up an increasing part of advertising today may continue to make prosumers obsolete. This is because the concept of prosumer is strongly related to Web 2.0 tools, but it could become less relevant in a context in which big data have taken the leading role. On the other hand, when considering the co-creation of consumer experiences, the developments noted in this chapter could open the door to considering consumers' own activity as the key source for effective advertising discourse in the form of signification advertising. In any case, these new developments intensify the use of emotional elements in building brand imagery that had been observed in the first stage of experience creation, while also expanding the constructed nature of the consumer identity based on the consumption experience.

Finally, from the existential, constructive, non-essentialist, and ontological point of view that corresponds—as has already been shown in different sections—to the signification processes taking place in the context of an updated semiotic production of the brand during the second stage of the notion of experience as brand equity, consumption would have to be considered beyond an operation of simple identification. Therefore, first, it would be necessary to note how consumers' emotional ties to the brand imaginary takes place through an imaginative activity that promotes and stimulates consumers' own creative activity. And, second, one must also note ways in which such activity constitutes a step forward in the evolution of the representative function of the brand, which continues to shift from agency to consumer.

References

Barthes, Roland. 1957. *Mythologies*, Paris, Éditions du Seuil.

———. 1982. *L'Obvie et l'Obtus*. Paris: Éditions du Seuil.

Baudrillard, Jean. 1977. *Pour une critique de l'économie politique du signe*. Paris: Gallimard.

Benjamin, Walter. 2005. *Libro de los pasajes*. Madrid: Akal.

Bermejo, Jesús. 2013. "Nuevas estrategias retóricas en la sociedad de la neopublicidad." *Icono 14. Revista de comunicación y tecnologías emergentes* 11(1): 99–124.

Bourdieu, Pierre. 1991. *La distinction*. Madrid: Taurus.

Campbell, Colin. 2004. "I Shop Therefore I Know that I Am: The Metaphysical Basis of Modern Consumerism." In *Elusive Consumption*, edited by K. M. Ekström and H. Brembeck, 27–44. New York: Berg.

Caro, Antonio. 1993. *La publicidad de la significación (marco, concepto y taxonomía)*, Madrid: Servicio de Publicaciones de la Universidad Complutense de Madrid.

———. 1994. *La publicidad que vivimos*. Madrid: Celeste Eresma.

———. 1998. "La marca como mito" In *Mitos*, edited by T. Blesa, 683–89. Actas del VII Congreso Internacional de la Academia Española de Semiótica, Tomo I, Asociación Española de Semiótica y Universidad de Zaragoza.

———, ed. 2009. *De la mercancía al signo/mercancía. El capitalismo en la era del hiperconsumismo y del desquiciamiento financiero*. Madrid: UCM.

———. 2010. *Comprender la publicidad*. Barcelona: Universitat Ramon Llull.

Davenport, T. H. and J. C. Beck. 2001. *The Attention Economy. Understanding the New Currency of Business*. Boston: Harvard Business School.

Denison, R. 2011. "Anime Fandom and the Liminal Spaces between Fan Creativity and Piracy." *International Journal of Cultural Studies* 14(5): 449–66.

Deuze, Mark. 2008. "Corporate Appropriation of Participatory Culture". In *Participation and Media Production: Critical Reflections on Content Creation*, edited by Nico Carpentier and Sonia Livingston, 27–40. Newcastle upon Tyne: Cambridge Scholars Publishers.

Eguizábal, Raúl. 2007. *Teoría de la publicidad*. Madrid: Cátedra.

———. 2009. *Industrias de la conciencia*. Barcelona: Península.

Ewen, Stuart. 1991. *Todas las imágenes del consumo*. México: Grijalbo.

Floch, Jean-Marie. 1990. *Sémiotique, marketing et communication*. Paris: Presses Universitaires de France.

Fowles, J. 1996. *Advertising and Popular Culture*. London: Sage.

Gobé, Marc. 2005. *Branding emocional*. Barcelona: Divine Egg.

Goldman, Robert. 1992. *Reading Ads Socially*. London: Routledge.

Goldman, R. y S. Papson. 1996. *Sign Wars. The Cluttered Landscape of Advertising*, New York, The Gilford Press.

———. 2011. *Landscapes of Capital. Representing Time, Space, and Globalization in Corporate Advertising*. Cambridge: Polity Press.

Ibáñez, Jesús. 1994. *Por una sociología de la vida cotidiana*, Madrid: Siglo XXI.

Jameson, Fredric. 1991. *Postmodernism; or the Cultural Logic of Late Capitalism*. Durham: Duke University Press.

Jenkins, Henry. 2008. *Convergence Culture. La cultura de la convergencia de los medios de comunicación*. Barcelona: Paidós.

Jhally, Sut. 1987. *The Codes of Advertising*. London: Routledge.

Keslen, Keith. 2010. *Unleashing the Power of Digital Signage. Content Strategies for the 5th Screen*. Burlington: Focal Press.

Lash, S., and J. Urry. 1994. *Economies of Signs and Space*. London: SAGE.

Leiss, W. Kline, S. and Jhally, S. *Social Communication in Advertising. Persons, Products and Images of Well-Being*, Ontario, Nelson Canada, 1990.

Lenderman, M. 2006. *Experience the Message. How Experiential Marketing Is Changing the Brand World*. New York: Carroll & Graf Publishers.

Levine et al. 2000. *Cluetrain Manifesto*. Deusto: Barcelona.

Lindström, M. 2012. *Buyology. Verdades y mentiras de por qué compramos*. Barcelona, Booket.

Maffesolí, M. 1990. *Los tiempos de las tribus*. Barcelona: Icaria.

Magariños de Morentin, J. A. *1984. El mensaje publicitario*. Buenos Aires: Hachete.

Mayer-Schönberger, V. and Kenneth Cukier. 2013. *Big Data: A Revolution That Will Transform How We Live. Work and Think*. London: John Murray.

Michelli, J. A. 2007. *La experiencia Starbucks. 5 principios para convertir lo ordinario en extraordinario*. Barcelona: Granica.

Norman, Donald A. 2004. *Emotional Design*. New York: Basic Books.

Ollé R. and D. Riu. 2000, 2009. *El nuevo Brand Management. Cómo plantar marcas para hacer crecer negocios*. Barcelona: Gestión.

Péninou, G. 1972. *Intelligence de la publicité*. Paris: Laffont.

Pine, B. J. and J. H. Gilmore. 1999. *The Experience Economy*. Boston: Harvard Business School Press.

Prahalad, C. K. and V. Ramaswamy. 2004. "Co-Creation Experiences: The Next Practice in Value Creation." *Journal of Interactive Marketing* 18(3): 5–14.

Press, Mike, and Rachel Cooper. 2003. *The Design Experience*. Burlington: Ashgate.

Potts, J. et al. 2008. "Consumer Co-Creation and Situated Creativity." *Industry and Innovation* 15(5): 459–74.

Rifkin, Jeremy. 2001. The Age of Access. Los Angeles: Tarcher.

Roberts, K. 2004. *Lovemarks*. New York: PowerHouse Books.

Rodríguez, R. et K. Mora. 2002. *Frankenstein y el cirujano plástico. Una guía multimedia de semiótica de la publicidad*. Alicante: Universidad de Alicante.

Sanders L. and G. Simons. 2009. "A Social Vision for Value Co-creation in Design." *Open Source Business Resource*. http://timreview.ca/article/310 [Access: 30/10/2015].

Schaeffler, J. 2008. *Digital Signage. Software, Networks, Advertising and Displays. A Primer for Understanding the Business*. Burlington: Focal Press.

Schmarzo, B. 2014. *Big Data. El poder de los datos*. Madrid: Anaya.

Schmitt, B. H. 1999. *Experiential Marketing*. New York: The Free Press.

Schmitt, B.H., D. L. Rogers, y K. Vrotsos. 2004. *There's No Business That's Not Show Business. Marketing in an Experience Culture*. Upper Saddle River, NJ: Financial Times Prentice Hall.

Scolari, C. A. 2013. *Narrativas transmedia. Cuando todos los medios cuentan*. Barcelona: Deusto.

Toffler, Alvin. 1980. *La tercera ola*. Bogotá, Plaza y Janés.

Twitchell, J. B. 2005. *Branded Nation*. New York: Simon & Schuster.

Van Dijk, J. 2009. "Users Like You? Theorizing Agency in User-Generated Content." *Media, Culture & Society* 31(1): 41–58.

Veblen, T. *Teoría de la clase ociosa*, México, Fondo de Cultura Económic, 1974.

Vidal, Felip. "La (co) creación ficcional de la autenticidad vivencial como valor de marca en la Web 2.0: el caso *Bench*", Klaus, Z., Cuenca, J. and Rom, J. (eds.)

Breaking the Media Value Chain, Barcelona, Universidad Ramon Llull, 2013, 283–292.

Vidal, Felip. "Media and the Creation of Brand Value in "Signification Advertising": Defining a Model and Case Studies: Muji, Moleskine, Bench". Klaus, Z. et Cuenca, J. *Media Business Models: Breaking the Traditional Value Chain*, Peter Lang, New York (in print), 2016.

Williams, R. "Advertising: The magic system". *Problems in Materialism and Culture*, London, Verso, 1980, 170–195.

Williamson, J. *Decoding Advertisements*, London, Marion Boyards, 1978.

Zukin, S. *Point of Purchase. How Shopping Changed American Culture*, New York, Routledge, 2005.

12 Advertising and Photography in a Culture of Photo Sharing

Iben Bredahl Jessen

Photography is a dominant mode of communication in advertising. Since photographs in advertisements became widespread in illustrated papers and magazines between 1920 and 1930 (cf. Johnston 2005; Ramamurthy 2009), photographic images of products, persons, and settings have complemented the written word as persuasive means in different formats of advertising (see for example Leiss et al. 2005). In digital media, social software facilitates new ways of communicating by means of photographs that have become popular not only among individual users, but also among companies to advertise products and brands. Photo sharing platforms and features such as liking and hashtagging allow marketers to use photos to connect with consumers and to involve consumers' photos in advertising campaigns, for example by arranging photo contests or by promoting hashtags with brand names or slogans to be connected with consumers' photos. In these ways, photo-sharing platforms suggest new kinds of photographic practices and photographic images in advertising.

Accordingly, this chapter addresses how to understand advertising photography in the wake of a culture of photo sharing. It approaches doing so by reassessing theoretical standpoints to the advertising photograph within text-oriented, interpretative research traditions. The first part of the chapter reviews prevailing understandings of the advertising photograph and how it creates meaning. Attention is given to Barthes's analysis of the photographic message in advertising as a means of reflecting on the status of the advertising photograph and the photographic medium more broadly (Barthes 1997b), Scott's critique of the natural visual sign (Scott 1994), Goffman's analysis of gender display in advertising photographs (Goffman 1987), Messaris's analysis of semantic properties in advertising imagery (Messaris 1997), and Pateman's suggestion of a pragmatic perspective in understanding advertisements (Pateman 1983). These perspectives help illuminate important aspects of the advertising photograph in a context of photo sharing culture. Following this theoretical discussion, the chapter then discusses new kinds of photographic images and photographic practices in advertising with the example of the mobile photo sharing application Instagram. Upon considering functions of hashtagging, the chapter suggests a broadened definition of the advertising photograph and discusses its implications for critical analyses of advertising photography.

Understanding Advertising Photographs

Advertising photographs are commercial images aimed at a public audience with the purpose of promoting products, services, or brands (cf. Goffman 1987, 10). This definition points to advertising photography as a distinct sub-category of photographic images. They differ from images belonging to categories such as art photography, press photography, or amateur snapshot photography, yet at the same time may share features of these as well as those of other kinds of images. In that connection, advertising photography has been characterized as parasitic (Ramamurthy 2009, 217)—not in a negative sense, but as a communicative practice that draws on conventions from a variety of cultural resources (see also Cook 2001). This makes it difficult to differentiate advertising photographs from other categories of photographic images simply on the basis of appearance or formal characteristics. Instead, advertising photographs are better identified at the level of role and function. The accompanying components in the advertising text—mainly caption and logo or brand name—as well as the context assist in identifying photographs as *advertising* photographs. More generally, recognizing advertising texts has been argued to be dependent on our knowledge and expectations of this specific communicative practice (Nöth 1987; Pateman 1983).

The relational constitution of advertising photographs raises important issues. In Barthes's essay *Rhetoric of the Image*, the signification of the advertising image is underscored as highly intentional and "formed with a view to the optimum reading" (1977, 33). This characterization points to a fundamental debate about the meaning of the advertising photograph and how it can be claimed to convey messages. First, and as already noted, advertising photographs are determined by relationships to other elements. For example, accompanying text points out specific meanings in the advertising photograph, which—in Barthes's characterization—is otherwise "polysemous" (1977b, 39). Inspired by ideas from structural linguistics, Barthes describes signs in the image as unstable, which makes the meaning of the image difficult to determine. Moreover, in contrast to the linear structure of language, there is no particular order or accepted syntax with which to "read" an image. Given this instability, Barthes emphasizes the importance of text as a means of specifying the meaning of the signifiers in the image, with "anchorage" and "relay" as two distinctive functions of the linguistic message to accomplish this (1977b, 38–39). Where relay is defined as a complementary relationship between the linguistic message and the image (Barthes 1977b, 41), anchorage works on a denotative as well as a connotative level of meaning, linguistic messages can either point out or identify elements in the image (denotation) or they can guide the reader's interpretation of the image (connotation). In this way, Barthes argues, the function of anchorage is ideological, since it directs the reader to pay attention to some meanings and overlook or discount others (1997b, 40).

However, others are more pessimistic. A critical contrast to Barthes's somewhat optimistic view of text as capable of fixing the meaning of the image is Pateman's (1983) pragmatic or contextual perspective in the analysis of advertisements. When considering the relation between the written word and the image, Pateman argues that "verbal messages are neither necessary nor sufficient to achieve disambiguation" (1983, 197). The point here is that the meaning of the advertising text cannot be determined solely by the structural relationships in "the text itself" (see also Slater 1983). Rather, the meaning of an advertisement must be considered in relation to the various kinds of pragmatic knowledge needed to understand the advertisement, for example: "pragmatic knowledge about texts in general and advertisements in particular" (Pateman 1983, 194). In this connection, Pateman even suggests that the function of anchorage is an illusion: "the 'anchorage' is only of use to those who know how to anchor" (1983, 194).

In addition to questions about relations between photographs and text, others exist regarding the advertising photograph in isolation and how it can be claimed to convey messages. For these questions, the discussion of the photographic "code" and the role of the photographic medium itself become central. In contrast to the digital code of language, which is based on double articulation, Barthes considers the "coding" of the photograph as analogical (1977b, 32). In other words and following Barthes, the photograph is seen to "re-present" or imitate reality by means of non-arbitrary signs. The relation between signifier and signified is regarded as motivated due to the nearly "accurate" mechanical reproduction of reality provided by the photographic medium. This does not mean that the photograph is—or is like—reality (Barthes has elsewhere emphasized the photograph as a "perfect *analogon*," see 1977a, 17, emphasis in original), or that the photograph is not arranged or staged in any way. However, compared to the combinatory logic of language, Barthes asserts a principal non-coded iconic nature of the photographic image (1977b, 36).

Accordingly, photographs are argued to have a denoted, literal meaning based on a non-coded message, while aspects such as framing and style reside to connotation (Barthes 1977b, 44).[1] At the same time, Barthes points to this understanding as an analytical construct, which even includes a paradox. On the one hand, the "reading" of the denoted photographic message involves knowledge connected to our perception of the world (Barthes 1977b, 36). This relates to our ability to identify basic visual elements in the photograph. On the other hand, Barthes argues, the denoted, literal message cannot be read without the connoted, symbolic (and hence coded) message. In fact, the two levels of meaning are read simultaneously, and their separation is utopian; a pure literal message does not exist (Barthes 1977b, 42). This paradox makes it difficult even to define the literal message, and according to Barthes, "the characteristic of the literal message cannot be substantial but only relational" (1977b, 42). Consequently, reading an advertising photograph requires an investment of knowledge on both levels of meaning, which include cultural (and other kinds of) knowledge (Barthes 1997b, 46).

The conception of analogical representation and the idea of a non-coded iconic message have been criticized within semiotic research (see for example Eco 1979, 191) as well as from other sides. In relation to the advertising photograph, Scott emphasizes the photographic medium enabled by the camera as inherently biased and irredeemably cultural: "We must learn to understand cameras not as machines that record the world as it is (or even as we see it) but as machines designed to represent the world in the manner we have learned to *show* it" (1994, 261, emphasis in original). In this respect, advertising photographs cannot be regarded as analogical representations, but rather as symbolic constructs based on cultural conventions (Scott 1994, 252). To the extent that this standpoint suggests a critique of Barthes's conception of analogical representation—Scott refers to a long tradition of "copy theory" in western culture; a critique of Barthes is implied (see Scott 1994, 259)—the idea of the photographic paradox seems not to be embraced. However, Scott's definition of the visual symbol as "denotation by agreement or convention, a sign produced by culture, not nature" (1994, 263) in many ways resembles Barthes's description of the photographic paradox (see also Barthes 1977a, 19). As mentioned, Barthes acknowledges the cultural framing of the utopian, literal message. However, what Barthes perhaps overlooks—and that Scott wisely points to when calling for an understanding of "the camera"—is a conception of the photographic medium *as medium*, neither neutral nor objective.

Similar considerations of the importance of recognizing the photographic medium as a medium are implicitly present in Goffman's (1987) discussion of the relation between the photographic picture and what he—with reference to his theatrical metaphor (see Goffman 1959)—calls a "real-life scene." Photographs are not neutral, because the human vision of a real-life scene and the mechanical reproduction of the camera are qualitatively different processes (Goffman 1987, 12). Furthermore, Goffman points to a confusion often connected to the photograph, namely that what the image is a "subject of" and the material "model of" the photograph are easily mistaken (1987, 13).

A more explicit consideration of the medium is present in Messaris's (1997) study of advertising imagery, which also suggests a different approach to the iconic. Drawing on the general semiotics of Peirce, Messaris considers the semantics of the advertising image in terms of iconicity and indexicality (cf. Peirce 1978). While the iconic quality of the advertising image is established by the sign representing its object on the basis of likeness or analogy, iconicity can also be established through more abstract means by showing, for example, structural resemblance (Messaris 1997, ix). On the one hand, Messaris emphasizes the incapability of photographs for reproducing three-dimensional space of reality (see also Eco 1979, 193; Goffman 1987, 12; Scott 1994, 260–61). However, on the other hand, this lack of "perfect analogical representation" (cf. Barthes above) does not make the idea of iconicity irrelevant. Based on insights from cognitive psychology, Messaris argues that "even a very rudimentary match between image and reality (e.g., a simple sketch or a stick figure) is enough for the brain to be able to employ its real-world processes of visual interpretation" (1997, ix). In this way, iconicity is a quality related to various categories of images that can be used in advertising to create attention and evoke emotions (Messaris 1997, 4).

Messaris's and others' comments about the more abstract nature of iconicity raises yet more substantial issues by suggesting how attention paid to the non-coded iconic nature of photographs may be misplaced altogether. Perhaps what differentiates the photograph from other categories of images is not so much its iconic quality but, more precisely, the indexical quality of the medium. As pointed out by Goffman, the photograph needs a material "model," of which the photograph is a "model" (1987, 13). In terms of Peirce's index, the mechanical reproduction of the model by the photographic medium can be regarded as a trace or imprint (Messaris 1997, x). A similar point is made in Berger's description of the photograph as an actual trace of its subject to which it directly *"belongs"* (2013, 63).[2] Although this trace does not imply any direct correspondence to the represented object (cf. smoke is not the same as fire), the photographical index is closely related to the myth of the photograph as proof or evidence that often comes into play in advertising imagery (Messaris 1997, 130).

Speaking more generally, the iconic and indexical qualities of the advertising photograph can be argued to be connected to (or confused with) the idea of the photograph as an expression (or subject) *of* something in the social world (cf. Goffman, mentioned above). For Barthes, the reading of an advertising photograph as an expression of something is explained through the structural mechanisms of signification. According to Barthes, the photographic paradox comprises a connection between "spatial immediacy and temporal anteriority," which implies a sense of *"having-been-there"* (1977b, 44, emphasis in original). An important point in relation to this simultaneous "real" and "unreal" character of the photograph is the working of the denoted/connoted message in order to produce "natural" meanings on the basis of what is in fact constructed. Barthes holds that the literal, denoted message *naturalizes* the connoted, symbolic message (1977b, 45) and that this structural relationship becomes an ingredient in the production of ideology. Ideology here refers to the "common domain of the signifieds of connotation" (Barthes 1977b, 49), which again are related to so-called "connotators," which Barthes explains as the "signifiers of connotation" (1977b, 49). When Barthes—as in the title of his essay—refers to a *rhetoric* of the photographic image, he is pointing to these "connotators" as the "signifying aspect of ideology" (1977b, 49). In structural terms, Barthes describes the rhetoric of the photographic image according to the paradigmatic relation of connotation and the syntagmatic relation of denotation that, due to the non-coded, literal message, makes meaning seem "real" or "natural" (1977b, 51).

At the same time, Barthes calls for further effort to produce a metalanguage to describe this rhetoric, with contributions by classical rhetorical figures proposed as a field to be explored in relation to images (1977b, 50). While this challenge has received much attention within advertising research, visual rhetoric has been studied with different accentuations on representation and persuasion. With examples of advertising images, Durand (1970) takes up Barthes's idea for creating a general classification of figures based on type of rhetorical operation (addition, suppression, substitution, exchange) and type of relation between elements in the image (identity, similarity, difference, opposition) (see also Durand 1987). Here the structural system of signification is explained as a formal repertoire of "creative methods" used in advertising images (Durand 1970, 91), including figures such as comparison, hyperbole, metaphor, metonymy, etc. Other approaches with focus on a "rhetoric of the advertising image" have stressed the rhetorical operations in a consumer perspective and how figural constructions of the advertising image may be connected to consumer processing and response (McQuarrie and Mick 2003; Phillips and McQuarrie 2004). In this line of research, textual and cognitive aspects related to the advertising image are combined. However, the interest in the rhetorical is not oriented toward the advertising image as an expression *of* something (for example, in terms of ideological functions), but focuses instead on the links between visual structure and affect. Such a perspective can be connected to Scott's accentuation of the rhetorical as a matter of persuasion, not representation (1994, 260).

Goffman's analysis of gender display in advertisements in relation to the conception of the advertising photograph as an expression of social matters seems to be articulated somewhere in between representation and persuasion. The connection of the advertising photograph to a "real-life scene" is, as has been mentioned above, not conceived as a straightforward relation, but as a "hyper-ritualization" of social behavior (1987, 84). Advertising photographs do not represent actual gender behavior but rather "advertisers' view of how woman can be profitably pictured" (Goffman 1987, 25). Advertisers employ various visual methods to simulate real-life scenes but, according to Goffman, to do so they draw on ritualized patterns of actual gender expressions that are themselves artificial (1987, 27). Goffman even concludes that social performance *is* a commercial: "Whether we pose for a picture or execute an actual ritual action, what we are presenting is a commercial, an ideal representation under the auspices of its characterizing the way things really are" (1987, 84). This understanding is related to Goffman's theory of display and self-presentation, which—following the proposed metaphor of "the commercial"—is stated to (also) follow a logic of advertising. In this view and broadly speaking, we present or "advertise" ourselves in the best and most convincing ways in order to be read "optimally."

New Kinds of Photographic Images and Photographic Practices in Advertising

Granting the value of this work, theoretical perspectives on the pre-digital, pre-social advertising photograph have begun to be challenged by the emergence of online photo sharing culture. Developments in camera equipment and new ways of producing, storing, and sharing photographs have altered the ways people use photography in everyday life. For example, the mobile camera phone (Gye 2007) is always at hand to document everyday experiences. Online photo sharing platforms have broadened the reach and audience of photographs previously conceived as private pictures, which mostly were shown to family and friends inside the home (Berger 2013, 63; Chalfen 1987, 8; Goffman 1987, 10). Photographs are still used to preserve memory of the past and communicate with and present oneself to others, but such practices are emerging in altered forms (Van Dijck 2008; Van House 2011). For example, compared with Barthes's understanding of the photograph as an expression of "having-been-there" (see above), photography is now (also) used to communicate experiences "here-and-now" (Van Dijck 2008, 62; Gye 2007, 285). Moreover, we are witnessing new kinds of photographic trends such as selfies (Rettberg 2014) and pictures of the mundane, such as the food on one's dinner plate (Murray 2008).

As a key photo-sharing platform, Instagram invites individual users as well as brands to create an account and communicate with other users by sharing photos and other visual content such as videos. It is used by marketers to distribute what can be considered as advertising photographs.[3] As a key difference to pre-digital advertising photography, the ability to add searchable metadata to a photo challenges theorizations of the photos as "advertising photographs" in a traditional sense as consisting of clearly defined and isolated text elements. Corresponding with the above-mentioned use of photography to communicate experience "here-and-now," Instagram describes the platform as a way to "experience moments in your friends' lives through pictures as they happen" (Instagram 2016a). To commercial users, Instagram is promoted as a platform to "Inspire People Visually with Your Business' Story" (Instagram 2016b). Furthermore, in Instagram's tips for getting started, commercial users are urged to use their account to engage with their community by using available tagging functions that elaborate if not complicate pre-digital notions such as anchorage: "Engage with comments and questions on your own posts and use hashtags, location tags and Photos of You to discover and join the conversation on other community members' posts about your brand" (Instagram 2016c).

On the one hand, photos posted by commercial users on Instagram conform to prevailing definitions of advertising photographs as a category of commercial images (cf. Goffman 1987, 10). Accordingly, even if such photos appear different than photographs in printed advertisements (an important area for future scholarly research), the commercial interest related to such photos at least becomes visible by the surrounding brand name or logo connected to the advertiser's account. On the other hand, the function of hashtagging challenges the definition of advertising photographs as (only) commercial images. The promotion of brand-related hashtags encourages users to hashtag their own photos with, for example, a brand name or a campaign slogan, potentially producing heterogeneous aggregates of brand-related content that also operate in relation to the advertising text. However, if connected consumer photos are regarded as part of the advertising text, they are perhaps not as easily recognized *as advertising* as presumed by Pateman (1983) and Nöth (1987). For example, a consumer photo could appear as a personal snapshot—a category of private pictures usually described as requiring some kind of knowledge available to the portrayed and/or to the photographer (Berger 2013, 63; Goffman 1987, 17). While this point argues in one sense against embracing consumers' photos as part of the advertising text, doing so would neglect otherwise important functional conditions of the photo-sharing platform and neglect the platform as an environment in which genre boundaries may seem less clear, for example as regards the distinction between private and public pictures (Goffman 1987, 10). Furthermore, the inclusion of consumer photos as part of the advertising text challenges Barthes's description of the advertising photograph as highly intentional and "formed with a view to the optimum reading" (1977b, 33). In fact, consumers' photos may potentially blur, distort, or even contradict what can be considered as the intended meaning of the photograph or the "campaign idea."

Photo sharing on Instagram and the invitation to commercial users to "join the conversation" with other users' photos about their brands (cf. Instagram 2016c) is only one of many examples of the importance of the debate about the meaning of the advertising photograph. First, shared photos need to be recognized as a particular category of images, namely *digital* photographs. Although realistic (or "analogical") in appearance, the digital photograph is articulated on the basis of a coded system (binary coding), which makes editing and manipulation possible on the levels of camera equipment, storage medium, and distribution platform—which, in the case of Instagram, are integrated in the same device, the mobile camera phone. It follows that Barthes's conception of a non-coded message is even more problematic than before, effacing the argument of a photographic paradox (if this has ever existed; cf. Scott 1994). In addition, the indexical characteristic of the photograph is difficult to justify due to its digital context. For example, when taking into account the algorithmic processes of photographic software, it becomes clear that photographic sign production is symbolic. In this way, the myth of the photograph as proof or document continues to fade (Van Dijck 2008, 66).

At the same time, what remains important for an understanding of advertising photographs, chemical or digital, is Barthes's and others' admonishment to always consider the various kinds of knowledge needed to understand the advertising photograph. When this is done, the problem presented by consumers' online and shared photos becomes clear. If they are included in an enlarged definition of the advertising photograph, claims of the general comprehension of the photograph is even more problematic due to its re-contextualized and changed function (cf. Goffman 1987, 17). Who or what is portrayed? How is the photo related to the brand hashtag? In this way, hashtagging photos has implications for connotative analysis. An important resulting question is how might consumers' photos be decoded, if one lacks knowledge of the context in which they are taken or what has motivated the consumer to use the hashtag. In this connection, it seems that the linguistic message not only points *into* the text by anchoring or adding new meanings to the image (cf. Barthes 1977b), but may also provide the image with more subjective meanings that point *out of* the text (to the creator of the posted photo) and can hardly be understood without contextual knowledge (cf. Schlesselman-Tarango's (2013) distinction between descriptive and identity-based tags). Moreover, Pateman's critique of anchorage as a textual function that requires knowledge about reading texts draws attention to another area in need of investigation: Structurally connected (advertising) photos that can be juxtaposed, compared, differentiated, etc. apparently require new kinds of interpretive work that are also deserving of much more scholarly attention (cf. Van Dijck 2008, 65).

Beyond these complexities, the hashtag function needs to be considered beyond its meaning vis-à-vis the individual photo in order to investigate its contextual meanings as a photographic collaboration or co-creation of brand meaning. Moreover, the hashtag function needs to increasingly be understood not (only) from a perspective of "reading," but as related to common persuasive intentions within advertising such as creating attention (cf. Messaris 1997) and achieving consumer response (cf. McQuarrie and Mick 2003; Phillips and McQuarrie 2004). Where attention-creation basically is about "being seen," consumer response in a context of Instagram is linked to endeavors of generating likes and followers. In this sense, a rhetoric of the advertising image is intertwined with the functional features of the platform.

Finally, accepting an expanded definition of the advertising photograph that involves consumers' photos makes social critiques difficult if they operate solely at the level of representation. Here, again, an understanding of the advertising photograph needs to be developed, one that includes a conception of the photographic medium and how the photo-sharing platform provides and is employed by users to construct messages and social interaction. At the very least, critical analyses should begin to include the conditioning—or framing—aspects of the platform and take into account its social (contextual) uses and how the platform supports particular photographic practices such as self-portraying and presentations of everyday experiences with products and brands.

Conclusion

The proposed extended conception of the advertising photograph in a culture of photo sharing exemplifies the need to consider structural relations between photos in co-creating brand meanings. Doing so suggests a move away from classic text-oriented analyses of internal structural relations in the photographs in, for example, terms of rhetorical figures. Nevertheless, such analyses are still valuable for understanding the "expressiveness" of particular image practices related to advertising on photo-sharing platforms. In this connection, measures of likes and followers may turn out to be an important analytical tool in studies of visual advertising rhetoric and consumer response. However, beyond such quantitative measures, what also needs to be investigated is how brand-related content is exchanged and negotiated among individual and commercial users and how they collaborate in creating meanings for the brand. In this way, analyzing advertising photographs in a context of photo sharing becomes difficult without a consideration of the platform and how it frames conversations about products and brands. Based on the discussion here of prevailing approaches to the advertising photograph, at least three areas of future scholarly attention present themselves, in relation to hashtagging: 1) the hashtag function as a textual relation that not only adds meaning to the photograph, but also connects it with other photographs, 2) the hashtag function as a challenge to connotational analysis, and 3) the hashtag function and its implications for a social critique of advertising photography.

Notes

1. Barthes considers this absence of coding as exclusive to the photographic image. Other visual modes of communication such as drawings are described as coded messages also on the level of denotation (Barthes 1977b, 43).
2. Berger refers to Sontag's discussion of the nature of the photographic image and its relation to the real (cf. Sontag 2008).
3. Besides having an account from which photos (and videos) can be posted, marketers can create adverts on Instagram (marked as sponsored content) by using Facebook's advert services (see Instagram 2016d). This service will not be taken into account here.

References

Barthes, Roland. 1977a. "The Photographic Message." In *Image – Music – Text*, edited by Stephen Heath, 16–31. New York: Hill and Wang.
———. 1977b. "The Rhetorique of the Image." In *Image – Music – Text*, edited by Stephen Heath, 32–51. New York: Hill and Wang.
Berger, John. 2013. "Uses of Photography." In *Understanding a Photograph*, edited by Geoff Dyer, 62–71. London: Penguin.
Chalfen, Richard. 1987. *Snapshot Versions of Life*. Bowling Green: Bowling Green State University Press.

Cook, Guy. 2001. *The Discourse of Advertising* (2nd edition). London: Routledge.

Durand, Jacques. 1970. "Rhétorique et image publicitaire." *Communications* 15: 70–95.

———. 1987. "Rhetorical Figures in the Advertising Image." In *Marketing and Semiotics: New Directions in the Study of Signs for Sale*, edited by Jean Umiker-Sebeok, 295–318. Berlin: Mouton De Gruyter.

Eco, Umberto. 1979. *A Theory of Semiotics*. Bloomington: Indiana University Press.

Goffman, Erving. 1959. *The Presentation of Self in Everyday Life*. London: Penguin Books.

———. 1987/1976. *Gender Advertisements*. New York: Harper & Row.

Gye, Lisa. 2007. "Picture This: The Impact of Mobile Camera Phones on Personal Photographic Practices." *Continuum: Journal of Media & Cultural Studies* 21(2): 279–88.

Instagram. 2016a. "Instagram | FAQ." Accessed March 21. https://www.instagram.com/about/faq/.

———. 2016b. "Instagram Business." Accessed March 21. https://business.instagram.com/.

———. 2016c. "Instagram Business | Getting Started." Accessed March 21. https://business.instagram.com/gettingstarted/.

———. 2016d. "Instagram Business | Advertising on Instagram." Accessed March 21. https://business.instagram.com/advertising/.

Johnston, Patricia. 2005. "Advertising Photography." In *The Oxford Companion to the Photograph*, edited by Robin Lenman and Angela Nicholson. Oxford: Oxford University Press.

Leiss, William, Stephen Kline, Sut Jhally, and Jacqueline Botterill. 2005. *Social Communication in Advertising. Consumption in the Mediated Marketplace* (3rd edition). New York: Routledge.

McQuarrie, Edward F., and David Glen Mick. 2003. "The Contribution of Semiotic and Rhetorical Perspectives to the Explanation of Visual Persuasion in Advertising." In *Persuasive Imagery. A Consumer Response Perspective*, edited by Linda M. Scott and Rajeev Batra, 191–221. Mahwah, NJ: Lawrence Erlbaum Associates.

Messaris, Paul. 1997. *Visual Persuasion. The Role of Images in Advertising*. Thousand Oaks, CA: Sage.

Murray, Susan. 2008. "Digital Images, Photo-Sharing, and Our Shifting Notions of Everyday Aesthetics." *Journal of Visual Culture* 7(2): 147–63.

Nöth, Winfried. 1987. "Advertising: The Frame Message." In *Marketing and Semiotics: New Directions in the Study of Signs for Sale*, edited by Jean Umiker-Sebeok, 279–94. Berlin: Mouton De Gruyter.

Pateman, Trevor. 1983. "How Is Understanding an Advertisement Possible?" In *Language, Image, Media*, edited by Howard Davis and Paul Walton, 187–204. Oxford: Basil Blackwell.

Peirce, Charles S. 1978. *Collected Papers of Charles Sanders Peirce, Vol. II*, edited by Charles Hartshorne and Paul Weiss. Cambridge, MA: The Belknap Press of Harvard University Press.

Phillips, Barbara J., and Edward F. McQuarrie. 2004. "Beyond Visual Metaphor: A New Typology of Visual Rhetoric in Advertising." *Marketing Theory* 4(1/2): 113–36.

Ramamurthy, Anandi. 2009. "Spectacles and Illusions. Photography and Commodity Culture." In *Photography: A Critical Introduction* (4th edition), edited by Liz Wells, 205–56. London: Routledge.

Rettberg, Jill W. 2014. *Seeing Ourselves through Technology. How We Use Selfies, Blogs and Wearable Devices to See and Shape Ourselves*. Basingstoke: Palgrave Macmillan.

Schlesselman-Tarango, Gina. 2013. "Searchable Signatures: Context and the Struggle for Recognition." *Information Technology and Libraries* 32(3): 5–19.

Scott, Linda M. 1994. "Images in Advertising: The Need for a Theory of Visual Rhetoric." *Journal of Consumer Research* 21(2): 252–73.

Slater, Don. 1983. "Marketing Mass Photography." In *Language, Image, Media*, edited by Howard Davis and Paul Walton, 245–63. Oxford: Basil Blackwell.

Sontag, Susan. 2008. *On Photography*. London: Penguin.

Van Dijck, José. 2008. "Digital Photography: Communication, Identity, Memory." *Visual Communication* 7(1): 57–76.

Van House, Nancy A. 2011. "Personal Photography, Digital Technologies and the Uses of the Visual." *Visual Studies* 26(2): 125–34.

13 A Consideration of the Needs, Opportunities, and Challenges for a Critical Advertising Pedagogy

Silke Lissens & Joke Bauwens

Contextualizing the Need for Critical Advertising Pedagogy

The hyper-mediatization of children's lives, at least in affluent parts of the world, and the altered nature of advertising reinvigorate concerns about how children become engaged in consumerism early on in life. Of course, the commercialization of childhood is not a recent development, with its modern beginnings in the 18th century, when industrialization processes enabled the mass production of consumer goods (Murphy 2000; Plumb 1976). The trend accelerated in the 1950s (Wasko 2008), followed by an escalation in the 1980s (Levin and Linn 2004). What makes the issue pressing nowadays is children's intensifying and increasing media use (see for example Kaiser Family Foundation 2010), for they are continuously exposed to the consumerist attitudes and images the media promote (Hill 2011). The social pleasures, democratic gains, and educational opportunities of contemporary media thus come at a steep price.

At the same time, the proliferation of media platforms and the rapid succession of technological innovations facilitate the omnipresence and perpetual reinvention of one of commercialization's most effective tools, i.e., advertising. Online environments in particular have changed the features and characteristics of advertising. They facilitate immersive and interactive configurations, making it very difficult to detect where advertising is present (Martin and Smith 2008; Nairn and Dew 2007) and how to distinguish between informational and/or entertainment substance and commercial content. Online, embedded advertising such as advergames, advertising in social games or on social networks, and in-game advertising are more difficult to capture precisely because of their interactive and affect-based nature (An, Jin, and Park 2014; An and Stern 2011; Owen et al. 2013; Van Reijmersdal, Rozendaal, and Buijzen 2012). Accordingly, advertising regulations, guidelines, and controls applicable to traditional media lag behind due to their incompatibility to the technological, economic, and political economy of online media (e.g., Drumwright and Murphy 2004). Inasmuch as governments and regulators cannot keep up with media developments and calls for renegotiation or revision of acceptable practices (Freestone and Mitchell 2004), the Internet will remain *"the Wild West"* of advertising (Drumwright and Murphy 2004, 87).

Interventionist research concludes that children's advertising literacy concerning those new advertising techniques and formats lags when compared to conventional (broadcast television) advertising (An, Jin, and Park 2014; An and Stern 2011; Owen et al. 2013; Van Reijmersdal, Rozendaal, and Buijzen 2012). And advertising literacy's current conceptualization does not guarantee its effectiveness (e.g., Rozendaal et al. 2013). Occasionally, advertising literacy is even linked with more positive brand attitudes or increased purchase intentions (Livingstone and Helsper 2006; Rozendaal, Buijzen, and Valkenburg 2009, Van Reijmersdal et al. 2012). As argued by others, being media savvy does not necessarily amount to critical media literacy (Teurlings 2010, 368).

This is where the issue of critical advertising pedagogy surfaces. Indeed, advertising texts are frequently the subject of media literacy and analyses of marketing as the whole (see for example Šramová 2014). Furthermore, the notion of (over-) consumption has instigated arguments for critical pedagogies (see for example Sandlin and McLaren 2010). Contemporary critical pedagogy perspectives often criticize schools—mainly public ones (Kirylo et al. 2010) for prioritizing facts, figures, values, and roles that service and legitimate capitalist, consumerist societies (see for example Jaramillo and McLaren 2009).

This chapter addresses arguments for a critical advertising pedagogy that critically examines commercialization, commodification, and the pivotal role of advertising therein. We bring together insights from media-effect studies to cultural studies-inspired research to present an account of not only what is to be criticized, but also what is to be celebrated. Precisely this double-sided perspective is at the heart of critical pedagogy. Finally, particular guidelines are presented as to what critical advertising pedagogy's theorization should and its operationalization could entail.

The Basics of Critical Pedagogy

Critical, also engaged, radical, liberatory/emancipatory, and humanizing (cf. Giroux 1989; Kiryo et al. 2010) pedagogy gained significant momentum with the 1970s' translation and dissemination of Freire's *Pedagogy of the Oppressed* (Kirylo et al. 2010, 332). Having experienced firsthand the repercussions of a disadvantaged background on academic performances and life opportunities, the Brazilian educator developed a critique of *"the banking system"* of education (Freire 1970). This metaphor emphasized that canonical data was deposited in students and merely needed to be spent later at times of testing, without accounting for their particular contexts, the curriculum's relevance for their individual and social life struggles, and the legitimation or contestation of dominant power systems reinforced by such a pedagogical approach. A *"culture of silence"* (Freire 1970) was imposed upon the (primarily oppressed and disadvantaged) students. Important contributions to critical pedagogy come from Giroux (1989, 1997). Although his original readings are situated within the 1980s USA late-Cold War context, his analysis of the school system still applies to the current argument. Rather than encouraging social justice and change, schools had become conservative bastions (Giroux 1989, 8) and company stores (ibid., 18) contributing to economic growth and cultural uniformity. The principles of morality, civic courage and social compassion had shifted toward mastery, efficiency, and control (ibid., 18) or how to function within the dominant corporate order (ibid., 113).

Critical pedagogy, then, requires the introduction of a language of critique and a language of possibility. The language of critique exposes political and social power relations and struggles present within society and schools alike. It questions the role of teachers as purely agents of transmission and the role of pedagogy as a memory machine that reproduces history while ignoring subordinate voices and meanings (Giroux 1989). The language of possibility therefore gives students hope that citizens can exert political power (e.g., unions, ibid., 16) and that societal change is possible. Teachers need to be encouraged to become agents of transformation, providing the knowledge and tools to understand ideological processes and the complex system of representation through which selves and social relations are experienced (ibid., 16).

Such a goal can be worked toward through a triple discursive analysis that relies on a Foucauldian (2002) deconstruction of institutionalized knowledge to be found in verbal, visual, written, and other semiotic events. First, discourses of production question the organizational conditions of schools (i.e., presence of books, hot meals, ICT, role of the teachers) and society on the macro level for they are shaped by and endorse existing, unequal power relations. Second, discourses of texts address the question of what voices and values are represented within the school curricula. Third, discourses of lived cultures presuppose incorporating students' experiences, with special regards to minority backgrounds. Concretely, the student's, teacher's, and the school's voices should be taught and analyzed, for each is characterized by specific interests and contexts. Emancipatory potential arises when individual values and interests, teacher roles, and school features (i.e., how the school is organized, what content is offered, which social practices need to be followed) and their mutual interaction coincide (Giroux 1989, 143).

The Translation into Critical Advertising Pedagogy

Besides focusing on advertising as the main purveyor of "messages of consumerism" (Murphy 2000), critical advertising pedagogy addresses enabling and disabling content, strategies, and techniques of advertising. Additionally, such an approach does not consider the industry from a mere deterministic viewpoint and its impact as a mechanical certainty. Instead, it incorporates the accountability of young people as in how they reproduce advertising and consumerism's legitimacies on the one hand but also resist them on the other.

Recognizing that defining critical pedagogy might be counterproductive to its radical agency (Kirylo et al. 2010, 332), in what follows we provide ideas and suggestions that illustrate and explore how a critical pedagogic approach to advertising can actually be implemented in classroom practices.

The Language of Critique within Discourses of Production

One fundamental level of analysis consists of discourses of production. Advertising to children as one of the most controversial areas of marketing (Bakir and Vitell 2010) creates direct contact between advertising professionals, working on behalf of their clients, and vulnerable youngsters. Typically, this takes the form of advertising augmenting or exacerbating the importance of brand consumption for young people as a means of joining and belonging to certain groups (see for example Elliot and Leonard 2004; Pilcher 2011; Roper and Shah 2007). A second key level of analysis concerns covert advertising. Advertising strategies and formats such as premiums (Nairn 2008), character branding or celebrity endorsement (Danovitch and Mills 2014; Nairn 2008), product placements—including in-game advertising (Terlutter and Capella 2013)—stealth (Martin and Smith 2008) or viral marketing, associative marketing (Nwachukwu et al. 1997), quick pressure sales techniques (Nairn 2008), and personalized advertising through online data-tracking (Tucker 2014) should be identified and analyzed for how they try to appeal to and shape children's needs and wishes and make use of their social contacts and networks.

As has been noted, schools are not immune to these pressures. As a result, actual school surroundings require scrutinizing. Declining financial resources have pushed numerous school officials to accept company funding (Schor 2004) in exchange for the incorporation of commercial messages into school books and classes, and/or appearances on the level of infrastructure in such forms as ICT hard- and software, sports fields, and vending machines (e.g. Hill 2011; Molnar 2013; Quart 2004; Schor 2004). Students need to be sensitized to the extent of entanglement between commercial and educational institutions and the repercussions thereof.

Finally, existing regulatory frameworks defining legal advertising practices need to be addressed as well, because these rules and regulations help determine power relations. Interpreting whether advertising laws and policy principles correspond to the prevailing necessities and opportunities of both producers and (child) consumers, or arguing for their reconsideration and reformulation should not be restricted to advertising professionals, scholars, and legislators alone (see for example Arnold and Oakly 2013; Cutler and Nye 1997; Drumwright and Murphy 2004; Krueger 1998). Even six year olds have shown the ability to reason morally on the social beneficence or unjustness of laws (Helwig and Jasiobedzka 2001). Children must be given the chance to scrutinize how and to what extent they are protected or over- or under-protected by advertising laws, i.e., laws focusing on the principles of identification and separation (Audiovisual Media Services Directive, Directive on electronic commerce) in the context of their lived realities as children, consumers, and citizens.

The Language of Critique within Discourses of Texts

Discourses of texts concern how advertising is elaborated upon in classrooms. First, as has been shown frequently, the content often raises ethical questions. Due to the pressure to convey clear messages in as little time as possible within a competitive environment and an overabundance of information in general, advertising tends to present sound bites, clichés, stereotypes, and generally oversimplified images of the social world, which are then linked to the features and characteristics of the advertised products. Critical advertising pedagogy, then, intersects with research on the truthfulness or credibility of and skepticism toward advertising (see for example An, Jin, and Park 2014; Derbaix and Pecheux, 2003; Obermiller and Spangenberg 2000; Terlutter and Cappella 2013). Such claims also activate biased ideas, norms, and values. Regarding gender, for example, a wealth of scientific research can be built upon (see for example also Bakir, Blodgett, and Rose 2008; Browne 1998) to stimulate children's experiences with and thinking about how often gender is represented, what gender roles are attributed, and how the gendered appearances and attributions in advertising might affect social interactions and life expectations. The representation of ethnicity and social constructs like childhood, friendship, love, beauty, and success can raise critical questions as well. The over-representation of majority ethnic backgrounds and the marginalization of others, the absent or limited interracial interactions in advertising, and/or the links with particular product types (see for example Bailey 2006; Maher et al. 2008) contribute not only to children's current conceptions of selves and others, but also to lifelong ones. Regarding perspectives on generations and childhood, food advertising to children has been accused of instigating anti-adultism (Schor and Ford 2007). Many foods are made attractive to children to counterbalance the reluctance of parents to buy them, often for reasons of low nutritional value. Similar to general media exposure (see for example Derenne and Beresin 2006), advertising generates and reinforces ideas on how people should look and what they should have or wear to be beautiful and successful or popular and cool (Hill 2011; Quart 2004; Vermeir and Sompel 2014).

Second, the commodities themselves require consideration. Much research focuses on so-called sinful products that cause detrimental effects on consumers' health. Of primary concern for children have always been tobacco, alcohol, and drugs (see for example Freeman et al. 2009). In the past decade, however, an alarming rise of obesity in minors has also prompted public, policy, and academic debates on sugar-rich and fatty foods and beverages (see for example Livingstone & Helsper 2006; Roberts & Pettigrew 2007). Critical advertising pedagogy has to explicate the arguments underlying these moral panics, yet at the same time it has to stimulate children's personal opinions and priorities about what products and commodities are considered sinful, why so, and what rules and regulations could be appropriate concerning advertising for these products in order to build critical self-awareness.

The Language of Critique within Discourses of Lived Cultures

Discourses of lived cultures address children's daily life experiences of brands, advertising and consumer culture, most particularly those of the *silenced* in advertising. These are often minority groups in society constituted by ethnicity, gender, age, or health issues. How do children of such groups think about the ideas proposed in advertising? Do they feel left out or, contrarily, do they feel stigmatized? In this case, though, the minority groups most silenced within consumer societies are determined by social class. Teachers can provide both the place and space for disadvantaged children to express authentic experiences with advertising and consumer cultures or assume a guiding role in examining all children's sensitivities to the problems that arise under such conditions.

Discourses of lived cultures also consider behavioral issues that are detrimental to individuals. Targeting children erodes the structure of childhood, depriving them of experiences that differentiate them from the adult world (Hill 2011, 348). However, whereas children should be permitted their life worlds and corresponding learning pace, these distinctive environments should not be considered in opposition to those of adults, often caused by the aforementioned anti-adultism (Quart 2004), or exhibited in family conflicts because of consumption decision making (Buijzen & Valkenburg 2003; Hamilton 2009; Nairn 2008).

Stimulating consumerism exploits children's psychological vulnerabilities (Hill 2011; Nairn 2008). They learn that happiness results from material goods and that self-worth depends on what one has, rather than relying on creativity and social interaction to attain these feelings (Hill 2011). A form of "caste snobbery" arises, with youngsters judging each other on what they wear and how much money their family has (Quart 2004). Evidently, those unable to consume sufficiently suffer stigmatization, discrimination, and exclusion (Hamilton 2009). Sustaining certain lifestyles or trying to keep up with the perceived consumption standards gets young consumers increasingly into trouble. Adolescent consumers are the fastest-growing group in debt (Quart 2004) and, to pay off these debts and continue their upscale lifestyles, some turn to criminal activities (e.g., Hamilton 2009; Quart 2004). Critical advertising pedagogy can build on these studies and dig into children's experiences with advertising and consumer cultures and the associated repercussions on an individual, family, and societal level in order to sensitize them to their own and others' struggles. Thereby it is not solely the advertising industry that should be scrutinized. The social uses of advertising and (non-) participation in consumer cultures also deserve attention.

The Language of Possibility within Discourses
of Production, Texts, and Lived Cultures

The constructive approach upon which critical pedagogy is built opens up new spaces from which children can develop their senses of agency, not only by coping with or resisting the disabling sides of advertising (indicated in the language of critique), but also by making the most of advertising's enabling aspects.

This necessary nuance to the analysis is due to the fact that power relations do not work one-directionally from the producers/advertisers to the consumers. Indeed, both the changing nature of advertising and institutional control mechanisms allow for consumers to intervene. Online word-of-mouth marketing (Berger and Milkman 2012; Camarero and San José 2011; Gunawan and Huarng 2015), for example, enables consumers to take up a more active, sometimes empowered, role. For example, engagement with advertising increasingly has become a matter of "pulled exposure" (Schlosser, Shavitt, and Kanfer 1999; Wolin and Korgaonkar 2003), resulting in more selective exposure to commercial messages, where marketers and advertisers depend on consumers' willingness and connectedness to spread these messages. Likewise, advertisers rely on the consumers' interpretations of their messages. For meanings are "uncontrollable"; they can be transformed and transcended, with alternative readings or unintended messages spreading rapidly (see for example Blichfeldt and Smed 2015). Hence, consumers can give readings to advertising texts and brand identities that deviate from the advertisers' and marketers' intentions. In a more structural, institutionalized way, consumers can make formal complaints whenever they feel advertising practices are offensive or unfair (i.e., the JEP or Jury for Ethical Practices in case of advertising in Belgium, own translation). Finally, the notion of de-commodification, for some exemplified by initiatives of fair trade, microfinance, open source and social enterprises (e.g., Vail 2010) or individual and group behaviors going from consumer activism to taking on simple lifestyles (e.g., Helm, Moulard, and Richins 2015), could reduce the market's influence and bring its relationship with society into greater balance.

Second, issues discussed through the language of critique can also be acknowledged for their benefits. Although advertising offers stereotyped and idealized notions of gender, age, ethnicity, beauty, and success, it can also foster counter-stereotype and aspirational content on all of these aspects (e.g. Meijer 1998). Next, apart from criticizing advertising's presentation of harmful commodities and the use of fear or threat appeals, critical advertising pedagogy should incorporate persuasive messages communicated within the context of corporate social responsibility like anti-alcohol and anti-smoke or smoke cessation campaigns (see for example Durkin, Biener, and Wakefield 2009; Niederdeppe et al. 2011) and anti-obesity messages (Charry and Demoulin 2012; Charry, De Pelsmacker, and Pecheux 2014). And, taking on an instrumental perspective, questionable fear or threat appeals in the end do serve welfare goals. In this sense, the discourse of production reappears, but in such cases consumers are provided with essential information and can feel empowered because of it.

Last, the analysis strongly builds upon advertising's production and diffusion of symbolic resources or its performances as a "vital semiotic tool" that provide people with language and meaning making texts (Gustafson 2001; Preston 2004). Advertised brands and products on the one hand and the vocabulary and scripts advertising contains on the other often function as the basis for individual identity construction and social interaction and identification (Quart 2004; Schor 2004). According to Meijer (1998) it is advertising more than any other genre or form of communication that plays a major role in the construction of subjectivities and individualities because of its utopian, optimistic narratives. For instance, advertising induces laughter and irritation among young children (Martinez, Jarlbro, and Sandberg 2013). Among adolescents, it was found to be a prerequisite to participate in group-conversations, as it was considered a common subject matter (Ritson and Elliot 1999). Having seen the advertising text, having "experienced" it, however, is only a start. Continued interaction depends on the "interpretation" (giving it meaning), "evaluation" (indicating its coolness or conventionality), and "application" (using it in a new context) of the texts (1999). The "ritualization" of the text (1999), enacted by what Bartholomew and O'Donohoe (2003) call "performance masters," instigates and inspires social interaction through the re-enactment of advertising stories, characters, jingles, and slogans. As expected, the real products, in combination with and thanks to the appeals that are used for their advertising, help consumers to construct the identity/ies to which they aspire. Brands and products allow for the communication of one's individual and group memberships, tastes, lifestyles, and class (e.g. Berger 2005; Quart 2004; Ritson and Elliot 1999; Schor 2004).

Concluding Discussion

Despite all the work done in critical pedagogy of advertising, two main challenges remain. The first tackles its place in relation to critical media pedagogy. Is one a substitute for the other, or do they complement each other? For some scholars, the ongoing commodification of society underscores the comparative importance of critical media pedagogy. However, whereas advertising texts are often the point of departure for media literacy analysis (see for example Hobbs 2004), advertising offers levels of analysis and application far beyond those of critical media pedagogy. Critical advertising pedagogy not only covers similar themes and topics (e.g., content analysis in function of representations of all kind), the powers of production and reception (e.g., the discourses of lived cultures), and the technological innovations and proliferation (e.g., the altering nature of advertising).

It also incorporates critical media pedagogy's forms of participatory culture (see for example Jenkins et al. 2009) and offers more opportunities for cross-curricular approaches and topics such as economics (i.e., income, market mechanisms, poverty rates) and norms and values as conditions for/within social interaction. As such, it contributes to Meijer's (1998) advertising citizenship by celebrating the performative power of consumer culture and the democratization of citizenship.

Closely connected is the question of where in the educational process critical advertising pedagogy could or should be enacted. Arguments for critical pedagogy (Giroux, 1989) and evaluations of critical media pedagogy (see for example Hammer 2011) often focus on secondary or even higher education levels. Yet, besides works within the critical pedagogy tradition (see for example Christensen and Aldridge 2012), we find claims that critical advertising pedagogy should begin in the last years of elementary education. An analysis of 25 years of child-consumer socialization research (John 1999) concludes that from the age of 11 children appertain to the reflective stage. This implies a heightened awareness for the social aspects of being a consumer and creating identities along the way. Also, scholars advocating media literacy/pedagogy approaches (see for example Buckingham 2003; Hobbs and Moore 2013) demonstrate that creative, interactive ways on how to understand, analyze, and create media (texts) work well even with very young children.

The second challenge relates to the incomplete operationalization of critical advertising pedagogy. Even if a comprehensive definition was possible at this point, it could not stand the test of time. For critical pedagogy requires constant reinvention because of the numerous communities and collective struggles involved (Kirylo et al. 2010, 332), more so in the light of the fast-changing nature of advertising, the rapid shifts in consumer fads (Berger 2004), the internationalization of companies, the proceedings in advertising policy and regulation, and the motions in socio-economical situations that affect the power relations at stake. This unceasing need to address existing realities demands a lot from the pedagogical staff. As with general critical pedagogy and critical media pedagogy, appropriate training is required. Teachers need to be accommodated with the analytical tools to address the three discursive languages (see for example Giroux 1988) in order to teach students how to do so. This necessitates the knowledge and skills to know and evaluate the external world of advertising and consumption and a form of self-reflexivity about how they as consumers relate to all of this.

Acknowledgments

This text was produced within the framework of AdLit, an interdisciplinary research project on advertising literacy funded by VLAIO (Vlaams Agentschap Innoveren en Ondernemen).

188 *Silke Lissens & Joke Bauwens*

References

An, Soontae, Hyun Seung Jin, and Eun Hae Park. 2014. "Children's Advertising Literacy for Advergames: Perception of the Game as Advertising." *Journal of Advertising* 43(1): 63–72.

An, Soontae, and Susannah Stern. 2011. "Mitigating the Effects of Advergames on Children." *Journal of Advertising* 40(1): 43–56.

Arnold, Denis G. and James L. Oakly. 2013. "The Politics and Strategy of Industry Self-Regulation: The Pharmaceutical Industry's Principles for Ethical Direct-to-Consumer Advertising as a Deceptive Blocking Strategy." *Journal of Health Politics, Policy & Law* 38(3): 505–44.

Bailey, Anthony, A. 2006. "A Year in the Life of the African-American Male in Advertising - A Content Analysis." *Journal of Advertising* 35(1): 83–104.

Bakir, Aysen, Jeffrey G. Blodgett, and Gregory M. Rose. 2008. "Children's Responses to Gender-Role Stereotyped Advertisements." *Journal of Advertising Research* 48(2): 255–66.

Bakir, Aysen, and Scott Vittell. 2010. "The Ethics of Food Advertising Targeted toward Children: Parental Viewpoint." *Journal of Business Ethics* 91(2): 299–311.

Bartholomew, Alice, and Stephanie O'Donohoe. 2003. "Everything Under Control: A Child's Eye View of Advertising." *Journal of Marketing Management* 19(3–4): 433–57.

Berger, Arthur A. 2004. *Ads, Fads, and Consumer Culture. Advertising's Impact on American Character and Society.* Lanham: Rowman & Littlefield.

———. 2005. *Shop 'till You Drop. Consumer Behavior and American Culture.* Lanham: Rowman & Littlefield.

Berger, Jonah, and Katherine L. Milkman. 2012. "What Makes Online Content Viral?" *Journal of Marketing Research* 49(2): 192–205.

Blichfeldt, Bodil S., and Karina M. Smed. 2015. "'Do It to Denmark': A Case Study on Viral Processes in Marketing Messages." *Journal of Vacation Marketing* 21(3): 289–301.

Browne, Beverly A. 1998. "Gender Stereotypes in Advertising on Children's Television in the 1990s: A Cross-National Analysis." *Journal of Advertising* 27(1): 83–96.

Buijzen, Moniek, and Patti Valkenburg. 2003. "The Effects of Television Advertising on Materialism, Parent-Child Conflict, and Unhappiness: A Review of Research." *Applied Developmental Psychology* 24(4): 437–56.

Camarero, Carmen, and Rebeca San José. 2011. "Social and Attitudinal Determinants of Viral Marketing Dynamics." *Computers in Human Behavior* 27(6): 2292–2300.

Charry, Karine M., and Nathalie T. M. Demoulin. 2012. "Behavioral Evidence for the Effectiveness of Threat Appeals in the Promotion of Healthy Food to Children." *International Journal of Advertising* 31(4): 773–94.

Charry, Karine, Patrick De Pelsmacker, and Claude Pecheux. 2014. "How Does Perceived Effectiveness Affect Adults' Ethical Acceptance of Anti-Obesity Threat Appeals to Children? When the Going Gets Tough, the Audience Gets Going." *Journal of Business Ethics* 124(2): 243–57.

Christensen, Lois McFadyen, and Jerry Aldridge. 2012. *Critical Pedagogy for Early Childhood and Elementary Educators.* London: Springer.

Cutler, Tony, and David Nye. 1997. "Subjects and Accomplices: Regulation and the Ethics of Cigarette Advertising." *International Journal of Health Services* 27(2): 329–46.

Danovitch, Judith H., and Candice M. Mills. 2014. "How Familiar Characters Influence Children's Judgments about Information and Products." *Journal of Experimental Child Psychology* 128: 1–20.

Derbaix, Christian, and Claude Pecheux. 2003. "A New Scale to Assess Children's Attitude toward TV Advertising." *Journal of Advertising Research* 43(4): 390–99.

Derenne, Jennifer L., and Eugene V. Beresin. 2006. "Body Image, Media and Eating Disorders." *Academic Psychiatry* 30(3): 257–61.

Directive 2010/13/EU of the European Parliament and of the Council of 10 March 2010 on the Coordination of Certain Provisions Laid down by Law, Regulation or Administrative Action in Member States concerning the Provision of Audiovisual Media Services (Audiovisual Media Services Directive), OJ L 95.

Directive 2000/31/EC of the European Parliament and of the Council of 8 June 2000 on Certain Legal Aspects of Information Society Services, in Particular Electronic Commerce, in the Internal Market ('Directive on Electronic Commerce'), OJ L 178.

Drumwright, Minette. E., and Patrick. E. Murphy. 2004. "How Advertising Practitioners View Ethics: Moral Muteness, Moral Myopia, and Moral Imagination," *Journal of Advertising* 33(2): 7–24.

Durkin, Sarah J., Lois Biener, and Melanie A. Wakefield. 2009. "Effects of Different Types of Antismoking Ads on Reducing Disparities in Smoking Cessation Among Socioeconomic Subgroups." *Research & Practice* 99(12): 2217–23.

Elliott, Richard, and Clare Leonard. 2004. "Peer Pressure and Poverty: Exploring Fashion Brands and Consumption Symbolism among Children of the 'British Poor'." *Journal of Consumer Behavior* 3(4): 347–59.

Freestone, Oliver, and Vincent-Wayne Mitchell. 2004. "Generation Y Attitudes toward e-Ethics and Internet-Related Misbehaviors." *Journal of Business Ethics* 54(2): 121–28.

Freeman, Dan, Merrie Brucks, Melanie Wallendorf, and Wend Boland. 2009. "Youth's Understandings of Cigarette Advertisements." *Addictive Behaviors* 34(1): 36–42.

Freire, Paulo. 1970. *Pedagogy of the Oppressed*. New York: Continuum.

Foucault, Michel, and Sheridan Smith, transl. 2002. *The Archaeology of Knowledge*. London: Routledge.

Giroux, Henry A. 1988. *Teachers as Intellectuals: Toward a Critical Pedagogy of Learning*. London: Bergin & Garvey.

———. 1989. *Schooling for Democracy. Critical Pedagogy in the Modern Age*. London: Routledge.

———. 1997. *Pedagogy and the Politics of Hope. Theory, Culture, and Schooling*. Boulder, CO: Westview Press.

Gunawan, Dedy D., and Kun-Huang Huarng. 2015. "Viral Effects of Social Network and Media on Consumers." *Journal of Business Research* 68(11): 2237–41.

Gustafson, Andrew. 2001. "Advertising's Impact on Morality in Society: Influencing Habits and Desires of Consumers." *Business & Society Review* 106(3): 201–23.

Hamilton, Kathy. 2009. "Low-Income Families: Experiences and Responses to Consumer Exclusion." *International Journal of Sociology & Social Policy* 29(9): 543–57.

Hammer, Rhonda. 2011. "Critical Media Literacy as Engaged Pedagogy." *E-Learning & Digital Media* 8(4): 357–63.

Helm, Amanda E., Julie G. Moulard, and Marsha Richins. 2015. "Consumer Cynicism: Developing a Scale to Measure Underlying Attitudes Influencing

Marketplace Shaping and Withdrawal Behaviors." *International Journal of Consumer Studies* 39(1): 515–24.

Helwig, Charles C., and Urszula Jasiobedzka. 2001. "The Relation between Law and Morality: Children's Reasoning about Socially Beneficial and Unjust Laws." *Child Development* 72(5): 1382–93.

Hill, Jennifer Ann. 2011. "Endangered Childhoods: How Consumerism Is Impacting Child and Youth Identity." *Media, Culture & Society* 33(3): 347–62.

Hobbs, Renee. 2004. 'Does Media Literacy Work? An Empirical Study of Learning How to Analyze Advertisements." *Advertising & Society Review* 5(4): downloaded from:https://muse-jhu-edu.kuleuven.ezproxy.kuleuven.be/journals/advertising_and_society_review/v005/5.4hobbs.html.

Hobbs, Renee, and David C. Moore. 2013. *Discovering Media Literacy: Teaching Digital Media and Popular Culture in Elementary School*. Thousand Oaks: Corwin.

Jaramillo, Nathalia E., and Peter McLaren. 2009. "From the Imaginary to the Real: Towards a Critical Teacher Education." *International Journal of Educational Policies* 3(1): 5–19.

Jenkins, Henry, Ravi Purushotma, Margaret Weigel, Katie Clinton, and Alice J. Robison. 2009. "Confronting the Challenges of Participatory Culture: Media Education for the 21st Century." The John D. and Catherine T. MacArthur Foundation Reports on Digital Media and Learning. Cambridge: MIT Press.

John, Deborah R. 1999. "Consumer Socialization of Children: A Retrospective Look At Twenty Five Years of Research." *Journal of Consumer Research* 26(3): 183–213.

Kaiser Family Foundation. 2010. "Generation M2: Media in the Lives of 8- to 18-Year-Olds." Kaiser Family foundation Study. Last Consulted December 4th, 2015. https://kaiserfamilyfoundation.files.wordpress.com/2013/04/8010.pdf.

Kirylo, James D., Vudya Thirumurthy, Matthew Smith, and Peter McLaren. 2010. "Critical Pedagogy: An Overview." *Childhood Education* 86(5): 332–34.

Krueger, David. 1998. "Ethics and Values in Advertising: Two Case Studies." *Business and Society Review* 99(1): 53–65.

Levin, Diane, and Susan Linn. 2004. "The Commercialization of Childhood: Understanding the Problem and Finding Solutions." In *Psychology & Consumer Culture*, edited by Tim Kasser and Alan D. Kanner, 213–32. Washington DC: American Psychological Association.

Livingstone, Sonia and Ellen J. Helsper. 2006. "Does Advertising Literacy Mediate the Effects of Advertising on Children? A Critical Examination of Two Lined Research Literatures in Relation to Obesity and Food." *Journal of Communication* 56(3): 560–84.

Maher, Jill K., Kenneth C. Herbst, Nancy M. Childs, and Finn Seth. 2008. "Racial Stereotypes in Children's Television Commercials." *Journal of Advertising Research* 48(1): 80–93.

Martin, Kelly D., and Craig N. Smith. 2008. "Commercializing Social Interaction: The Ethics of Stealth Marketing." *American Marketing Association* 27(1): 45–56.

Martinez, Carolina, Gunilla Jarlbro, and Helena Sandberg. 2013. "Children's Views and Practices Regarding Online Advertising." *Nordicom Review* 34(2): 107–21.

Meijer, Irene C. 1998. "Advertising Citizenship: An Essay on the Performative Power of Consumer Culture." *Media, Culture & Society* 20(2): 235–49.

Molnar, Alex. 2013. *School Commercialism: From Democratic Ideal to Market Commodity.* New York: Routledge.

Murphy, Patricia L. 2000. "The Commodified Self in Consumer Culture: A Cross-Cultural Perspective." *The Journal of Social Psychology* 140(5): 636–47.

Nairn, Agnes. 2008. "It does my head in … buy it, buy it, buy it!" The Commercialization of UK Children's Web Sites." *Young Consumers* 9(4): 239–53.

Nairn, Agnes, and Alexander Dew. 2007. "Pop-ups, Pop-unders, Banners and Buttons: The Ethics of Online Advertising to Primary School Children." *Journal of Direct, Data and Digital Marketing* 9(1): 30–46.

Niederdeppe, Jeff, Matthew C. Farrelly, Kevin C. Davis Nonnemaker, and Lauren Wagner. 2011. "Socioeconomic Variation in Recall and Perceived Effectiveness of Campaign Advertisements to Promote Smoking Cessation." *Social Science & Medicine* 72(5), 773–80.

Nwachukwu, Saviour L.S., Scott J. Vitell, Faye W. Gilbert, and James Barnes. 1997. "Ethics and Social Responsibility in Marketing: An Examination of the Ethical Evaluation of Advertising Strategies." *Journal of Business Research* 39(2): 107–18.

Obermiller, Carl, and Eric R. Spangenberg. 2000. "On the Origin and Distinctness of Skepticism toward Advertising." *Marketing Letters* 11(4): 311–22.

Owen, Laura, Charlie Lewis, Susan Auty, and Moniek Buijzen. 2013. "Is Children's Understanding of Nontraditional Advertising Comparable to Their Understanding of Television Advertising?" *Journal of Public Policy & Marketing* 32(2): 195–206.

Pilcher, Jane. 2011. "No Logo? Children's Consumption of Fashion." *Childhood* 18(1): 128–41.

Plumb, J. H. 1976. "The Commercialization of Childhood." *Horizon*: 62–66.

Preston, Chris. 2004. "Children's Advertising: The Ethics of Economic Socialization." *International Journal of Consumer Studies* 28(4): 364–70.

———. 2005. "Advertising to Children and Social Responsibility." *Young Consumers: Insight and Ideas for Responsible Marketers* 6(4): 61–67.

Quart, Alissa. 2004. *Branded. The Buying and Selling of Teenagers.* New York: Basic Books Perseus Books Group.

Ritson, Mark, and Richard Elliott. 1999. "The Social Uses of Advertising: An Ethnographic Study of Adolescent Advertising Audiences." *Journal of Consumer Research* 26(3): 260–77.

Roberts, Michele, and Simone Pettigrew. 2007. "A Thematic Content Analysis of Children's Food Advertising." *International Journal of Advertising* 26(3): 357–68.

Roper, Stuart, and Binita Shah. 2007. "Vulnerable Consumers: The Social Impact of Branding on Children." *Equal Opportunities International* 26(7): 712–28.

Rozendaal, Esther, Moniek Buijzen, and Patti Valkenburg. 2009. "Do Children's Cognitive Advertising Defenses Reduce Their Desire for the Advertised Products?" *Communications* 34(3): 287–303.

Rozendaal, Esther, Matthew A. Lapierre, Eva A. Van Reijmersdal, and Moniek Buijzen. 2011. "Reconsidering Advertising Literacy as a Defense against Advertising Effects." *Media Psychology* 14(4): 333–54.

Rozendaal, Esther, Noortje Slot, Eva A. Van Reijmersdal, and Moniek Buijzen. 2013. "Children's Responses to Advertising in Social Games." *Journal of Advertising* 42(2–3): 142–54.

Sandlin, Jennifer A., and Peter McLaren., eds. 2010. *Critical Pedagogies of Consumption: Living and Learning in the Shadow of the "Shopocalypse."* New York: Routledge.

Schlosser, Ann E., Sharon Shavitt, and Alaina Kanfer. 1999. "Survey of Internet Users' Attitudes toward Internet Advertising." *Journal of Interactive Marketing* 13(3): 34–54.

Schor, Juliet. 2004. *Born to Buy*. New York: Scribner.

Schor, Juliet, and Margaret Ford. 2007. "From Tastes Great to Cool: Children's Food Marketing and the Rise of the Symbolic." *Journal of Law, Medicine & Ethics* 35(1): 10–21.

Šramová, Blandina. 2014. "Media Literacy and Marketing Consumerism Focused on Children." *Procedia – Social & Behavioral Sciences* 141: 1025–30.

Terlutter, Ralf, and Michael L. Capella. 2013. "The Gamification of Advertising: Analysis and Research Directions of In-Game Advertising, Advergames, and Advertising in Social Network Games." *Journal of Advertising* 42(2–3): 95–112.

Teurlings, Jan. 2010. "Media Literacy and the Challenges of Contemporary Media Culture: On Savvy Viewers and Critical Apathy." *European Journal of Cultural Studies* 13(3): 359–73.

Tucker, Catherine. 2014. "Social Networks, Personal Advertising, And Privacy Controls." *Journal of Marketing Research* 51(5): 546–62.

Vail, John. 2010. "Decommodification and Egalitarian Political Economy." *Politics & Society* 38(3): 310–46.

Van Reijmersdal, Eva A., Esther Rozendaal, and Moniek Buijzen. 2012. "Effects of Prominence, Involvement, and Persuasion Knowledge on Children's Cognitive and Affective Responses to Advergames." *Journal of Interactive Marketing* 26(1): 33–42.

Vermeir, Iris, and Dieneke Sompel. 2014. "Assessing the What Is Beautiful Is Good Stereotype and the Influence of Moderately Attractive and Less Attractive Advertising Models on Self-Perception, Ad Attitudes, and Purchase Intentions of 8–13-Year-Old Children." *Journal of Consumer Policy* 37(2): 205–33.

Wasko, Janet. 2008. "The Commodification of Youth Culture." In *The International Handbook of Children, Media and Culture*, edited by Kirsten Drotner and Sonia Livingstone, 460–74. London: Sage.

Wolin, Lori D., and Pradeep Korgaonkar. 2003. "Web Advertising: Gender Differences in Beliefs, Attitudes and Behavior." *Internet Research: Electronic Networking Applications and Policy* 13(5): 375–85.

Part IV

Critical Discursive/Rhetorical Analysis

14 Crossing the Borders

A Theory of Hybrid Advertising Formats

Nils S. Borchers

Since the end of the 1980s, hybrid advertising formats like advertorials, native advertising, product placements, advergames, search ads, brand postings in discussion forums, or fake online reviews have steadily gained in popularity. Hybrid formats are marketers' reaction to the decreasing effectiveness of traditional formats. By blurring the borders to their environment, especially to information and entertainment, hybrid formats discourage consumers from activating advertising-specific reception strategies. Such strategies reduce the probability of successful persuasion because they take into account that the communicator is self-interested and thus acts strategically. Yet, while serving the purposes of marketers, hybrid formats have far-reaching negative impacts on society. They erode willingness to trust corrupted communication forms such as journalistic articles or blogs, and they delegitimize modern society's foundations by fostering forms of fake rationality.

Despite their popularity and despite their negative impacts, hybrid advertising formats are surprisingly under-theorized. In this article, I will develop the theoretical concept of mimicry and position it as an analytical category in critical advertising studies. I do so because an adequate theoretical conceptualization of hybrid formats is important for a comprehensive understanding of the phenomenon.

The remainder of the article is organized as follows: I will start with an overview of existing theoretical concepts of hybrid advertising formats. Based on a critical discussion of these concepts, I will present the concept of mimicry as an alternative and, as I will argue, more apt approach to theorizing hybrid advertising formats. To do so, I will first introduce an advertising definition that is grounded in the perspective of consumers. I will then employ this definition to develop the mimicry concept and demonstrate its potential by discussing advertorials and fake online reviews as prime examples of hybrid formats. This discussion makes it possible to criticize mimicry strategies on the grounds of their social impacts. Finally, I will conclude by discussing policy implications.

Hybrid Formats as a Combination of Advertising and Publicity

Advertising has a long tradition of mimicking other communicative formats. Observing this tradition, Wyss (1998) uses the metaphor of advertising mimicry to denote the imitation of other television texts in TV commercials as intertextual references. For example, Wyss speaks of mimicry if a commercial imitates specific content characteristics of a soap opera. At this level of mimicry, however, TV commercials can still be identified as advertisements easily because they retain the external features typical of TV commercials such as their short length, condensed narratives, the identification of a sponsor, and contextual clues such as being shown within a clearly designated commercial break.

Yet, advertising's mimicry attempts reach well beyond such cases of intertextual references. Hybrid formats also intermingle with their environments by adapting the external features of other communicative genres and by obliterating contextual clues (Matteo and Dal Zotto 2015). This deeper level of mimicry fuels the debate on hybrid advertising formats.

Studies on hybrid advertising tackle issues such as identifiability (cf. Tutaj and van Reijmersdal 2012), effects on decision making (cf. Kim, Pasadeos, and Barban 2001), and ethical implications (cf. Köberer 2014). But although these studies have improved our understanding of hybrid formats considerably, much less effort has been devoted to strengthening our conceptual understanding.

A notable exception is Serazio's work on guerilla marketing, which he introduces as a "label for nontraditional communications between advertisers and audiences that rely on an element of surprise or surreptitiousness in the intermediary itself" (2013, 3). Borrowing from Foucault's theory of power (2000), he argues that instead of controlling consumers, guerrilla marketing seeks to govern them by surreptitiously structuring consumers' fields of action. In this way, marketers try to circumvent consumers' ad-avoidance strategies because recipients experience their own agency without noting the structuring of their actions. Although Serazio's approach does not offer a clear-cut definition of guerilla marketing, it still gives ample scope for strengthening the conceptual basis of hybrid formats by explaining how they can be successful in persuading their audiences.

In his approach to hybrid formats, Balasubramanian (1994) takes a different angle by describing them as a fusion of advertising and publicity, with hybrid formats combining the advantages of both. While marketers pay for the publishing of hybrid messages and hence exert control on content and form, they are not identified as sponsors, with the result that their messages are processed with less skepticism. Accordingly, Balasubramanian (30) defines hybrid formats as *"paid attempts to influence audiences for commercial benefit using communications that project a non-commercial character."*

While Balasubramanian's concept provides a sound foundation for theorizing hybrid formats, it remains within the boundaries of a marketing framework that in many ways is too restrictive from the perspective of communication scholars whose reference point often is society as a whole and not the interests of specific organizations (Borchers 2014; Krallmann, Scheerer, and Strahl 1997). Two shortcomings should be noted. First, hybrid formats are not limited to organizations' mass-mediated communication efforts. Second, hybrid formats blur the borders with many phenomena other than journalism. For example, even Balasubramanian (1994, 32) identifies as a hybrid format the case of a physician who secretly receives payments for transferring patients to cooperating hospitals.

The balance of this article reformulates Balasubramanian's ideas in a more abstract way to overcome their shortcomings. In doing so, I will take up Wyss's metaphor of advertising mimicry, generalize it beyond its original context of presentation strategies in TV commercials, and provide it with a solid theoretical foundation. This way, mimicry can be developed into an analytical category that can be employed for examining various hybrid advertising formats.

Theorizing Mimicry Strategies in Advertising

Hybrid advertising messages owe their effectiveness to the manipulation of their targets' expectations. By mimicking non-advertising formats, hybrid messages seek to be seen as an instance of the mimicked communicative genre, e.g., a journalistic report, a blog post, or an online consumer review. If recipients do this, they will process the message using reception strategies that, depending on the socially shared expectations, are adjusted to the mimicked genre because they are based on socially shared expectations about that specific genre. The crux is that the expectations about advertising differ fundamentally from those about journalism and other genres. Unlike journalism, advertising is expected to have ulterior motives and thus is commonly met with more skepticism (Obermiller, Spangenberg, and MacLachlan 2005). Due to the crucial role of recipients' understandings of the messages, an explanation of hybrid formats requires an advertising concept that takes into account recipients' perspective.

This requirement disqualifies established marketing concepts of advertising from being a convincing foundation for theorizing hybrid formats. In marketing research, advertising is typically defined as "a paid nonpersonal communication from an identified sponsor, using mass media to persuade or influence an audience" (Richards and Curran 2002, 64). In adopting the perspective of marketers while ignoring that of recipients, such a definition exemplifies the goal of conventional marketing research, which is to explain the market performance of organizations. To do so, such a definition simply distinguishes advertising from other measures organizations can employ to influence their performance—the marketing tools (Borchers 2014). For example, in marketing research, advertising is defined as communication to distinguish it from marketing tools within the categories product, price, and place in the 4Ps marketing mix (Borden 1964). By calling attention to its distribution by mass media, advertising is distinguished from promotion tools that are not mass mediated such as personal selling and sales promotion, while payment is included to distinguish advertising from publicity/PR, which also are mass mediated but whose distribution is not paid for. In doing so, the marketing definition of advertising treats marketers' intentions to advertise as a key criterion for identifying a message as advertising.

In contrast to the marketing approach, an advertising concept that considers the recipients' perspective has to identify the criteria that motivate recipients to categorize a message as advertising (Borchers 2014). In doing so, it has to be grounded in recipients' life worlds. These life worlds are not limited to, but extend significantly beyond, organizational communication. Accordingly, a sociological approach to advertising seems to be most apt for developing a respective advertising concept because it takes into account the complexity of the social.

In the vein of sociologists such as Luhmann, Parsons, and Durkheim who assume that social order by chance or nature is unlikely and thus has to be explained, I ask how advertising contributes to the emergence of social order. The mere fact that advertising is ubiquitous suggests that it has a social function and contributes to solving an existing social problem. From the perspective of social systems theory as advanced by Luhmann (1995), the problem of the contingency of the future is what advertising seeks to solve. Communication as the basic element of social systems is not time persistent but disintegrates continuously. Social systems must re-produce communication to prevent their collapse. Yet, doing so is far from a trivial act. At every moment, only one of all potential options can be realized. Selecting an option hence means that other options are not selected. Furthermore, every option has its specific consequences, by leading to specific future options while not leading to others. Moreover, realizing an option is an irreversible process and so is the non-realization of the rejected options. When considering that social actors distinguish preferred from non- or less-preferred options, it is easy to see how risky choice eventually is. Therefore, it is rational to select options no randomly, but deliberately. Yet actors often have to make decisions under time pressure, because options have to be realized before they expire so the system will not collapse.

This combination of the complexity of decisions, the riskiness of selections, and the time pressure to make decisions renders actors susceptible to hints on specific options. Such hints highlight single options as preferable (or not preferable) and, in this way, they support actors with arguments for their selection. I refer to these hints as *appeals*. Appeals have the social function to motivate (or de-motivate) the selection of a specific connecting option. Thus, they make the re-production of communication more likely.

The specific appeals can be characterized by two criteria: self-interest and threat of sanction. The issue of self-interest is closely connected to the fact that oftentimes, an actor's decision determines the future options of other actors. In such cases, the other actors may suggest only those options from which they will benefit. If appealing actors benefit from the realization of options they suggest, they might be motivated to present the option as attractively as possible and to exploit the decider's susceptibility for hints on how to evaluate the preferability of a specific option. In terms of Marxist theory (Haug 1971), the appealing actor is interested in the exchange value of the option and, thus, will attempt to maximize its use-value promise. By contrast, impartial appellators take the perspective of a peer user and therefore focus on the use value.

Orientation toward use value or exchange value in turn can motivate different appeals. If appellators estimate that the use value of option A is higher than that of option B, they will propose realizing option A if they are impartial, but option B if they benefit from option B and thus are self-interested. Therefore, deciders are well advised to control for the appellator's motivation. The risk of exchange-value oriented biases can only be ruled out if the appellator is not motivated by self-interest. Accordingly, the criterion of self-interest touches upon issues of trust.

Self-interest has already been acknowledged as a defining criterion of advertising. In macroeconomics, advertising is usually regarded as a source of market information. As such, it has to be distinguished from other sources, particularly from information by experts (e.g., product tests by consumer organizations) and by acquaintances (word-of-mouth). Compared to these two phenomena the existence of ulterior motives and thus of self-interest appear as constitutive trademarks of advertising (Kaldor 1950). The self-interest of advertising lies within the blind spot of marketing definitions because *all* marketing tools are self-interested.

A second criterion that can be used to characterize appeals is the threat of sanctions. The probability that a suggested option will be realized depends on possible negative sanctions for rejecting the suggestion. If deciders are not threatened with sanctions, it is easier for them to reject an appeal. While explicit threats can be made, the deciders' anticipation of sanctions is often sufficient, particularly if deciders feel they are relevant and their realization is possible. Since deciders are interested in avoiding sanctions they may be willing to accept even suggested options which they do not prefer. Thus, the criterion of negative sanctions touches upon issues of power.

Threat of sanctions has been acknowledged as a defining criterion of advertising. Approaches that identify advertising as a general mechanism for influencing the actions of others distinguish it from phenomena such as education, order, instruction, manipulation, and plea (cf. Lysinski and Seyffert 1920; Plenge 1922; Schweiger and Schrattenecker 2009, 385–90). In this context, freedom from coercion thus can be recognized as a constitutive trademark of advertising. Advertising's freedom from coercion lies within the blind spot of marketing definitions because—due to ideological factors—marketing regards all marketing tools as free from coercion.

The combination of the two criteria—self-interest and threat of negative sanctions—leads to four basic types of appealing communication: order, advertising, recommendation, and instruction (see Figure 14.1). The types differ in terms of the conditions under which a recipient makes a decision about accepting or rejecting a suggested option. Recipients activate type-specific reception strategies that account for the type-specific combination

		Threat of sanctions	
		+	–
self-interest	+	command	advertising
	–	instruction	recommendation

Figure 14.1 Basic types of appellative communication.

of power and trust. They do so on the basis of their individual understanding of a message. For example, if they understand a message as recommendation, they will use a recommendation-specific reception strategy. This implies that the intention of the communicator has only an indirect impact on the response; it may affect but does not determine the understanding of the message.

By using this theoretical framework, one can distinguish advertising from the other types of appeals and from other types of non-appealing communication. Advertising is the self-interested attempt to motivate (or de-motivate) the selection of an option without the threat of negative sanctions. This recipient-based concept of advertising helps in turn to theorize mimicry strategies as the underlying principle of hybrid advertising formats. Compared to other types of appeals, advertising has the most challenges to meet. In contrast to recommendations, advertising is seen to be self-interested and therefore biased in its own favor. And, in contrast to commands, advertising cannot levy sanctions against deciders who reject its proposal. To overcome these challenges, appellators can communicate their suggestions in a format typical not of advertising but of recommendation, command, or instruction. They do so in the hope that the recipients will categorize the message as the respective type and thus process it in a non-advertising-specific way.

This theoretical framework helps ultimately generate a clearer understanding of mimicry as an advertising strategy. I define mimicry as a communicator's attempt to provoke a desired understanding of a message by employing a message format that prompts a categorization of the communicated information that differs from the communicator's own understanding of the message. The use of mimicry strategies thus lies at the core of hybrid advertising formats.

From the perspective of advertising, it is possible to distinguish strategies of recommendation mimicry, command mimicry, and instruction mimicry— depending on the appeal type the message format mimics. Moreover, appellators can even mimic seemingly non-appellative, entertainment-based message formats like movies, computer games, or vlogs. For example, if a vlog by a popular YouTuber features a specific product, the viewers might infer that it is part of the YouTuber's brand world. If they decide to act on the grounds of this information, they treat the respective detail of the video as an appeal.

Appellators use mimicry strategies to increase the probability that the option they propose will be selected. Mimicry strategies increase this probability in two steps. First, they increase the probability that recipients pay attention to an appeal because many recipients avoid messages only because they identify them as advertising messages (Ducoffe and Curlo 2000). Second, mimicry strategies increase the probability that the appellator's proposal will be accepted because they indicate an orientation toward the use value of the option (recommendation mimicry) or the danger of being sanctioned (command mimicry), or both (instruction mimicry).

Recommendation Mimicry

Mimicry strategies offer marketers the advantage of higher efficiency due to greater effectiveness. However, from the perspective of the recipients, they have serious disadvantages. Recommendation mimicry is probably the most popular strategy among marketers. As command and instruction require threatening credibility with negative sanctions, they are harder to mimic than recommendations, which "only" require the depiction of impartiality. This is not to say that command and instruction mimicry would be irrelevant. Even if the straightforward appeal to fear has become rather unusual in mainstream advertising, marketers often employ less-obvious threats. The ideal worlds that commercials present refer at least implicitly to the negative consequences of rejecting the suggested options. They claim that if we simply used this shampoo, wore these sneakers, and drank this beer we would be attractive, popular, and successful. However, as Möller (1970) highlights, all these promises imply the threat that if we refuse to do so, we will be unattractive, unpopular, or unsuccessful. It is an empirical question whether some recipients identify the implicit references as a credible threat of negative sanctions. In the following, I discuss two popular formats of recommendation mimicry in order to demonstrate both the relevance and the explanatory power of the mimicry concept.

Advertorials, as one of the most popular hybrid advertising formats, mimic the form and style of their journalistic environment. Communicating a suggestion as advertorial can be identified as mimicry strategy, because appellators try to prompt an understanding of the message as impartial journalistic recommendation. Studies on the reception of advertorials show that a many readers mishandle the challenge of identifying a persuasive intent in the messages. Wilkinson, Hausknecht and Prough (1995) report a share of 27 percent of study participants who did not identify a specific advertorial as advertising. Baerns and Lamm (1987) find that 44 percent of participants repeatedly categorize advertorials as journalistic articles, and only 29 percent identify all presented advertorials as advertising. Kim, Pasadeos, and Barban (2001) distinguish labeled from unlabeled advertorials, with respective identification rates of 89 percent and 72 percent. In the Internet, borders between original content and advertising are even more blurred than in print. Tutaj and van Reijmersdal (2012) examine the identification of a labeled advertorial on the website of a news portal, finding that only 55 percent of the participants identify the advertorial as advertising.

The identification of such items as advertising is required in many countries and can serve as contextual clue. However, as the cited studies show, while common labeling formats might help some of the recipients to identify the advertising intention, they do not guarantee that all readers will identify the intention. One reason is the variety of labeling. For example, in Germany, advertorials might be labeled as "advert," as "special publication" (sometimes noting as well "of the advertising department"), as "promotion" or even as "advertorial" (a term not even most of my communication students are familiar with). Furthermore, the label is often placed in an unobtrusive spot, printed in small letters and without any further emphasis. Finally, publishers regularly fail to label advertorials in traditional media and online (Cameron, Ju-Pak, and Kim 1996; Klimmt et al. 2012).

A less obvious, but nevertheless widely spread, hybrid advertising format is the fake online review on specialized review portals (e.g. Yelp, Glassdoor) or retailer homepages (e.g., Amazon, Booking). As these reviews have become an important source of market information, some companies try to influence the reviews on the options they provide. The most aggressive way of influencing is the posting of fake reviews (Godes et al. 2005). In a pioneer study, Hu et al. (2012) estimate that reviews on every tenth book are manipulated on Amazon.com.

As a second type of mimicry strategy, fake online reviews are composed by review authors who pose as impartial peer consumers, peer patients, or peer employees and thus conceal their self-interest in order to encourage an understanding of their proposal as a disinterested recommendation. Success at detecting fake online reviews is quite low. Pioneering studies show that consumers' success rate is only slightly better than the chances of random guessing (Huang et al. 2012; Ott et al. 2011). A key reason is the general lack of contextual clues. While portal operators seek to provide such clues by establishing comment functions, reputation systems, reviewer profiles, and "certified purchase" badges and while they even develop algorithms for identifying fake reviews (Mukherjee et al. 2013), operators have not succeeded in making their portals fraud-safe.

Social Impacts of Mimicry Strategies

From the perspectives of the recipients, it is possible to identify three negative social impacts of mimicry strategies. On the micro level, mimicry strategies are a form of deception. On the macro level, mimicry strategies erode trust while delegitimizing modern society's foundations. Because critics have discussed the first two impacts in some length, I will only briefly touch upon these impacts before turning to a more substantial discussion of the third effect, which is the delegitimizing effect of mimicry strategies.

The criticism that mimicry strategies are deceptive is based on the fact that these strategies obscure the marketer's persuasive intention (cf. Hackley, Tiwsakul, and Preuss 2008; Martin and Smith 2008). As a result, they motivate decisions that may have been different if the marketer's intention had been explicit. Thus, consumers can be harmed because they invest resources to realize proposals they might not have realized under conditions of transparency.

The second criticism that mimicry strategies erode trust is an often-addressed long-term effect. For example, if the consequences of decisions made on the basis of online reviews repeatedly turn out to be unsatisfactory but deciders do not notice that mimicry strategies have been employed to corrupt the reviews, they will be less willing to trust particular online review portals, reviews in a particular area of life (e.g., physician reviews), or online reviews in general. As online reviews serve a social function—as digital knowledge commons, they support decision-making processes—employing mimicry strategies provokes social dysfunctions. This is also true in regard to other mimicked forms such as journalistic reports (Cameron, Ju-Pak, and Kim 1996; Eckman and Lindlof 2003) or advice by friends and acquaintances (Martin and Smith 2008; Serazio 2013). Therefore, mimicry strategies are seen to destroy established mechanisms for coping with world complexity—with the only objective to advance short-term self-interests.

The third criticism of mimicry strategies is that they undermine the foundations of modern society. This becomes apparent when analyzing modern society as "bourgeois society," seen as built on presumptions of romanticism and Enlightenment thought (Fischer 2004). The bourgeois society incorporates the Enlightenment's idea of rationally acting human beings, which is translated into the core values of self-reliance, maturity, and individual responsibility (Aßländer 2007). Despite important exceptions—most notably in love and religion—the idea of rational actors has become prevalent in most areas of our lives. It is generally expected that decisions are intentionally rational (Weber [1921] 1968, 26) and that "the end, the means, and the secondary results are all rationally taken into account and weighed."

The assumption that individuals (can) act rationally has had far-reaching consequences in social history, because it provides the grounds for a shift in the main mechanism for emerging social processes: from tradition to individual decision. In the course of this shift, the social perception of time has changed as well. Today, the future appears to be less determined by the past, but rather open and therefore rationally plannable (Aßländer 2007; Beck 1992, ch. 4), which leads to a shift in the perception of responsibility. Instead of holding God, fate or—in a secular version—society (e.g., class) responsible, individual lives seem to depend on individual decisions, which make individuals responsible for their own successes and failures. This is a key feature of modern society's architecture, and it is legitimized by the idea of human beings as rational decision makers.

Given the constant need created by the Western "multi-optional society" (Gross 1994) for good decisions, deciders need to evaluate all possible actions clearly. As aids to this need, appeals reduce the complexity of decisions because individuals can ideally rely on them to help evaluate and thus facilitate rational decisions. However, as argued above, it makes a difference whether the appeals are motivated by self-interest, i.e., whether they are oriented toward the use value or exchange value. Their orientation indicates which aspects should better be controlled: the evaluation's relevance according to personal criteria (in case of no self-interest) or additionally the evaluation's validity (in case of self-interest). For example, as long as a consumer can presume that an online reviewer of a hotel is competent, it is not necessary to question the description itself because it is assumed to be based on the use value. In contrast, a clearly self-interested source such as the homepage of the hotel prompts a consumer to consider possible biases.

By adopting a form that suggests impartiality, consumers accept proposals through mimicry strategies as rational, even though the appellator is self-interested and acts strategically. This constellation transforms the presumed rationality into a fake rationality: Deciders realize a proposed option, which they would not have realized or would have realized in different terms if assuming self-interest. For example, fake rationality can be observed if deciders decide to book a hotel after considering the advantages and disadvantages depicted in online reviews without noticing that one or more of the decisive reviews were published by the hotel management. By obscuring self-interest, recommendation mimicry encourages decision making under inadequate assumptions (i.e., deciding without controlling for possible biases toward the exchange value). It obstructs rational decisions and thus threatens the success of life plans for which the deciders are responsible.

Some commentators have argued that consumers have the moral right to know when they are targeted by marketers because only then can they be saved from deception (cf. Nebenzahl and Jaffe 1998). It is necessary to demand this moral right as well in respect to the ideal of rational decisions. Only under the conditions of transparency can individuals be made responsible for their decisions. And only under these conditions is it legitimate to base society on the assumption of rationally acting actors.

Conclusion and Implications

Hybrid advertising formats continue to gain in popularity during the last few decades, with little end in sight. Marketers employ them in an attempt to counterbalance the decreasing efficiency of traditional formats while the Internet affords technical, legal, and social opportunities for creating and employing new hybrid formats. Additionally, financial pressures have increased the readiness of media organizations to weaken the strict separation of editorial and sales and thus to agree on publishing hybrid advertising messages. Some publishers have already begun offering native advertising services, among them such established organizations as *The New York Times*, *The Washington Post,* or *Le Monde* (Matteo and Dal Zotto 2015).

Given the negative social impacts of mimicry strategies, researchers and lawmakers alike need to pay more attention to hybrid formats. While much research focuses on the efficiency of hybrid messages, it implicitly legitimizes the use of mimicry strategies because it is undertaken from the perspective of marketers who seek to market products efficiently. Apart from this research, there is a smaller, but nevertheless strong, tradition of scrutinizing the use of hybrid formats more critically, on the grounds of both their limited distinguishability and their negative social impacts. These critical approaches can benefit from adopting the concept of mimicry, because it allows a more comprehensive analysis of hybrid advertising formats. Conceptualizing hybrid formats on an abstract level and grounding them in the broader framework of appealing communication captures hybrid formats beyond mass media and economic objectives without forfeiting theoretical perspicacity.

Lawmakers should regulate the use of mimicry strategies more tightly. Although there appear to be clear rules for labeling mimicry strategies in most countries, lawmakers fail to keep step with the fast evolution of advertising formats, especially in the field of online communication. As a result, legislation is often merely reactive. Moreover, violations of the labeling regulations are hardly ever persecuted. Marketers do not hesitate to exploit the practically existing leeway, particularly as ethical issues are systematically blocked out in the advertising industry (Drumwright and Murphy 2004).

But the hiding of a persuasive intention can be accomplished even within legal borders. For example, the European Union's jurisdiction is based on the assumption of a model consumer who is averagely informed, attentive, and conscientious (Lange 2012, Rn. 387). This model establishes relatively high requirements from the perspective of the consumers by shifting a huge share of the responsibility to identify mimicry strategies onto the consumer while exonerating marketers and cooperating distributers—and this despite the studies discussed above that demonstrate the great difficulty people have in doing so. Some commentators have therefore argued for strengthening the advertising literacy of consumers (cf. Cornish 2014; Köberer 2014). However, even this strategy upholds the shift of responsibilities onto the consumers.

Against this background, there is the need to introduce a "polluters pay" principle also in regard to advertising. Individuals should be relieved from coping with the persuasion attempts of a multi-billion dollar industry by themselves—an industry that systematically tries to circumvent consumers' persuasion knowledge by means of permanent innovation. Advertising messages have to be labeled in a way that makes their persuasive intention transparent immediately, even in moments of distraction. Only such a transparency allows for averting the negative consequences of mimicry strategies.

References

Aßländer, Michael S. 2007. "Die Geburt der Ökonomie aus dem Geist der Aufklärung." In *Kultur - Ökonomie - Ethik*, edited by Mi-Yong Lee-Peuker, Fabian Scholtes, and Olaf J. Schumann, 287–311. München: Hampp.

Baerns, Barbara, and Ulrich Lamm. 1987. "Erkennbarkeit und Beachtung redaktionell gestalteter Anzeigen: Design und Ergebnisse der ersten Umfrage zum Trennungsgrundsatz." *Media Perspektiven* no Vol. (3): 149–58.

Balasubramanian, Siva K. 1994. "Beyond Advertising and Publicity: Hybrid Messages and Public Policy Issues." *Journal of Advertising* 23(4): 29–46. doi: 10.2307/4188949.

Beck, Ulrich. 1992. *Risk Society: Towards a New Modernity.* London: Sage.

Borchers, Nils S. 2014. *Werbekommunikation: Entwurf einer kommunikationswissenschaftlichen Theorie der Werbung.* Wiesbaden: Springer VS.

Borden, Neil H. 1964. "The Concept of the Marketing Mix." *J.Advert.Res.* 4: 2–7.

Cameron, Glen T., Kuen Ju-Pak, and Bong-Hyun Kim. 1996. "Advertorials in Magazines: Current Use and Compliance with Industry Guidelines." *Journalism & Mass Communication Quarterly* 73(3): 722–33.

Cornish, Lara S. 2014. "'Mum, can I play on the Internet?' Parents' Understanding, Perception and Responses to Online Advertising Designed for Children." *International Journal of Advertising* 33(3): 437–73.

Drumwright, Minette E., and Patrick E. Murphy. 2004. "How Advertising Practitioners View Ethics: Moral Muteness, Moral Myopia, and Moral Imagination." *Journal of Advertising* 33(2): 7–24.

Ducoffe, Robert H., and Eleonora Curlo. 2000. "Advertising Value and Advertising Processing." *Journal of Marketing Communications* 6(4): 247–62.

Eckman, Alyssa, and Thomas Lindlof. 2003. "Negotiating the Gray Lines: An Ethnographic Case Study of Organizational Conflict between Advertorials and News." *Journalism Studies* 4(1): 65–77.

Fischer, Joachim. 2004. "Bürgerliche Gesellschaft: Zur historischen Soziologie der Gegenwartsgesellschaft." In *Die bürgerliche Gesellschaft und ihre Avantgarden,* edited by Clemens Albrecht, 97–118. Würzburg: Ergon.

Foucault, Michel, Paul Rabinow, and James D. Faubion. 2000. *Power. The Essential Works of Michel Foucault, 1954–1984 3.* New York: New Press.

Godes, David, Dina Mayzlin, Yubo Chen, Sanjiv Das, Chrysanthos Dellarocas, Bruce Pfeiffer, Barak Libai, Subrata Sen, Mengze Shi, and Peeter Verlegh. 2005. "The Firm's Management of Social Interactions." *Marketing Letters* 16(3/4): 415–28.

Gross, Peter. 1994. *Die Multioptionsgesellschaft.* Frankfurt am Main: Suhrkamp.

Hackley, Chris, Rungpaka A. Tiwsakul, and Lutz Preuss. 2008. "An Ethical Evaluation of Product Placement: A Deceptive Practice?" *Business Ethics* 17:109–20.

Haug, Wolfgang F. 1971. *Kritik der Warenästhetik.* Frankfurt am Main: Suhrkamp.

Hu, Nan, Indranil Bose, Noi S. Koh, and Ling Liu. 2012. "Manipulation of Online Reviews: An Analysis of Ratings, Readability, and Sentiments." *Decision Support Systems* 52(3): 674–84.

Huang, Yun K., Wen I. Yang, Lin, Tom M. Y., and Ting Y. Shih. 2012. "Judgment Criteria for the Authenticity of Internet Book Reviews." *Library & Information Science Research* 34(2): 150–56.

Kaldor, Nicholas. 1950. "The Economic Aspects of Advertising." *The Review of Economic Studies* 18: 1–27.

Kim, Bong-Hyun, Yorgo Pasadeos, and Arnold Barban. 2001. "On the Deceptive Effectiveness of Labeled and Unlabeled Advertorial Formats." *Mass Communication & Society* 4(3): 265–81.

Klimmt, Christoph, Florian Hirt, Felix Keldenich, Konrad Mischok, Ina v. Salzen, Julia Sponer, and Maike Engelmann. 2012. "Netzfreiheit und Online-Werbung: wie Unternehmen der Regulierung vorauseilen: eine Chance für die Kommunikationswissenschaft." *Publizistik* 57: 259–69.

Köberer, Nina. 2014. *Advertorials in Jugendprintmedien: Ein medienethischer Zugang.* Wiesbaden: Springer VS.

Krallmann, Dieter, Ralph C. Scheerer, and Christoph Strahl. 1997. "Werbung als kommunikative Gattung." [Advertising as communicative genre]. *Sociologia Internationalis* 2: 195–216.

Lange, Paul. 2012. *Marken- und Kennzeichenrecht.* 2. Aufl. München: Beck.

Luhmann, Niklas. 1995. *Social Systems.* Stanford: Stanford University Press.

Lysinski, Edmund, and Rudolf Seyffert. 1920. "Begriff, Arten, allgemeine Bedeutung und Anwendungsbereiche der Werbung." *Zeitschrift für Handelswissenschaft und Handelspraxis* 12(4/6): 65–69.

Martin, Kelly D., and N. C. Smith. 2008. "Commercializing Social Interaction: The Ethics of Stealth Marketing." *Journal of Public Policy & Marketing* 27(1): 45–56.

Matteo, Stéphane, and Cinzia Dal Zotto. 2015. "Native Advertising, or How to Stretch Editorial to Sponsored Content within a Transmedia Branding Era." In *Handbook of Media Branding*, edited by Gabriele Siegert, Kati Förster, Sylvia M. Chan-Olmsted, and Mart Ots, 169–85. Cham: Springer.

Möller, Carola. 1970. *Gesellschaftliche Funktion der Konsumwerbung.* Tübingen: Poeschel.

Mukherjee, Arjun, Vivek Venkataraman, Bing Liu, and Natalie S. Glance. 2013. "What Yelp Fake Review Filter Might Be Doing?" In *Proceedings of the International Conference on Weblogs and Social Media.* http://www2.cs.uh.edu/~arjun/papers/ICWSM-Spam_final_camera-submit.pdf.

Nebenzahl, Israel D., and Eugene D. Jaffe. 1998. "Ethical Dimensions of Advertising Executions." *Journal of Business Ethics* 17(7): 805–15.

Obermiller, Carl, Eric Spangenberg, and Douglas L. MacLachlan. 2005. "Ad Skepticism: The Consequences of Disbelief." *Journal of Advertising* 34(3): 7–17.

Ott, Myle, Yejin Choi, Claire Cardie, and Jeffrey T. Hancock. 2011. "Finding Deceptive Opinion Spam by Any Stretch of the Imagination." In *ACL 2011: Proceedings of the 49th Annual Meeting of the Association for Computational Linguistics*, edited by Dekang Lin, 309–19. Stroudsburg, PA: Association for Computational Linguistics.

Plenge, Johann. 1922. *Deutsche Propaganda: die Lehre von der Propaganda als praktische Gesellschaftslehre.* Bremen: Angelsachsen.

Richards, Jef I., and Catharine M. Curran. 2002. "Oracles on "Advertising": Searching for a Definition." *Journal of Advertising* 31(2): 63–77.

Schweiger, Günter, and Gertraud Schrattenecker. 2009. *Werbung: Eine Einführung.* Stuttgart: Lucius & Lucius.

Serazio, Michael. 2013. *Your Ad Here: The Cool Sell of Guerrilla Marketing.* New York: New York University Press.

Tutaj, Karolina, and Eva A. van Reijmersdal. 2012. "Effects of Online Advertising Format and Persuasion Knowledge on Audience Reactions." *Journal of Marketing Communications* 18(1): 5–18. doi: 10.1080/13527266.2011.620765.

Weber, Max. (1921) 1968. *Economy and Society.* Berkeley: University of California Press.

Wilkinson, J. B., Douglas R. Hausknecht, and George E. Prough. 1995. "Reader Categorization of a Controversial Communication: Advertisement versus Editorial." *Journal of Public Policy & Marketing* 14(2): 245–54.

Wyss, Eva L. 1998. *Werbespot als Fernsehtext: Mimikry, Adaptation und kulturelle Variation.* Tübingen: Niemeyer.

15 Class and Advertising

Matthew P. McAllister and Anna Aupperle

In the long tradition of condiment advertising, one stands out: a Grey Poupon television commercial, debuting in 1981 and continuing for many years (Kanner 1986). In the spot, a chauffeur drives a Rolls Royce. A narrator explains as chamber music plays in the background: "The finer things in life. Happily, some are affordable," including, of course, this mustard. As the driver reaches with his gloved hand for a jar of the mustard that is kept, comically, in the glove compartment, it is revealed that his upper-class employer—a middle-age white male in a business suit—is eating a full meal in the back of the car. When the car stops, another Rolls pulls up. A similarly elite male rolls down the window and asks, "Pardon me, would you have any Grey Poupon?" "But of course," the first man replies, passing a jar through the cars' windows. "One of life's finer pleasures" is both stated by the narrator and written in an on-screen graphic. The campaign led to a significant selling surge and established Grey Poupon as a brand more upscale than its main competitor, French's. But, arguably, the campaign did more than that. A marketing executive for the campaign claimed that "We're not selling mustard here. Rather, we're selling an accessible taste of the good life" (19).

This ad associates the brand with the upper class in a tongue-in-cheek way. The commercial is filled with icons of the economically wealthy—luxury cars, full-time servants, expensive suits, and a demographic association of the economically privileged with a particular gender and age—all connected to Grey Poupon. These icons are presented as desirable and elite. The ad is striking, too, for its explicitness: We see these icons, but both narration and on-screen graphics solidify the message that Grey Poupon = upper-class status and pleasure.

Although not always as obvious as this ad, class is a key dynamic in the cultural meanings and economic elements of advertising. However, class is also arguably under-researched in critical media and advertising studies (Callier 2014; Foster 2005), perhaps due to the complexity of its depiction. Contradictions about class in advertising abound. Often the portrayal of class is so pervasive and uniform that it is invisible (Callier 2014). Claims in ads make suggestions about the accessibility of class mobility, exemplifying what Foster calls a "both mutable and rigid" depiction of class as generally presented in media (2005, 8). This chapter will explore some of the key concepts, examples, contradictions, and ideological significance of class in advertising as both a symbolic and political economic system and will argue that class in advertising is worthy of additional scholarly attention.

Class in Early Consumer Culture and Advertising

The study of class in advertising commonly combines historical, sociological, and textual analysis. This is because of the multifaceted presence of class. One way class is commonly conceptualized is as a series of hierarchical categories defined by socio-economic status (Thomas and Gruys 2015). Typical categorizations include lower class, middle class, and upper class, with occupational variations including working class and professional class. Because it is rooted in material inequity, class often leads to differences in access to income, property, location, education, and occupation. However, class also has a symbolic dimension that varies by culture, including class markers such as physical appearance (especially clothes), speech patterns, geographic areas (ranging from neighborhoods to countries), and types of housing. Class, then, not only marks one's socio-cultural position and identity, but it also is produced in systems of representation. Recent theoretical attention to intersectionality (Crenshaw 1991) notes the collusion of class with other systems and symbols of inequity, such as race, gender, and nationalism. For example, in the Grey Poupon commercial noted above, elite status is symbolized by a particular privileged combination of gender (male), race (white), and of course, class (upper).

Building upon the multifaceted nature of the concept, the study of class in advertising has commonly consisted of a combined historical and textual approach that lends itself to analytic comparisons between conditions and depictions at and between points in time. Critical approaches to advertising that center on class analysis typically draw upon Marxism and much of critical theory to highlight the structural inequities built into capitalism and the resulting group differentiations between the proletariat (workers, masses) and the bourgeoisie (owners, elite). Marx also believed that the unsustainable imbalances inherent to capitalism would eventually lead to increased proletarian alienation from the system but also class-consciousness, triggering a major rupture (or revolution) in the economic system. Although income may have risen for many people at the end of the 19th century, and many service and professional workers moved into the middle class, their mobility and autonomy were limited by severe industrial-era work requirements and constraints. And, of course, for many, severe economic disadvantages continued to characterize lives in capitalism. However, a general lack of strong class-consciousness and revolutionary impulse among the proletariat in Western societies (Borland 2008) suggests to Ewen (1976) and other cultural critics that the development of industrial-era consumer culture and advertising helped mitigate class resentment during this era. Packaging, retail display, and advertising of mass-produced consumer goods promised an equality and class mobility that became a powerful and enduring socio-cultural force that may have dampened social dissatisfaction and resentment (see also, Cross 2000).

Such an approach is useful for studying how class manifested itself in early-20th century print advertising in the US. A key way of differentiating products in the same category was through the development of brands—the symbolic construction of specific products and commodities in advertising and other marketing techniques. Then, as now, advertisers worked to link their products with values and well-known symbols—including desirable class-based symbols—to create positive meanings for the brand. Prior to the rise of consumer culture, values of convenience and leisure were mostly associated with the rich (Strasser 2003). However, with the rise of mass production, mass marketing addressed a wider range of people, including those of different classes, than in the early 1800s, when many fine, hand-crafted goods were sold only to the wealthy (Ewen 1976, 24). For instance, Kodak camera ads helped universalize photography, which was an expensive hobby before the availability of the mass-produced and affordable "Brownie" camera (Kotchemidova 2005). The values of convenience and leisure therefore became more universal as advertising associated them with their brands, stating that such brands offer to everyday consumers the privileges of the rich. Soap and appliance brand advertising promised to make household tasks so convenient that it would be like having servants in the consumer's home, no matter the consumer's class (Strasser 2003).

Early print advertising in the US also relied upon images of the well-to-do, as advertisers presented the brands with clearly very rich people using them, a class of people several rungs above the targeted consumer group. For example, the campaign for the patent medicine Lydia Pinkham portrayed rich women at the opera, despite the product's market of working- and middle-class women (Burt 2013). In such ads, the rich are portrayed as thin, impeccably dressed, elegant, and white. The tactic of showing the extremely rich using a product, without satire, would be less common today; notwithstanding Grey Poupon's famous commercial, modern advertising tends to use a "one-step-up" rule in elevating the status of a brand—associating the brand with people in a slighter higher status than the desired consumer—rather than with portrayals of the super-rich (Laird 1998). However, as we will see, lifestyle ads targeted at the affluent may still contain such images, if a bit more muted.

The working class also appeared in many early ads as servants in friendly support of the rich people using the brands (Burt 2013). During the Depression, maids—at least when portrayed as racially white—often were similar in physical appearance to the women they served, implying the possibility of class mobility (Marchand 1985). African Americans in advertising were typically portrayed as friendly servants for well-to-do white people (O'Barr 1994). The use in advertising of friendly servant-class people who looked out for the consumer continued through the television era and is found today, although these servants are now more typically in support of middle-class customers rather than the rich. Madge the manicurist for Palmolive dish-washing liquid was common in 1960s television, convincing her clients of the soothing properties of the soap by soaking their fingers in it. The Maytag Repairman—a slightly gruff, overweight white male in a work uniform— was unfulfilled at his job and desperately lonely, because Maytag appliances never broke (or so the commercials claimed). The modern equivalent of such servant-class characters may be found in Jan, the friendly receptionist in Toyota commercials, AT&T's blue-shirted Lily, and Flo for Progressive Insurance (McAllister, Cooke, and Buckley 2015).

US advertising not only romanticized class differences, but also implied that these distinctions could be eroded by the use of particular brands. The sheer magnitude of products available for purchase was part of this mes-sage, as were the common portrayals of the rich, helped by servants, using these affordable goods in ads. Many ads also promised to deliver the life-styles of the rich to the common person through stories of new adventures (cars, photography) and the elimination of cleaning and cooking drudgery. Collectively, then, advertising offered class mobility through consumption. Marchand (1985) labeled this message "the parable of the democracy of goods," where "no discrepancies in wealth could prevent the humblest citi-zens, provided they chose their purchases wisely, from retiring to a setting in which they could contemplate their essential equality, through possession of an identical product, with the nation's millionaires" (218).

When network television was introduced in US society in the late 1940s to early 1950s, it adopted the sponsorship model from radio in which one advertiser's name would be strongly connected with a program, such as *I Love Lucy*, sponsored by the cigarette company Phillip Morris, and *Texaco Star Theater*. The sheer number of television commercials and the melding of brands into television programming—through such techniques as host selling and product placement—visually offered the promise of the American Dream as a (nearly exclusively white) middle-class life embed-ded with brand-name appliances, foods, and cars. This televisual abundance may also have turned around tendencies toward thrift that were encour-aged because of decreased incomes triggered by the Great Depression and rationing during World War II (Samuel 2001). This basic middle-class dynamic of broadcast network commercial television still exists, as will be developed in a later section.

Class Hierarchy and "Shaming" in Advertising

While some aspects of consumer culture presented a class-mobile society that seemed to erode distinctions, other elements in marketing accentuated class differences. Cross writes that shopping "was a defensive reaction to insults from the class above or an offensive response to the classes below" (2000, 22). The same might be said about other elements of consumer culture, including advertising. The works of Thorstein Veblen and Pierre Bourdieu help to explain this class dynamic in consumer culture.

Veblen's work sought to investigate systematically the social and cultural life of commodities. In *The Theory of the Leisure Class*, Veblen (1922) takes note of several differences in consumption patterns among the lower and upper classes. He called wealthy people's obvious display of fine goods "conspicuous consumption," whereby the "Unproductive consumption of goods is honourable, primarily as a mark of prowess and a perquisite of human dignity; secondarily it becomes substantially honourable in itself, especially the consumption of the more desirable things" (69). Other patterns he noted distinguished what is considered socially appropriate to be consumed by the differing social classes. The consumption of high-end goods is reserved for certain genders (men) and more specifically, for some social classes (upper class men only, 69–70). When culture evolves to a "peaceable" state, allowing for men of upper-class status to become "gentlemen of leisure," these men are expected to eat and drink the highest quality of goods and surround themselves with the highest quality items of consumption (73).

Another of these distinct patterns of consumption is the difference between urban and rural populations. Veblen argues that urban-dwellers are forced to spend more on items of conspicuous consumption because of the need to "keep up a decent appearance," where rural residents do not have the same requirement (87). Because of the need to keep up appearances, urban residents are less likely to save money and more likely to spend it on fashionable goods, as they are forced to continue buying to compete with other city-dwellers.

Veblen also notes distinct differences in the ways in which men and women consume in relation to their class status. In earlier cultures, Veblen posits, women were the ones in charge of production, and it was up to men to do the major activities of consumption (69). When culture develops, it eventually becomes the woman's place to do the consuming for the entire family, at the expense of men and their place in the workforce. Even in lower-middle-class families where the capacity for consumption is quite low, men (and often children) are expected to do without so that the woman of the house can retain its "reputability" for the entire family (80–85).

However, all members of society are expected to participate in the consumption, albeit unequally. Subsequently, the goal of this consumption becomes emulation of those in a higher financial position, through aspirational attempts to purchase their way to the top of the social strata. Conspicuous consumption, as a result, fulfills other societal needs, such as the need to present a perfect self-appearance even if the end goal—increased financial wealth—is never achieved (84).

A similar intention of understanding class differences in relation to advertising, marketing, and consumption underlies sociologist Pierre Bourdieu's work, *Distinction* (excerpted in Bourdieu 2004). In his discussion of the "aesthetic sense," Bourdieu argues that taste "unites all those who are the product of similar conditions while distinguishing them from all others" (205). The practice of creating an aesthetic is by its nature upper class. In particular, the likes and dislikes of the working class are meant to tell middle- and upper-class citizens what they should aesthetically avoid, so as to not be associated with the working class (206–207). Bourdieu notes that the most important aesthetic distinctions, or "taste cultures," come between two closely related classes, as they have the most direct competition with each other (209).

Critiques of the concepts of conspicuous consumption and taste cultures often note how the meaning of brands and products is not given simply by the marketers, but also by consumers, who through alternative use and display may redefine the class-based or hierarchical connotations of established brands (Paterson 2006). Similarly, the hierarchical assumptions of brands may be gleefully rejected, as when consumers revel in their working-class identity and ridicule the rich. The advertising industry recognizes such dynamics and will often try to influence how people use brands. Such strategies include both the celebration of "elite luxury" (with a subsequent demeaning of the working class) and the "common sense" of the working class (with an implied ridicule of the rich).

Modern advertising thus often positions brands by not only associating them with upper-class icons and luxury, but doing so in ways that intersect with gender and other social categories. Sometimes these associations can be explicitly normative, even to a point where "class shaming" seems to occur with one class framed as clearly superior. One example of overt taste culture comparisons in advertising is the campaign for satellite provider DirecTV featuring actor Rob Lowe, airing in the US from 2014 to 2015. These ads were designed to counter the class image of garish satellite TV dishes as something found in working-class neighborhoods. In the commercials, Lowe plays two versions of himself: one who subscribes to DirecTV, and one who has cable. The DirecTV version is of course the preferred, and the class differences that are often shown between the two are an indication. In one version, DirecTV Lowe is contrasted with "Total Deadbeat Rob Lowe." Viewers know immediately as the two versions are shown side by side that there are normative class differences. Regular Lowe is clean-shaven, in a fine suit coat with matching shirt. "Total Deadbeat" wears a suede jacket and a Hawaiian shirt with a white t-shirt or tank top underneath them, a gold chain, and has patterned baldness with long hair, a mustache, and a "soul patch." Instead of being in a spacious modern home with a view of the mountains as DirecTV Lowe is, "Total Deadbeat" plays craps in a dirty alley behind a Chinese restaurant with the servant class (cooks and wait staff). He yelps loudly and with exaggerated body motions when he wins at craps, unlike the measured speech patterns of DirecTV Lowe. These two caricatures, then, reinforce class stereotypes in clearly hierarchical ways: upper-class Rob Lowe represents the preferred elite taste culture (which includes DirecTV), while "Total Deadbeat" performs a lower-class "trash" taste culture. DirecTV Lowe also watches television with large groups of friends at social gatherings, "consuming conspicuously" his satellite goods with his peers. Cable Lowe literally has "poor taste"—he has the look, mannerisms, and cultural preferences of the economically impoverished.

Conversely, ads may also poke fun at the snooty practices of the elite, emphasizing the "common sense" of the average person, especially for certain mass-marketed goods (or, as seen later, brands targeted for a working-class market). A Miller Lite commercial from 2015, part of a campaign that takes place in a convenience store with the same recurring store clerk (who, like Deadbeat Lowe above, has a mustache that indicates his class status, although in this case framed as favorable), illustrates this branding strategy. In this commercial, the clerk notices a regular customer uncharacteristically browsing through the wine selections. When asked by the clerk about this, the woman replies glumly, "Chardonnay party." "The Helen I know," he says, "brings a sledge hammer to a thumbtack. She brings a flamethrower [showing her a six-pack of Miller Lite] to a bonfire." Helen states the obvious conclusion: "She brings beer to a chardonnay party" and takes the six-pack. A male narrator sums up, "As long as you are you, it's Miller Time." So here the "true to yourself" message is enacted by violating the class status of a gathering: not snobby Chardonnay, but the "normal person" beer in which masculine metaphors (sledgehammer, flamethrower) convey this class disruption.

A 2014 TV ad for the non-Lite Miller High Life equates happiness of the working class with that of the rich. Titled "I Am Rich," the commercial uses irony to juxtapose the main character's words with black-and-white screen images. The working-class point-of-view of the ad is reinforced by background music with a honky-tonk twang. The character narrates the ad with such accompanying visuals as "I am rich" (20-something white male with a beard, jeans, and untucked shirt is shown, presumably the narrator), "I live in a luxury penthouse overlooking Central Park" (looks out the window of a modest apartment, looking down on a few trees lining a small street), "at my country club, we play parlor games with members of the royal family" (playing with large men in tank tops at a pool hall), "yes, I am rich. That's why I drink the Champagne of Beers" (sits on a throne, facing the camera, with a bottle of Miller beer). The ad mildly criticizes the rich with the juxtaposition of images, comparing the everyday working-class setting and life with uncommon privileges such as penthouses and country clubs. But in large part, this ad offers the two taste cultures as functionally equivalent: being "rich" with friends, dogs, shooting pool, and of course Miller beer, is just as rewarding as being literally rich with country club access, Central Park addresses, and (literal) champagne. As will be discussed in the conclusion, such comparative messages that attempt to establish hierarchies or equivalencies between classes and their taste cultures have ideological implications for how we may view economic difference.

The "Invisible" and The Lifestyle in Modern Advertising

The above examples where different classes are explicitly compared in advertising are rare. One of the reasons that class as a concept in advertising may be under-researched in many Western liberal democracies such as the US is that it often is invisible. The default characterization of people in mainstream advertising is upper-middle or professional class and, like the racialized concept of whiteness or the gendered concept of patriarchy, this class-based depiction of the "normal" identity makes it difficult to see (Foster 2005). Callier (2014) posits that in media representations such as modern advertising, non-normative class positions like the working class are "marked" in particular ways—where attention is especially called to it—while the middle class is "unmarked," where no explicit class markers are used, and such representations are presented as "average." The middle or professional class, then, is often indicated by the absence of what are commonly seen as class-based symbols: yachts, tailored suits, celebrity trappings (for the rich); corner bars, plaid work shirts, and football fandom (for the working class). For example, when customers interact with receptionist Jan in Toyota commercials, none of them wears shorts/t-shirts (too working class) or business suits (too upper class); none of them speaks with a Southern accent (too working class) or British accent (too upper class); none of them belches (working class) or sips tea (upper class). Instead, everyone looks, talks, and acts "normal," which presents, unassumingly, a middle-class lifestyle. This middle-class orientation, as noted earlier, was established in the early days of television and continues today for many advertising campaigns, especially for commercials on broadcast network television and in most general-interest consumer magazines such as *People*. One group is absent: in commodity-based advertising, the truly poor are rarely seen. They are visible in public service announcements for organizations like Christian Children's Fund, but in commercials for branded products, the impoverished do not ostensibly exist.

When modern advertising deviates from the middle-class symbols and orientation of most marketing, it is often designed to reach particular "niched" consumer groups in the form of lifestyle marketing. As Turow explains, such marketing is designed "to reach different groups with specific messages about how certain products tie into their lifestyles," albeit idealized versions of these lifestyles (Turow 1996, 4). So here class is used less to elevate a brand's status for all consumer groups than to target and appeal to members of a specific group that especially identifies with and sees itself belonging to the representations being presented in the campaign. Often, class symbols are a key way to constitute and target the brand's consumer group.

An early example of how a brand changed its lifestyle orientation largely by changing its class orientation is Marlboro cigarettes. It was introduced as "America's Luxury Cigarette"—a pricey, if underselling, filtered cigarette targeting well-to-do women smokers. Its vaguely British-sounding name also signaled an upper-class association. Ads featured women of elegance, in some cases smoking Marlboros with a cigarette holder, and told potential consumers, "Taste—not money—dictates the choice of Marlboros: only a tiny difference in price for a world of difference in pleasure." In the 1950s, the brand was re-targeted for a male consumer base, a challenge for a filtered cigarette that was not considered masculine. Ads at first featured a series of white working-class male hunters, tattooed men, sailors, and of course cowboys smoking Marlboros. The latter became most associated with the brand as the "Marlboro Man," shown wrangling and riding horses, lighting cigarettes with a stick over a campfire, leaning against a barn while smoking, and like the stereotype of the taciturn working man never speaking. Although this campaign is most noted for its construction of masculinity, it accomplished it through working-class symbolism, eventually focusing on that of the Western ranch hand (for discussions of the Marlboro Man, see Sivulka 2012; Twitchell 2000).

Today class symbols in lifestyle ads are typically conveyed visually—that is, not explicitly verbally expressed. Upper-end advertising uses symbols of the rich: yachts, tailored suits, small groomed dogs, and pearls. One common and perhaps more nuanced way to signify an elite and privileged class is through the use of particular celebrities, especially Hollywood stars. A 2015 magazine ad for diamond-encrusted "Ladymatic" Omega watch—listed at $17,000—tells us that the brand is "Nicole Kidman's Choice." The advertisement shows the Australian actress in lighting that emphasizes clean, almost pore-less skin, wearing the watch with an elegant white shirt and gold bracelet on the other hand.

Ads targeting working-class males use very different symbols to imply a lifestyle for their target market. A print advertisement for Copenhagen smokeless tobacco informs us that, despite its European name, it is "100% American Grown," a nationalistic claim that seems more "salt of the earth" conservative than the use of foreign actresses. Reinforcing this is the visual image in the ad: a close-up of dirty, scarred, work-worn, white male hands, gripping the Copenhagen tin. The dirt, scars, and worn nails of the hands indicate a workingman, one who is most likely to use such a product. These hands contrast very sharply with the fine, clean, and braceleted hands of Nicole Kidman—they both signal particular intersectional associations with nationalism, gender, class, and lifestyle.

Advertising's Influences on Class Biases in Media Content

An emphasis on the "invisible" middle and professional class is seen not just in advertising, but also in the non-advertising content of advertising-supported media, and it is not an accident that there is a similarity in classed portrayals in advertising and non-advertising messages. Butsch (2011) argues that much of media entertainment tends to under-represent working-class characters and over-represent professional-class characters when compared to their distribution in the US population. Many reasons for this exist, including potential ethnocentrism of professional-class media creators and the recycling of established formulas for content creation (thus slowing diversity in character types). But another reason is the long-term effect of advertising on programming. In addition to being a symbolic system, advertising is also a funding system, with commercial broadcasting, websites, and magazines significantly or entirely dependent on advertising revenue. In such cases, advertisers, not audiences, are the customers and income source of the media system. Although some may argue that advertising's involvement subsidizes the costs of media and makes it more affordable, it also steers media into the patterns of class discussed above. Much of the work about class orientations of media content focused on traditional analog media (television, film, magazines). A valuable research agenda, beyond the scope of this chapter, would be to examine whether the much-vaunted emergence of digital advertising deviates at all from this pattern.

The dominance of upper-middle and professional-class characters and settings in programming fulfills key needs of advertisers who want and pay for access to consumers who 1) can afford the products being advertised and 2) are receptive to consumption-oriented messages in commercials (Baker 2002; Hardy 2014). Such class-based orientations attract audiences from that category (or wish to be in that category, evoking the "one-step-up" principle mentioned earlier). Media content featuring characters using commodity goods associated with those classes integrates well with the accompanying advertising (Budd, Craig, and Steinman 1999).

As an illustration, the five most expensive US broadcast network scripted programs on which to advertise in 2015 featured characters who were more diverse in terms of gender, race, and sexual orientation than they are in class. These programs, in order, were about music industry executives (*Empire*), science professors (*The Big Bang Theory*), law professors (*How To Get Away with Murder*), middle- and upper-class families (*Modern Family*), and crisis management executives/politicians (*Scandal*) (Poggi 2015). These characters generally dress nicely, have nice things, eat in nice restaurants, and drive nice cars, with the exception of characters in *The Big Bang Theory*, who are obsessed with collectibles and popular culture. Commercials, then, for brands like Macy's, Apple, Olive Garden, Buick, and Star Wars fit right in with the lifestyles portrayed in such programs. *Modern Family*, especially, creates whole episodes around brands like the iPad, as consumption and leisure are central to the characters' class-oriented lifestyles (Steinberg 2012).

The working class does appear in television entertainment and other advertising-supported media. Programs such as the family sitcom *The Middle* earnestly reflect on economic hardship, especially during the Global Recession of 2008 in which programs such as this may thrive (Spangler 2014). However, others have noted the long history of television stereotypes of working class fathers as buffoons, as in the case with *The Honeymooners*, *The Flintstones*, *All in the Family*, and *The Simpsons* (Butsch 2011). Reality programs such as *Here Comes Honey Boo Boo* reinforce a hegemonic message of the immutable nature of southern working-class white people. Like *The Beverly Hillbillies* before them, even when characters like Mama June from *Honey Boo Boo* or the Robertsons from *Duck Dynasty* come into money, they do not change their taste culture: they still perform a "white trash" or hillbilly persona, often through the excessive consumption of vulgar "trashy" items like junk food (Rennels 2015). In such ways, class hierarchies are reinforced even in seemingly sympathetic portrayals.

Conclusion

Advertisements are a form of narrative storytelling and media finance that influence other stories that surround advertising. Advertising is first and foremost designed to sell products, but this does not mean that the stories they tell have meanings beyond what brands to buy. The stories told in advertising and advertising-supported media—digital and otherwise—have characters, settings, and perhaps most importantly, morals. Such morals and conclusions can be about what certain people are like, what they value, and how we should conceptualize happiness. All of these can include what role class plays in our lives: how we think of our own class, what class we aspire to, and what other classes are like. Grey Poupon wants us to think of its brand as elite, but in doing so it offers us meanings about how the rich live, what they value, and ultimately sends a message that we should be like them, that we should want their version of "the good life."

Sometimes the ideological meanings and messages we receive about class in advertising are contradictory, where the working class is stigmatized, stereotyped, and shamed as crass, lazy, and undesirable (DirecTV with Rob Lowe) or the rich framed as snooty and snobby (Miller Lite). But is this an equal ridiculing? The different levels of privilege indicate that the poor are more vulnerable and damaged by images of social "othering" and the blaming for their circumstances (why not just buy DirecTV?, such ads imply) than the wealthy.

Ads like Miller's "I Am Rich," on the other hand, perform images of "the happy poor" (Spangler 2014) that reinforce the economic status quo of capitalism and justify class inequity. The main character in the ad does not need material wealth to be "rich." Although certainly human happiness may be achieved in a variety of ways, by equating different levels of economic circumstance, it also erodes the real and significant advantages those with higher levels of material resources may access.

The middle-class bias of advertising and advertising-supported content may also stigmatize those less economically privileged as "not normal" and create debt-inducing expectations for access to material goods and the connection of these goods to living a satisfying life and the ability to consume these goods conspicuously as a display of desired lives. Lifestyle ads and ads that use classed-marked people as part of their brand associations (like Progressive's Flo) may also offer stories about what the rich and the working class look and sound like, sometimes associating stereotyped images of gender and race, as well. Enabled by the extensive data collection of consumer behavior offered by interactive and digital media, advertising will become increasingly target-market oriented into smaller lifestyle groups (for a general discussion, see Gehl 2014). In such cases, we may see even more specific combinations of social categories, including race, gender, and class.

This chapter argues that class, although perhaps not always as obvious as race and gender and not as extensively studied, is nevertheless a salient and ideologically significant element in advertising. The stories that advertising tells about class should continue to be interrogated and documented and their implications debated in our digital age.

References

Baker, C. Edwin. 2002. *Media, Markets and Democracy*. New York: Cambridge University Press.

Borland, Elizabeth. 2008. "Class Consciousness." In *Encyclopedia of Social Problems*, edited by Vincent N. Parrillo, 134–35. Los Angeles: Sage.

Bourdieu, Pierre. 2000. "The Aesthetic Sense as the Sense of Distinction." In *The Consumer Society Reader*, edited by Juliet Schor & Douglas B. Holt, 205–11. New York, NY: New Press.

Budd, Mike, Steve Craig, and Clay Steinman. 1999. *Consuming Environments: Television and Commercial Culture*. New Brunswick, NJ: Rutgers University Press.

Burt, Elizabeth V. 2013. "Class and Social Status in the Lydia Pinkham Illustrated Ads: 1890–1900." *American Journalism* 30(1): 87–111.

Butsch, Richard. 2011. "Ralph, Fred, Archie, Homer, and the King of Queens: Why Television Keeps Re-creating the Male Working-Class Buffoon." In *Gender, Race, and Class in Media: A Critical Reader*, edited by Gail Dines & Jean M. Humez, 101–109. Los Angeles: Sage.

Callier, Patrick. 2014. "Class as a Semiotic Resource in Consumer Advertising: Markedness, Heteroglossia, and Commodity Temporalities." *Discourse & Society* 25(5): 581–99.

Crenshaw, Kimberle. 1991. "Mapping the Margins: Intersectionality, Identity Politics, and Violence against Women of Color." *Stanford Law Review* 43(6): 1241–99.

Cross, Gary. 2000. *An All-Consuming Century: Why Commercialism Won in Modern America*. New York: Columbia University Press.

Ewen, Stuart. 1976. *Captains of Consciousness: Advertising and the Social Roots of Consumer Culture*. New York: McGraw-Hill.

Foster, Gwendolyn Audrey. 2005. *Class-Passing: Social Mobility in Film and Popular Culture*. Carbondale, IL: Southern Illinois University Press.

Gehl, Robert W. 2014. *Reverse Engineering Social Media: Software, Culture, and Political Economy in New Media Capitalism*. Philadelphia: Temple University Press.

Hardy, Jonathan. 2014. *Critical Political Economy of the Media: An Introduction*. New York: Routledge.

Kanner, Bruce. 1986. "When You're Haute, You're Hot." *New York*, January 27, 14, 16, 19.

Kotchemidova, Christina. 2005. "Why We Say 'Cheese': Producing the Smile in Snapshot Photography." *Critical Studies in Media Communication* 22(1): 2–25.

Laird, Pamela Walker. 1998. *Advertising Progress: American Business and the Rise of Consumer Advertising*. Baltimore, MD: The Johns Hopkins University Press.

Marchand, Roland. 1985. *Advertising the American Dream: Making Way for Modernity, 1920–1940*. Berkeley, CA: University of California Press.

McAllister, Matthew P., Tanner R. Cooke, and Catherine Buckley. 2015. "Fetishizing Flo: Constructing Retail Space and Flexible Gendered Labor in Digital-era Insurance Advertising." *Critical Studies in Media Communication* 32(5): 347–62.

O'Barr, William M. 1994. *Culture and the Ad: Exploring Otherness in the World of Advertising*. Boulder, CO: Westview.

Paterson, Mark. 2006. *Consumption and Everyday Life*. London: Routledge.

Poggi, Jeanine. 2015. "TV Ad Pricing Chart: 'Sunday Night Football,' 'Empire' Are Broadcast's Most Expensive Ad Buys." *Advertising Age*, September 24. Accessed January 4, 2016 at http://adage.com/article/media/ad-pricing-chart-sunday-night-football-empire-broadcasts-most-expensive-ad-buys/300516/.

Rennels, Tasha R. 2015. "*Here Comes Honey Boo Boo*: A Cautionary Tale Starring White Working-Class People." *Communication and Critical/Cultural Studies* 12 (3): 271–88.

Samuel, Lawrence R. 2001. *Brought To You By: Postwar Television Advertising and the American Dream*. Austin, TX: University of Texas Press.

Sivulka, Juliann. 2012. *Soap, Sex, and Cigarettes: A Cultural History of American Advertising*. Boston, MA: Wadsworth.

Spangler, Lynn C. 2014. "Class on Television: Stuck in *The Middle*." *The Journal of Popular Culture* 47 (3): 470–88.

Steinberg, Brian. 2012. "Many Brands Bid for Product Placement on 'Modern Family,' But So Few Make It. *Advertising Age*. Accessed January 4, 2016 at http://adage.com/article/media/brands-products-modern-family-make/232271/.

Strasser, Susan. 2003. "The Alien Past: Consumer Culture in Historical Perspective." *Journal of Consumer Policy* 26(4): 375–93.

Thomas, Jacob, and Kjerstin Gruys. 2015. "Class." In *The Wiley Blackwell Encyclopedia of Consumption and Consumer Studies*, edited by Daniel Thomas Cook & J. Michael Ryan, 86–89. Oxford, England: Wiley-Blackwell.

Twitchell, James B. 2000. *Twenty Ads that Shook the World*. New York: Three Rivers Press.

Turow, Joseph. 1996. *Breaking Up America: Advertisers and the New Media World*. Chicago: University of Chicago Press.

Veblen, Thorstein. 1922. *The Theory of the Leisure Class: An Economic Study of Institutions*. New York: B.W. Huebsch.

16 Advertising Ethics

The Bounds of Deceptiveness and the Endless Virtues of Rhetorical Strategies

Paulo M. Barroso

In contemporary Western societies and industrialized cultures, globalization increases both the quantity and variety of products for satisfying psychological and material needs (i.e., commodities, services, and brands), as well as the number of messages in the public space about these products. The seductive and appealing signs, images, and meanings of advertising that surround us appeal to our consumption, satisfaction, pleasure, comfort, happiness, or social success.

Considering such profusion of products and messages, Baudrillard (1998, 50) designates the contemporary Western and industrialized societies as "the consumer society" and Lipovetsky (1986, 19) designates the same societies as "post-modern societies," with a global trend to reduce the authoritarian relations and add private options, stimulating the diversity. According to this latter perspective, seduction has nothing to do with false representation and alienation of consciousness (Lipovetsky, 1986, 19); seduction builds and remodels our world according to a systematic process of customization, which is essentially based on the multiplication and diversification of offers (i.e., offering more and more and allowing people to decide more, replacing uniform subjection with free choice, uniformity with plurality, austerity with the fulfilment of desires). However, contrary to Lipovetsky's claim, advertising strategies of seduction are not only effective but also create precisely the illusion of something attractive in a product for which consumers should be persuaded. Due to this close relationship between strategies of false representation and illusion, alienation and seduction, critiques of the persuasive power and effectiveness of advertising necessarily invoke questions about ethical issues and social values.

But is the profusion of advertising messages the cause or the effect of massiveness? The answer to this question is complex and corresponds to the social and cultural transformations of societies and cultures due the globalization, which is per se another complex process. For Giddens, the concept of globalization is linked to the idea of a constant and rapid set of worldwide transformations, with changes affecting people everywhere (2000, 15).

As one such consequence of globalization, increased individualism is the result of the fragmentation of community life, and thus the denial of any form of ethics, because ethics presupposes alterity. The crisis of modernity is linked to the development of the subjectivity, in which the human being builds private aims for life, forgetting completely the other. As another consequence, the increasing spread of modernity brings with it secularization as the loss of social values and moral principles.

If globalization and modernity lead to a crisis of values and principles or to the end of ideologies, narratives and myths of the modern world, Nietzsche's *The Birth of Tragedy* (1999, 111) associates the demise of myth and the secularization of everything. This association represents a cultural decline of the world, where nothing is left that is mysterious or sacred, including nature, which is also subject to human manipulation. The idea of "secularization" (from the Latin *saecularis*) corresponds to a particular kind of temporality that denies history, a constitutive feature of modernity.

The use of persuasive techniques in advertising cannot be independent from rhetorical strategics. Such use makes public discourse more performative and the public space more secular. The issue of ethics brings the rise of individualism and secularization into relation with advertising, with rhetoric being a powerful technique or tool to influence or to persuade no matter what. It does so in ways quite different from the ancient ideals of its republican genesis, mentioned by Nietzsche's *On Rhetoric and Language* "as an essentially *republican art*" (1989, 3). Indeed, the profusion of messages leads to mass, unconscious, and conspicuous consumption, which apparently fulfills individual self-realization: the expectation of achieving happiness consistent with advertising claims and due to consumption. For example, Baudrillard criticizes the way consumer society produces signs and images of consumption that profoundly transform the sociocultural ecosystem. Also regarding this mass, unconscious, and conspicuous consumption, Veblen (2007, 60) points out the central role of advertising and consumption in individualist and secular societies due to exposing "individual[s] to the observation of many [other] people who have no other means of judging of his reputability than the display of goods." More generally, globalization, individualism, and secularization impair the ethical substance of social relations, which are manifest in less concern about social values and moral principles and the use of any means to achieve desired ends. Public discourse is more disposed toward the performative efficiency and effectiveness of what is said or transmitted, instead of truth as an absolute value of ethics. Signs of secularization include emphases on the materiality, possession, and appearance of brands the messages and public speeches appeal to and standardize.

By using seductive signs and images, advertising messages become fleeting and hedonist while also producing different conceptions of the present time and space and producing an increasingly image-centric popular culture. In order to consider these interlocking processes through the lens of rhetoric and ethics, this chapter analyses from an ethical perspective how advertising communicates and persuades using rhetorical strategies to construct seductive messages in a more and more secular, visual, and popular culture. In doing so, it also examines the profuse uses of advertising on screens in the public space as signs and images of secularization. This chapter regards visual, popular, and secular cultures as primarily shaped by advertising discourses. It is based on a conceptualization of the mutual relations among advertising, ethics, and rhetoric and public uses in producing a visual, popular, and secular culture.

Advertising and Ethics

Ethics deals with all human action, including the ubiquitous and persuasive forms of language use. Any action (the means) carried out for the sole purpose of achieving something else (an end) implies ethics, because ethics is mainly based on the relation between liberty of action (e.g., speech acts) and responsibility. In producing and transmitting public discourses, the mass media have important social and ethical implications, including *inter alea* the conferral of social status and the enforcement of social norms, actions, and fashions. In so doing, mass media reshape and restructure patterns of social and cultural life by providing not only information, but also models of behavior, social roles, and lifestyles. This ethical dimension of mass media is perhaps the most critical in regards to advertising. The goal of advertising is not truth, social values, or moral principles, but selling an idea, a concept, a product, a service, or a brand. Furthermore, advertising acts not just individually but socially by consumption while extolling certain social values and cultural patterns (beauty, success, wealth, youth, etc.). Thus, advertising messages produce a secular and popular culture from the early 20th century onwards by becoming a fully integrated part of it. A key way this is done is through the growth of displays and screens in the public space that convey attractive and seductive messages while establishing collective ways of seeing and understanding them as well as collective ways of thinking and taking actions.

Seen in this way, advertising ethics is a contradiction. While advertising uses seductive strategies of every kind to disarm reflection in its quest to persuade and sell, ethics has moral concerns and aims to be a critical and independent reflection on our actions, behaviors, and attitudes. Advertising disarms ethical reflection by suggesting a gap, a lack, or a need for consumers. Such a strategy is a perverse way to satisfy people's needs because it is a negative way to present what is taken as a positive good. In addition, advertising lies or deceives when it says what is convenient for one, which is the opposite of the truth (what is convenient for all). In the more general sense, one way advertising is unethical is by seeking to create false needs. As Marcuse (2007, 7) argues, false needs "are those which are superimposed upon the individual by particular social interests in his repression," with common ones being "to relax, to have fun, to behave and to consume in accordance with the advertisements, to love and to hate what others love and hate." Advertising encourages people to develop false needs and to satisfy such needs by purchasing non-essential commodities (Leiss et al. 2005, 83).

Such advertising practices are unethical because they are governed by particular benefits and specific interests instead of general, public, and disinterested consequences. Advertising is also unethical due to being designed to evoke passionate reaction instead of intellectual comprehension, which is no surprise for an industry devoted to using any means as long as it is effective. As Key (1976, xi) argues, advertising messages are composed to evoke emotions instead of thought. Speaking more generally, persuasion can often be more effective and unethical by using hidden and subliminal meanings. Perception is subconscious; people don't realize it. Meanings reach the subconscious in a way inimical to reason as Grijelmo (2000, 15) argues. As such, subliminal advertising is an ethically questionable way to manipulate and transform rational and critical people into an uncritical buying public.

Advertising not only affects consumers. It also affects other public communication processes through the adoption of similar strategic styles and uses of signs (words and images) to produce intended meanings or arguments (Bulmer and Oliver 2006, 55). To the extent that aesthetic elements (shapes, shadows, colors, saturation, depth, movement, etc.) and semantic elements (e.g., encoding levels and meaning or cultural systems) derived from advertising are used in other forms of public communication, advertising creates a generalized visual rhetoric that downplays if not ignores social values and moral principles of ethics.

While its genesis and implications are modern, advertising appropriates ancient persuasion techniques. For example, a Diet Coke commercial from the 1990s uses the message "It's 11:30 ladies! ...," which means "Diet Coke break." The message includes the song "I just want to make love to you" by Etta James (an original of Muddy Waters) in order to provoke desire, stimulate body attraction, and seduce. The advertisement treats women as targets for seduction by presenting stereotypes of sweaty and muscular workmen. Popular seduction of such kinds invades the private spaces of homes through the TV screen.

Advertisements awaken all sorts of feelings, from affection or pleasure to grief or disgust, by using images that provoke such reactions. Various Benetton campaigns in the 1990s also evoked feeling as a way to capture attention. Such advertising raises ethical issues due to its misappropriation of images that convey inappropriate social values while not transmitting moral social principles such as friendship and solidarity. Other examples show the use of deception within a polemic. An example is an advertisement for Weatherproof with the headline "The Leader in Style," which shows US President Barack Obama wearing a coat of this brand. According to *The New York Times* (dated January 7, 2010), the billboard, which was placed in Times Square in New York, consists of a photograph of Obama taken during his visit to the Great Wall of China, but which was used without his consent or knowledge in order to promote a jacket.

Due to how it "models the consciences" (Breton 2002, 60), advertising can produce spurious needs and desires in people by fostering an increasingly post-modern or secular, hedonistic, and consumerist society. For example, the concept of "Italianness" or "Italianicity" (i.e., the Italian character or quality or the state of what belongs to Italy or "what is coded as Italian") has been exploited by several advertising campaigns, one of which is a recent Dolce & Gabbana campaign, which displayed an Italian way of life, the fashion style, and the daily cultural lifestyle. In this case, advertising links a product or a brand with a clear and stereotyped cultural or national identity (Edensor 2002).

Ethics after Advertising: The Bounds of Advertising's Deceptiveness

Like any social and communicative activity, advertising should be evaluated using ethical norms, i.e., socially shared rules of behavior or action expressing what one ought and ought not to do under certain circumstances. Norms are authoritative rules or standards (of right and wrong or truth and falsehood) by which someone or something is judged and on that basis approved or disapproved. They are the set of conventional procedures (obligations, permissions, and prohibitions) that embody key social/cultural values and virtues. In addition, norms can be enforced by internal sanctions (e.g., feelings, awareness) or by external sanctions by being made mandatory rules established by the state. Either way, they provide rules for social coexistence and the guiding of action by showing what (and how) we should and should not do as moral or immoral.

The significance of norms for action is not purely theoretical. Norms shape social behaviors and constrain human actions according to the dichotomy of right and wrong. We consider our behaviors or actions in light of them and choose how to perform but with virtue. Behaviors and actions commit us and speak for us in the light of the existing norms. As Aristotle suggests in *Nicomachean Ethics*, we don't act virtuously in order to acquire knowledge, but to become good people (Aristotle 2004b, 1103b). Acting in accordance with norms is thus acting for the right reasons.

Thinkers as different from Aristotle as Parsons and Durkheim also see action as shaped by shared norms and values: The mere existence of norms entails, primarily, automatic compliance with them (Parsons 1967, 251), because norms are the basis of contractual relations, exercising an important regulatory action on us (Durkheim 1997, 161). Key foundational works in sociology view social norms as efficient means of achieving desirable ends such as social order and regulation, cooperation and retribution, and welfare maximization.

However, it is important to note that norms are normative. People do not always follow norms in practice (Smith 2004, 85). If norms are rules that prescribe or proscribe social behavior or action, they depend upon the possibility of violation as well as of adherence. It is here that norms raise problems of freedom and responsibility. If people act in accordance with prevailing norms, it is because (at least theoretically) they might also not act in accordance with them. This problem extends to ethics. The relation between normative standards and actual practice is necessarily tense and confrontational. For this reason, norms must be unconditional and clear. If they are not generally enforced and followed, they lose their strength to impose what they prescribe or proscribe. At the same time, norms change just as society and culture change. In this sense, norms are also relative, varying as they do from society to society and from culture to culture. Despite the differences, norms still regulate action and ensure mutual respect, because norms should ethically benefit everybody and reduce the risk of exploitation.

Mass media contribute to the formation and spread of norms (McQuail 2010, 433). Audiences demand good taste and morality, while other norms prevent the damage that unethical media can cause (McQuail 2010, 410). Foundational work in mass-media functionalist sociology makes this claim as well. Lazarsfeld and Merton outline three social functions of mass media, all of which (status conferral, enforcement of norms, narcotizing dysfunction) center on norms and issues of social cohesion (Lazarsfeld & Merton 2002, 20–23; Laughey 2007, 23). Writing in the 1960s, technological determinists such as McLuhan also focused on the importance of norms, their ethical import, and mass media. Television was seen to be restructuring patterns of social interdependence while forcing people to reconsider practically every thought, action, and institution formerly taken for granted (McLuhan 1967, 8). McLuhan's thesis was based on the idea that electronic *media* would transform and remake tribal our cultural ecosystem, because the mass media provide not only information, but also models of behavior, attitudes, social roles, and lifestyles (McLuhan 1962, 112).

As a particularly influential form of mass media, advertising promotes particular norms, which are ethically questionable. People are persuaded to accept the offers of the market. Certain corresponding, but unethical, norms are extolled such as the value of beauty, success, wealth, and youth.

Issues of norms and actions in relation to rhetorical practice such as advertising in our own time date back to Greek classical culture. Ethics has to do with the scrupulous guidance of one's life in order to act virtuously. According to Aristotle (2004b, 1098b, and 1101a), being ethical and virtuous also means being happy. However, problems occur whenever issues of virtue are separated from matters of happiness, as well as that of virtue and the law separated from the pursuit of pleasure and success. For this reason, Aristotle's rhetoric is a total art, because it assimilates ethics and the use of certain techniques. It is a *tekhné rhétoriké*. The main issue, whether regarding advertising or any action, is to know and to do what is necessary to become ethical. The difficulty with advertising from this view is that, by promoting a fantastic idyllic world, it hyperbolizes this world in order to ostensibly solve people's everyday problems. In this way, advertising messages are the product of rhetorical techniques. They use text and image to become aesthetically more appealing and believable (Grunig 1990, 8).

However, advertising messages invade the public space in a strategic and self-interested way, showing and disseminating unethical instead of ethical norms and values.

Recognizing how advertising relies on and conveys norms takes the argument about ethics into the realm of applied ethics. Advertising and applied ethics is controversial, because advertising as has already been noted concerns instrumental means and self-interested and thus unethical ends. Advertising effectiveness does not necessarily depend on morality; contents may be moral or immoral. Due to using the power of speech, advertising is a rhetorical action that requires ethical caution, because ethically speaking the ends should not justify the means. By taking a cunning, fallacious, or deceptive strategy in the service of self-interested ends, advertising refutes ethics. Thus, advertising and morality are two distinct domains.

The Endless Virtues of Rhetorical Strategies

Now that issues of advertising, ethics, norms, and morality have been discussed, the chapter turns to the implication of these conceptions on time and space and their remaking in part through advertising as also an ethical dilemma. As has been noted above, time and space today are increasingly global and secular, thus reshaping contemporary Western societies and industrialized cultures in profound ways. They are also revealed and produced in rhetoric techniques and strategies used in advertising discourses. Establishing this credibility depends not simply on showing the product; as has been noted above, the use of signs and images of seduction is much more effective (Greene 2003, 139). Discourses that convey modernist norms of time and space seduce by being epideictic as well as apodictic, seeking to emphasize the current moment of a rhetorical act while asserting the message's indisputable truth. When used in advertising, such messages create a false appearance of great importance or worth. They also develop new secular, visual, and popular forms of life that in turn rely on modernist forms of time and space.

One way this can be seen is in the semantic conversion of "ancient" via the dichotomy of ancient versus modern (or tradition versus modernity). Here, too, long-standing notions of rhetoric remain active and important today, consistent with Barthes's (1993, 19) claim that "the world is incredibly full of ancient rhetoric."

As an art of enunciating, rhetoric (from the Greek *retoriké*, the art of discourse) is traditionally regarded as the study of as well as the ability to persuade or motivate receivers of a message. As the art of effective speech, rhetoric is the supreme good that gives domain over other people, as Plato argues in *Gorgias* (2004, 452e). Similarly, in *Phaedrus*, Plato (1997, 261a) defines the art of rhetoric as a force for influencing the mind by means of words about any subject anywhere, in public or private spaces. Plato distinguishes *Gorgias*'s "bad rhetoric" from *Phaedrus*'s "good rhetoric" or *psychagogia* ("soul-leading"). According to *The Art of Rhetoric* of Aristotle (2004a, 1355b), the latter, virtuous use of rhetoric (as a careful and conscientious use for good purposes) is "the ability to discover what is appropriate in each case in order to persuade." Thus, from the beginning (*circa* 2,500 years ago) in Ancient Greece, rhetoric is the organized use of written, spoken, and visual language to fulfil certain intentions. Choosing the appropriate expression to communicate the best arguments is essential to persuading people about any subject.

Recalling Aristotle's perspective on rhetoric and ethics helps clarify the relation of both to advertising. While rhetoric is viewed as a productive or poetic science, ethics falls into the practical (or action guidance) sciences (Barroso 2014, 364). The relevance of rhetoric for ethics and vice versa is justified by the idea of truth. Whether emphasizing rhetorical speech production art or principles and values of truth and justice, advertising messages deviate from Aristotelian guidelines in an accepted yet unethical way. Advertising rhetoric is in opposition to ethical ideals of truth, because it neglects the rules and procedures that lead to the good use of argumentation, i.e., to the fair, accurate, and persuasive use of rhetoric.

In this way, ancient understandings of rhetoric continue to be relevant today for understanding the ethical lapses of advertising. As Packard (2007, 31) points out, "many of us are being influenced and manipulated, far more than we realize, in the patterns of our everyday lives." Persuasion itself is not unethical; however, as the Aristotelian strictures suggest, persuasion that does not embody good use of argumentation is. Advertising messages use rational but also irrational techniques of persuasion, which are impossible to perceive at the conscious level of awareness, thus becoming ethically suspect. People are manipulated by advertising messages, and this manipulation requires exerting a shrewd influence for someone else's advantage, convenience, or interest. Considered this way, manipulation can be understood as the cleavage of rhetoric from ethics. As a technique, rhetoric manipulates with words and with the way words are enunciated; as an orientation to action (mainly to speech acts), ethics is based on moral values and ideas of right and wrong, which are the opposite of manipulative actions.

Because public discourses should be regulated by truth criteria, ethics condemns manipulation. While ethics is a thoughtfulness and consciousness about what we responsibly do concerning and caring for other people, rhetoric is the art of speech no matter what is said and no matter the means to the ends.

One can see the resulting dilemma of this separation of rhetoric and ethics in the particularly modern phenomenon of simulacra, which in one sense are based on appearances, artifices, and illusions that deny their own historicity. Simulacra are produced by signs that convey peculiar rules and ways of thought (Baudrillard 1990, 21). However, Baudrillard doesn't recognize the imposition or seduction of simulation as power. Instead, discourses of simulation by virtue of their form alone produce a simulacrum of affect, desire, or libidinal investment, themselves produced by a world in which the need for these is cruelly felt. In simulations, signs recreate reality as an illusion, and as an enchanted world suggested by the idyllic fairy-tale end typical of advertising messages, in which products or services solve all problems. Advertising tools provide continually new ways of persuasion, manipulation, and simulation. One example of doing this is to reconfigure the distinction of true from false. "Do not lie" is different from "do not tell the whole truth," but both sentences are typical speech acts of influence or decision-making processes in social relations.

Manipulation and simulation presuppose misleading, a false conscience of transformation based on an illusion that nevertheless is dependent on a truth of desire and need. As Eco notes, ideology is only recognizable when it is socialized and cultured, i.e., converted into a social, cultural, and con- ventional code of meanings and practices. Seen from a Marxist notion of ideology as false conscience, advertising is an ideological discourse, in which a factual description tries "to justify it theoretically, gradually being accepted by society through a process of overcoding" (Eco 1976, 290). Eco quotes Jaspers's description of ideology as an "unconscious codeswitching," seen as "the complex of thoughts and representations appearing as an Absolute Truth to the thinking subject for the interpretation of the world" but "producing a self-deception, a concealment, an escape (from reality)" (Eco 1976, 312).

Simulation and simulacra also depend on a modernist proliferation of images, which also obscures by dehistoricizing needs and desires. Similar to Deleuze's "civilization of image" as a civilization of cliché (1985, 20), the ubiquity of images was previously diagnosed by Debord's *Society of the Spectacle*. In accordance with Debord (1995, 12), the whole life of society itself is an accumulation of spectacles, a concrete inversion of life, and as such, the autonomous movement of non-life, which if true is nevertheless represented as false.

In this way, advertising fosters and reproduces the "civilization of cliché" particular to the present modernist moment and global geography. Public discourses represent what a given culture values while also homogeniz- ing it. The more rhetorical, visual, and seductive advertisements are, the more hedonistic, consumerist, popular, and generalized cultures are. More seductive and public messages mean more distractive and spectacular social life. Image-based advertising presupposes the omnipresence of a corporate commodity culture. And all of these developments as seen from a critical point of view embedded in rhetoric and ethics reveal a characteristic tak- ing advantage of people, satisfying one's own intentions by manipulating others, or persuading others through unethical argumentation.

Conclusion

As has been argued here, persuasive forms of language are everywhere. Yet, as one central way that people are constantly trying to influence each other, advertising does so in subtle or subliminal ways instead of explicit and honest ways, thus seeking to affect people's opinions no matter the truth of the claim and no matter the means as long as the desired ends are achieved. Furthermore, modern advertising strategies are primarily visual. The public space overflows increasingly with advertising signs and images showing secular, unethical, tautological, hyperbolized, ephemeral, immediate, ideological, and new meanings. These new meanings in turn create new norms as ways of thinking, acting, speaking, and feeling.

However, despite the complexities noted above, advertising's ethical problems are at root due to lies, manipulation, excesses, failures, and simulations. When advertisements say "this car flies," "use this perfume and you will conquer all women," or "lose 60 pounds this week easily while eating what and when you like: just take a diet pill," it remains an important problem that many people do not regard these messages as false by understanding them figuratively instead of literally. Exaggeration is part of advertising techniques to influence and affect the public. These messages are effective and everywhere; they have persuasion power and a vast reach and influence.

Due to possessing such power and influence, advertising requires ethical reflection on its effects, with such reflection immeasurably deepened through attention to rhetoric. The rhetorical means by which advertising so effectively persuades today the world over depend in turn on individualism and secularization. As Camps (1996, 61) notes, "secularization [has] privatized or individualized everything," insofar as "everything is relative, including those values our culture and our tradition conceived as universal." We live in a given confusion where our own moral values become relative, subjective, and less credible.

Life in a democratic system and an information society paradoxically means greater freedom, media plurality, mass messages, and transparency but also the proliferation of more manipulative strategies. Advertising does not annihilate the public space of discussion and criticism, but it amplifies false values while releasing certain references and celebrities into circulation. In doing so, it renders the superficial as substantial while standardizing desires, uses, tastes, and fashions.

Advertising has the strategic power to redefine lifestyles but only centered on what it benefits from, which is consumption. Advertising devalues saving while it values spending and immediate enjoyment (Lipovetsky, 1996, 264). It disseminates a hedonistic culture dependent upon isolated individuals, while it accelerates the search for personality and new forms of expression.

As advertising's purpose is clearly to affect and influence people, it deserves greater scrutiny if not regulation of its role and responsibility. To limit ethical issues to the discussion about the imposition of deontological norms in a professional context is to disregard the application of ethics and its values. While deontology has to do with the imposition of norms to frame professional exercise, ethics belongs to the realm of the axiological ground and reflection, based on a collective definition of the system of values that regulate social interaction, including through public speeches. Therefore, ethics should be a *conditio sine qua non* to produce advertisements. However, advertisements will be ethical only if people who produce and consume them—as well as the dominant values in a given society—are also ethical. Ethics should be present in all human dimensions because, as Wittgenstein (1999, § 6.421) notes, "ethics must be a condition of the world."

References

Aristotle. 2004a. *The Art of Rhetoric*. London: Penguin Classics.

———. 2004b. *Nicomachean Ethics*. Cambridge University Press.

Barthes, Roland. 1993. *La Aventura Semiológica*. [Spanish edition of *The Semiotic Challenge*]. Barcelona: Ediciones Paidós.

Barroso, M. Paulo. 2014. "The Ethical Primacy of Advertising Rhetoric." *Journal of Communication and Society* 25: 360–75.

Baudrillard, Jean. 1982. *A L'Ombre des Majorités Silencieuses – La Fin du Social*. Paris: Éditions Denoël/Gonthier.

———. 1990. *Seduction*. Montreal: New World Perspectives.

———. 1998. *The Consumer Society*. London: Sage.

Breton, Philippe. 2002 *A Palavra Manipulada*. Lisboa: Caminho.

Bulmer, S., & M. B. Oliver. 2006. "Visual Rhetoric and Global Advertising Imagery." *Journal of Marketing Communications* (12–1).

Camps, Victoria. 1996. *El Malestar en la Vida Pública*. Barcelona: Grijalbo-Mondadori.

Debord, Guy. 1995. *The Society of the Spectacle*. New York: Zone Books.

Deleuze, Gilles. 1985. *Cinema 2: L'image-Temps*. Paris: Les Editions de Minuit.

Durkheim, Émile. 1997. *The Division of Labor in Society*. New York: Macmillan.

Eco, Umberto. 1976. *A Theory of Semiotics*. Indianapolis: Indiana University Press.

Edensor, Tim. 2002. *National Identity, Popular Culture and Everyday Life*. Oxford: Berg.

Giddens, Anthony. 2000. *O Mundo na Era da Globalização*. [Portuguese edition of *Runaway World – How Globalisation is Reshaping Our Lives*] Lisbon: Editorial Presença.

Greene, Robert. 2003. *The Art of Seduction*. London: Penguin Books.

Grijelmo, Álex. 2000. *La Seducción de las Palabras*. Madrid: Santillana Ediciones Generales.

Grunig, Blanche. 1990. *Les Mots de la Publicité*. Paris: CNRS.

Key, Wilson Bryan. 1973. *Subliminal Seduction*. Englewood Cliffs, NJ: Prentice-Hall.

Key, Wilson Bryan. 1976. *Media Sexploitation*. Englewood Cliffs, NJ: Prentice Hall.

Laughey, Dan. 2007. *Key Themes in Media Theory*. London: McGraw-Hill.

Lazarsfeld, Paul, & R. K. Merton. 2002 "Mass Communication, Popular Taste, and Organized Social Action," in *Media Studies – A Reader*, edited by Paul Marris & Sue Thornham, 18–30. New York: New York University Press.

Leiss, William, Stephen Kline, Sut Jhally, & Jacqueline Botterill. 2005. *Social Communication in Advertising – Consumption in the Mediated Marketplace*. New York: Routledge.

Lipovetsky, Gilles. 1986, *La Era del Vacío – Ensayos sobre el Individualismo Contemporáneo*. Barcelona: Editorial Anagrama.

———. 1996. *El Imperio de lo Efímero: La Moda y su Destino en las Sociedades Modernas*. Barcelona: Editorial Anagrama.

Marcuse, Herbert. 2007. *One-Dimensional Man. Studies in the Ideology of Advanced Industrial Society.* New York: Routledge.

McLuhan, Marshall. 1962. *The Guterberg Galaxy.* Toronto: University of Toronto Press.

———. 1964. *Understanding Media.* New York: McGraw-Hill.

———. 1967. *The Medium Is the Message.* New York: Bantam Books.

McQuail, Denis. 2010. *Mass Communication Theory.* London: Sage.

Nietzsche, Friedrich. 1989. *On Rhetoric and Language.* Oxford: Oxford University Press.

———. 1999. *The Birth of Tragedy.* Cambridge: Cambridge University Press.

Packard, Vance. 2007. *The Hidden Persuaders.* New York: Ig Publishing.

Parsons, Talcott. 1967. *The Structure of Social Action.* New York: Simon & Schuster.

Plato. 1997. *Phaedrus.* Cambridge: Cambridge University Press.

———. 2004. *Gorgias.* London: Penguin Classics.

Smith, Michael. 2004. *Ethics and the A Priori – Selected Essays on Moral Psychology and Meta-Ethics.* Cambridge University Press.

Veblen, Thorstein. 2007. *The Theory of the Leisure Class.* Oxford: Oxford University Press.

Wittgenstein, Ludwig. 1999. *Tractatus Logico-Philosophicus.* London: Routledge.

Part V

Emotion, Mood, Affect

17 The Mood of Information in an Age of Empathic Media

Andrew McStay

Around 35 years ago, literary and media critic Raymond Williams wrote that the real business of the historian of advertising is:

> to trace the development from processes of specific attention and information to an institutionalized system of commercial information and persuasion; to relate this to changes in society and in the economy; and to trace changes in method in the context of changing organizations and intentions. (2005 [1980], 170)

The proposition is right in that critical approaches to advertising should consider how ads influence and inform in relation to larger political, economic, and social structures. Clearly, advertising institutions are greatly different today from when Williams wrote this, but the methodological principle remains correct: We should situate our immediate experiences of advertising in the context of business practice, new technologies, social norms such as privacy, data protection, and as this chapter will explore, the nature and political economy of networked life. The final point on "intentions" in the quote above is key because, although today's behavioral advertising and automated data gathering is a relatively recent development, I argue that we are living through a pivotal moment of advertising history. As this chapter will detail, the intention for advertising today is to make use of sentiment, moods, emotions, and moments of experience. This is a topic that I began to address in the late 2000s in regard to online behavioral advertising, but within the last 10 years there have been significant developments in this domain. These include the range of data sources used to target advertising, the spilling over from our personal screens into public brick-and-mortar spaces, and the increasing interest in using data about emotions for both targeting and creating advertising. The chapter begins by recounting the behavioral context of modern advertising, the potential for programmatic techniques, the interest in not just life-stages but moments of experience, the role of soft biometrics and emotion-tracking, and what I term "empathic" media.

Web-Based Behavioral Advertising: Toward Real-Time Feedback and Moods

Until relatively recently, critical advertising scholarship has focused on the social significance of ads themselves. This canon, almost without fail, equates advertising with being visual. It makes extensive use of textual analysis to understand the historical, social, political, and cultural contexts from which ads derive their potency, inspire desire, and perpetuate brand mythologies. This approach sees advertising primarily as a symbolic practice interested in meaning making and sign play, and practitioners of advertising as handsomely paid bricoleurs employed to create novel combinations of symbols to engage and influence consumers. Through this semiotic-led tactic, critical studies focus on *reading* advertisements (Williamson 1978; Vestergaard and Schroder 1985; Jhally 1990; Goldman 1992; Dyer 1993 [1982]; Goldman and Papson 1996; MacRury 2012).

This is more sophisticated than it may at first appear because "reading" means coming to grips with the governing realities that lie beneath the surface of the text. In other words, it is a study of how meaning is made and why advertising resonates with us. Inspired by linguistics, this involves attention to visual and verbal grammar and rules governing interrelations of elements within ads; detection of the appropriation of signs from one domain, which are then leveraged within an ad; consideration of the socio-political nature of images and phrases; and arguments about the commodity sign and the ideological nature or the broader worldview promoted by ads. In addition to questions of how meaning is made and representations that distort reality and self-perception, another root of critical concerns about advertising is the way in which ad makers use what we hold dear. This entails the appropriation of important elements of cultural iconography and personal and collective experience. This includes raids on the highbrow arts, but also more fundamental experiences such as motherhood, sporting endeavors, meeting a loved one, first kisses, and even anti-advertising sentiments. As cultural practice and life experiences are appropriated and commodified, signs are re-articulated to influence and sell. As such, to an extent we behave, see ourselves, and play out life depicted by brands and advertising. The effect of this is to transform experience into cliché.

In *The Mood of Information* (McStay 2011), I departed from this canon of advertising criticism. I argued that greater attention should be paid to technologies used to deliver advertising, particularly behavioral techniques that involve tracking users' browsing activity over a period of time for the purposes of serving advertising tailored to what advertising networks working on behalf of advertisers assume are users' interests. This is what we could phrase as a *post-representational* perspective. Behavioral advertising has less to do with playfulness, depth, richness, humor, unusual perspective, intertextuality, juxtaposition, optical illusions, provocation, and means of seduction that draw on collective reservoirs of social and cultural references than with maximizing *relevance* to the viewer. A post-representational approach acknowledges the mechanics, processes, and impetus toward accountability, informatization of human action, and precision targeting deemed through orientation of the user, time, and location. This is less about advertising as a spectacular practice, as envisaged by critics inspired by Guy Debord and Roland Barthes, and what I argue to be a subtle channeling of consumer desire achieved by an exponential increase of information about us.

This requires attention to how this information is generated, what is done with it, the legal and regulatory context, social norms surrounding data generation, and close understanding of the industries themselves. Attention to the industry itself is something that symbol-led accounts of advertising had little interest in, perhaps believing that the cultural languages that govern texts are more important than authorship. Analysis of the behavioral advertising assemblage addresses the infrastructure that both supports advertising and is supported by it. This includes: *hardware* (machines, networks, and client-server data relationship); *software and applications* (most obviously web browsers and apps that support advertising); *businesses* (ad networks, ad agencies, online publishers, and advertisers); and *regulatory structures* (of national, regional, and self-regulatory design). We might also add *cultural dimensions*, particularly conceptualizations of privacy and data protection. Note that these elements of the assemblage do not exist in isolation, but interact in many ways. Also, lest we forget, behavioral advertising represents an important phenomenon for examination because it is the principle determinant of which businesses are viable or not on the web. This has implications for how we search and disseminate information, communicate, and socialize.

Heterogeneity and Feedback

In the *Mood of Information*, I accounted for how automated advertising processes quantify qualitative factors such as interests, feelings, expressions, and moods by converting behavior into digital and thereafter quantitative data. The opposite applies too as analytics provide media experiences that are increasingly meaningful and tailored and, when the technology works, may offer appearances of understanding our subjective selves and the circumstances we are in at a particular time and place. My argument was deeply constructivist in that it was premised on the logic that behavioral advertising is user centric. The theory is that a person's entire media environment reacts to his or her own input, with our very presence affecting the way that our informational environment appears to us. In other words, it is our informational being that affects the nature of "there." Nowadays the discourse of personalization is well known, and the fact that ads we receive are dictated by our input, clicks, and expressed interests is a relatively banal fact.

The principle of heterogeneity over homogeneity is key to keep in mind though, particularly as we consider the future of advertising. The turn from mass media experience and subsequent media fragmentation (proliferation of channels) to co-produced heterogeneous advertising experiences can only continue, intensify, and expand from our devices into our environments. The analytics can only improve too as the ability to infer interests, preferences, wishes, desires, disposition, and orientation allows us to speak of "moods of information." In addition to relevance to a person's interests, this is the affective and emotional tone of interactions we have with screens, sensors, digitally mediated environments, and networked systems.

The fact that heterogeneous reactivity happens in real time provides a liquid character to media and advertising experiences. The key is in feedback. Although this word may appear inextricably digital, it is something that audience-research organizations, advertisers, and advertising agencies have depended upon since their inception. Indeed, the business activities and writings of Daniel Starch (1914) and Claude Hopkins (1998 [1923]) were utterly based on laws of automation and feedback. However, the real-time nature of feedback is much more recent. Whereas Hopkins's understanding was broadly Newtonian in character in that it theorized feedback in advertising in terms of mechanics and causes and effects, an evolutionary approach provides a better diagnosis of contemporary advertising. This maintains an interest in feedback but recognizes the co-productive dimension of behavioral advertising in which one's input into the system affects the experience of one's environment. The key to this is in the process of coupling (or total state of relations between users and advertising systems) and co-production as we post, tweet, share, forward, like, create, search, read, buy, peruse, and click online content. As online advertising spending overtook that of television in 2011 in the UK (IAB 2014), the dominant logic of advertising today is one in which we more clearly inscribe ourselves on the advertising we receive.

This principle will outstrip any given device, technique, or platform. It reflects the changing form of capitalism wherein we take an even more active role in the creation of the commodity form than has historically been the case. This connects with audience-as-commodity concerns, although there are fundamental differences. For example, Dallas Smythe in the 1970s and 1980s argued that the audience is "more a statistical abstraction than are, for example, the audience of the live or motion picture theatre because they have no possibility of simultaneously and totally interacting internally to create an audience mood or affect" (1981, 49). Today this is quite wrong because today's social media platforms are based on users who are core and immanent parts of the system. Further, text, image, video postings, and dialogue generate the nature of the environment that they experience (expressed in terms of interests, moods, and tone). This in turn is closely analyzed by platforms and analytics firms (such as Cluep, Crimson Hexagon, Datasift, Ditto, Gnip, MutualMind, or Piqora) who each offer advertisers the ability to monitor online conversations and understand what people are posting and saying, where they are saying it, and how they feel about it in order to understand the impact of campaigns, to recognize who is influencing conversations, and to be able to ascertain how campaigns and brands are performing in relation to the competition.

Programmatic Logic: A Twist on the Experience Economy

Programmatic advertising (or "programmatic," as the ad industry refers to it) allows advertisers to automatically target consumers across a range of devices. It promises advertisers the ability to deliver the right message to the right person at the right moment. Receivers of advertising are assured that this is a preferable system because by understanding on- and offline behavior across their devices, this granular picture means they only receive advertising related to their interests. However, the efficiency of this system as it currently exists is questionable, not least because of poor inventory (ad stock), adblocking, and automated ad fraud (McStay 2016). But programmatic advertising remains important because it is the next step in behavioral techniques as it reaches across devices, apps, websites, and platforms to contact people with static ads, videos, rich media, native ads, and even promoted tweets. Readers of this book should be familiar with third-party tracking cookies, but programmatic uses a more diverse range of data sources than behavioral techniques that rely solely on tracking web browsers. It allows web publishers and advertisers to combine their own first-party data with third-party data. The former gives insight into purchase behavior and how people behave both in stores and on a company's websites. Retailers for example hold colossal databases about consumers' histories and interests (that are mined for correlations and things of potential interest to consumers). Third-party data includes data from behavioral ad networks, but there is more to it. Third-party data is bought from Data Management Platforms (sometimes known as Data Aggregators), such as eXelate, Lotame, and Bluekai, who deal with a large number of websites in order to gain a big-picture view of users (by means of cookies *and* IDs on mobile phones). Third-party data is derived from online tracking, but also website registration data, publically available demographic data, mobile phone data, insights gleaned from apps and social media, anonymous credit card data, and offline transaction data such as loyalty cards.

What programmatic offers is the possibility of combining these data streams to build richer pictures of target audiences (McStay 2016). The point about device types is key, because reaching us on our phones and tablets grants greater access to when we are most likely to spend and a greater understanding of which stimuli were influential in getting us to click or buy. In sum, programmatic advertising facilitates merging first- and third-party data (that is derived from a myriad of sources) to create more detailed pictures of device users than has hitherto been possible.

Not Just Targeting and Delivering, but Creating

These are early days for programmatic approaches, but programmatic advertising companies such as Adobe offer "dynamic creative optimisation." This allows brands to have their ads *automatically* (without human intervention) optimized to account for the type of viewer and contextual factors such as situation, location, time of day, and weather. The automated point is very important because what is at hand is not just automated real-time targeting and delivery, but *automated creativity*. Although creative agencies have nothing to fear just yet, it is reasonable to assume that low-rent advertising will increasingly be farmed out to machines. By "low-rent," I mean advertising that makes people aware of the latest and best deals, new products, or location/time sensitive advertising for stores nearby to where a shopper happens to be. This automated content contrasts with advertising that focuses on branding, storytelling, and semiosis (the production of meaning and significance). Should automated creativity seem fanciful, automated journalism is already used by respected news agencies such as the Associated Press to provide detail-heavy news (such as quarterly earnings coverage) not requiring human context, interpretation, or analysis.

The broader point is that automation in creating, targeting, serving, and collecting data about the reception of advertising gives rise to dynamic media environments. This is where words such as "virtual" and even "online" lose meaning because the future of behavioral advertising is based on programmatic targeting and optimization so to interact with us on a moment-by-moment basis. An example is Google and its Micro-Moments, which began to be promoted in 2015. This is their worldview of mobile-enabled advertising whereby individual customer "journeys" are tracked. What Google sells to its advertisers is the possibility of reaching people when there is strong intent to buy and opportunity to influence decisions. Thus, for example, when out and about and in need of coffee, Dunkin' Donuts is there to show us the quickest route to their outlets (and even line wait times). Sephora, a cosmetics and beauty products store, uses mobile communication to help customers while in a store decide which products are best for them. The company also uses Google's local inventory ads to target customers who are browsing for products nearby. Coca Cola also uses mobile, but this time to target teenagers whom they see as constantly using the Google search engine. This is an extension of their Share a Coke campaign whereby people buy Coca Cola with their name on the bottle. Thus, when in a store, they can search other stores to see if there is one in stock with their name in it (and even order one, if not). These examples tell us that mobile can be used to enable advertisers to reach their consumers where they are.

Programmatic logic and interest in Micro-Moments is deeply reminiscent of phenomenological interest in personal experience, questions of how we navigate spaces and places, and how we appreciate time. Indeed, Google's promotional video for Micro-Moments tells us that life is not lived in years, days, or even hours, but rather moments. It depicts memorable moments as people enjoy time with friends, watch firework shows, dance at festivals, put on new running shoes for the first time (Nike), break hairdryers (time for a new one), work out what car engine part is needed, wake and see snow has fallen (time to buy a sled), have successes (opportunity to go out and celebrate), fail in cooking attempts (let's eat out instead), decide to stay in town another day (hotel required), and find themselves being new parents (help from childcare stores needed). In most of the cases listed here, there will be no ad popping up to provide a solution (yet). However, it is the big picture rather than the detail that is significant. Not only does it lay out Google's strategy, it sets the mold for others to follow. This is deeply phenomenological in that it is about interacting with lived experiences and fleeting moments. But, paradoxically, this will be done with large and diverse types of data that Google can make sense of and react to in real time.

If linking advertising, phenomenology, and philosophies of experience together seems a stretch, consider the following quote from phenomenologist Alfred Schutz, who suggests that "experience in duration is not a being that is discrete and well-defined but a constant transition from a now-thus to a new now-thus" (1967, 45). The interest in Moments is not just a technological and business shift to mobile, but rather a philosophical and ontological progression to interact (and profit) from life seen as a "perpetual now." Where once marketers spoke of life-stages, the rally cry is different today: "Every moment, a new opportunity!"

Empathic Media

In theory, this moment-by-moment psycho-technological approach to advertising is based on shopping as a frictionless and fluid experience. It fits within a larger picture of personal device-based payment for goods, retail techniques that merge on- and offline opportunities, enhanced user experience of on- and offline environments, ubiquitous connectivity, increased data about behavior, recommendations, and relevance. Data-powered ads do not interrupt as much as they enable and guide need, desire, and intent along preferred channels to one's own stores, products, and checkouts. For this seamless vision of fluid capitalism to be realized, we have to be able to interact with our devices and environments in more natural ways. This brings us to the third part of this chapter as we consider the trajectory of behavioral and automated advertising. So far we have considered the prominence of tracking, targeting, and the way in which this has segued into programmatic and an interest in Micro-Moments. The next dimension to this narrative is an interest in emotional life.

Elsewhere I have used the term *empathic media* to refer to technologies that discern emotions and intentions, understand what is significant for people, and act on their emotional states (McStay 2014, 2016, 2017). These are wide-ranging and include: facial coding of peoples' expressions with cameras; voice analytics (not just what we say, but how we say it); sentiment analysis (of social media and images we post online); and wearable devices that record a wide range of information that indicates emotion (such as heart rates, respiration, galvanic skin responses, and what we look at). In general (with the exception of sentiment analysis), they use soft biometrics to infer emotional life. One might refer to it as artificial emotional intelligence.

I use words such as "infer" and "understand" loosely. Machines do not comprehend emotions in the same way as people do because, although they can track indicators of emotion, they cannot appreciate the fullness of emotion. At best there is verisimilitude of understanding, or a passing off of it, for our technologies to engage and immerse themselves into our lives. As John Searle puts it in relation to artificial intelligence, "you cannot milk semantics out of syntactical processes alone" (1998, 12). A spike of hate for example may make our face contort in ungainly ways, but this outward expression by muscle movement is only a small part of the biological and cognitive processes taking place during emotional states (not to mention the primacy of lived mental experience). However, we should be careful not to lapse into an interior/exterior binary regarding the truthfulness of emotion. Many head-based wearable devices, such as headbands, track electro-encephalogram (EEG) signals to infer mood. Others track respiration and other internal bodily indicators of emotion.

In advertising, tracking of emotions is used in two ways. One is in-house research, where research firms such as Millward Brown use facial coding, EEG signals, and other intimate means of analysis to assess our bodies and brains for reactions to advertising. This is much less about what we say and much more about how we react. Marketers and advertising agencies typically use these services to understand how people feel about brands, or to optimize big budget branded advertising to elicit high levels of emotional reactions. In practice, this might entail changing parts of the ad, altering music, amending the narrative, or even removing a character.

The second way of tracking emotion is by sensors in our devices, homes, and environments. Focusing on public environments and emotion-sensitive out-of-home advertising, in London 2015, M&C Saatchi (partnering with Clear Channel and Posterscope) produced an ad that evolves unique ads based on people's facial reactions. Placed on Oxford Street and Clapham Common (a district of London), it used hidden Microsoft Kinect cameras to infer viewers' emotions. The ad reacted over a period of views according to whether people's facial expressions were happy, sad, or neutral. This is done by identifying features and muscles on a person's face, tracking their movement, and thereafter correlating this movement with named emotional conditions. The ad was a test for a fictional coffee brand named Bahio that, ostensibly, was produced to gauge public reaction to this novel emotion-sensitive advertising. There are several notable features of this campaign. By reacting to emotional facial expressions, the ad optimized itself so to be more effective (by replacing elements of the ad that fail to trigger positive engagement so only the strongest elements survive). Behavioral advertising took place without personal devices and no personally identifiable information was collected or produced (important from a regulatory point of view). Thus, emotional life was commodified for the first time by automated means.

The "commodification of emotional life" is not especially new. Any student or scholar familiar with the *Journal of Advertising* or *Journal of Advertising*

Research will be aware that academic and industrial research into emotional reactivity to advertising has been taking place since the inception of the professional advertising industry. It is not even the interest in data and feedback that is significant because, as mentioned above, the earliest successful practitioners recognized that advertising can be treated as a science (entailing testing, iterations, feedback, data, and improvement). The capacity for automation, self-learning, and self-correction is the significant dimension to this story. The Bahio campaign should be seen in context of a wider array of emotion-sensitive and artificial intelligence technologies. Indeed, the campaign itself only used a very basic version of facial coding (to track whether people are happy, neutral, or sad), and other more sophisticated offerings are available from companies such as Affectiva, Emotient, and RealEyes who each draws upon seven facial expressions (joy, surprise, sadness, anger, fear, disgust, and contempt). This methodology derives from the psychological and anthropological work of Paul Ekman and Wallace Friesen (1971, 1978).

The reason for interest in this class of data is that emotions are critical to decision making. If emotions can be understood and reached in Micro-Moments, there is opportunity to influence us. Indeed, ad men such as Ogilvy and Mather's Rory Sutherland, who adheres to nudge architecture approaches (Thaler and Sunstein 2008), argues that emotional life provides such a strong steer on behavior that rationality is simply post-event justifications for behavior driven at a pre-cognitive level. This recognizes the failings of rational choice theory and puts to work insights developed by behavioral economists, such as Daniel Kahneman (2011), who study biases in intuition, heuristics in decision making, the role of emotions in prescribing thought, and problems with the belief that the human mind is cool and logical. Seen this way, the nub of empathic media for Adland is that mediated insight into emotional life grants greater capacity to affect decision making. As discussed in McStay (2013), this line of affect-based accounts of emotions fits within the neuroscientific worldview popularized by Antonio Damasio (2011) who argues that "somatic markers" and emotions play a pivotal role in reasoning and decision making, particularly when all other things are equal and there is no obvious decision to be made. The capacity to understand and harness people's emotions has less to do with suggestion or persuasion (a form of argumentation) than the intention to affect emotions so to steer decision making at a pre-conscious level (a form of control). It is to return to the long-standing matter of influence over social life and subversion of rational faculties at key moments.

We are still in the early days. So far, the use of empathic media in advertising is limited. However, when seen against the backdrop of increased commercial use of artificial intelligence, neural networking, automated pattern recognition, self-learning, improvements in natural language processing, predictive analytics, increased use of personal biometric devices, continued use of sentiment analysis, and emotional heat-maps of private spaces (such as stores) and public spaces (such as cities), there is a degree of inevitability about its use. The possibilities are far-reaching, particularly when we consider that cues perceived by empathic media include physiological change (for example pupil dilation, pulse, heart rate, blood pressure, body temperature, or respiration), electrodermal responses, pheromones, galvanic skin responses such as sweat, facial/body expressions, sound and voice inflection, and speech and language selection.

An understanding of how far-reaching these possibilities are can be enhanced by returning to programmatic advertising and what I phrased above as programmatic logic. If data management platforms seek to build complete pictures of their consumers, we can see the preferred direction of travel for Adland and marketers. The data-management platform eXelate claims to offer "unified customer profiles" that understand people across all of their devices and use of first-party data (our interactions with companies) and third-party data (brought in from a range of sources). Firms such as Kinetic (who specialize in out-of-home advertising) are developing programmatic ways to plan and buy out-of-home ad spaces. Although, at the time of writing in early 2016, emotion-sensitive approaches are not planned, Kinetic (and others) seek to make use of more precise audience targeting (which entails audience profiling and analytics) and real-time optimization of ads themselves. Although Kinetic has not yet started to use biometric data (but does use online sentiment analysis), the potential is clear. As it stands, personally identifiable information is not being used (at least in the case studies I have examined here and elsewhere), but it is reasonable to believe this will soon not be the case. Consider for example retail spaces where we give device-level data away in exchange for free Wi-Fi. Once we "consent," it is a very short step to connect our devices with in-store location, camera tracking, facial coding, assessment of interactions with store elements (such as products and assistants), and to thereafter use data about emotional reactions in tandem with other device-level indicators. This principle is intensified if we are already registered customers of a given retailer because it will have access to purchase histories and other first-party data.

Privacy vs. Intimacy

While speculative, I would not bet against this outcome. What we *do* have today is advertising that makes use of intimate, but not personal, information. My argument is based on a critical interest in intimacy over privacy. Is automated use of emotion profiling something we are comfortable with, even if the data is in no way personally identifiable? As this spans psychology and technology, we can borrow from Bernard Stiegler (2010, 2013) his notion of psycho-technology and thereafter questions of bio-politics (that entails a very wide range of investigations into how bodies are regulated). The broader point for us is that human activity, emotional life, and biometrically inferred presence of our bodies in public spaces is put to work for ends other than our own.

The bio-political dimension is an important one because empathic media bring the body into renewed focus. In relation to advertising we see this because we are less interested in: a) symbols (traditional advertising) or b) data and privacy (behavioral advertising) but c) tracing the body to track emotions and intentions. One notable feature of this modern situation and interest in soft biometrics is that we do not have the legal and regulatory frameworks in place to address this new relationship between bodies and public spaces. This is not just a question of legal coverage, updates, detail, or articles and clauses, but jurisprudence and philosophy. This is because data protection laws are wedded to privacy understood in terms of the possibility of identification. Empathic media currently have less to do with questions of privacy than intimacy. This refers to physical and emotional life and the fact that we can be affected without being personally identified.

My argument is not that privacy is now less important, but that it has come under strain in the context of contemporary advertising business practice and new technologies. As such, we now have to think "beyond privacy" and focus on the affective qualities of information in terms of intended and unintended consequences. As it stands in Europe, laws, directives, and parts of the General Data Protection Regulation relevant to advertising and data tracking are based on identification and privacy. Despite Europe's possessing what is routinely argued to be the strictest data protection regime in the world, commercial use of data about emotions is legal on the basis that no personal data is being used. This is so if: a person cannot be identified from given data; no code is generated about a person when data is collected; and persons are not singled out in any way (even if this "singling out" cannot be linked back to a real living person). If these criteria are met, data about emotions can be used without first requiring consent. The net result is that public spaces can be used to mine aggregated data about citizens' emotions by means of tracing faces, bodies, and behavior. How will this affect our relationship to public spaces? I suggest that by basing data protection on privacy, this leaves the door open to informational harm, not least regarding: how people relate to their environments; chilling effects (inhibition of behavior); and the lure of connecting emotional data with personal information in a situation where the possibility of meaningful consent is dubious. At a very basic level, even if not strictly speaking a privacy issue, tracking of emotions in public settings involves interacting, interfacing, and taking something without our say so.

Conclusion

This chapter has assessed recent trends in behavioral advertising. It has reflected on web-based cookie-enabled advertising, the reach and logic of programmatic applications, interest in mobile Micro-Moments, and more recent developments in emotion-sensitive out-of-home advertising. Critical approaches to digital technologies and privacy frequently invoke the specter of Orwell, but for those interested in advertising it is to Aldous Huxley we should turn. This is because the Brave New World he foresaw was based on control through pleasure and plenty. This is intensified when we consider Huxley's fascination with Pavlovian notions of conditioned reflexes and behavior and today's popular psychology based on nudges, behavior change, and the embedding of prompts into communication and environments to steer people toward a desired end. There is an important point here in that social control does not have to be oppressive, mechanical, or militarized, but can be made of the tiniest prompts (aimed to influence at the Micro-Moments just before decisions are made).

Thus, if we understand control to be about intentional influence toward a predestined goal and place, and if we place this understanding alongside the implementation of programmatic logic, we can see the future trajectory of advertising. Of course, pragmatism should prevail, and it is important that we do not lapse into dystopian narratives, but the theory (if not lived reality) of modern advertising is based on programmatic logic. This is characterized by desire for informational transparency of human demography, interests, location, time sensitivity, and situation. The arrival of out-of-home emotion-sensitive advertising portends a great deal for advertising and marketing (for the latter, particularly in-store analysis). Although Adland has long recognized the role of emotions in decision making, the fact that today data about emotions is being put to work to target, evolve, and create advertising in an automated manner is worthy of critical scrutiny.

As this chapter has indicated, bio-political theorization has much to offer in the way of diagnosing the nature of the problems. Privacy theory, too, can assist in terms of how we understand public and private spaces, although this runs into problems at the level of policy and regulation. If critical scholars and students agree that empathic media and emotion-sensitive advertising is cause for concern, we should be lobbying our policy makers and regulators to make them aware that intimacy as well as privacy matters.

References

Damasio, Antonio. 2011. *Self Comes to Mind: Constructing the Conscious Brain.* London: Vintage Books.

Dyer, Gillian. 1993 [1982]. *Advertising as Communication.* London: Routledge.

Ekman, Paul, and Wallace V. Friesen. 1971. "Constants across Cultures in the Face and Emotion." *Journal of Personality and Social Psychology* 17(2): 124–29.

———. 1978. *Facial Action Coding System: A Technique for the Measurement of Facial Movement.* Palo Alto: Consulting Psychologists Press.

Hopkins, Claude. 1998 [1923]. *My Life in Advertising & Scientific Advertising.* Chicago: NTC Business Books.

IAB. 2014. *IAB / PwC UK Digital Adspend Study Full Year 2013*, http://www.iabuk.net/research/library/2013-full-year-digital-adspend-results, accessed 20/01/15.

Goldman, Richard. 1992. *Reading Ads Socially.* London: Routledge.

Goldman, Robert, and Stephen Papson. 1996. *Sign Wars: The Cluttered Landscape of Advertising.* New York: Guildford.

Jhally, Sut. 1990. *The Codes of Advertising: Fetishism and the Political Economy of Meaning in the Consumer Society*. New York: Routledge.

Kahneman, Daniel. 2011. *Thinking, Fast and Slow*. New York: Farrar, Straus and Giroux.

Leys, Ruth. 2011. "The Turn to Affect: A Critique." *Critical Inquiry* 37(3): 434–72.

MacRury, Iain. 2012. *Advertising*. Oxon: Routledge.

McStay, Andrew. 2011. *The Mood of Information: A Critique of Online Behavioural Advertising*. New York: Continuum.

———. 2013. *Creativity and Advertising: Affect, Events and Process*. London: Routledge.

———. 2014. *Privacy and Philosophy: New Media and Affective Protocol*. New York: Peter Lang.

———. 2016. *Digital Advertising*. London: Palgrave-Macmillan.

———. 2017. *Empathic Media: The Surveillance of Emotional Life*. London: Sage.

Schutz, Alfred. 1967. *Phenomenology of the Social World*. Dekalb, IL: Northwestern University Press.

Searle, John. R. 1998. *The Mystery of Consciousness*. London: Granta Publications.

Smythe, Dallas Walker. 1981. *Dependency Road: Communications, Capitalism, Consciousness, and Canada*. New Jersey: ABLEX.

Starch, Daniel. 1914. *Advertising: Its Principles, Practice, and Technique*. New York: Appleton.

Stiegler, Bernard. 2010. *For a New Critique of Political Economy*. Cambridge: Polity.

———. 2013. *What Makes Life Worth Living: On Pharmacology*. Cambridge: Polity.

Thaler, H. Richard, and Cass. R. Sunstein. 2008. *Nudge: Improving Decisions about Health, Wealth and Happiness*. London: Penguin.

Vestergaard, Torben, and Kim Schroder. 1985. *The Language of Advertising*. Oxford: Basil Blackwell.

Williams, Raymond. 2005 [1980]. *Culture and Materialism*. London: Verso.

Williamson, Judith. 1978. *Decoding Advertisements: Ideology and Meaning in Advertising*. London: Boyars.

18 Affect Theory and Advertising

A New Look at IMC, Spreadability, and Engagement

Emily West

Critical scholars of advertising have long been attuned to emotion and affect. For example, the development of brands in the late 19th and early 20th century was predicated on creating a sense of trust and intimacy between consumers and particular companies or products (Cross 2000). Repeated exposures to the Quaker of Quaker Oats are designed to produce an affective response, which one could argue either subverts "rational" decision making (lowest price for best value) or produces a different, affectively based consumer logic. Scholars have consistently attended to how advertisers seek to create positive associations with consumers or how they have tried to articulate their brand with existing affects. Whether creating "brand tribes" (Maffesoli 1996), "Dreamworlds" (Jhally 1994), or other aspirational images (Lears 1994; Marchand 1985), both the practice and analysis of advertising have long left behind the view that advertising is a matter of rational persuasion about the objective features of products. In addition, one of the oldest critical theories we work with—that of Marx's (2001/1887) commodity fetishism—emerges from an emotionally inflected analysis of the human condition, wherein the creation of distance between the self and the fruits of one's labor, or between the self and the people that produce the things that we use, is fundamentally alienating. When we mistake our relationship with things as *social* and our relationship with people (workers) as *instrumental*, then commodities (and, subsequently, advertising) have played a trick on us that, according to Marx, disrupts our emotional well-being as humans.

In recent years we have seen an "affective turn" (Clough and Halley 2007) in critical theory. As Reber (2012) argues, "Emotion has been there all along; its status has simply experienced an epistemic shift, and scholars are, in effect, returning to the Western canon to give the presence of emotion a new epistemic interpretation" (89). While some of the concerns of affect theory are continuous with established theorizations of capitalism and advertising, others take us in new analytic directions. This chapter briefly reviews the developments in affect theory that are most relevant to the study of advertising and then demonstrates the fit between the analytic tools of affect theory and contemporary developments in advertising.

Affect theory is particularly useful for understanding people's encounters with advertising as lived experience, in space and time (McStay 2013).

Beyond focusing on advertising as representation, and our analytic activity on parsing how these representations work semiotically, the study of affect draws our attention to how a series of encounters with a brand, through various modes and channels, accumulates into a dynamic affective *relation* between consumer and brand. In this way, it has analytic fit with the industry practice of IMC (Integrated Marketing Communications) and helps us understand the importance of media buying and placement, behavioral targeting, and out-of-home, sponsorship, and mobile advertising—arguably all under-studied aspects of contemporary advertising practice. Further, affect theory can help us gain greater purchase on the power of virality, or spreadability, as Jenkins, Ford, and Green (2013) argue we should call it: how advertising that is passed among people through their social networks, especially with speed, acquires an affective intensity that may not be apparent just from analyzing the promotional image or text. An affective conceptualization of advertising also helps us understand the industry shift from seeking consumer attention to cultivating consumer engagement with brands.

Affect Theory in Critical Cultural Studies

In the last 30 years, affect theory has emerged as a major trend in critical cultural studies. Rooted in the resistance to mind-body dualism espoused by 17th century philosopher Spinoza, and subsequently shaped by psychoanalytic theories and autonomous Marxism, contemporary articulations of this theory draw our attention to energy, flows, movements, and intensities that exceed representation. Contemporary theorists including Deleuze & Guattari (2004/1987), Massumi (2002), Sedgwick and Frank (1995), and Clough (2010) have found affect theory useful for understanding our contemporary world, particularly for questions about power, global connections, mobility, social change, and the ever-proliferating ways that we connect with and affect, or are affected by, people and things.

Affect is usually defined in contrast to the more familiar category of emotion. Scholars have distinguished between the category of emotion—which is socially recognized and for which there are available discourses in the public sphere—and the category of affect, which is experienced and the effects of which may be observed, but for which there may not be labels or recognizable cultural forms (Kavka 2008; Wetherell 2012). Emotion is available to consciousness and can be narrated but therefore is already captured in a sense by ideology (Grossberg 2010) or organized by "emotional regimes" as Reddy (2001, xiii) would argue. In Grossberg's (2010, 318) formulation (drawing on Williams), it points to what is not yet sayable but is nonetheless "livable." Therefore, the examination of affect is often motivated by critical scholars who seek the ground zero of social change in some sense—where it exists as incipient affective energy that has yet to manifest as recognizable "politics."

In critical-cultural studies and media studies, the lens of affect has been turned onto politics (Ahmed 2004), labor (Hardt 1999), cinema

(Marks 2000; Sobchack 2004), and the consumption of popular culture (Gibbs 2011; Grossberg 2010; Kavka 2008). We might argue that cultural studies has long attended broadly to questions of affect, for example in its focus on structures of feeling (Williams 1977), questions of pleasure in popular culture (Modleski 2008; Radway 1991), and attention to the sociality of cultural consumption (Hebdige 1979; Morley 1986). However, affect theory, even though it is arguably still emergent and therefore still somewhat unclear in its boundaries, brings explicit attention to aspects of media and culture that are beyond language, representation, and signification. As Grossberg (2015) has remarked, signification and representation don't get at intensities, or the *quantitative* aspect rather than the qualitative aspect of communication. Indeed, the fuzziness that continues to characterize affect theory is precisely because it seeks to engage that which is beyond (or before) language and cognition, while having to use language as its explanatory and analytic mode (hence the move by some scholars toward alternative modes such as performance). Swenson (2008, 315) acknowledges that, "Affective change is difficult to pinpoint" and asks, given its ineffable qualities, "How do we discuss affect?" The answer, Swenson says, inspired by Althusser's (1971) comments on the unconscious, is that while we may not be able to language or observe affect itself, we can attend to its "effects" (315). Along these lines, affect theory directs our attention to movement (or flows, or fluxes, according to Gibbs 2011) and to contagion among people and things. As Seigworth and Gregg (2010, 9) explain, affect is associated with the shareable, the mimetic, the collective, and "stickiness." It focuses on the body in these processes, as source, recipient, and conduit of affect.

Affective and Emotional Capitalism

Many theorists have considered the place of affect and emotion in capitalism. The autonomous Marxists have argued that affect has economic value and is of increasing interest to capital (Hardt 1999; Terranova 2000). Hardt (1999) argues that affective labor is one of the primary forms of immaterial labor that drives our service, information, and experience-focused economy. While it is still possible, Hardt contends, for the fruits of people's affective labor to remain "autonomous" from capital—and perhaps to even be the source and means for "liberation" (100)—increasingly the value of affect is recognized, and exploited by, capital. This is particularly true in the culture industries, such as advertising, and underlies the analysis of scholars like Arvidsson (2005) who conceptualize consumers' immaterial, affective labor as central to the generation of brand value. Consumer activities ranging from purchase and use to displaying and advocating for the brand in social networks, responding to invitations from the brand to participate in events and online communities, and generally embedding the brand in their everyday lives, can be understood as necessary affective labor without which the brand has no sustainable value.

From a different perspective than the autonomous Marxists, Ahmed (2004) looks to Marx to understand how, while we misrecognize emotions as "belonging" or "attaching" to objects or persons (in her case, the case of "hate" toward groups seen as "other"), in fact our sense of this is only produced through an "affective economy" created by the *circulation* of affect, across discursive moments through time. She argues that just as the circulation of money-capital-money leads to the accumulation of value, so does the circulation of affective discourse accumulate into what is experienced as emotion. Along these lines Hearn (2015) argues that the "perpetual circulation of emotion and expressivity is new fuel for capitalism." Just as capital "gains its power through circulation" (Swenson 2008, 319), so does affect accumulate its power through circulation, sometimes culminating in an "affective epidemic" (Gibbs 2011, 257). Patricia Clough (2010) elaborates on the role of circulating affect in advertising in particular, saying "the circuit from affect to emotion is attached to a circulation of images meant to simulate desire already satisfied, demand already met, as capital extracts value from affect – around consumer confidence, political fears, and so forth ..." (220). Capital not only "extracts" affect, but magnifies its impacts and unleashes its productive capacities through processes of circulation.

Advertisers like scholars have broadened their emphasis beyond just storytelling and image making about brands and products, toward the generation of affect: between consumers and brands and among consumers, through a wide array of techniques. We can see this shift through book titles of the last 15 years or so, such as *Creating Brand Loyalty* (Ciernawski and Maloney 1999), *Emotion Marketing* (Robinette, Brand, and Lenz 2001), *Firms of Endearment* (Sisodia, Sheth, and Wolfe 2014), and *Marketing: A Love Story* (Jiwa 2014). In 2012, Garfield and Levy argued in *Advertising Age* that the era of product positioning, in which the attributes of a product are carefully positioned to be semiotically unique relative to competing products, has ended in favor of the era of relationship marketing. Their article was responding to the growing ability of consumers to make or break brands through the exponential power that social media and other forms of digital communication give to word-of-mouth, as well as the success of brands that have focused more on providing a consistent and coherent consumer experience than on persuasion through paid media. Garfield and Levy argued that, while until recently brands could make appeals based on consumer emotion, desire, or aspiration through logos, images, and stories told through traditional advertising vehicles, now the media environment no longer supports that kind of strategy, and further, consumers are looking to deal with brands that they trust.

So what does affect theory offer to the theorization of advertising and promotional culture that is new? Following from scholars such as Ahmed (2004), Clough (2010), and Gibbs (2011), I would point to the importance of *circulation, movement,* and the *accumulation* of affect in space and time. This approach focuses on the body as it affects the world and as it receives affect from people and things around it. Andrew McStay (2013) argues that the era of affective advertising has arrived, in which we should "consider creative advertising less in terms of abstraction but more in terms of stimulation and sensation—or that which is experienced in a lived and embodied place, time, field of movement and action, and is engaged with" (4). It follows that our tools for the critical analysis of advertising must be re-examined, or at least expanded. In order to understand advertising and society, we must study advertising *in* society. The significance of a given ad or campaign may not be apparent without understanding how actual consumers encounter it, the various ways in which they are exposed, and how they subsequently engage (McStay 2013). There are three emergent aspects of advertising that affect theory is uniquely positioned to help us understand better: the rise of Integrated Marketing Communications (IMC), the importance of spreadability through social media for promotion, and the shift from consumer attention to engagement as a valued metric.

Integrated Marketing Communications (IMC)

Integrated Marketing Communications, or IMC, is a term-of-art coined in 1989 by the 4As (American Association of Advertising Agencies) to describe a promotional plan in which all communication and customer service aspects of a business or brand have a consistent message and, in the definition of the American Marketing Association (2015), "all brand contacts received by a customer or prospect for a product, service, or organization are relevant to that person and consistent over time." Gaining particular relevance in a world where online and offline forms of marketing can too easily become disparate, especially given the siloed nature of many agencies, IMC argues for the need to *integrate* these aspects of a brand's communications, since they will *become* integrated by the consumer, who lives simultaneously in online and offline spaces. Conceived as a "360 degree media plan" that encompasses multiple points of contact beyond just media, IMC ideally doesn't just consider the story or image of the brand but how a relationship is built with the consumer, in time and space. Facebook interactions, Twitter outreach, print and TV ad buys, Out-of-Home (OOH) ads on public transportation or on billboards, and sponsored events can be part of this mix. Behavioral targeting, where ads are customized down to the individual level based on behavioral information left by our digital traces, allows ads to be delivered in a timely or spatially relevant manner via mobile, the mail, or online. IMC draws the advertiser's attention to how contacts with a brand or campaign play out in the customer's embodied, lived experience. The sensory aspects of these interactions start to loom larger, so it's not just the story, image, or slogan that is seen as impactful, but the pacing, the scale, the "touches" and contacts.

A notable example illustrates how IMC anticipates how consumers will encounter a brand or campaign in time and space, across online and offline contexts. An annual campaign "Small Business Saturday" started in the US in 2010 by American Express OPEN encourages consumers to kick off their holiday shopping at local, independent businesses on the Saturday after Thanksgiving, thereby reinforcing positive relations between American Express and its small business cardholders. Campaign media include traditional ad buys, online, and social media plus a public relations campaign fueled by supportive tweets from Barack Obama (reported on CNN.com by Diaz, November 28, 2015) and even the imprimatur of Congress who announced it to be an official holiday in 2012 (reported in Adage.com by Rupal Parekh and Kunur Patel, June 18, 2012). However, beyond media and PR, the campaign operates as an embodied, time-sensitive event. American Express converts small business owners and fans of local and independent business into brand advocates as they take to their Facebook and Twitter accounts to promote Small Business Saturday to their own networks. Reflecting on the multidimensional nature of IMC, *Advertising Age* reports about the initial planning of Small Business Saturday: "The question was, how could they get consumers and small businesses to actively participate in marketing and promoting the idea to make it a national success? The answer? With a million tiny details," including social media toolkits and promotional materials such a logos, posters, and buttons (Bulik 2015). The goal for such an integrated campaign is that when people go out in their community to "shop small," and see others doing the same, they will, it is hoped, feel the affective contagion and energy produced by like-minded people acting in concert.

This campaign is affective not just in design, but in content. Small business signifies in particular ways: as nostalgic, independent, sustainable, and responsible, while the people who shop at small businesses are imagined to be virtuous and community-minded. In a context in which it is well known that the confluence of big box stores and e-tailing are threatening small businesses on our main streets, Small Business Saturday becomes an example of cause marketing (Bulik 2015). However, the way in which Amex gets linked to community-mindedness through embodied, coordinated experience in time can't be simply read off the logo or taglines. Affect theorists would argue that we have to tap into the lived experience of this campaign to understand its power. However, while we may not be able to observe "affect" itself, we can point to its "effects" as Swenson (2008) suggests—such as high awareness of the event, rapidly increasing participation, and dollars spent year to year in the short life of the campaign in the US, with an estimated $16.2 billion spent as a result of the campaign in 2015 (according to Nicole Leinbach-Reyhle in *Forbes.com*, December 1, 2015), and almost 3.5 million "likes" on Facebook. By conceptually putting the consumer at the center of the campaign, Integrated Marketing Communications attends to embodiment and anticipates the ways in which campaign "touches"—both digital and in-person—will accumulate in the individual through time.

Spreadability: Promotion by the People

Marketers have long been aware of the power of word-of-mouth, certainly before the digital era (Katz and Lazarsfeld 1955). But digitally networked publics now make the snowballing of affect a much more rapid, visible, and seemingly measurable phenomenon. While the rapid diffusion of memes across the Internet via social media has long been called "going viral," Jenkins, Ford, and Green (2013) convincingly argue that we should refer to such content as "spreadable" rather than "viral." Carefully unpacking the metaphor, they point out that virality places agency in the "virus" itself, making the people who pass it along to others unwitting, even unwilling conduits. This metaphor is misleading. While certain kinds of content or affect may be more "spreadable" than others, depending on their properties and resonance, people have the agency to spread it or not throughout their e-mail lists, social media accounts, and blogs. Affect theory helps us gain greater purchase on how advertising that people share through their social networks, especially with speed or on a large scale, acquires an affective intensity that may not be legible from the promotional image or text alone.

Gill and Elias (2014) have commented on the affective power of spreadable content with Dove's Real Beauty Sketches campaign, which was pronounced the most viral ad campaign of the year in 2013 by marketing research firm Visible Measures (*Advertising Age*, December 16, 2013). The campaign featured a short film of an FBI sketch artist drawing portraits from two descriptions: one how a woman describes herself and the second how another person describes the same woman. In every instance, the portrait resulting from the stranger's description is more attractive than the one supplied by the woman herself. This contrast dramatizes the damage done to women's self-esteem and self-image by beauty culture. Gill and Elias (2014) point out that when brands such as Dove create highly emotional pieces of content, people are much more likely to share them with friends and on their social networks than just a standard promotional video. Responding to the 62 million views that the Real Beauty Sketches video had received so far on YouTube, they write that, "the fact of receiving it from a friend with a message such as 'You must watch this—it made me cry' is believed by advertisers to heighten viewers' receptiveness as compared with traditional forms of advertising" (Gill and Elias 2014, 182).

An added benefit of creating branded content that people participate in or spread through their social networks is that these behaviors, especially in many digital spaces, are observable, measurable, and sometimes even newsworthy. In the case of both Small Business Saturday and Dove's Real Beauty campaign (which goes well beyond the "Sketches" video), the brands have received considerable press coverage and buzz, which can create a multiplier effect for attention. It helps that both campaigns also intersect, even obliquely, with cause marketing, in that they both articulate their brands with a known social issue. In the context of the newsworthiness of the likes, hits, and other metrics of participation, it's crucial to bear in mind that these metrics are not foolproof indicators of consumer participation. In light of online robots, or "bots," fake and inactive social media accounts, the ways that brands can seed and promote their content with known "influencers" and "advocates," and other ways of gaming the system through an assertive public relations campaign, the extent to which promotional content has "naturally" struck a chord with the public should be taken with a grain of proverbial salt (Barger and LaBrecque 2013).

On the other hand, while publicly visible digital activity can easily be overestimated and even manufactured, it's likely that the majority of sharing about brands that occurs among individuals online goes unmeasured. Characterized as "dark social" by Madrigal (2012), the informal word-of-mouth and sharing of links, information, and preferences that occurs via e-mail, texting, and instant messenger applications is not measurable because it isn't public or on a platform that collects that data and sells it to brands (Barger and LaBrecque 2013). Websites measure this as "direct" traffic even though it has often resulted from someone following a link that was shared with them by someone they know. The significance of dark social becomes clear given that multiple measurement firms estimate that about 70 percent of social shares are "dark" (Madrigal 2012; Stanislaw 2015).

Whatever the means of distribution, a shared video accumulates authenticity and a sense of urgency, as well as the sensation of responding in concert with like-minded others. As emotionally powerful as the videos themselves might be, what we can't read from them is the experience of encountering them in different places or receiving them as links from multiple friends, all in a relatively short time period. The sensation of movement—also the term for "a group of people working together to advance their shared political, social, or artistic ideas" according to Google's 2015 definition—adheres to the Real Beauty Sketches video, for example, as it travels through cyberspace and contributes to the construction of an imagined community that shares similar ambivalences about beauty and femininity. Creating content that consumers will feel compelled to spread is a prominent strategy that brands use to foster not just exposure to their message, but engagement.

Consumer Engagement: New Metrics

Advertising clutter, along with the industry shift from an "advertising" to a "branding" mentality, has meant greater industry interest in audience engagement, rather than merely audience exposure (McAllister 2000). As Mark Stewart, then-Vice President of global media services at Kraft Foods said, "Exposure has absolutely nothing to do with engagement," hence their shift from "blasting an ad out to the masses" to making them "react" (quoted in Steinberg for *Adage.com*, May 10, 2010). Of course, ideally most brands are aiming for both: engaging advertising that works at scale.

What is "engagement"? If the measurement of audience attention was itself an inexact science (Napoli 2003; Steinberg 2010), then defining and measuring audience engagement with a form of media, or consumer engagement with a brand, has proven to be even less exact (Schultz and Peltier 2013). No standard metric exists. Facebook measures engagement with ads through comments, likes, and shares of paid content (*Advertising Age*, November 26, 2012). Barger and LaBrecque (2013) define the measurement of engagement with social media generally as "The number of comments on, replies to, likes of, and shares of a given post," acknowledging that the opportunities for engaging and responding to a brand's content vary with the social media form in question. Schultz and Peltier (2013), in contrast, argue that the new focus on specific forms of online behavior loses sight of the traditional understanding of consumer engagement, which focuses on individuals who use a brand or product and then engage in advocacy, be it online or offline, with members of their social networks.

Amex's Small Business Saturday uses IMC to achieve a high level of engagement with both consumers and "partners," or local businesses and business organizations that help promote the event and to whom this campaign is also targeted. Some of these metrics used to measure engagement with the campaign and track growth from year to year include number of Tweets and re-Tweets, Facebook likes, Facebook posts, number of people joining Facebook groups, number of businesses requesting promotional packets, and measured recall of TV ads. But both the quality and quantity of engagement is arguably difficult to capture in any one metric, or even in an index of metrics.

By contrast, when spreadability is about whether a campaign "moves" consumers and audiences to play a role in distributing promotional content, and therefore a way in which people offer their "free" affective labor to brands (Terranova 2000), the concept of consumer engagement encompasses more broadly the character of interactions between brand and consumer. For many years, Special K invited women to take the Special K Two Week Challenge, in which replacing two meals a day with Special K products was meant to yield a six pound weight loss. In positioning itself as an authoritative source of information and on-going support in weight management, the brand provided online tools including meal planners and weight trackers. As Special K brand manager Jose Alberto Duenas put it, the brand was no longer a cereal but a "weight-loss partner" (quoted by Newman in the *New York Times*, 2010) for women, allowing considerable brand extensions into other products like energy bars, meal replacement drinks, and even chips. Special K built a whole ecosystem of ways that women could engage with the brand, through multiple products, a variety of online and mobile tools, and in differing ways throughout the calendar year, from New Year's to bikini season. It was a prime example of relationship marketing, where inducing consumers to interact and engage with the brand across time generates affect and attachment that is worth its weight, no pun intended, in gold.

The brand's commitment to engagement over branding can also be seen in an initiative called The Victory Project, which briefly aired during commercial spots on morning talk shows in 2010, followed by a more extended web presence (PR Newswire, January 5, 2010). The 30-second TV spots featuring "real women" trying to lose weight had essentially no branding. Duenas said that "showing no Special K products or even a logo in ads was unprecedented for the brand" (quoted in Newman 2010). It wanted to avoid "the piece feeling overwhelmed by what the brand brings to the table. If you want to make a connection, you have to give consumers a chance to take part of the spotlight. Authenticity is what we're looking for" (quoted in Newman 2010). Even the name of the web presence for the campaign did not include the brand: "the victoryproject.msn.com" (Newman 2010). Amex uses a similar "low branding" strategy for Small Business Saturday. Campaign ads generally do not display American Express branding; only when people connect to the campaign's webpage does the American Express sponsorship become clear, although still in a visually reduced way. On the Small Business Saturday homepage, for example, the logo for American Express is very small and tucked into the top righthand corner of the page. For both The Victory Project and Small Business Saturday, though, the cause-marketing brand echoes the color scheme of the underlying commercial brand.

While Special K's Victory Project and Amex's Small Business Saturday may be on the far end of the spectrum, in terms of their willingness to dial down their branding in favor of cultivating multidimensional consumer engagement, they illustrate an advertising logic that emphasizes on-going, time-sensitive, customized engagement with consumers. Brands aren't just trying to tell stories that will create a one-time affective response in the consumer; rather, they are seeking forms of interaction that will create a more lasting affective bond, because it is rooted not just in the reception of content, but in concrete consumer engagement.

Conclusion: Brand Intimacies

An urgent question among scholars in recent years has been exactly how brands persuade consumers to do their promotional work for them. What are the incentives for us to provide free affective labor (Andrejevic, 2008; Cohen 2013)? Although an important question, affect theory leads to a question that perhaps logically precedes this one: How is intimacy—a certain kind of affect—cultivated between people and brands? The study of affect allows us to see how the sensation of a social relationship, even a sense of intimacy, develops between people and brands. Considering the emphasis in affect theory on the accumulation of affect through circulation, critical approaches to advertising should look at interactions with a brand over time, a sense of the brand being with us on our phones or other devices, the tactility of items we engage with from the brand (i.e., products), and the sensation of responsiveness when a brand anticipates or acknowledges our needs or desires. It's an *ecological* rather than *representational* approach to analyzing, and producing, advertising (McStay 2013). In our digital, interactive, mobile media environment, the opportunities for customized interaction herald the potential for brand intimacies never before imagined. The possibilities for circulation and flow—between consumer and brand, and among consumers, in both online and offline spaces—facilitated by digital technologies are likely to only intensify affective relations in consumer culture, according to affect theory. Of course, the capacities for backlash and resistance to brands are similarly bolstered by the same tools, the subject for future study.

What are the implications of analyzing advertising using affect theory? Theories of affect, as McStay (2013) has argued, encourage us to expand our analysis of advertising beyond the meaning of promotional texts and images, to attend further to how advertising circulates in our society and how people encounter ads and brands in an embodied way, in time and space. Changes in advertising brought about by the fragmentation of the media environment, the rise of digital and mobile communication technologies, and the resulting ascent of Integrated Marketing Communications should have already encouraged scholars to decenter the singular advertising text in their analysis, in favor of the campaign, the space, or the individual as their object of analysis. While the emotional appeals of ads and brands remain relevant, they are just part of the story of affect, which speaks more broadly to questions of attachment, trust, and the somewhat mysterious energy that puts people and things into motion, be it through purchases, online forms of expression, or seeking out other consumers.

References

Ahmed, Sara. 2004. "Affective Economies." *Social Text* 22(2): 117–39. doi: 10.1215/01642472-22-2_79-117.

Althusser, Louis. 1971. *Lenin and Philosophy, and Other Essays,* translated by Ben Brewster. New York: Monthly Review Press.

American Express. 2014. "Small Business Saturday®: About the Day." Accessed May 10 2015. https://www.americanexpress.com/us/content/small-business/shop-small/about/?linknav=us-open-shopsmall-homepage-about.

Andrejevic, Mark. 2008. "Watching Television without Pity: The Productivity of Online Fans." *Television and New Media* 9(1): 24–46. doi: 10.1177/1527476407307241.

Arvidsson, Adam. 2005. "Brands: A Critical Perspective." *Journal of Consumer Culture* 5(2): 235–58. doi: 10.1177/1469540505053093.

Barger, Victor A., and Labrecque, Lauren. 2013. "An Integrated Marketing Communications Perspective on Social Media Metrics." *International Journal of Integrated Marketing Communications* Spring 2013: 64–76. Available at SSRN: http://ssrn.com/abstract=2280132.

Bulik, Beth Snyder. 2015, February 3. "American Express: Small Business Saturday." The 15 Best Ad Campaigns for the 21st Century – So Far. Accessed December 29. http://adage.com/lp/top15/#smallsaturday.

Cierniawski, Richard D., and Maloney, Michael W. 1999. *Creating Brand Loyalty.* New York: Hudson House Publishing.

Clough, Patricia Ticineto. 2010. "The Affective Turn: Political Economy, Biomedia, and Bodies." In *The Affect Theory Reader,* edited by Melissa Gregg and Gregory J. Seigworth, 206–25. Durham, NC: Duke University Press.

Clough, Patricia Ticineto, and Jean Halley, Eds. 2007. *The Affective Turn: Theorizing the Social.* Durham, NC: Duke University Press.

Cohen, Nicole S. 2013. "Commodifying Free Labor Online: Social Media, Audiences, and Advertising." In *The Routledge Companion to Advertising and Promotional*

Culture, edited by Matthew P. McAllister and Emily West, 177–91. New York: Routledge.

Cross, Gary. 2000. *An All-Consuming Century: Why Commercialism Won in Modern America*. New York: Columbia University Press.

Deleuze, Gilles, and Guattari, Félix. 2004/1987. *A Thousand Plateaus: Capitalism and Schizophrenia*. Trans. and foreword by Brian Massumi. New York: Continuum.

Garfield, Bob, and Doug Levy. 2012. "Ignore the Human Element of Marketing at Your Own Peril." *Advertising Age*, January 2. http://adage.com/article/news/dawn-relationship-era-marketing/231792/.

Gibbs, Anna. 2011. "Affect Theory and Audience." In *The Handbook of Media Audiences*, edited by Virginia Nightingale, 251–66. Malden, MA: Wiley-Blackwell.

Gill, Rosalind, and Ana Sofia Elias. 2014. "Awaken Your Incredible": Love Your Body Discourses and Postfeminist Contradictions." *International Journal of Media & Cultural Politics* 10(2): 179–88. doi: 10.1386/macp.10.2.179_1.

Grossberg, Lawrence. 2010. "Rediscovering the Virtual in the Actual." In *The Affect Theory Reader*, edited by Melissa Gregg and Gregory J. Seigworth, 309–38. Durham, NC: Duke University Press.

———. 2015. Plenary Talk Presented at the WTF Affect Theory Conference, Lancaster, PA, October 15.

Hardt, M. 1999. "Affective Labor." *Boundary 2* 26(2): 89–100. Academic Search Premier, EBSCOHost (2259981).

Hearn, Alison. 2015. "Verified: Twitter, Identity Management, and Affective Capitalism." Paper Presented at the WTF Affect Theory Conference, Lancaster, PA, October 16.

Hebdige, Dick. 1979. *Subculture: The Meaning of Style*. New York: Routledge.

Jenkins, Henry, Sam Ford, and Joshua Green. 2013. *Spreadable Media: Creating Value and Meaning in a Networked Culture*. New York: New York University Press.

Jhally, Sut. 1994. "Intersections of Discourse: MTV, Sexual Politics and Dreamworlds." In *Reconceptualizing Audiences*, edited by Jon Cruz and Justin Lewis, 151–68. Boulder, CO: Westview Press.

Jiwa, Bernadette. 2014. *Marketing: A Love Story: How to Matter to your Customers*. Australia: The Story of Telling Press.

Katz, Elihu, and Paul F. Lazarsfeld. 1955. *Personal Influence: The Part Played by People in the Flow of Mass Communications*. Glencoe, IL: Free Press.

Kavka, Misha. 2008. *Reality Television: Affect and Intimacy*. New York: Palgrave Macmillan.

Lears, T. J. Jackson. 1994. *Fables of Abundance: A Cultural History of Advertising in America*. New York: Basic Books.

Madrigal, Alexis C. 2012. "Dark Social: We Have the Whole History of the Web Wrong." *The Atlantic*, October 12. http://www.theatlantic.com/technology/archive/2012/10/dark-social-we-have-the-whole-history-of-the-web-wrong/263523/.

Maffesoli, Michel. 1996. *The Time of the Tribes: The Decline of Individualism in Mass Society*. Thousand Oaks, CA: Sage Publications.

Marchand, Roland. 1985. *Advertising the American Dream: Making Way for Modernity, 1920–1940*. Berkeley: University of California Press.

Marks, Laura U. 2000. *The Skin of the Film: Intercultural Cinema, Embodiment, and the Senses*. Durham, NC: Duke University Press.

Marx, Karl. 2001/1887. *Capital: A Critique of Political Economy, Volume 1*. Trans. Samuel Moore and Edward Aveling, edited by Frederick Engels. London: Electric Book Co.

Massumi, Brian. 2002. *Parables for the Virtual: Movement, Affect, Sensation*. Durham, NC: Duke University Press.

McAllister, Matthew P. 2000. "From Flick to Flack: The Increased Emphasis on Marketing by Media Entertainment Corporations." In *Critical Studies in Media Commercialism*, edited by Robin Andersen and Lance Strate, 101–22. New York: Oxford University Press.

McStay, Andrew. 2013. *Creativity and Advertising: Affects, Event, and Process*. New York: Routledge.

Modleski, Tania. 2008. *Loving with a Vengeance: Mass-Produced Fantasies for Women*. 2nd edition. New York: Routledge.

Morley, David. 1986. *Family Television: Cultural Power and Domestic Leisure*. London: Comedia Publishing Group.

Napoli, Philip. 2003. *Audience Economics: Media Institutions and the Audience Marketplace*. New York: Columbia University Press.

Newman, Andrew Adam. 2010. "Pitching a Product, without Showing It," *The New York Times*, January 4. http://www.nytimes.com/2010/01/05/business/media/05adco.html.

Radway, Janice. 1991. *Reading the Romance: Women, Patriarchy, and Popular Literature*. Chapel Hill: University of North Carolina Press.

Reber, Deidra. 2012. "Headless Capitalism: Affect as Free-Market Episteme." *differences: A Journal of Feminist Cultural Studies* 23(1): 62–100. doi 10.1215/10407391-1533529.

Reddy, William M. 2001. *The Navigation of Feeling: A Framework for the History of Emotions*. Cambridge: Cambridge University Press.

Robinette, Scott, Claire Brand, with Vicki Lenz. 2001. *Emotion Marketing: The Hallmark Way of Winning Customers for Life*. New York: McGraw-Hill.

Schultz, Don E., and James Peltier. 2013. "Social Media's Slippery Slope: Challenges, Opportunities, and Future Research Directions." *Journal of Interactive Marketing* 7(2): 86–99. doi 10.1108/JRIM-12-2012-0054.

Sedgwick, Eve Kosofsky, and Adam Frank, Eds. 1995. *Shame and Its Sisters: A Silvan Tomkins Reader*. Durham, NC: Duke University Press.

Seigworth, Gregory J., and Melissa Gregg. 2010. "An Inventory of Shimmers." In *The Affect Theory Reader*, edited by Melissa Gregg and Gregory J. Seigworth, 1–25. Durham, NC: Duke University Press.

Sisodia, Rahendra S., Jagdith N. Sheth, and David B. Wolfe. 2014. *Firms of Endearment: How World-Class Companies Profit from Passion and Purpose*. 2nd edition. Upper Saddle River, NJ: Pearson Education.

Sobchack, Vivian. 2004. *Carnal Thoughts: Embodiment and Moving Image Culture*. Berkeley: University of California Press.

Stanislaw, Brewster. 2015, September 9. What Is "Dark Social" and Is It Something You Should Care About? *The Simply Measured Blog*. http://simplymeasured.com/blog/what-is-dark-social-and-is-it-something-you-should-care-about/#sm.00000fhs7vxb5he4asu7hp6rgf5eu.

Swenson, Kristin. 2008. "Capitalizing on Affect: Viagra (In)Action." *Communication, Culture & Critique* 1(3): 311–28. doi: 10.1111/j.1753-9137.2008.00025.x.

Terranova, Tiziana. 2000. "Free Labor: Producing Culture for the Digital Economy." *Social Text,* 18(2): 33–58. doi: 10.1215/01642472-18-2_63-33.

Wetherell, Margaret. 2012. *Affect and Emotion: A Social Science Understanding*. London: The Open University Press.

Williams, Raymond. 1977. *Marxism and Literature*. New York: Oxford University Press.

19 A Critique of the Advertising Consumer as "Target"

Addressing Advertising's Reflective Audience

Tony Wilson, Choy Tuck Yun, Sia Bee Chuan, Tan Teck Hong, and Michael Tiong Hock Bing

A swift digital download of advertising industry talk exhibits the metaphor of "targeting" as dominant. "Targeting consumers in all the right places." "Targeting consumers where they spend time." "Attitude replaces age for targeting consumers."[1] Consumers are presented here as passive recipients of stimuli, prodded, pushed, penetrated, or worse with objectifying, reifying zeal.

In this chapter we argue rather for the real consumer as active, as everywhere exercising an interpretive understanding of surroundings, not least advertising, both routinely and reflectively. To do so, we mobilize the philosophical opposition to positivism—phenomenology. While positivists construct their law-like generalities on a little discussed bedrock of data divorced from its specific cultural context, phenomenologists acknowledge seeing the world to be culturally situated.

We shall draw (not uncritically) upon a currently marginalized stream of advertising thought initiated some 25 years ago, often referred to as interpretive marketing theory underwritten by hermeneutic phenomenology. Hermeneutic marketing theory in its fuller formulation (an account we will discuss) is a narrative of active consumer practices. Subverting dominant talk of "targeting," this "presences" or "remembers" the embodied, equipped habituated narrative of routine consuming, which nonetheless tacitly and without reflection emplaces or puts in place consumer perspectives, affective "horizons of understanding" (Gadamer 1975). In advertising, our consumer horizons need respect. Qualitative consumer psychology listens to focus group participants (Wilson 2013, 2015).

Consumer reflection needs to be accommodated within this framework of everyday tacit practice—as individuals reflecting in the parallel discipline of organization studies to which we will refer later in the chapter. The discussion of mall visitor cellphone photography in a subsequent section is intended to demonstrate this siting of reflection within habituated tacit activity, a point so appropriately exemplified by a Malay female research participant. Hermeneutic phenomenology as distinct from its descriptive counterpart retains an interest in consumer iterative or individual story, not unlike the concern with narrative structures evident within ethnomethodology.

Active Consumers: A Hermeneutic Perspective

> You mean this sort of thing goes on all the time?
> (Question at recent Business School Conference)

Advertising research on interpreting consumers has been structured by hermeneutic theory for more than two decades, drawing upon writing by Heidegger, Gadamer, and Ricoeur, occupying a major role in qualitative psychology studies. This chapter seeks to advance that role by (re)turning to core concepts in hermeneutics' philosophical basis. Consumer responses to marketing in a massive multi-purpose Malaysian mall—displays designed to deliver equally massive visitor numbers—are considered to be embodied interpretative practices equipped by celebratory marketing. What is the psychology of such audience reception of advertising? Far from a stimulus-response or a positivist model of advertising cause and its audience effect, one can here incorporate consumer reflection. Is there a place in hermeneutic marketing theory for a consumer reflecting on embedded or emplaced affective horizons of understanding—while habitually engrossed in the mall?

In this chapter the question asked of advertising—not least as place branding in shopping malls—concerns whether it can address reflective consumers, enabling a recipient to enjoy escaping from (or transcending) habituated mundane consumption. Critically, can hermeneutic marketing theory—so prevalent in qualitative advertising and audience research—accommodate reflective escaping in the midst of everyday consuming? Here a qualitative psychology of consumer practices in response to marketing displays interprets them as: 1) embodied habituated (hence tacit) generic narratives (e.g., taking celebratory pictures), 2) enabled by equipment, and 3) emplacing a sometimes reflectively considered affective horizon of understanding (e.g., as "bonding"). Practices are familiar, habituated.

> (I) came back to the homeland, feeling so warm and so comfortable and glad to be back to the surroundings where I was grown up.
> (Chinese Malaysian female, 2014, Kuching)

Familiarity is the foundation of everyday life—constituting our life worlds. Yet advertising frequently features the extraordinary: "Your Unique Shopping Adventure." In this chapter, we extend the range of "adventure," exploring materially enabled, habituated, or mundane consumer behavior, going to a shopping mall, yet characterized by celebratory aspect or moment. Critically considering ubiquitous hermeneutic marketing theory, we ask where is the place for reflection practices—equipped, routine consumer engaging with product in response to marketing? To do so we draw on hermeneutic philosophy's own critique of positivism in foregrounding fundamentally the temporal dimension of everyday behavior as instantiating a tacit generic awareness of appropriate activity—or practices. Every day we walk in the familiar mall without reflecting on rule following.

Custom, then, is the great guide of human life. It is that principle alone which renders our experience useful to us, and makes us expect, for the future, a similar train of events with those which have appeared in the past.

(Hume 1748, Edinburgh)

Immersion in "custom" (Hume 1748)—our inductive generalization from past particulars as ground for anticipating the future—relies on familiar experience, underwriting the very possibility of understanding daily life. Without "tradition" (Gadamer 1975) enabling recognition, experiencing "surroundings" as fundamentally our hermeneutic "homeland," we could not actualize being-in-the-world as always already meaningful participatory modes of consuming addressed by advertising.

From a hermeneutic perspective, routine activities, undertaken with minimal self-monitoring as instantiating familiar or "fore-understood" (Heidegger 1962) genres, but nonetheless configuring narrative, are practices—or "ready-to-hand" (ibid.) equipped action—enabling (or indeed disabling) "being-with-others" (ibid). Hammering (Heidegger's example) can produce—eventually!—a house. In practices theory, "things also appear as always-already-interpreted—but here they are things to be handled and constitutive elements of forms of behaviour" (Reckwitz 2002, 253).

People are always already engaging in practices, producing a meaning for entities (apples, narrative) as equipment from collective horizons of understanding. Echoing this analysis, Schatzki argued in his early defining practice theory (2005) that the "social is a field of embodied, materially inter-woven practices centrally organized around shared practical understandings" (12). A practice's "constitutive elements" are "meanings, competences, materials" (Shove 2012, 5).

Hermeneutics considers how such (narrative) meaning is built, with tacit anticipating resting on generic assumptions about the world or "custom" (Hume 1748)—"projection" from a "horizon of understanding"—and integrating expectation with events. Practices so investigated hermeneutically range from the very activity of consumer and advertising researchers [which it is possible to regard reflexively through a "perspectival" lens (Bettany and Woodruffe-Burton 2009, 671–72)] to the genre of commonplace behavior this chapter considers, visitors taking their photographs in a seasonally splendidly decorated suburban shopping mall. For this study, the hermeneutic account of habituated activity as tacitly generic, enabling presumed, projected, and produced behavior, focuses further on consumer "enduring habits" (Üstüner and Thompson 2012).

These pages explore being "comfortable" with habituated practices (such as taking a picture). For mundane activities can nonetheless—as in our snapshot here of visiting a shopping mall—enable consumers' celebratory moments of reflective insight. The latter, particularly in pictorial form, we suggest should take a more prominent position in promotions.

Taking pictures involves a tacit set of shared assumptions: neither the activity (swiftly "taking a snap") nor assumptions (or "prefiguring") are likely to be explicitly reflected upon—unless issues or illuminating insight arises in the process.

Within thinking about advertising, it is important that consumers' 1) tacit understanding of practices (in which little self-monitoring occurs) be not conflated with 2) a transformative (albeit transitory) celebratory and critical considering. Both modes of understanding need in turn to be distinguished from 3) narrative contributions as participants to research focus groups/interviews and 4) their theoretical interpretation as "secondary derivatives" (Alvesson and Skoldberg 2009, 95). In short, acknowledging that a hermeneutic perspective includes our habitual behavior, rather than a seamless presenting of participants' narratives, this chapter proposes that such biographies of consuming contain a conjunction of tacit and—where appropriate—transformative meaning making. Consumers' reflectively configuring the latter is an appropriate celebratory subject for advertising.

In the ensuing chapter, we draw upon wider business and management studies to delineate consumers' habituated understanding-in-practice—their tacitly generic engaging with equipment in presuming, projecting, and producing a narrative—to provide a behavioral bedrock supporting our considering reflection as a suitable focus for advertising. We continue with a study—albeit short—of media consuming in a mall, so extending a hermeneutic practices perspective. In our following such a route, the philosophical "language-game" of a hermeneutic focus on understanding everyday life at a shopping mall is advanced through empirical experiment.

In this exploratory experiment of photography as a popular activity by mall consumers, we recognize that such devices shape practice in the market (Pantzar and Ruckenstein 2015). Holding familiar cell phone cameras (branded for smooth simplicity in use), consumers snap ready-to-hand shots—with attention focused on potential outcome (the picture) not easily managed equipment.

Embodied, Equipped, Emplaced Consumer Reflection as a Suitable Case for Advertising

A comparison of business school disciplines reveals mobilization of a hermeneutic practices perspective in management and organization study, most notably by Yanow and Tsoukas (2009) and Nicolini (2012). In their conceptual discussion, the former present an important distinction between "reflection-on-action" (such as when participants talk in research focus groups) and "reflection-in-action"—a celebratory or critical reflecting "in the midst of" habitual behavior. Analyzing the latter assumes an adequate account of routine activity. Thus aligning with a hermeneutic perspective on habitual practices as socially embedded, embodied, and equipped, these authors present their thesis that a "phenomenological view of reflection-in-action, such as the one we propose here, emphasizes its embedded (social), engaged (practice), and embodied (material) aspects" (1342).

Distinguishing between these modes of reflecting in/on action, then, is underwritten by the profoundly practices concept of "embodied" or habituated understanding. As the authors argue, their presentation of "reflection-in-action" points to momentary challenging of "ready-to hand" (Heidegger 1962) accustomed activity, in a "further theorizing of the character of surprise" (1339). Yanow and Tsoukas approach management study from a hermeneutic perspective incorporating understanding-in-practice. Likewise, Lai et al. (2007) are "challenging the dominant dualist influence of Cartesian philosophy in marketing" from a "hermeneutic perspective" incorporating the "embodied self."

In advertising or marketing theory, Thompson's contribution initiated hermeneutic inquiry. However, here, embodied, equipped reflection— presenting "horizons of understanding" (Gadamer 1975) in the midst of habituated behavior rather than subsequently in focus groups—is absent. No reference appears to hermeneutic grounding of activity as "primordial" tacit understanding-in-use.

Writing a year after Wilson's (1993) media studies of "hermeneutics, reception and popular culture," the paper by Thompson et al. (1994) references Heidegger's *Being and Time* (1962) to posit this philosophy's fundamental claim: "Interpretation is taken to be a necessary and inevitable aspect of scientific understanding," "preconceptions provide a necessary frame of reference rather than act as distorting 'biases' that hinder understanding" (433). *Contra* positivism, the consumer's "horizons of understanding" (Heidegger) from which practices theory asserts meaning is projected receive first recognition as a topological metaphor for exploring the construction of our intelligible experience. Nonetheless, no mention is made of Heideggerian phenomenology's equally fundamental claim in dismissing Cartesian dualism, that humanity primordially understands entities as equipment (Zeug). "Zeug basically means 'things' or 'stuff,' and in Heidegger's use more specifically 'something for such-and-such an activity or use.'" (Parkes 1992, 112) Our core awareness is tacit and teleological: "temporality and the spatiality of human activity are teleological phenomena" (Schatzki 2009, 38).

Given marketing's main orientation to addressing the consumer as user, this is an important omission. A paper by Thompson and Hirschman the following year (1995) on the "socialized body" ironically discusses the "several multi-billion-dollar industries that have an explicit body focus, such as diet programs, fitness equipment and services" (139) (emphasis added). Thompson's later (1997) article "Interpreting Consumers: A Hermeneutical Framework for Deriving Marketing Insights from the Texts of Consumers' Consumption Stories" neglects habituated tacit understanding in equipment use to refer only to the hermeneutic circle and "historically established understanding" (443). When Betty (a research participant) discusses her habit of dining out ("I usually do it [eat out for dinner] on days when I've just been working so hard and the thought of having to come home and to just work harder still is just more than I can take"), analysis of her "narrative frames" (445) or horizons of understanding considers only her subsequent reflection in talking to Thompson. Yet this narrative also involves reflection upon the activity within her accustomed practice—to "eat out for dinner"—a "thought" of avoiding further engaging with equipment—to "work harder still" (cf. Wilson 2012). It is not difficult to imagine restaurant marketing addressing such liberating consumer reflection.

Where research on advertising pursues consumer response as being "historically established understanding" (Thompson 1997), the latter needs to be necessarily grounded in the embodied and little-reflected-on habituated generic substratum of consumption as a site of narrative production. To illustrate such an inclusion, we make a sharp turn empirically to outline a current Malaysian media and mall research project on visitor behavior. In doing so, we further recent study of multi-cultural motivation in mall consuming (Farrag, El Sayed, and Belk 2010).

In *Practice Theory, Work, and Organization*, Nicolini remarks on phenomenology's practices perspective (following Heidegger's analysis of understanding and interpretation in *Being and Time*): "for reflexive, investigative, theoretical knowledge to come into play, something previously usable must become unusable" (2012, 34). But functional entities can also enable enlightening or insight, offering liminal possibility (Turner 1967) beyond both practical and propositional understanding of "identity exploration, self-focus, instability" (Marchant and O'Donohue 2014).

Everyday activity is immersively goal-directed, not least in producing intelligible meaning: "humans are always operating within an horizon of projection and concerns (Besorgen); that is, they are absorbed and caught up with things to do and achieve" (Nicolini 2012, 36). We can pass beyond unreflectively employing entities merely as functional equipment to momentarily regarding them as supporting celebration. In this complex behavioral play of switching meaning—crossing borders—the liminal (Kupers 2011) is foregrounded, the "edges" in transitory modes of consumer experience.

Seeking to evaluate this hermeneutic practices perspective on empirical research data, a pilot project exploring the liminal interface—or interweaving—of consumer ready-to-hand and reflected-upon experience was arranged in a large suburban mall. This multi-level building with its wide walkways contains among its many shops, around 150 food and beverage outlets along with 10 entertainment clubs, bowling and gym sports facilities, and a cinema complex. Space is distinguished by considerable investment in seasonal celebrations (e.g., for Chinese New Year).

Rather than interrupt consumer progress or walking with mall visitors (Lowrey, Otnes, and McGrath 2005), a small booth was established with the permission (and preference) of management where passing consumers were invited by students staffing the stand to share mall photographs and so participate in this project on consumer activities. Potential contributors were invited to talk at a later date about cell phone photos they had previously taken (already in their cameras), and in so doing respond to the topic, "what does the mall mean to you?" Photography of this architecturally splendid mall is widespread, a habituated practice evident on visually oriented social media.

As Jansson argues, "media consumption weaves together with other forms of consumption, thus exposing the inseparability of these two domains" (2002, 6–7). Likewise, mobile phones have been previously cast as an "emergent technology" for use in marketing research among consumers (e.g., Hein, O'Donohoe, and Ryan 2011) —see also "participant-led photography," Penaloza 1998; Vince and Warren 2012; Warren 2002). Screen immersion in shopping malls is ubiquitous.

This initial phase of inviting people to participate in media-led reflection on visiting the mall occupied a weekend. A subsequent four-week correspondence online ensued, arranging a mutually convenient meeting between consumers and the researchers. Participants discussed 25 photographs, individually and as a group (six persons): female and male, ranging in ages from 20 to 51, Chinese, Indian, as well as Malay, contributors included new graduates, account executive, management trainee, and teacher. In group discussion, people were asked to consider the photographs they had taken as signaling "themes" they wished to consider (e.g. "bonding"). Where consumers met a researcher individually, discussion revolved around "feelings," specific memories prompted by the pictures, and short descriptions of their content.

Subsequent to these "face-to-face" meetings between mall visitors and researchers, a further 12 online as virtual Facebook and WhatsApp "chats" were arranged with one of the chapter's co-authors in three groups discussing photographs of memorable moments in the mall. Participants of both genders were exclusively Chinese, with one exception (Bidayuh) and included a businessman, dentists, doctor, housewife, students, and lecturers: they were recruited as friends of friends. These contributions to both "real" and virtual meetings were all fully transcribed.

Talking here provided accounts of customary consumer visits to the mall, or in hermeneutic terms enabled narrative "presencing" pre-reflective or "ready-to hand" (Heidegger 1962) behavior. Reference was made to concurrent reflection, enlightened moments, a transcending "clearing" (ibid.) in mall consumers' everyday awareness. Distributed across genres or modes of immersion in the mall (such as "enjoying the crowd," the "health option," taking pictures), reflection-in/on-practices occurred spontaneously or it could constitute remembering, prompted by the mall's being "lighted up," celebrating the nation's diverse multi-cultural festivals—"spectacle" (Sherry et al. 2001). Here, mall spatial design and themes (Firat, Pettigrew, and Belk 2011; Van Marrewijka and Broosa 2012) prevailed as materially (in)forming affective horizons of understanding this place:

> At 'Chinese New Year, the lights … erm now look at this (photograph) is just that, I think it just, just brightens the day with the lights and … with the lanterns, so it is like more of a … like leading the path kind

of stuff, showing the way because it's lighted up', an older male Indian responds, reflecting on the mall's festive orientation as both materially and metaphorically illuminating, encouraging visitor affective perspectives.

Embodied horizons of understanding cell phone photography are brought to the fore. "I love candid shots. It seems to capture a moment in time, a real moment:)" (male, Chinese visitor) Or as female Chinese mall visitors enthused, a "precious moment," a "remarkable moment" of equipment use. In the following section, we consider taking such pictures in this mall as being an embodied habituated practice suspended momentarily in consumers' celebratory reflecting on participatory "being-there." Such celebration, we submit, is a suitable if neglected case for advertising, recognizing consumers as actively reflecting, transcending the mundane, rather than penetrated passive "targets."

Reflection-in-Practices: A Clearing in Consumers' Habituated Practical Understanding

Participants presented their narratives of why they visited the mall, constructing its vast space as a place familiar from frequent visiting. The mall was viewed from articulately mapped shared horizons of understanding this "habitat" (Bloch, Ridgway, and Dawson 1994), evident in collective behavior. Perceiving this urban space from adjacent points on these metaphorically spatial horizons of embodied anticipation, it was a place understood (or "projected") as enabling visitors to configure modes of generic being (such as "bonding" and "hanging out"), participatory involvement or "being-with-others" (Heidegger 1962), close friends, and companions in practices.

During an interview, one participant talks of her photograph taken after meeting a friend, "when we meet, that time you know, it was like, like after letting out everything": the photograph "was a closing of our meeting." "It was a happy ... happiness but is something more because I remember at this moment when we took the picture it was something that you want it to last ..." (female, Malay).

Surprised by "something more" than simply "happiness," in this brief introspective narrative (Caru and Cova 2008), she switches for a "moment" from habituated ready-to-hand experience of mall visiting to reflecting within the practice, regretting its transitory quality, wanting "it to last." In this temporary but transformative longing, she crosses the liminal borders between tacit immersion and thoughtful if passing inspection. From a hermeneutic perspective, both are modes of ludic (play-like) projecting and producing participatory intelligibility—so immersively integrating an existential narrative (Gaviria and Bluemelhuber 2010). A mall is thereby momentarily experienced differently, "reframed" (Schon 1983) from briefly changing horizons of understanding, regarded not as a place of passing consumption but of more prolonged pleasure through using this "singularized object," a cell phone camera (Epp and Price 2009). In taking a photograph, tacit pre-reflective consumption 1) has been transformed by a moment of reflection-in-practice 2) regarding ("remembering") affective embodied horizons of understanding "bonding," emplaced or put in place through habituated visits. "At this moment," this Malay woman presences a renewed sense of her "self-understanding" (Arnold and Fischer 1994, 55), celebrating "communitas" (Turner 1967).

Here we have closely observed memory, a presencing in/of a tacitly configured practice or generic habitual behavior ("ok, why not we just take one of those pictures?") by a consumer who considers this mall as enabling a "bonding session." Her narrative vividly accompanies concurrent celebration, refiguring its reception: "It was something that you want it to last." Pictures record that "something," "place ballet" (Seamon 1979)—a transcending display of her embodied cultural capital.

At this "moment" (hermeneutic as well as human) of reunion, rekindling and relief, one photograph shows behind the close friends a women's lingerie shop as a mall mise-en-scene, which serves to underwrite the occasion's "sense-content" (Ricoeur 1981) of intimacy, warmth, comfort, and solidarity in bonding. Such reflective images are a suitable focus for activity advertising.

Participating in the mall from a shared horizon of understanding it as a "superb hanging out place" (female, Chinese), this Malay woman produces (behaviorally or implicitly in her action, and explicitly in later talk) an account integrating expectation with later event. A celebratory moment is marked by closing equilibrium: it was "a relief after finishing," in their re-affirming close friendship. Here, indeed, "materiality and human relationships are inextricably intertwined" (Price 2013, 304).

Celebratory reflecting-in-practices can be a momentary enlightening amidst a forest of habit. But it may also be behaviorally evident as in a visitor taking photographs. The mall's aquatic and historical displays offered empowerment and peace to an older male Indian: "The water, to a large extent has a kind of soothing effect on the soul." He reflects in taking his distinctive photograph on the detailed decoration ["the stuff that (they) put there"] as equipping "different" activity, as mapping out alternative horizons of understanding embedded in behavior other than "just the norm."

His action belongs to the genre of evaluative comment rather than photography epitomizing representation. In subsequent reflection he attributes the "force of agency" (Epp and Price 2010) to the subject seen, understood in his narrative to manifest a preferred reading as a "challenge." It is a marketing construct also, we suggest, addressing the active consumer transcending habit: A display "has quite lot of history background to the early days when they use the sail boats and the journeys that the Chinese did during that era. (…) I think it, it kind of challenge(s) us to do something different other than just the norm." (male, Indian) Displays shape "different" practices, emplacing progressive horizons of understanding.

Switching from Reflection-in-Practices to Subsequent Reflection-on-Practices

The habituated practice of ludic immersion in the mall enabling their behavioral projection and production of narrative is considered by other contributors to interviews. This can be a delayed reflection-on-practices during discussion with the researcher (we "just come here, see, look and then just enjoy the crowd") rather than the Malay woman's earlier reflection momentarily in the midst of a shared practice. Equally subsequent to visiting, a Chinese woman for whom the hugely distinctive "Egyptian look" of this suburban mall is "very unique, lah. ... I mean you don't find it in other place(s) in Malaysia, right?" acknowledges that a presence in the place enables her to "catch up with old friends" (laughing) "like reunion." "Decoration" signals celebratory difference, drawing "the crowd": "sometimes we don't come here for shopping" but rather the "atmosphere, lah."

In other regularities of returning to this massive mall, a male Chinese celebrated the "health option," "bowling, exercise or the gym" as providing "for you to enjoy your healthy living styles." Here, he again projects and produces a participatory narrative with enabling equipment. Potential and actual activity could both be enjoyed. Reflecting on his desire, this visitor confessed, "Firstly I don't know how to play ice skating but I saw people playing with their friends with joy and fun." Reflecting upon her repeated visit, a female Chinese lecturer invests in stereotype to express excitement. "This place never fails to make me feel excited about shopping. It brings out the Asian in me." She looks to her horizons of self-understanding in mapping out cultural identity.

An older female Chinese teacher clearly visits the mall from a horizon of ludic expectation focused on equipment ["I always come to (the mall) actually," 'oh, ya, (its) mega lane"], producing in Seamon's terms a "place ballet" of vivid consumption ("every Thursday we have our bowling lesson here"). She is celebrating strength in overcoming chronic illness, especially when a mall's Chinese New Year decorations promote positive anticipation if not utopia (Murtola 2010):

> We are having a team called Pink Power. I'm a cancer survivor actually so we Pink Power are the cancer survivors team.

In all of these instances of "voicing out," reflection does not momentarily suspend a habitual practice but rather occurs in discussion, subsequent to people visiting the mall and engaging with its variety of circulating crowds and sometimes serious play. Here it constitutes *post eventum* reflecting—frequently a subject matter for arranging and analysis in much mainstream marketing hermeneutic research and sufficiently remarkable to be celebrating in advertising respecting the audience.

Conclusion: Advertising Addressing Reflective Consuming

In this chapter, we have turned to philosophical hermeneutics to re-conceptualize "habituated orientations" (Arnould and Thompson 2007, 11) on behavior. In doing so, we have sought to show how "individuals use consumer culture to transcend" (ibid.) habit can be addressed in advertising.

Consumer culture theory has much acknowledged the interweaving of marketing and material culture. The chapter has explored whether considering this dialectic from our hermeneutic practices perspective enhances research and advertising activity. From such a viewpoint, consumers engage in equipped, embodied mobility, habituated, hence tacit practices—generic if variously instantiated behavior—emplacing little reflected on horizons of comprehending, yet supporting celebration and criticism. Their subsequent reflection on a practice (such as ubiquitous photography in a mall) may be advanced in a focus group exploring horizons of expectation and their social embeddedness. Interviewing mall visitors, this chapter has sought to affirm consumer reflection as a suitable focus for advertising. We have argued for a "psychology" of the thoughtful consumer:

1 "dwelling" or immersed in a familiar mall, consumers' ready-to-hand understanding (unreflected on/incorporated in practices) is of entities as "equipment" (*Zeug*) rather than objects *simpliciter*;
2 celebratory or critical consumer reflecting within practices (insight or a momentary clearing in the mundane) may be enabled by refreshing displays or being spontaneous, a passing self-awareness;
3 creating this momentary clearing in otherwise unreflective everyday awareness is manifested in participatory activity of reflecting, captured in consumers' photography;
4 rather than seamless narratives of self-reporting by our participants in research categorized as being "hermeneutic," contributors should be encouraged to present celebratory and critical moments within habituated practices. "I remember at this moment when we took the picture it was something that you want it to last." These can constitute remarkable images in advertising consuming.

Incorporated in circulating around this mega-mall, consumer narrative practices construct a diverse material culture of response to concretized display, in which personal and professional goals are integrated—or occasionally involved in challenge. From a marketing perspective, its perceived promise of festive decorating, "great innovative ideas on each festive celebration," "creativity comes every festive season" (male, Chinese visitor) is particularly encouraging of mobile practices where "making know-how known" (Chia and Holt 2006, 642) is clearly understood and achieved.

The mall enables both ready-to-hand immersion and reflection-in-practices, with visitors momentarily switching in a liminal crossing between these modes of experience, as well as their subsequent reflexive accommodation. These categories rest on a hermeneutic practices perspective, which foregrounds for advertising celebratory moments transcending mundane activity—equipped reflection subverting corporate advertising talk of stimuli "targeting" passive consumers to purchase.

Acknowledgement

A much-appreciated conversation with Nicholas Davey, Professor of Philosophy at the University of Dundee, Scotland, cleared the path to an understanding of Lichtung (Heidegger's "Enlightening").

Note 1: Targeting Websites

<https://www.clickz.com/clickz/column/1691159/targeting-consumers-all-right-places>
<https://www.boundless.com/marketing/textbooks/boundless-marketing-textbook/social-media-marketing-15/social-media-and-technology-trends-99/targeting-consumers-where-they-spend-time-489-1299/>
<https://www.marketingweek.com/2015/11/05/attitude-replaces-age-for-targeting-consumers/>

References

Alvesson, Mats, and Kaj Skoldberg. 2009. Reflexive Methodology: New Vistas for Qualitative Research. London; Sage.

Arnold, Stephen J., and Eileen Fischer. 1994. "Hermeneutics and Consumer Research." *Journal of Consumer Research* 21 (June): 55–71.

Arnould, Eric, and Craig Thompson. 2007. "Consumer Culture Theory (and We Really Mean Theoretics): Dilemmas and Opportunities Posed by an Academic Branding Strategy." In *Consumer Culture Theory: Research in Consumer Behavior*, edited by R.W. Belk and J.F. Sherry, Jr., Volume 11, 3–22. Amsterdam: Elsevier.

Bettany, Shona, and Helen Woodruffe-Burton. 2009. "Working the Limits of Method: The Possibilities of Critical Reflexive Practice in Marketing and Consumer Research', *Journal of Marketing Management* 25(7–8): 661–79. doi: 10.1362/026725709X471550.

Bloch, Peter, Nancy M. Ridgway, and Scott A, Dawson. 1994. "The Shopping Mall as Consumer Habitat." *Journal of Retailing* 70(1): 23–42.

Caru, Antonella, and Bernard Cova. 2008. "Small versus Big Stories in Framing Consumption Experiences." *Qualitative Market Research: An International Journal* 11(2): 166–76. doi: org/10.1108/13522750810864422.

Chia, Robert, and Robin Holt. 2006. "Strategy as Practical Coping: A Heideggerian Perspective" *Organization Studies* 27(5): 635–55. doi: 10.1177/0170840606064102.

Epp, Amber M., and Linda L. Price. 2009. "The Storied Life of Singularized Objects: Forces of Agency and Network Transformation." *Journal of Consumer Research* 36, February, 820–37. doi/pdf/10.1086/603547.

Farrag, Dalia A., Ismail M. El Sayed, and Russell W. Belk. 2010. "Mall Shopping Motives and Activities: A Multimethod Approach." *Journal of International Consumer Marketing* 22: 95–115. doi: 10.1080/08961530903476113.

Fırat, Fuat, Simone Pettigrew, and Russell W. Belk. 2011. "Themed Experiences and Spaces." *Consumption, Markets and Culture* 14(2): 123–24. doi: 10.1080/10253866.2011.562014.

Gadamer, H.G. 1975. *Truth and Method*. London: Sheed and Ward.

Gaviria, Pilar R., and Christian Bluemelhuber. 2010. "Consumers' Transformations in a Liquid Society: Introducing the Concepts of Autobiographical-Concern and Desire-Assemblage." *Journal of Consumer Behaviour* 9(2): 126–38. doi: 10.1002/cb.309.

Heidegger, Martin. 1962. *Being and Time*. New York: Harper and Row.

Hein, Wendy, Stephanie O'Donohoe, and Annmarie Ryan. 2011. "Mobile Phones as an Extension of the Participant Observer's Self: Reflections on the Emergent Role of an Emergent Technology." *Qualitative Market Research: An International Journal* 14(3): 258–73. doi: 10.1108/13522751111137497.

Hume, David. 1748. *Philosophical Essays Concerning Human Understanding*. London: Millar.

Jansson, Andre. 2002. "The Mediatization of Consumption: Towards an Analytical Framework of Image Culture." *Journal of Consumer Culture* 2(1): 5–31.

Küpers, Wendelin. 2011. "Dancing on the Līmen~~~Embodied and Creative Inter-Places as Thresholds of Be(com)ing: Phenomenological Perspectives on Liminality and Transitional Spaces in Organization and Leadership." *Tamara - Journal for Critical Organization Inquiry* 9(3–4): 45–59.

Lai, Ai-Ling, Janine Dermody, and Stuart Hanmer-Lloyd. 2007. "Exploring Cadaveric Organ Donation: A 'Mortal Embodiment' Perspective." *Journal of Marketing Management* 23(5–6): 559–85. doi: 10.1362/026725707X212838.

Lowrey, Tina M., Cele C. Otnes, and Mary A. McGrath. 2005. "Shopping with Consumers: Reflections and Innovations." *Qualitative Market Research: An International Journal* 8(2): 176–88. doi: org/10.1108/13522750510592445.

Marchant, Caroline, and Stephanie O'Donohue. 2014. "Edging out of the Nest: Emerging Adults' Use of Smartphones in Maintaining and Transforming Family Relationships." *Journal of Marketing Management* 30(15–16): 1554–76. doi: 10.1080/0267257X.2014.935798.

Murtola, Anna-Maria. 2010. "Commodification of Utopia: The Lotus Eaters Revisited." *Culture and Organization* 16(1): 37–54. doi: 10.1080/1475955090 3558078.

Nicolini, Davide. 2012. *Practice Theory, Work, and Organization: An Introduction*. Oxford: OUP.

Pantzar, Mika, and Minna Ruckenstein. 2015. "The Heart of Everyday Analytics: Emotional, Material and Practical Extensions in Self-Tracking Market." *Consumption Markets and Culture* 18(1): 92–109. doi: 10.1080/10253866. 2014.899213.

Parkes, Graham. 1992. "Thoughts on the Way: Being and Time via Lao-Chuang." In *Heidegger and Asian Thought*, edited by G. Parkes, 105–44. Honolulu: University of Hawaii Press.

Penaloza, Lisa. 1998. "Just Doing It: A Visual Ethnographic Study of Spectacular Consumption Behavior at Nike Town." *Consumption, Markets and Culture* 2(4): 337–400.

Price, Linda L. 2013. "Family Stuff: Materiality and Identity." In *The Routledge Companion to Identity and Consumption*, edited by A.A. Ruvio and R.W. Belk, 302–12. Oxford and New York: Routledge.

Reckwitz, Andreas. 2002. "Toward a Theory of Social Practices: A Development in Culturalist Theorizing." *European Journal of Social Theory* 5(2): 243–63.

Ricoeur, Paul (1981) "The Model of the Text: Meaningful Action Considered as a Text." In *Paul Ricoeur: Hermeneutics and the Human Sciences*, edited by J.B. Thompson, 197–221. Cambridge: Cambridge University Press.

Schatzki, Theodore R. 2005. "Introduction: Practice Theory." In *The Practice Turn in Contemporary Theory*, edited by T.R. Schatzki, K.K. Cetina, and E. Von Savigny, 10–23. London: Routledge.

———. 2009. "Timespace and the Organization of Social Life." In *Time, Consumption and Everyday Life Practice, Materiality and Culture*, edited by E. Shove, F. Trentmann, and R. Wilk, 35–48. New York and Oxford: Berg.

Schön, Donald A. 1983. *The Reflective Practitioner*. New York: Basic Books.

Seamon, David. 1979. *A Geography of the Lifeworld*. London: Croom Helm.

Sherry, John F. Jr., Robert V. Kozinets, Diana Storm, Adam Duhachek, Krittinee Nuttavuthisit, and Benét Deberry-Spence. 2001. "Being in the Zone: Staging Retail Theater at ESPN Zone Chicago." *Journal of Contemporary Ethnography* 30(4): 465–510. doi:10.1177/089124101030004005.

Shove, Elizabeth. 2012. "Putting Practice into Policy: Reconfiguring Questions of Consumption and Climate Change." *Contemporary Social Science: Journal of the Academy of Social Sciences*. doi:10.1080/21582041.2012.692484.

Thompson, Craig J. 1997. "Interpreting Consumers: A Hermeneutical Framework for Deriving Marketing Insights from the Texts of Consumers' Consumption Stories." *Journal of Marketing Research* 34(4): 438–55.

Thompson, Craig J., and E.C. Hirschman. 1995. "Understanding the Socialized Body: A Poststructuralist Analysis of Consumers' Self-Conceptions, Body Images and Self-Care Practices." *Journal of Consumer Research* 22(2): 139–53.

Thompson, Craig J., H.R. Pollio, and W.B. Locander. 1994. "The Spoken and the Unspoken: A Hermeneutic Approach to Understanding the Cultural Viewpoints that Underlie Consumers' Expressed Meanings." *Journal of Consumer Research* 21 (December): 432–53.

Turner, Victor. 1967. *The Forest of Symbols*. Ithaca: Cornell University Press.

Üstüner, Tuba, and Craig J. Thompson. 2012. "How Marketplace Performances Produce Interdependent Status Games and Contested Forms of Symbolic Capital." *Journal of Consumer Research* 38(5): 796–814.

Van Marrewijka, Alfons, and Maaike Broosa. 2012. "Retail Stores as Brands: Performances, Theatre and Space." *Consumption, Markets and Culture* 15(4): 374–91. doi: 10.1080/10253866.2012.659438.

Vince, Russ, and Samantha Warren. 2012. "Participatory Visual Methods." In *Qualitative Organizational Research: Core Methods and Current Challenges*, edited by G. Symon and C. Cassell, 275–95. London: Sage.

Wilson, Tony. 1993. *Watching Television: Hermeneutics, Reception and Popular Culture*. Cambridge, UK and US: Polity-Blackwell.

———. 2012. "What Can Phenomenology Offer the Consumer?" *Qualitative Market Research: An International Journal* 15(3): 230–41. doi.org/10.1108/13522751211231969.

———. 2013. *Global Advertising, Attitudes and Audiences*. New York and London: Routledge.

———. 2015. *Media Consumption in Malaysia: A Hermeneutics of Human Behaviour*. New York and Oxford: Routledge.

Yanow, Dvora, and Haridimos Tsoukas. 2009. "What is Reflection-in-Action? A Phenomenological Account." *Journal of Management Studies* 46(8): 1339–64. doi: 10.1111/j.1467-6486.2009.00859.

List of Contributors

Anna Aupperle is a doctoral student in the College of Communications at the Pennsylvania State University. Her research interests are in financial structures of media production, historical media industrial structures, and political economy of the media, with an academic background in music business/sound recording, media studies, and television production. Her previous research focuses on online fandom communities and their experiences with social activism and consumerism.

Felip Vidal Auladell received his PhD in Communication Studies from the Complutense University of Madrid, with a dissertation entitled "The Value of Experience in Signification Advertising." He graduated in Law from Girona University and in Philosophy from UNED. He has an MA in History of Philosophy, Aesthetics and Culture Theory, from Barcelona University. His research interests include advertising theory, branding, semiotics and cultural theory. He has published several articles on the new forms of advertising and media culture. He is a member of the research group ARPA (Analysis of Audiovisuals Screens Reception) at the Girona University, and he is also on the Editorial Board of the *Communication Papers; Media Literacy & Gender Studies*.

Paulo M. Barroso holds a PhD in Philosophy and has served as a post-doctorate researcher (6 years) in Communication Sciences. Since 2009, he has been an Assistant Professor of Public Higher Education at the Higher School of Education, Viseu, Portugal, where he teaches Advertising Semiotics, Sociology of Communication, and Ethics. He also serves as an integrated researcher at the Communication and Language Studies Center on the Faculty of Social Sciences and Humanities, New University of Lisbon. His current research interests are in semiotics, philosophy of language, argumentation and rhetoric, ethics, media languages, and theories and models of communication, fields in which he has published several articles.

Joke Bauwens is a Senior Lecturer at the Department of Communication Studies at the Vrije Universiteit Brussel (Free University Brussels). Drawing upon media-sociological, media-theoretical and media-philosophical approaches, her research and publications examine young people's engagement with media, the relation between online media and morality, and the digitization of media and culture (e.g., broadcasting). She also heads the research center for Culture, Emancipation, Media and Society (CEMESO).

Michael Tiong Hock Bing is the Head of the School of Accounting and Business, Nusantara Institute of Information Technology (NIIT), Malaysia. He graduated from Universiti Malaysia Sarawak with a Master's degree in Marketing in 2013. He obtained his Bachelor's Degree of Business Administration with Honours (Marketing) from Universiti Malaysia Sarawak in 2010. His main research interests are advertising and interpretive marketing. He is particularly interested in how consumers understand and assess media advertising.

Robert Bodle is an Associate Professor of Communication and New Media Studies at Mount St. Joseph University and Adjunct Professor in the Department of Media, Journalism, and Film at Miami University. He has published extensively on the ethical and human rights implications of social media design, governance, and use, focusing primarily on privacy and freedom of expression. He served as Co-Chair of the Internet Rights and Principles Dynamic Coalition (2013–2015) at the UN Internet Governance Forum, and as a steering committee member of the IRP Coalition since 2010.

Nils S. Borchers is a researcher and lecturer at the Institute of Communication and Studies at the University of Leipzig, Germany. In his dissertation, he developed a communications approach to theorizing advertising that employs constructivist reasoning for emancipating itself from marketing theory. His current research focuses on advertising's wider impacts on society, advertising literacy, and the empowerment effects of peer-to-peer communication on the Internet. He served as young scholars' representative in the Advertising Research group of the European Communication Research and Education Association (ECREA).

Sia Bee Chuan is the Dean at the Faculty of Accountancy and Management, Universiti Tunku Abdul Rahman (UTAR), Malaysia. She received her PhD degree in Marketing from Cardiff University in 2013, and her Master's and Bachelor's of Business Administration from Wichita State University, USA. Upon return, she worked in the private sector within the banking industry and also as a business consultant. Her current areas of research are consumer behavior, cultural consumption, tourism, sustainability management, and particularly qualitative studies.

Olga Fedorenko is an Assistant Professor/Faculty Fellow at the Department of East Asian Studies at New York University. She received her PhD from the East Asian Studies Department at the University of Toronto. Her articles appear in *The Korean Popular Culture Reader* (eds. Kyung Hyun Kim and Youngmin Choe, Duke University Press) and *Feminist Media Studies*. She is currently working on a book manuscript, entitled "Flower of Capitalism: South Korean Advertising at a Crossroads." She also holds

MBA from Yonsei University in Seoul, South Korea, and BA in Korean Studies from Moscow State University in Russia.

James F. Hamilton is the James Kennedy Professor of New Media, Head of the Department of Entertainment and Media Studies, and Director of the New Media Institute at the University of Georgia. He has published broadly in the areas of democratic communications and alternative media. Among his published work is *Democratic Communications; Formations, Projects, Possibilities* (Lexington Books, 2009) and *Alternative Journalism* (Sage, 2009), co-written with Chris Atton.

Jonathan Hardy is Reader in Media Studies at the University of East London and teaches political economy of media at Goldsmiths College, University of London. He is the author of *Critical Political Economy of the Media* (Routledge, 2014), *Cross-Media Promotion* (Peter Lang, 2010), and *Western Media Systems* (Routledge, 2008) and co-editor of *The Advertising Handbook* (Routledge, 2009). He teaches and writes on political economy of media, media and advertising, communications policy and regulation, and international and comparative media. He is secretary of UK media reform group, the Campaign for Press and Broadcasting Freedom (www.cpbf.org.uk).

Nicholas Holm is a Lecturer in Media Studies at Massey University in New Zealand where he teaches courses in advertising, popular culture, and introductory media studies. His research addresses the political role of aesthetics, in particular the aesthetics of popular culture, which he has explored in published articles in terms of mediated humour, urban wildlife, comic books and the transnational adaptation of film. He is currently writing a textbook addressing advertising and capitalist culture for Palgrave Macmillan.

Tan Teck Hong is Visiting Professor, Henley Business School, University of Reading Malaysia. His main research interests include real estate marketing. Some of his latest papers have been published in international refereed journals such as *Social Indicators Research, Habitat International, Cities, Journal of Real Estate Research*, and *International Journal of Housing Market and Analysis*.

Iben Bredahl Jessen is an Associate Professor of Media and Communication at the Department of Communication and Psychology, Aalborg University, Denmark. Her research addresses market communication and aesthetics in digital media. International publications include "The Aesthetics of Web Advertising" (in *Web History*, edited by N. Brügger, Peter Lang, 2010) "Sounds of Web Advertising" (with N. J. Graakjær in *Handbook of Research on Digital Media and Advertising*, edited by M. S. Eastin et al., Information Science Reference, 2010), "Cross-media Communication in Advertising" (with N. J. Graakjær in *Visual Communication*, 2013) and "Reconsidering Display in Online Testimonial Advertising" (in *Advertising & Society Review*, 2014).

Ezequiel Korin is a PhD student in the Grady College of Journalism and Mass Communication at the University of Georgia.

Silke Lissens is a PhD student at the Department of Communication Studies at the Vrije Universiteit Brussel (Free University Brussels), a member of the research group CEMESO (the center for Culture, Emancipation, Media and Society) and a junior researcher within the interdisciplinary AdLit project (Advertising Literacy). Building on experiences gained in the educational field, her main interests are situated within the context of critical pedagogy, children and empowerment, consumer culture in general, and the commercialization of childhood in particular.

Matthew P. McAllister is a Professor of Communications in the Department of Film-Video & Media Studies at Pennsylvania State University. His research interests are in critical advertising studies and political economy of the media. He is the author of *The Commercialization of American Culture*, and the co-editor of *The Advertising and Consumer Culture Reader* (with Joseph Turow) and *The Routledge Companion to Advertising and Promotional Culture* (with Emily West). He has also published about advertising and promotional culture in such venues as *Journal of Communication*, *Critical Studies in Media Communication*, and *Popular Communication*.

Lee McGuigan is a PhD student in the Annenberg School for Communication at the University of Pennsylvania. He holds a Master's degree from the Faculty of Information and Media Studies at the University of Western Ontario. McGuigan is co-editor (with Vincent Manzerolle) of *The Audience Commodity in a Digital Age: Revisiting a Critical Theory of Commercial Media* (Peter Lang, 2014). His work has been published or is forthcoming in journals such as *New Media & Society*, *Media, Culture & Society*, *Television & New Media*, and the *Journal of Communication Inquiry*.

Andrew McStay is Senior Lecturer in Media Culture at Bangor University and is also author of *Digital Advertising* (2009); *The Mood of Information: A Critique of Online Behavioural Advertising* (2011); *Creativity and Advertising: Affect, Events and Process* (2013); and *Privacy and Philosophy: New Media and Affective Protocol* (2014).

Chris Miles is Lecturer in Marketing & Communication at the School of Business and Management, Queen Mary University of London, where he teaches modules on digital marketing and persuasive strategies. Much of his research investigates the rhetorical strategies employed by marketing practitioners and marketing academics and has been published in such journals as *European Journal of Marketing*, *Journal of Marketing Management*, and *Marketing Theory*. His book, *Interactive Marketing: Revolution or Rhetoric?* was published by Routledge in 2010.

Anthony Nadler is an Assistant Professor of Media and Communication Studies at Ursinus College. His work has been published or is forthcoming in *Politics & Culture, The Communication Review, Flow*, and *Cultural Studies*. Nadler is finishing a book exploring how U.S. news organizations have shaped popular interest in politics and public life as they have oriented news values toward a market-driven philosophy. With Julie Wilson, Anthony is co-founder of teachingmedia.org.

David B. Nieborg is an Assistant Professor at the University of Toronto and former a Postdoctoral Fellow with the University of Amsterdam and the Massachusetts Institute of Technology. He graduated cum laude at Utrecht University and holds a PhD from the University of Amsterdam. He has published on digital culture and games and has a particular interest in the political economy of the game industry. Nieborg is a contributing editor for the leading Dutch newspaper *NRC Handelsblad*. In 2013 he was awarded a three-year postdoctoral grant by the Netherlands Organisation for Scientific Research (NWO) to investigate "app economics," the political economy of mobile gaming. For more information see http://www.gamespace.nl.

Brice Nixon is an adjunct instructor in the Department of Media Studies and Production Temple University and a visiting scholar at the Annenberg School for Communication at the University of Pennsylvania. His research concerns the political economy of communication, and the history of media and cultural studies. His work has been published in *Media, Culture & Society,* and *tripleC: Communication, Capitalism & Critique*.

David J. Park is an Associate Professor in the School of Journalism and Mass Communication at Florida International University. Author of *Conglomerate Rock: The Music Industry's Quest to Divide Music and Conquer Wallets* (Lexington Books), his research interests include media technologies, political economy, media and culture, environmental sustainability, consumerism and international communication. His scholarship appears in a variety of journals and book chapters, while he also serves on the editorial boards of various journals.

Emily West is an Associate Professor of Communication at the University of Massachusetts, Amherst. Her research and teaching are in the areas of consumer culture, audience research, cultural studies, and health. She is the co-editor of *The Routledge Companion to Advertising and Promotional Culture* (2013) and the author of several journal articles on greeting cards as an emotional commodity. Her current research focuses on consumerism in health care in the United States, both among users of health care and as an aspect of policy and promotional discourses of health.

Tony Wilson has taught audience and consumer, marketing and media research at postgraduate and undergraduate levels in Australian, English and Scottish universities, as well as private and public sectors of Malaysian higher education. He holds a PhD from Glasgow University and has published many papers on responses to mediated practices of advertising and the wider provisions of screen content, as well as six monographs, two with Blackwell, two with Routledge and one with August, Malaysia and Hampton Press, USA, respectively. His work is informed by philosophical hermeneutics.

James H. Wittebols is a Professor of Political Science and Graduate Studies Chair at the University of Windsor. He received his PhD in Sociology from Washington State University in 1983. His research focuses on the intersection of media, culture and politics and has published in numerous communication journals. He has published two books *Watching M*A*S*H*, *Watching America: A Social History of the 1972–1983 Television Series* (McFarland, 1998) and *The Soap Opera Paradigm: Television Programming and Corporate Priorities* (Rowman and Littlefield, 2004). He has been studying the promotional culture industry's use of authenticity for the last decade.

Choy Tuck Yun is a Chartered Marketer, CIM (UK) and Senior Lecturer, Sunway University Business School. He worked in sales, marketing and operations for Malaysian and international firms for 21 years in both commercial and industrial sectors. Then he taught in universities for 15 years in Malaysian, UK and Australian tertiary and post-graduate business programs. His DBA is from the University of Newcastle, Australia, with research interests in services and entrepreneurship.

Index

Printed in the United States
by Baker & Taylor Publisher Services